PERVASIVE PROBLEMS
IN INTERNATIONAL ARBITRATION

International Arbitration Law Library

Series Editor Dr. Julian D.M. Lew QC

In the series *International Arbitration Law Library* this book,
Pervasive Problems in International Arbitration, is the fifteenth title.

The titles published in this series are listed at the end of this volume

PERVASIVE PROBLEMS
IN INTERNATIONAL ARBITRATION

Edited by Loukas A. Mistelis and Julian D.M. Lew, QC

School of International Arbitration

KLUWER LAW
INTERNATIONAL

A C.I.P. catalogue record for this book is available from the Library of Congress.

ISBN 90 411 2450 0

Published by:
Kluwer Law International
P.O. Box 316
2400 AH Alphen aan den Rijn
The Netherlands

Sold and distributed in North, Central and South America by:
Aspen Publishers, Inc.
7201 McKinney Circle
Frederick, MD 21704
United States of America

Sold and distributed in all other countries by:
Turpin Distribution Services Ltd
Stratton Business Park
Pegasus Drive
Biggleswade
Bedfordshire SG18 8TQ
United Kingdom

Printed on acid-free paper

FOREWORD

The School of International Arbitration, at the Centre for Commercial Law Studies (CCLS), Queen Mary University of London celebrated its twentieth anniversary in 2005. On this occasion we decided to look into the future and identify issues which are pervasive and topical in international arbitration.

This volume is a distillation of ideas discussed in a three day symposium held in London from 10 to 12 April 2005. This was attended by many of the leading academic and practising arbitration specialists from around the world. There were over 320 participants from 71 countries at the conference.

A wide area of specialist contributors undertook the task of taking a fresh look at some of the legal and practice issues which frequently occur in international arbitration. These discussions demonstrated over the three days not only the increasing breadth and scope of the subject, but also the way in which many of its themes and issues cross legal and disciplinary boundaries and pose questions for the future of the law and arbitration practice in an internationalised world.

International arbitration is at the junction of national, international and conflicts laws, public and private law and substantive and procedural law. The conference and this book illustrate the combination of the scholarly and the highly practical approach which characterises the mission of the School of International Arbitration and CCLS since their inception.

We owe a number of debts. The conference could not have taken place and this book published without the generosity of the contributors who enthusiastically gave their time to prepare their contributions, participate in the conference and finalise their chapters. This alone stands as testimony to the high regard in which the School is held nationally and internationally.

Loukas A. Mistelis and Julian D.M. Lew (eds), Pervasive Problems in International Arbitration, v–vi
© 2006 Kluwer Law International. Printed in the Netherlands

Particular thanks are due to the Rt Hon Lord Justice Bernard Rix, Chairman of the CCLS Advisory Council who chaired the conference, Professor Sir Roy Goode, the founding Director of CCLS and a constant inspiration for our activities, Professor Marise Cremona, the head of the CCLS Unit which includes the School; Sandra Baird and Sarah Batty for their administration and organisation of the Conference. Stavros Brekoulakis, a research fellow at the School of International Arbitration, has assisted with editing the book and prepared the subject index.

As always, it has been a pleasure to work with Kluwer on the project. Our publisher, Bas Kniphorst, has shown patience as deadlines have passed. His encouragement and support are much appreciated.

Loukas A Mistelis
Clive M Schmitthoff Professor of
Transnational Law and Arbitration
Director of Studies, School of
International Arbitration

Julian D M Lew QC
Visiting Professor

Head, School of International
Arbitration

3 February 2006

TABLE OF CONTENTS

Chapter 8
The Role of National Courts and *Lex Fori* in International Commercial Arbitration 155
Wang Shengchang and Cao Lijun

Chapter 9
Provisional Measures — **185**
Ali Yesilirmak

Chapter 10
Reflections on the Use of Anti-Suit Injunctions in
International Arbitration — **201**
Emmanuel Gaillard

TABLE OF ABBREVIATIONS

INSTITUTIONS, ORGANIZATIONS AND RULES

The Institution may import the Rules

AAA	American Arbitration Association
ABA	American Bar Association
ASA	Swiss Arbitration Association
CIETAC	China International Economic and Trade Arbitration Commission
CRCICA	Cairo Regional Centre For International Commercial Arbitration
DIS	Deutsche Institution für Schiedsgerichtsbarkeit
EC	European Community
EEC	European Economic Community
EU	European Union
HKIAC	Hong Kong International Arbitration Centre
IBA	International Bar Association
ICC	International Chamber of Commerce
ICCA	International Council for Commercial Arbitration
ICDR	American Arbitration Association International Center for Dispute Resolution
ICSID	International Centre for the Settlement of Investment Disputes

IFCAI	International Federation of Commercial Arbitration Institutions
JCAA	Japan Commercial Arbitration Association
LCIA	London Court of International Arbitration
OECD	Organisation for Economic Co-operation and Development
PCA	Permanent Court of Arbitration (The Hague)
SCC	Stockholm Chamber of Commerce Arbitration Institute
SIAC	Singapore International Arbitration Centre
UNCITRAL	United Nations Commission for International Trade Law
UNIDROIT	International Institute for the Unification of Private Law
Vienna	Austrian Federal Economic Chamber in Vienna
WIPO	World Intellectual Property Organisation

GENERAL ABBREVIATIONS

AC	Law Reports, House of Lords (Appeal Cases)
ADRLJ	Arbitration and Dispute Resolution Law Journal
ALI	American Law Institute
All ER	All England Law Reports
Am J Comp L	American Journal of Comparative Law
Am J Int'l L	American Journal of International Law
Am Rev Int'l Arb	American Review of International Arbitration
Ann IDI	Annuaire de l'Institut de droit international
Arb Int	Arbitration International
Arbitration	Arbitration, Journal of the Chartered Institute of Arbitrators
ASA Bulletin	Swiss Arbitration Association Bulletin
Asian DR	Asian Dispute Review

ATF	Arrêts du Tribunal Fédéral Suisse
BGB	Bürgerliches Gesetzbuch (German Civil Code)
BGE	Entscheidungen des schweizerischen Bundesgerichts
BGHZ	Sammlung der Entscheidungen des Bundesgerichtshofs in Zivilsachen
BIT	Bilateral Investment Treaty
Boston U Int'l L J	Boston University International Law Journal
Brooklyn J Int'l L	Brooklyn Journal of International Law
BYBIL	British Yearbook of International Law
CA	Court of Appeal of England and Wales
CC	Code civil, codice civile, civil code
CCLS	Centre for Commercial Law Studies
CCP	Code of Civil Procedure
CISG	United Nations Convention on the International Sale Goods
CLR	Commonwealth Law Reports
Clunet	Journal de droit international
Columbia J Transnat'l L	Columbia Journal of Transnational Law
Con LR	Construction Law Reports
CPR	Civil Procedure Rules (England)
Disp Res J	Dispute Resolution Journal
Duke L J	Duke Law Journal
ECHR	European Convention on Human Rights
ECJ	Court of Justice of the European Communities
ECR	Report of Cases before the Court of Justice of the European Communities
EHRR	European Human Rights Reports
EJCL	Electronic Journal of Comparative Law
ER	English Reports
EWCA Civ	Neutral citation for England and Wales Court of Appeal civil division decisions
F 2d	The Federal Reporter Second Series
F 3d	The Federal Reporter Third Series

FAA	United States Federal Arbitration Act
FS	Festschrift
F Supp	Federal Supplement
Geo Wash J Int'l L & Eco	George Washington University Journal of International Law and Economics
Hastings Int'l & Comp L Rev	Hastings International and Comparative Law Review
HKHC	Hong Kong High Court
HL	House of Lords
IBA Rules	IBA Rules on the taking of Evidence in International Commercial Arbitration, 1999
ICC Bulletin	International Chamber of Commerce International Court of Arbitration Bulletin
ICLQ	International and Comparative Law Quarterly.
ICSID Rev-FILJ	ICSID Review – Foreign Investment Law Journal
IECL	International Encyclopaedia of Comparative Law
InsO	Insolvenz Ordnung
Int ALR	International Arbitration Law Review
Int'l Bus Law	International Business Lawyer
Int'l Law	International Lawyer
ILA	International Law Association
ILM	International Legal Materials
ILR	International Law Reports
IPRax	Praxis des internationalen Privat- und Verfahrensrechts
Iran-US CTR	Iran-US Claims Tribunal Reports
JBL	Journal of Business Law
J Int'l Arb	Journal of International Arbitration.
Law & Policy in Int'l Bus	Law & Policy in International Business
Lloyd's Rep	Lloyd's Law Reports
LNTS	League of Nations Treaty Series
Louisiana L Rev	Louisiana Law Review

Loy LA Int'l & Comp LJ	Loyola Los Angeles International and Comparative Law Journal
Mealey's IAR	Mealey's International Arbitration Reports
Michigan J Int'l L	Michigan Journal of International Law
Minn L Rev	Minnesota Law Review
Model Law	UNCITRAL Model Law on International Commercial Arbitration adopted 21 June 1985
MR	Master of the Rolls
NCPC	French Code of Civil Procedure (Nouveau Code de Procedure Civile)
New York Convention	1958 New York Convention on the Recognition and Enforcement of Foreign Arbitral Awards
NY	New York
NYAD	New York Appellate Division
NYLJ	New York Law Journal
NY L Sch J Int'l & Comp L	New York Law School Journal of International and Comparative Law
OJ	Official Journal of the European Communities
OLG	Oberlandesgericht
PC	Privy Council
PECL	Principles of European Contract Law
PIL	(Swiss) Private International Law
QBD	Queen's Bench Division
RCADI	Recueil des Cours de l'Académie de Droit International de la Haye / Collected Courses of the Hague Academy of International Law
RDAI/IBLJ	Revue de droit des affaires internationales / International Business Law Journal
Rep	Report
Rev Arb	Revue de l'arbitrage
Rev crit dip	Revue critique de droit international privé
Rome Convention	EC (Rome) Convention on the Law Applicable to Contractual Obligations 1980
SchiedsVZ	Zeitschrift für Schiedsverfahren

S Ct	Supreme Court of the United States
SDNY	Southern District of New York
SIA	School of International Arbitration, Queen Mary University of London
Stanford J Int'l L	Stanford Journal of International Law
Texas Int'l LJ	Texas International Law Journal
Tulane L Rev	Tulane Law Review
U Cin L Rev	University of Cincinnati Law Review
U Ill L Rev	University of Illinois Law Review
UKPC	Neutral citation for decisions of the Privy Council
UNCITRAL Notes	UNCITRAL Notes on Organizing Arbitral Proceedings
Unif L Rev	Uniform Law Review
UNTS	United Nations Treaty Series
Vanderbilt L Rev	Vanderbilt Law Review
WAMR	World Arbitration and Mediation Report
Washington Convention	Washington Convention on the Settlement of Investment Disputes between States and Nationals of other States 1965
WIPO Expedited Rules	WIPO Expedited Rules
WL	Westlaw
WLR	The Weekly Law Reports
WTAM	World Trade and Arbitration Materials
Yale LJ	Yale Law Journal
YBCA	Yearbook of Commercial Arbitration
ZPO	German Code of Civil Procedure (ZPO)
	European Human Rights Reports

Julian D.M. Lew QC*

INTRODUCTION

FUNDAMENTAL PROBLEMS
IN INTERNATIONAL ARBITRATION

1. The School of International Arbitration was created in 1985 by the Centre for Commercial Studies, Queen Mary, University of London. The then Director of the Centre, Professor Roy Goode, considered arbitration to be, and that it would become ever more so, an essential dispute resolution system for international commercial transactions. Accordingly, the School's aim was to undertake teaching and research into the developing law and practices of international arbitration. This would enable the School, and its alumni, to contribute to the knowledge of practitioners and users of international arbitration through its students and the content of the research and publications.

2. The approach of the School from the outset was to recognise that arbitration is an international, not a national, system of dispute resolution. The disputing parties, the subject matter of their disputes, their lawyers and the arbitrators, invariably transcended national boundaries. Arbitration is increasingly a transnational process, regulated by and following international and non-national rules and practices. This is in contrast to the previously prevalent view that every arbitration was inevitably governed and controlled by a national law, the law of the place or seat of the arbitration.[1]

3. To inaugurate the School, the Centre for Commercial Law Studies organised a conference held on 25-27 March 1985 with the title "Contemporary Problems in International Arbitration". The conference was attended by many of the leaders

---

* Head and Visiting Professor, School of International Arbitration, Centre for Commercial Law Studies, Queen Mary University of London; Barrister, 20 Essex Street.
[1] F A Mann, "Lex Facit Arbitrum", in Pieter Sanders (ed), *Liber Amicorum for Martin Domke*, (Martinus Nijhof 1967) 158; see also also Sauser-Hall, "L'arbitrage en droit international privé", 44 *AnnIDI* 520-2 (1952).

of international arbitration of that time: Professors Berthold Goldman, Pierre Lalive, Pieter Sanders and Clive Schmitthoff. They all offered advice, encouragement and support to the new institution.

4. Professor Pieter Sanders stated graphically that at the birth of the School

> [m]any fairy godmothers well known in the world of international arbitration stood at the cradle of the School. … There was no wicked fairy amongst them. On the contrary, they all wholeheartedly welcomed the newborn and contributed to her their gifts of arbitration-wisdom.[2]

5. Whilst many saw international arbitration as a purely procedural matter, subject tied to national procedural codes, the School has always considered and taught arbitration as an international and comparative law subject. This reflects the hope expressed that the School would be "truly international"[3] and "would attract participants from developing countries".[4] It was further added that back in 1985 there was "lack of international and comparative outlook".[5] In the 20 years since its establishment the School has achieved many of these goals with over 2500 students from over 80 countries, many from the developing world in Africa and Asia.

6. The 1985 inaugural conference had three main themes: the jurisdiction and authority of arbitrators; international arbitration procedure; and international arbitration involving states and state entities. The book published following the conference in 1986 had an added extra section entitled "The School of International Arbitration".

7. Whilst the themes considered at the 20th Anniversary Conference of the School of International Arbitration, held on 18-19 April 2005, were broadly the same as the 1985 themes, the specific topics differ greatly in content. This is because international arbitration has not only moved on; it has been revolutionised in many ways. Due to changing circumstances and increasing party autonomy and controls, arbitration has reinvented itself with new and different practices and problems.

---

[2] Pieter Sanders, "The Birth of the School of International Arbitration", in Julian D M Lew (ed), *Contemporary Problems in International Arbitration* (CCLS and Kluwer 1986) 9.
[3] Ibid, at 10.
[4] Ibid.
[5] Pierre Lalive, "International Arbitration – teaching and research", in Julian D M Lew (ed), *Contemporary Problems in International Arbitration* (CCLS and Kluwer 1986) 16, at 17.

8. What has changed in the last twenty years? To what extent is it a case of "*plus ça change plus la même chose*", i.e. the same problems with a new face? There have, however, been two enormous changes to the arbitration environment. First, the adoption of the New York Convention on the Recognition and Enforcement of Foreign Arbitral Awards 1958 by over 137 countries and the Washington Convention on the Settlement of Investment Disputes between States and Foreign Investors 1965 by more than 143 countries, including, in particular, the developing countries provides a public international law regulation for international arbitration. Second, the enormous success of the UNCITRAL Arbitration Rules and the UNCITRAL Model Law has given arbitration a new international and transnational dimension.

9. Many of our 1985 problems have changed dramatically. They cease to be a central issue or have been resolved or at least mechanisms for dealing with them have been developed. Today's problems are generated by greater acceptance of international legal instruments, changes in the world commercial structures, international commercial and political demographics, and the unintended result of the 1985 UNCITRAL Model Law on International Commercial Arbitration which has had a seismic influence on both the development of national laws and attitudes, and on the conduct of international arbitration.

10.   The changes are the result of several interlinked factors. First there has been a greater acceptance of and resort to arbitration for international business disputes. This is evidenced by the myriad of new international arbitration institutions, in many countries, all of which are providing a service to international business.[6]

11.   There is a genuine acceptance that there have been an increasing number of international arbitrations, of all kinds and under all systems. Whilst it remains difficult or even impossible to determine exact numbers the figures given by the major institutions suggest continuous growth in numbers. For example, in 1992 337 new arbitrations were filed with the ICC International Court of Arbitration. In 2004 this figure was 561.[7] In this same period the number of LCIA cases has increased from 21 to 87; American Arbitration Association international cases have increased from 204 to almost 700; Singapore International Arbitration

---

[6]   See, for example, the large IFCAI membership (of more than 60 full fee paying members) and the list of more than 200 arbitration institutions at www.kluwerarbitration.com.

[7]   For statistics of number and subject-matter of ICC arbitrations, the origin of the parties and the arbitrators, see annual spring issue of ICC Bulletin.

Centre figures have increased from 7 to 51; and Stockholm Institute cases have increased from 44 to 123.

12. The situation is similar with investment arbitration numbers. Although established in 1966, by 1985 only a couple arbitrations had been filed under the ICSID Rules. There were not many Bilateral Investment Treaties, and other regional multilateral dedicated investment treaties were not in the landscape. Last year there were 26 arbitrations filed with ICSID – there were 77 since 1995.

Table: Arbitration Cases in Selected Arbitration Institutions from 1992 to 2004

Institution	1992	1994	1996	1998	2000	2001	2002	2003	2004
AAA-ICDR[8]	204	187	226	387	510	649	672	N/A	N/A
CIETAC[9]	267	829	778	645	543	731	684	709	850
DIS[10]	20	30	31	42	62	58	N/A	N/A	N/A
HKIAC[11]	185	150	197	240	298	307	320	287	250
ICC[12]	337	384	433	466	541	566	593	580	561
JCAA[13]	5	4	8	14	10	17	9	14	21
LCIA[14]	21	39	37	70	81	71	88	104	87
SIAC[15]	7	22	25	67	55	56	46	41	51
SCC Arb Institute[16]	44	74	100	122	135	130	120	169	123
Vienna[17]	47	64	45	46	55	33	33	45	50
ICSID[18]				2	2	8	13	26	26

13. The many, almost constant, publications, seminars and conferences, all around the world, on all aspects of international arbitration manifest the increasing importance of the subject. This is evidenced further by the ever increasing number of students wishing to study the subject. From just 22 students in 1985

---

[8] American Arbitration Association International Center for Dispute Resolution: www.adr.org.
[9] China International Economic and Trade Arbitration Commission: www.cietac.org.
[10] Deutsche Institution für Schiedsgerichtsbarkeit: www.dis-arb.de.
[11] Hong Kong International Arbitration Centre: www.hkiac.org.
[12] ICC Court of International Arbitration: www.iccwbo.org/index_court.asp.
[13] Japanese Commercial Arbitration Association: www.jcaa.or.jp.
[14] London Court of International Arbitration: www.lcia-arbitration.com.
[15] Singapore International Arbitration Centre: www.siac.org.sg.
[16] Stockholm Chamber of Commerce Arbitration Institute: www.sccinstitute.com/uk/Home/. The numbers include both domestic and international cases.
[17] Vienna International Arbitration Centre: www.wk.or.at/arbitration/.
[18] International Centre for the Settlement of Investment Disputes: www.worldbank.org/icsid.

on the LLM course in "Commercial Arbitration", for the past 5 years, the School of International Arbitration has significantly over a hundred students each year. Although the School was the first dedicated institution to teach international arbitration at a post-graduate level, this subject is now taught by many universities in many countries around the world.

14. This publication contains the papers presented at the 20th Anniversary Conference of the School of International Arbitration. In view of the passage of time it is useful to contrast what was discussed in 1985 and the subjects of 2005. First, with respect to the "jurisdiction and authority of arbitrators", the interaction between party autonomy and the determination of the applicable law to substance and to procedure were of particular concern. What has changed?

15. Today party autonomy is universally recognised. It is the primary element that regulates all aspects of international arbitration. The authority of parties to submit to arbitration is no longer a real issue. Questions of arbitrability are of less significance and of a different nature. The doctrine of separability is almost universally accepted (at least by those systems that favour the international arbitration process). Choice of law is rarely an issue: arbitrators apply the law they think appropriate for the issue before them and are largely free from the artificial constraints of applying choice of law rules. Of course one can observe some disparity between developed and less developed systems and between liberal rules and more conservative laws. The law to govern procedure is no longer considered to be inevitably the law of the place of arbitration.

16. Applicable law issues today relate to factors different to how the substantive issues should be determined. Whatever law governs, major challenges emerge concerning the application of international standards, like international public policy (however that is defined) and the mandatory laws of the place of arbitration and the laws of the parties. The extent to which arbitration is a private and confidential process is increasingly controversial: as arbitration has become more widely used, so too it has been studied both empirically and from a legal point of view. If arbitration awards are to be public, and perhaps published, does that give the awards, the arbitrators' conclusions and findings any precedent value?

17. The so called "group of companies" doctrine is discussed widely. Contracting parties may be shell or special vehicle entities established specifically for the transaction in question. In practise however the contractual obligations are being, or are to be performed, or the actual business is being

5

done, by other companies in the same group or under common ownership or control. This occurs in many ways; for example, where different government ministries or controlled entities perform or interfere wrongly with the obligations of the state; where the seller of plant and systems agrees to provide intellectual property licenses even though the owner of intellectual property is another company in the group; where breaches by one party have to its knowledge caused damage to other companies in the contracting partner's group. Arbitrators applying international accepted principles have, in certain situations, extended their own jurisdiction and made awards to cover all relevant companies or entities involved in the transaction in dispute.

18. As international transactions become ever more complicated and involve more and more parties, parallel proceedings, both in court and in arbitration, have increased commensurately. Not only are there conflicts of jurisdiction but there are different interests to protect. As there is no *res judicata* rule in international arbitration, issues concerning conflicting decisions and contradictory evidence are of current concern. Furthermore, the assignment of contractual rights and obligations often include provisions for arbitration. This means that one contracting party can find itself in an arbitration with a party with whom it did not contract or expect or intend to refer disputes with to arbitration. This could have far reaching effects where the assignee carries on business or has its assets in a jurisdiction which is not party to the New York Convention.

19. The second part of this book is concerned with national and international regulation of international arbitration. Twenty years ago when we looked at international arbitration procedure, the first and principal influence was the law of the place of arbitration. This fundamental, nationalistic approach espoused by the Institut de Droit International and its rapporteur, Professor Sauser-Hall, spoke of the supremacy and control of the law at the place or *siege d'arbitrage*.[19] The argument was that parties intended and expected that the procedure at the place of arbitration should apply.

20. Institutional arbitration rules were drafted, and still are drafted, in very general terms. Interestingly the UNCITRAL Arbitration Rules probably have a little more substantive flesh on them but that is because they were originally intended for use in *ad hoc* arbitrations. The uncertainties and generalities of the

---

[19] Sauser-Hall, "L'arbitrage en droit international privé", 44-I *Ann IDI* 469-513 and 514-592 (1952); developed further in 47-II *Ann IDI* 394-496 (1957); 48-II *Ann IDI* 264-361 (1958).

arbitration rules were frequently relied on by arbitrators and parties to apply national procedures, except where the parties had agreed a procedure themselves.

21. Today international arbitration procedure has its own character and momentum. There is no, or an enormously reduced, tie to any national procedural system. There are now accepted procedures which are followed in most international arbitrations. The procedure is developed on a case by case basis. In the absence of agreement between the parties – alas too frequent – it is clear a tribunal has the power to fix a procedure which it considers appropriate to enable it to reach a determination of the issues in dispute. To do this the tribunal will take into account the origin of the parties and the arbitrators, the applicable arbitration rules, any intent expressed by the parties and the needs of the specific facts. Tribunals apply the generality of the arbitration Rules to enable them to fix or impose the procedure they think appropriate. These comprise some kind of procedural *lex mercatoria.*

22. Issues of great importance today concern standards for the presentation of evidence; the independence and impartiality of arbitrators, given particular profile and relevance due to the IBA Guidelines on arbitrators' conflicts of interests; the correct forum for the issuance of provisional relief; and anti-suit or anti-arbitration injunctions used to stop arbitration proceedings in favour of some national court or at least some other arbitration system. Whether third parties should be allowed to intervene, attend and be heard in private arbitrations is frequently raised.

23. In 1985 the concerns relating to state and state entity involvement in international arbitration related primarily to general commercial disputes and the use and abuse of sovereign immunity in disputes arising from transactions involving states, state entities and state controlled corporations. ICSID was then a fledgling institution with only limited experience.

24. In recent years we have witnessed an explosion of commercial and investment arbitrations involving states. ICSID has become a frequent selection for contracts with states which are party to the Washington Convention. Most of the awards made under the ICSID Rules are published officially or otherwise with the effect of a growing ICSID and investment arbitration jurisprudence. It is referred to as a definitive source of law to be applied by international arbitration tribunals. To what extent is it binding on the parties regardless of the otherwise applicable national or international law rules?

25. More importantly, the almost 2500 BITs which contain provision for alternative forms of arbitration in the event of disputes creates new arguments. These arbitrations are without privity: the former absolute requirement that there must be a clear agreement between the parties to submit their disputes to arbitration is no longer. Now the injured or aggrieved investor unilaterally concludes the separate arbitration agreement and chooses the form of arbitration according to the options in the relevant BIT and the general consent of the state party. This may have implications for the place of arbitration, the number and choice of arbitrators, the procedure to be followed, the degree of confidentiality the arbitration will receive and the law or rules to be applied to the substantive issues.

26. This form of arbitration has been enhanced by other forms of investment arbitrations such as the North American Free Trade Agreement (NAFTA) and the Energy Charter Treaty (ECT). The awards under these rules also have resulted in a body of decisions which are quoted and relied on in other arbitrations.

27. Perhaps the most interesting aspect of these arbitrations involving states or state entities, and investment arbitrations, is the interplay between commercial and investment issues, applicable national and international commercial law on the one hand, and public international law on the other hand. This gives rise to discussions whether in an ICSID arbitration or an arbitration brought under a BIT or the ECT and relating to an alleged breach of investment rights, claims for breach of the underlying contract can also be brought, or whether a claim under one head precludes or even excludes claims under the other head.

28. These contemporary and pervasive issues, which are the subject of this book, are at a stage of development. There a few definitive answers in a science that is constantly evolving. However these papers do represent a serious and valuable record of practical legal scholarship on issues which are frequently faced in international arbitrations.

PART I

INTERNATIONAL ARBITRATION AND POLICY ISSUES

Donald Francis Donovan* and Alexander K.A. Greenawalt**

CHAPTER 1

MITSUBISHI AFTER TWENTY YEARS: MANDATORY RULES BEFORE COURTS AND INTERNATIONAL ARBITRATORS

I. INTRODUCTION

1-1 "Arbitration is a creature of contract." So says the oft repeated maxim of U.S. judicial decisions confronting arbitration agreements.[1] Since the U.S. Congress passed the Federal Arbitration Act ("FAA") in 1925,[2] U.S. courts have held that if parties are free to enter into contractual obligations, they should also be free to provide contractually for a private dispute resolution mechanism to adjudicate legal disputes arising from those obligations. From that premise, and the U.S. Supreme Court's declaration of an "emphatic federal policy in favor of arbitral dispute resolution,"[3] there has emerged a network of statutory provisions and judicial precedents that not only enforce the right to enter into arbitration agreements, but also seeks to give meaning to that right through procedures, standards, and presumptions that aim to promote expeditious resolution of arbitrated disputes with minimal interference by the courts.

*   Partner, Debevoise & Plimpton LLP; Adjunct Professor of Law, New York University School of Law.

**   Associate, Debevoise & Plimpton LLP; Teaching Fellow, Columbia University School of Law (2005). The authors wish to thank their Debevoise colleagues Ethan Leib and Matthew Leonard for their generous research assistance.

[1]   See, e.g., *United Steelworkers of America v. American Manufacturing Co.*, 363 U.S. 564, 570 (1960) (Brennan, J, concurring). Writing in 1999, Stephen J. Ware found this phrase repeated 177 times in U.S. judicial precedents. Stephen J. Ware, "Default Rules from Mandatory Rules: Privatizing Law through Arbitration", 83 *Minn. L. Rev.* 703, 708 note 17 (1999). A search performed on 30 May 30, 2005 found it repeated 349 times.

[2]   Federal Arbitration Act (codified as amended at 9 U.S.C. §§ 1-307 (2005)).

[3]   *Mitsubishi Motors Corp. v. Soler Chrysler-Plymouth, Inc.*, 473 U.S. 614, 631 (1985)).

Loukas A. Mistelis and Julian D.M. Lew (eds), Pervasive Problems in International Arbitration, 11-60
© 2006 Kluwer Law International. Printed in the Netherlands

1-2 The U.S. policy in favor of arbitration applies with "special force"[4] in the context of international disputes governed by the United Nations Convention on the Recognition and Enforcement of Foreign Arbitral Awards (the "New York Convention"), which entered into force in the United States in 1970.[5] The FAA implements the Convention as U.S. law. The regime of the New York Convention creates an international system of dispute resolution in which parties to transnational transactions may commit to submit disputes to arbitrators selected by their agreed method, select the procedural rules that will govern the arbitration, select the juridical seat of the arbitration (and hence the national jurisdiction with primary supervisory authority over the proceedings and the award),[6] and, with limited exceptions, ensure that the award will be enforceable as a court judgment in any country that is a party to the Convention. When combined with the commonly recognized legal principle that courts must enforce the parties' choice of law, the New York Convention provides for an efficient and harmonized world of international commerce in which parties may reduce the uncertainty inherent in cross-border transactions by agreeing in advance to an exclusive forum in which to adjudicate their disputes and a single set of default rules that will govern the merits of the dispute.[7]

1-3 Over the last 30 years, arbitration has become an increasingly dominant form of dispute resolution, progressively displacing the role of courts in international commercial disputes. Commercial actors frequently find the

---

[4] *Mitsubishi*, 473 U.S. at 631; see also *Vimar Seguros y Reaseguros, S.A. v. M/V Sky Reefer*, 515 U.S. 528, 541 (1995); *Scherk v. Alberto-Culver Co.*, 417 U.S. 506, 515-18 (1974).

[5] United Nations Convention on the Recognition and Enforcement of Foreign Arbitral Awards, June 10, 1958, 21 U.S.T. 2517, 330 U.N.T.S. 38 (codified at 9 U.S.C. §§ 201-208).

[6] While the New York Convention does not regulate the national law under which the arbitration takes place, it does take account of the place in the enforcement scheme. Article I(1) provides that the Convention "shall apply to the recognition and enforcement of arbitral awards made in the territory of a State other than the State where the recognition and enforcement of such awards are sought," whereas Article V(1)(e) provides that one independent ground upon which a court may refuse to enforce an award covered by the Convention is that the award "has been set aside or suspended by a competent authority of the country in which, or under the law of which, that award was made." The effect of these provisions is to allow the law of the place of arbitration to impose restrictions on arbitral proceedings and the enforcement of arbitral awards that are otherwise forbidden by the Convention.

[7] On the ability of the New York Convention regime to create a harmonized world of international commercial dispute resolution, see generally Eric A Posner, "Arbitration and the Harmonization of International Commercial Law: A Defense of *Mitsubishi*", 39 *Va. J. Int'l L.* 647, 647-49 (1999).

prospective choice of an arbitral forum and governing law more attractive than exposure to the multiplicity of legal regimes and substantive bodies of contract law that might otherwise be brought to bear on disputes arising out of an international transaction. But this expansion lies in some tension with the rationale that arbitration is simply "a creature of contract." That rationale may apply comfortably to sophisticated commercial actors concerned exclusively with regulating their mutual relations. But fully to realize the efficiencies of this international system of private arbitration, it is also necessary to cede to arbitrators the authority to reach binding determinations of claims that implicate public rights, and not merely private rights.

1-4 The complication arises on account of what are commonly called mandatory rules. As the term suggests, mandatory rules are the opposite of default rules. They arise outside the contract, apply regardless of what the parties agree to, and are typically designed to protect public interests that the state will not allow the parties waive. Broadly speaking, mandatory rules could be said to include any number of laws, ranging from laws that regulate arbitration procedure to criminal laws. In the context of international commercial arbitration, however, the debate over mandatory rules focuses on substantive laws that may affect the enforceability of contracts or otherwise may regulate the transaction subject to arbitration. Mandatory rules that have a bearing on international commercial relationships include antitrust laws, securities laws, exchange control regulations, embargo regimes, and laws of a policing nature, such as prohibitions of bribery and corruption.[8]

1-5 Soon after the New York Convention became U.S. law, courts in the United States began confronting cases in which a party alleged that the arbitration agreement extended not only to pure contract disputes, but also to claims for which U.S. mandatory rules, such as those arising out of federal securities laws or antitrust laws, provided a private right of action. Thus arose a fundamental issue: if the courts were to refuse to enforce pre-dispute agreements to arbitrate such disputes, or were to allow de novo review of awards determining such claims, the efficiencies of arbitration would be lost. Any time parties to a contract with a broad arbitration clause found themselves in dispute, a party seeking to obstruct the arbitral process could force a separate court litigation on a mandatory rules claim arising from the same transaction or relationship and involving the

---

[8] See, *e.g.*, Marc Blessing, "Mandatory Rules of Law versus Party Autonomy in International Arbitration", 14(4) *J. Int'l Arb.* 23 (1997).

same nucleus of facts as the arbitrable contract dispute. Given that the U.S. discovery process alone is often more costly and time consuming than an entire typical arbitration process, this possibility would create enormous incentive for obstructionist parties to make claims based on mandatory rules. On the other hand, if the courts were to cede those disputes to arbitral determination, they would allow private arbitrators to displace the courts on matters of public law, thereby risking under-enforcement or erroneous application of U.S. public policy.

1-6 Twenty years ago, the U.S. Supreme Court confronted this issue in its landmark decision in *Mitsubishi Motors Corp. v. Soler Chrysler-Plymouth, Inc.*[9] A divided Court chose the latter course, ruling that parties could bind themselves in advance to submit claims arising under the Sherman Act to international arbitration, and that U.S. courts could not revisit the arbitrators' resolution of such claims as long as the arbitrators actually heard and decided the claims. U.S. courts have since extended this holding in both international and domestic disputes to other statutory claims, including claims arising under the securities laws,[10] antidiscrimination laws,[11] and antiracketeering statutes.[12]

1-7 The *Mitsubishi* decision provoked immediate debate and, we would argue, confusion. In fact, two distinct and largely separate debates have focused on the implications of *Mitsubishi*. One set of questions concerns how domestic courts should treat mandatory rules – specifically, whether arbitrators can be trusted to adjudicate claims arising under mandatory rules and what, if any, system of balancing arbitration against public rights might be preferable to the scheme set forth by *Mitsubishi*. A second set of questions asks how international arbitrators should treat mandatory rules in light of *Mitsubishi* and similar decisions from other countries – specifically, whether, in order justify the trust which courts have placed in arbitrators, or otherwise to protect the enforceability of arbitral awards, arbitrators must transcend their traditional role of heeding the parties'

---

[9] 473 U.S. 614 (1985).

[10] See *Shearson/American Express, Inc. v. McMahon*, 482 U.S. 220, 238 (1987) (Securities Exchange Act of 1934); *Rodriguez de Quijas v. Shearson/American Express, Inc.*, 490 U.S. 477, 484-86 (1989) (Securities Act of 1933).

[11] See, *e.g.*, *Gilmer v. Interstate/Johnson Lane Corp.*, 500 U.S. 20, 35 (1991) (Age Discrimination in Employment Act of 1967); *EEOC v. Luce, Forward, Hamilton & Scripps*, 345 F.3d 742, 748-49 (9th Cir. 2003) (Title VII of the Civil Rights Act of 1964); *Bercovitch v. Baldwin School, Inc.* 133 F.3d 141, 151 (1st Cir. 1998) (Americans with Disabilities Act of 1990).

[12] See *McMahon*, 482 U.S. at 238-42 (Racketeer Influenced and Corrupt Organizations Act (RICO)).

contractual expectations and instead enforce certain mandatory rules even where the arbitrators read the parties' agreement to preclude such claims.

1-8 With the benefit of some 20 years experience in the post-*Mitsubishi* world, this chapter considers the implications of the *Mitsubishi* decision for both debates. Although each debate raises distinct questions, they share common features. In both instances, commentators have been consumed with primarily theoretical risks. In the United States, critics of *Mitsubishi* have worried about the risk to the domestic public interest of ceding mandatory rules claims to privately appointed arbitrators, whereas practitioners and scholars of international arbitration have worried about the risk to the international arbitral system of declining to hear such claims, even if contractual analysis would support that decision. To a surprising extent, both debates appear to misconceive both the holding of the *Mitsubishi* case and the realities of the international arbitral system. A proper understanding of the *Mitsubishi* decision and its context, we argue, allows a defense of the *Mitsubishi* rationale without requiring, or even recommending, any change to the traditional modus of international arbitration.

1-9 The focus on theoretical risks is especially surprising in light of the experience under *Mitsubishi*. In the United States, fear of arbitral under-enforcement of mandatory rules stands in stark contrast to the virtual absence of case law challenging arbitral determinations concerning mandatory rules. In fact, the issue appears to have arisen directly only once, and there is no indication that the arbitral tribunal at issue in that case proved an unworthy custodian of U.S. public policy. In the arbitration world, moreover, the debate on mandatory rules has proceeded without much attention to the ways in which standard arbitration agreements actually authorize the broad application of mandatory rules, or to the apparent absence of cases in which an arbitral tribunal has actually applied mandatory rules not authorized by the parties to reach a result other than that authorized by the contract alone.

1-10 Part II of this chapter analyzes the *Mitsubishi* decision itself. After providing a brief background on the evolution of U.S. arbitration law, it analyzes the reasoning and outcome of the *Mitsubishi* decision, distinguishing the Court's core holding from the unusual factual background that has complicated discussion of the decision.

1-11 Part III considers the domestic debate in the United States over whether the *Mitsubishi* Court placed inordinate trust in the arbitral system as a means of protecting public rights arising under mandatory rules. While it is undeniable that a policy of deferring to arbitral decision-making creates a risk of erroneous determination in any individual case – whether or not mandatory rules are involved – we argue that the theoretical fear of systematic bias against enforcement of mandatory rules is misplaced given the specific holding of the *Mitsubishi* decision and the realities of the international arbitral system. Moreover, the paucity of actual cases confronting the question provides empirical evidence both that these theoretical concerns have proven exaggerated, and that alternate mechanisms, for example government enforcement actions and lawsuits initiated by third parties such as consumers or shareholders, should be adequate to prevent public harms in individual cases where the arbitrators do reach the wrong result. Of course, while we focus our analysis on *Mitsubishi* and the United States, the lessons should apply generally to the balance between the enforcement of arbitration agreements and the enforcement of public law.

1-12 Part IV looks to the debate in the international arbitration community concerning when arbitrators should apply mandatory rules. It argues that this debate is misconceived. Although the arbitrability principle established in the *Mitsubishi* decision allows parties to submit mandatory rules claims to arbitrators, there is nothing in the decision that requires or encourages arbitrators to exceed their authority by applying mandatory rules that the parties did not agree to subject to arbitration. Nor is there any reason, as a policy matter, why the traditional party-controlled system of arbitration is an inadequate vehicle for addressing such questions. Indeed, the primary argument in the literature for transcending the parties' own agreement is rooted in a consideration – the sense of an arbitral duty to issue enforceable awards – that applied in this context might actually give credence to *Mitsubishi's* critics by encouraging a bias against enforcing mandatory rules.

II. THE *MITSUBISHI* DOCTRINE

1. Background

1-13 The problem of mandatory rules arises in a world in which parties are permitted to enter into binding pre-dispute arbitration agreements. That was not always the case. In the 19th century, U.S. courts took the view that contractual arbitration clauses were nonbinding, and that arbitral decisions would be enforced only if the parties had agreed to submit the dispute to arbitration after it had arisen.[13] In this context, a post-dispute agreement to arbitrate could be viewed simply as a form of voluntary settlement, and parties concerned that a particular arbitral forum might not prove sympathetic to claims or defenses arising under particular mandatory rules could not be forced to abandon a judicial remedy for those claims.

1-14 This situation changed with the passage of the Federal Arbitration Act in 1925. The Act provides that an arbitration provision in a commercial contract "shall be valid, irrevocable, and enforceable, save upon such grounds as exist at law or in equity for the revocation of any contract."[14] For decades, the courts proved reluctant to extend this language to domestic disputes involving claims arising under mandatory rules. In its 1953 decision in *Wilko v. Swan*, for example, the U.S. Supreme Court refused to require arbitration of a shareholder's claim for damages under Section 12(2) of the Securities Act of 1933, holding that that statute created "a special right to recover for misrepresentation" which outweighed the policies underlying the FAA.[15] In the antitrust sphere, the U.S. Court of Appeals for the Second Circuit rendered an influential 1968 decision that refused on analogous grounds to enforce an agreement to arbitrate a claim arising under the Sherman Act.[16]

1-15 The U.S. Supreme Court would eventually rethink these decisions. The transformation began after the United States' accession to the New York Convention in 1970 as the Court assessed anew the relevance of mandatory rules within the specific context of international commerce. In 1972, the Court decided *The Bremen v. Zapata Off-Shore Co.*, in which, confronted with a contract for the shipment of a drilling rig from the United States to Italy, the Court enforced a forum-selection clause requiring that all disputes arising out of the contract be litigated in the English courts.[17] In language that the Court would later cite in the international arbitration context, it emphasized that

---

[13] See Robert B. von Mehren, "From *Vynior's Case* to *Mitsubishi*: The Future of Arbitration and Public Law", 12 *Brooklyn J. Int'l L.* 583, 589-90 (1986).

[14] 9 U.S.C. § 2 (2005).

[15] 346 U.S. 427, 431 (1953),

[16] *American Safety Equip. Corp. v. J.P. Maguire & Co.*, 391 F.2d 821 (2d Cir. 1968).

[17] 407 U.S. 1 (1972).

[t]he expansion of American business and industry will hardly be encouraged if, notwithstanding solemn contracts, we insist on a parochial concept that all disputes must be resolved under our laws and in our courts.[18]

1-16 Next, in its 1974 decision in *Scherk v. Alberto-Culver Co.*, the Court revisited the arbitrability of the U.S. securities laws in the context of an international commercial contract.[19] The case concerned a U.S. manufacturer, Alberto-Culver Co., and a German citizen, Fritz Scherk, who entered into an agreement by which Scherk transferred to Alberto-Culver his ownership of various enterprises organized under the laws of Germany and Switzerland. Scherk later sought to enforce an arbitration agreement after Alberto-Culver initiated a lawsuit in a federal district court in Illinois seeking damages for alleged fraudulent representations in violation of Section 10(b) of the Securities Exchange Act of 1934. After lower courts rejected Scherk's motion on the basis of the *Wilko* decision, the dispute reached the Supreme Court, which, reversing, enforced the agreement to arbitrate the securities claims. The case involved a different statutory provision than did the *Wilko* dispute, but the Court assumed arguendo that the provisions were the same. On that assumption, it distinguished the earlier case based on the international character of the transaction before it.[20] Contrasting the relative certainty as to the law applicable to domestic transactions with the uncertain landscape of international transactions, the Court observed that

[a] contractual provision specifying in advance the forum in which disputes shall be litigated and the law to be applied is, therefore, an almost indispensable precondition to achievement of the orderliness and predictability essential to any international business transaction.[21]

Concerned that a party in Scherk's position could seek a foreign injunction against Alberto-Culver's U.S. securities action, the Court invoked *The Bremen*, reasoning that

[a] parochial refusal by the courts of one country to enforce an international arbitration agreement would not only frustrate these purposes [of orderliness and predictability], but would invite unseemly and mutually destructive jockeying by the parties to secure tactical litigation advantages.[22]

---

[18] *Ibid.* at 9.
[19] 417 U.S. 506 (1974).
[20] *Ibid.* at 515.
[21] *Ibid.* at 516.
[22] *Ibid.* at 516-17.

This prospect, in the Court's view, rendered "chimerical" the advantages to claimants of securing court access under the securities laws and cautioned against any presumed exception to "the clear provisions of the Arbitration Act."[23]

1-17 The *Scherk* Court thus declared the securities claims arbitrable, but it went no further, omitting any discussion of when, if ever, it would refuse to order arbitration of such statutory claims or what, if any, judicial review would be available following the outcome of the arbitral proceedings. The Court did not reach those questions until its decision in *Mitsubishi*, which remains the Court's most comprehensive consideration of the relationship between arbitration and mandatory rules.

2. The Mitsubishi *Decision*

1-18 The dispute in *Mitsubishi* arose out of a transaction between a Japanese automobile manufacturer, the Mitsubishi Motors Corporation ("Mitsubishi"), and a Puerto Rican distributor, Soler Chrysler-Plymouth ("Soler"). The parties entered into a distribution agreement providing for the distribution of Mitsubishi vehicles by Soler within a designated area that included San Juan, Puerto Rico. They also executed a separate sales agreement providing for the direct sale of Mitsubishi products to Soler.[24] The sales agreement, but not the distribution agreement, included a third party, Chrysler, S.A. ("CISA"), a Swiss corporation registered in Geneva which, together with its joint venture partner Mitsubishi Heavy Industries, Inc., owned Mitsubishi. The sales agreement contained an arbitration clause, which provided that "[a]ll disputes, controversies or differences which may arise between [Mitsubishi] and [Soler] out of or in relation to" certain provisions of the agreement, or their breach, would be "settled by arbitration in Japan in accordance with the rules and regulations of the Japan Commercial Arbitration Association."[25]

1-19 A dispute arose when Soler became unable to meet its contractual minimum sales volume and Mitsubishi refused to permit Soler to transship vehicles for sale to the continental United States and Latin America. Invoking the arbitration clause in the sales agreement, Mitsubishi filed a request for arbitration before the Japan Commercial Arbitration Association and also commenced an action against Soler in the United States District Court for the District of Puerto Rico in

---

[23] *Ibid.* at 517-18.
[24] *Mitsubishi*, 473 U.S. at 617.
[25] *Ibid.*

which it sought an order to compel arbitration pursuant to the FAA.[26] Soler counterclaimed, alleging various breaches of the sales agreement and asserting various statutory causes of action, including a claim that Mitsubishi and CISA had conspired to divide markets in restraint of trade in violation of the Sherman Act.

1-20 The District Court granted Mitsubishi's motion to compel arbitration, holding that the majority of the counterclaims, including the antitrust claim, were both subject to the arbitration clause and arbitrable. With respect to the antitrust claim, the District Court relied on *Scherk* to find that the international character of the transaction required enforcement of the arbitration agreement. The U.S. Court of Appeals for the First Circuit agreed that the antitrust claims were subject to the arbitration agreement, but held *Scherk* inapposite. Instead, it followed *American Safety Equipment v. J.P. Maquire & Co.*,[27] in which the Second Circuit had refused to enforce a pre-dispute commitment to arbitrate antitrust claims.[28] The Supreme Court then reversed in an opinion by Justice Harry A. Blackmun.

1-21 Applying the established presumption that "any doubts concerning the scope of arbitrable issues should be resolved in favor of arbitration," the Court agreed with both the District Court and Court of Appeals that the arbitration clause did cover the Sherman Act claims.[29] It then explained why that contractual choice should be enforced. The Court first reviewed the same general considerations that it had found dispositive in *The Bremen* and *Scherk* and which, in its view, established a

> strong presumption in favor of enforcement of freely negotiated contractual choice-of-forum provisions . . . reinforced by the emphatic federal policy in favor of arbitral dispute resolution.[30]

It then proceeded to discount the concerns raised by the Second Circuit, in the *American Safety* decision, about the arbitrability of antitrust claims. Whereas the *American Safety* court had cautioned against the "strong possibility that contracts which generate antitrust disputes may be contracts of adhesion," the *Mitsubishi* Court maintained that the "mere appearance of an antitrust dispute does not alone

---

[26] *Ibid.* at 618-19.

[27] 391 F.2d 821 (2d Cir. 1968).

[28] *Mitsubishi Motors Corp. v. Soler Chrysler-Plymouth, Inc.*, 723 F.2d 155 (1st Cir. 1983).

[29] 473 U.S. at 626 (quoting *Moses H. Cone Mem'l Hosp. v. Mercury Constr. Corp.*, 460 U.S. 1, 24 (1983)).

[30] *Ibid.* at 631.

warrant invalidation of the selected forum" and pointed out that a party could override a specific forum selection clause upon a proper showing, for example where the agreement was affected by fraud or like contract defenses.[31]

1-22 Nor did the Court find the "potential complexity" of antitrust disputes troublesome. It observed that courts had already permitted post-dispute arbitration of such claims; that "adaptability and access to expertise are hallmarks of arbitration," where processes typically allow for parties to select appropriate arbitrators and provide for the assistance of party-appointed and tribunal-appointed experts; and that streamlined proceedings are often desirable to parties who wish "to keep the effort and expense required to resolve a dispute within manageable bounds."[32] Similarly, the Court

> reject[ed] the proposition that an arbitration panel will pose too great a danger of innate hostility to the constraints on business conduct that antitrust laws imposes.[33]

It noted in this respect that "[i]nternational arbitrators frequently are drawn from the legal as well as the business community" and that the parties or designated appointing authority could be expected to select appropriate arbitrators where a dispute has an important legal component. Thus, the Court

> decline[d] to indulge the presumption that the parties and arbitral body conducting the proceeding will be unable or unwilling to retain competent, conscientious, and impartial arbitrators.[34]

1-23 Having satisfied itself that none of these concerns posed a serious threat to arbitration of an antitrust claim, the Court then turned to what it considered "the core of the *American Safety* doctrine - the fundamental importance to American democratic capitalism of the regime of the antitrust laws."[35] The issue here is the one that typically dominates discussion of mandatory rules. Although the antitrust laws provide for a private remedy, they promote a deep public interest, converting the individual litigant into a "private attorney-general who protects the public's interest" with recourse to a treble-damages provision that serves as a "chief tool in the antitrust enforcement scheme, posing a crucial deterrent to

---

[31] *Ibid.* at 632.
[32] *Ibid.* at 633.
[33] *Ibid.* at 634.
[34] *Ibid.*
[35] *Ibid.* at 634-35.

potential violators."[36] Given this important public function, which transcends the rights of particular individuals, why should the courts cede supervision of the antitrust laws to privately appointed arbitrators?

1-24 The *Mitsubishi* Court gave three, largely independent answers to this question. *First*, it maintained, based on a review of the relevant legislative history, that the statutory treble-damages remedy sought by Soler was primarily compensatory, notwithstanding its "important incidental policing function."[37] *Second*, it observed that the "antitrust cause of action remains at all times under the control of the individual litigant," who is under no obligation to initiate a suit and remains free to reach a settlement without executive or judicial approval. Thus, the Court concluded that

> at least where the international cast of a transaction would otherwise add an element of uncertainty to dispute resolution, the prospective litigant may provide in advance for a mutually agreeable procedure whereby he would seek his antitrust recovery as well as settle other controversies.[38]

Finally, the Court returned to its fundamental point that arbitration was in fact a trustworthy means of resolving disputes, stating that

> so long as the prospective litigant effectively may vindicate its statutory cause of action in the arbitral forum, the statute will continue to serve both its remedial and deterrent function.[39]

1-25 Thus, as in *Scherk*, the Court ordered arbitration of the statutory claim, and it did so with a ringing endorsement of the methods and competence of the arbitral process. Unlike the *Scherk* decision, however, the *Mitsubishi* Court indicated in dicta that its decision was subject to two related qualifications.

1-26 *First*, in its much discussed footnote 19, the Court made clear that its holding hinged on the assumption that the Sherman Act claims were in fact before the arbitral tribunal sitting in Japan.[40] That the tribunal would have had authority to hear Soler's counterclaim was not altogether clear. The sales agreement contained a choice of Swiss law clause which raised the concern that the arbitrators might believe they lacked authority to apply the Sherman Act to

---

[36] *Ibid.* at 635 (internal citations not supplied).
[37] *Ibid.*
[38] *Ibid.* at 636.
[39] *Ibid.* at 637.
[40] *Ibid.* at 637 n.19.

Soler's antitrust claims.[41] In that event, the parties would have effectively contracted out of the Sherman Act by entering into an agreement that required arbitration of Soler's antitrust claims but subjected them to Swiss law. The Court noted this concern, but also took account of a representation by Mitsubishi that "American law applied to the antitrust claims."[42] Mitsubishi also represented that the claims had been submitted to the arbitrators and the Court found confirmation in the record that "the arbitral panel had taken these claims under submission."[43] The holding thus assumed that the arbitral tribunal would take cognizance of the antitrust claims, but the Court also cautioned that

> in the event the choice-of-forum and choice-of-law clauses operated in tandem as a prospective waiver of a party's right to pursue statutory remedies for antitrust violations, we would have little hesitation in condemning the agreement as against public policy.[44]

1-27 *Second*, the Court considered what subsequent commentators have called the "second look." It emphasized that under the New York Convention, U.S. courts would retain supervision over the arbitral process in the event that a party sought enforcement in the United States. But the Court made clear that any review of an award on the Sherman Act claims would be highly constrained, limited to ensuring that the antitrust claims were heard and decided:

> Having permitted the arbitration to go forward, the national courts of the United States will have the opportunity at the award-enforcement stage to ensure that the legitimate interest in the enforcement of the antitrust laws has been addressed. The Convention reserves to each signatory country the right to refuse enforcement of an award where the 'recognition or enforcement of the award would be contrary to the public policy of that country.' While the efficacy of the arbitral process requires that substantive review at the award-enforcement stage remain minimal, it would not require intrusive inquiry to ascertain that the tribunal took cognizance of the antitrust claims and actually decided them.[45]

---

[41] This clause provided that the agreement would be "governed by, and construed in all respects according to the law of the Swiss Confederation *as if entirely performed therein.*" *Ibid.* [emphasis supplied].

[42] *Ibid.* at 637.

[43] *Ibid.*

[44] *Ibid.*

[45] *Ibid.* at 638 [internal citations not supplied].

1-28 The *Mitsubishi* decision involved claims under the Sherman Act, but its rationale has since provided a general approach to arbitration of mandatory rules that Congress has not specifically made non-arbitrable.[46]

1-29 Criticism of *Mitsubishi* began with Justice Stevens's vigorous dissent, in which he declared that

> the elected representatives of the American people would not have us dispatch an American citizen to a foreign land in search of an uncertain remedy for the violation of a public right that is protected by the Sherman Act.[47]

3. *Understanding* Mitsubishi

1-30 Concerns about the effect of the *Mitsubishi* decision often appear to reflect confusion over its terms. We begin, therefore, by considering concretely what relationship between arbitration and court litigation the *Mitsubishi* decision embraced, and then consider both the theoretical and empirical implications of this model for the enforcement of U.S. mandatory rules.

1-31 The confusion arises from the interplay between the Court's core holding on arbitrability and its dicta concerning "prospective waiver" and the so-called "second look." Several commentators, for example, have questioned the coherence of requiring the invalidation of arbitration agreements that effect "prospective waiver" of mandatory rules.

1-32 In an article published not long after the *Mitsubishi* decision, Thomas E. Carbonneau criticized the decision for its

> [f]inding that an arbitration agreement is invalid because the principal contract refers to a governing law that lacks antitrust provisions.[48]

More recently, Eric Posner has argued that

---

[46] See *Shearson/American Express, Inc. v. McMahon*, 482 U.S. 220, 238-42 (1987) (extending *Mitsubishi* to RICO claims); *Vimar Seguros y Reaseguros, S.A. v. M/V Sky Reefer*, 515 U.S. 528, 541 (1995) (applying *Mitsubishi* to claims arising under Carriage of Goods at Sea Act). The Court has also extended *Mitsubishi* to domestic arbitration involving the Sherman Act, and it has explicitly overruled *Wilko v. Swan*, confirming that domestic securities law claims are also arbitrable. See *McMahon*, 482 U.S. 220.; *Rodriguez de Quijas v. Shearson/American Express, Inc.*, 490 U.S. 477 (1989).

[47] 473 U.S. at 666 (Stevens, J., dissenting).

[48] Thomas E. Carbonneau, "The Exuberant Pathway to Quixotic Internationalism: Assessing the Folly of *Mitsubishi*", 19 *Vand. J. Transnat'l L.* 265, 286 (1986).

footnote 19 is resoundingly ambiguous: either courts should enforce arbitration agreements routinely or only when they are sure that arbitrators will respect mandatory rules. Because the *Mitsubishi* Court assumed that the arbitrator in that case would respect American antitrust laws, the holding provides no direction for courts when the arbitrator's stance is in doubt.[49]

Posner further maintains that "[m]ost commentators believe that the holding of the majority and the dicta in footnote 19 contradict each other."[50]
Similarly, Andrew Guzman has identified an alleged contradiction in footnote 19:

> On the one hand, it indicates that arbitrators are to be given the benefit of the doubt and that arbitration agreements should be enforced. On the other hand, it indicates that such agreements will not be enforced when they represent a 'prospective waiver' of U.S. law.[51]

If these concerns have any validity, they necessarily call into question the practicability of requiring courts to use their "second look" to refuse enforcement of arbitration awards that effect such a waiver.

1-33 At root, these concerns appear to rest on a mistaken reading of *Mitsubishi*. Properly understood, the core principle of the case is a straightforward one: although parties may enter into pre-dispute agreements to arbitrate claims arising under mandatory rules, the courts should ensure that such agreements do not waive the right to have those claims heard and decided by the arbitral tribunal. The "prospective waiver" and "second look" doctrines operate to ensure that an arbitration agreement cannot be used to prevent such a hearing and decision.

1-34 What concretely does this mean? Consider the mechanics if a court were to identify the "prospective waiver" contemplated by the *Mitsubishi* dictum. Assume, for example, that the Mitsubishi sales agreement expressly authorized the arbitral tribunal to hear unfair competition claims but also contained an express proviso barring either the federal courts or the arbitral tribunal from hearing claims arising under the Sherman Act. In the views of the commentators just quoted, it would seem, the provision would then constitute a clear "prospective waiver," and *Mitsubishi's* footnote 19 would doom the entire

---

[49] Posner, supra note 7, at 650-51.
[50] *Ibid.* at 651.
[51] Andrew T. Guzman, "Arbitrator Liability: Reconciling Arbitration and Mandatory Rules", 49 *Duke L. J.* 1279, 1297 (2000).

arbitration agreement and empower the courts to hear the entire dispute, including both Mitsubishi's contractual claims and any applicable statutory claims that might be recognized by the tribunal.

1-35 But that would not be a fair reading of the decision when read in the context of the problem facing the Court as well the more general interplay of courts and arbitrators. In order to give effect to the principle set forth in footnote 19, the Court could simply sever the offending portion of the arbitration agreement from the unoffending portion, allowing the Sherman Act claims to go forward in U.S. court while consigning the rest of the dispute to arbitration, including any competition law claims that might arise under Swiss law. This is what courts commonly do when they confront arbitration clauses that are only partially enforceable.[52] In the *Mitsubishi* case itself, for example, the consequence of the First Circuit's prior determination that Soler's Sherman Act claims were inarbitrable was to deny arbitration of those claims, while enforcing the broader arbitration agreement.[53] Read in context, therefore, the Supreme Court's statement in footnote 19 that a "prospective waiver" would result in the condemnation of the "agreement" could only refer to that aspect of the agreement that purported to require arbitration of competition law claims but excluded application of the Sherman Act – that is, that aspect that effected the "prospective waiver" itself.

1-36 Of course, not all cases of "prospective waiver" will be as explicit as the hypothetical we have just outlined, and it is correct that the *Mitsubishi* Court did not itself set forth an explicit test for identifying such a waiver. But the *Mitsubishi* Court did signal the danger of premature speculation as to how an arbitral tribunal would interpret an ambiguous or vague contract, and in that context it adopted a permissive approach that gave arbitration the benefit of the doubt. That decision left open an obvious risk: namely, that after the Court referred Soler's Sherman Act claim to the tribunal, the tribunal would refuse to decide the claim. But the Court specifically responded to that risk by reminding the parties that the U.S. courts

---

[52] See, *e.g.*, *Dean Witter Reynolds Inc. v. Byrd*, 470 U.S. 213, 217 (1985) (holding that the "Arbitration Act requires district courts to compel arbitration of pendent arbitrable claims when one of the parties files a motion to compel, even where the result would be the possibly inefficient maintenance of separate proceedings in different forums")

[53] See *Mitsubishi*, 473 U.S. at 623.

would have the opportunity at the enforcement stage to ensure that the legitimate interest in the enforcement of the antitrust laws has been addressed.

1-37 Such review might occur in one of two ways. Soler independently might refile its Sherman Act claim following the conclusion of the arbitral proceeding, and Mitsubishi might raise as a defense the res judicata effect of the arbitral proceedings.[54] Or Mitsubishi might commence a proceeding to enforce the arbitral award in the United States, whereupon Soler might invoke the Sherman Act as a defense against such enforcement. In either event, the basic question would be the same: to determine whether Soler's statutory claim could go forward, the court would need merely to determine whether or not "the tribunal took cognizance of the antitrust claims and actually decided them."[55] In the event that the tribunal did not, the tribunal's award could not preclude Soler from pursuing that claim. However, there would be no reason not to let stand the tribunal's resolution of the others issues before it. The U.S. courts, of course, would need to determine what effect to give the award in the event that Soler prevailed in its claim for damages, but that is a standard question faced anytime that parties to a common transaction seek distinct remedies in different proceedings. Indeed, that enforcement stage question is no different than the one the courts would have faced in the uncontroversial scenario in which the parties had not agreed to arbitrate statutory claims but had instead entered into a narrower arbitration agreement that limited the arbitrators' jurisdiction to breach-of-contract claims.

1-38 Given the specifics of this interaction between the "prospective waiver" and "second look" doctrines, the prospect that a court may compel arbitration based on the incorrect prospective assumption that an arbitral tribunal will take cognizance of a mandatory rule is not especially consequential. In the event that the court guesses wrong, and mandates arbitration of a statutory claim that the

---

[54] See William W. Park, "Private Adjudicators and the Public Interest: The Expanding Scope of International Arbitration", 12 *Brook. J. Int'l L.* 629, 641-42 (1986).

[55] *Mitsubishi*, 473 U.S. at 638. Presumably for these purposes, the party resisting enforcement of the mandatory rule would also need to present evidence that it actually attempted to bring the relevant rule before the arbitrators. Otherwise, the award should benefit from the same principles of res judicata and issue preclusion that would apply to any domestic court decision. The FAA, in particular, provides that a U.S. court-confirmed arbitral award "shall have the same force and effect, in all respects, as, and be subject to all the provisions of law relating to, a judgment in an action; and it may be enforced as if it had been rendered in an action in the court in which it is entered." 9 U.S.C. § 13 (2005).

tribunal refuses to hear, the only issue is one of timing: the aggrieved party will have to wait to the end of the arbitral proceeding to pursue its statutory claim. Consistent with the Court's general view that ambiguities should be resolved in favor of arbitration, the *Mitsubishi* Court adopted a permissive approach to contractual ambiguity. And if the particular procedural facts of the *Mitsubishi* case raised doubts about how courts should approach future cases, subsequent case law clarified the question.

1-39 In *Vimar Seguros y Reaseguros, S.A. v. M/V Sky Reefer*, the Court ordered arbitration of a dispute arising out of a bill of lading notwithstanding the fact that arbitrators sitting in Japan would apply Japanese rules imposing a lesser standard of liability than those mandatorily imposed by the United States' Carriage of Goods by Sea Act ("COGSA").[56] Unlike in *Mitsubishi*, where the Court relied upon representations and evidence that the arbitrators would in fact entertain Soler's Sherman Act claim, the *Vimar* Court adopted a more explicit "wait and see" approach, declining to identify a "prospective waiver" where

> [a]t this interlocutory stage it is not established what law the arbitrators will apply to petitioner's claims or that petitioner will receive diminished protection as a result.[57]

Emphasizing that its holding turned on the availability of later review, the Court reasoned that

> [a]s the District Court has retained jurisdiction, mere speculation that the foreign arbitrators might apply Japanese law which, depending on the proper construction of COGSA, might reduce respondents' legal obligations, does not in and of itself lessen liability under COGSA § 3(8).[58]

1-40 None of this is to say that the *Mitsubishi* decision itself answers all questions of application. For example, how does a court assess at the "second look" stage whether a tribunal has actually decided a claim invoking a mandatory rule? Is it correct that *Mitsubishi*

---

[56] 515 U.S. 528 (1995).
[57] *Ibid.* at 540.
[58] *Ibid.* at 541.

may call for merely a mechanical inspection of the face of the award, which may not pose an obstacle to a savvy arbitrator who mentions the Sherman Act before rendering an award that misapplies the Act?[59]

Or does the "second look" require a more searching inquiry to confirm at least that the arbitrator provided meaningful consideration of the claim, as for example might be evidenced by a fully reasoned award? Might there be situations in which an arbitral tribunal so misstates the applicable legal standard that one might say the tribunal did not truly take cognizance of the claim?

1-41 A related set of questions goes to the interaction between the limited "second look" review of *Mitsubishi* and the more general standard under the New York Convention pursuant to which awards that violate public policy may be refused enforcement.[60] Could a court refuse enforcement of an arbitral award on the ground that the effect of enforcement would be to cause obvious injury to interests protected by a mandatory rule even if the tribunal rejected a claim or defense invoking that rule? If so, where does the court draw the line between protecting public policy and refusing to revisit the merits?

1-42 Notwithstanding these questions, the *Mitsubishi* holding maintains a basic logic: parties to international arbitration agreements maintain the substantive rights existing under mandatory rules. An agreement to forgo U.S. court adjudication of claims arising out of those rights will not be given effect unless the arbitrators actually entertain the claims (or, perhaps, apply other analogous laws that provide "adequate" protections[61]). If the arbitrators do entertain those claims, their decision will be enforced.

---

[59] Park, supra note 54, at 648-49.

[60] New York Convention, supra note 5, at art. V(2)(b).

[61] In a series of cases exemplified by *Roby v. Corp. of Lloyd's,* 996 F.2d 1353, 1361-66 (2d Cir. 1993), the federal courts of appeals have enforced arbitration and judicial forum selection agreements even on the assumption that English courts and arbitrators would not apply U.S. securities laws, on the ground that the English law of fraud provided "adequate remedies" for the alleged wrongdoing. See also *Haynsworth v. The Corp.,* 121 F.3d 956, 969-70 (5th Cir. 1997) ("The plaintiffs' remedies in England are adequate to protect their interests and the policies behind the statutes at issue."); *Allen v. Lloyd's of London,* 94 F.3d 923, 928-30 (4th Cir. 1996) ("British law . . . affords [plaintiffs] adequate remedies in the United Kingdom."); *Bonny v. Soc'y of Lloyd's,* 3 F.3d 156, 161-62 (7th Cir. 1993) ("[W]e are satisfied that several remedies in England vindicate plaintiffs' substantive rights while not subverting the [policies behind the U.S. securities laws]."). These cases raise an issue distinct from that addressed in this chapter, because those courts effectively held that there was no prospective waiver to bring *Mitsubishi* into play. Whether those holdings are consistent with *Mitsubishi* or correct on their own terms is a matter beyond the scope of this chapter.

III. THE COURTS' PERSPECTIVE

1-43 Arguments against judicial application of the *Mitsubishi* approach generally come in two forms. One is an argument in principle that objects to the improper delegation of public rights to private mechanisms. The other focuses on the practical consequences of that delegation and fears that arbitration is not an effective mechanism for vindicating public rights, particularly where the parties may have an incentive to waive those rights.

1. Improper Delegation

1-44 The "improper delegation" argument pervades much of the pre-*Mitsubishi* judicial skepticism toward arbitrating mandatory rules.[62] The argument has been well summarized by William Park, who describes it as

> a recognition that arbitrators are paid only to do justice between or among the parties before them. 'Public rights' belong not to the litigants, but to society at large. Society never signed the arbitration agreement, and is not a party to the arbitration. If the arbitration, which is a consensual process, affects only the consenting adults who signed the agreement, they alone are hurt by the arbitrators' folly. But if the dispute affects the property of one who never signed the arbitration agreement, the arbitration takes on a different cast. Indeed, the right to proper enforcement of antitrust laws may be analogous to a third person's property right. Furthermore, the societal interest in the vindication of claims relating to matters such as free economic competition and the securities markets belongs not to the businessmen in the controversy, but to a community which never agreed to arbitrate.[63]

---

[62] For example, in language quoted in Justice Stevens's *Mitsubishi* dissent, the *American Safety* Court urged that

> [a] claim under the antitrust laws is not merely a private matter. The Sherman Act is designed to promote the national interest in a competitive economy; thus, the plaintiff asserting his rights under the Act has been likened to a private attorney-general who protects the public's interest. . . . Antitrust violations can affect hundreds of thousands -- perhaps millions -- of people and inflict staggering economic damage. . . . We do not believe that Congress intended such claims to be resolved elsewhere than in the courts.

Mitsubishi, 473 U.S. at 655-65 (Stevens, J., dissenting) (quoting *American Safety*, 391 F.2d at 826-27).

[63] Park, supra note 54 at 638.

1-45 The intuitive appeal of this perspective comes from the suspicion that *Mitsubishi* trespasses upon the public/private distinction inherent in the notion that "arbitration is a creature of contract." The reality, however, is that this distinction is much murkier than might appear and – with or without the *Mitsubishi* decision – does not allow such absolute categorization. For starters, as the *Mitsubishi* decision itself observed, the "improper delegation" argument does not account for the circumstance that the delegation has in large part already occurred. The entire debate on mandatory rules and arbitration deals with a set of public rights that, by definition, the state has already entrusted to private litigants by providing private rights of action. If parties are free to decline enforcement of those rights, privately settle disputes concerning those rights, or enter into post-dispute agreements to arbitrate such disputes, does the public/private distinction provide a reliable basis for determining whether they should be permitted to execute contracts which commit them to arbitrate future disputes implicating mandatory rules?[64]

1-46 On the flipside, it would be wrong to assume that there are no public rights at issue in the resolution of even purely "private" disputes. When U.S. courts in the 19th century refused to enforce pre-dispute arbitration agreements, they did so on the basis of a mandatory rule: namely, that the right to court adjudication was too sacred to allow parties to forgo it in advance. In 1879, the U.S. Supreme Court justified this approach with the declaration that

> [e]very citizen is entitled to resort to all the courts of the country, and to invoke the protection which all the laws or all those courts may afford him. A man may not barter away his life or his freedom, or his substantial rights.[65]

Illustrating that principle, the Court noted that a party "may submit his particular [i.e., existing] civil suit by his own consent to an arbitration, or to the decision of a single judge" but he cannot "bind himself in advance by an agreement, which may be specifically enforced, thus to forfeit his rights at all times and on all occasions, whenever the case may be presented."[66]

---

[64] One can also think of certain analogies in purely public contexts - for example in administrative proceedings - in which adjudications concerning both public and private rights are subject to due process constraints that provide far less protection than a full trial.

[65] *Home Insurance Co. v. Morse*, 87 U.S. 445, 451 (1874).

[66] *Ibid.* See generally von Mehren, *supra* note 13, at 589-91.

31

1-47 The passage of the FAA, of course, changed this calculus, instituting a regime in which parties could make pre-dispute arbitration agreements. The statutory regime, along with the web of judicial holdings that have upheld and interpreted it, necessarily reflects a substantive judgment that arbitration provides adequate protection of the interests underlying rights that would otherwise be enforceable in court. And even today, this delegation is subject to limits that reflect the continued concern of the law to ensure the fairness of private dispute resolution. Soler and Mitsubishi could not, for example, have entered into an enforceable pre-dispute contract requiring any future breach of contract claims to be decided by a coin toss. The legal presumption that pre-dispute arbitration agreements will provide an adequate means of dispute resolution hinges, moreover, on the assumption that the agreement has been freely negotiated by parties capable of protecting their interests. Therefore, as the Court noted in *Mitsubishi*, Soler could have resisted enforcement of the arbitration agreement had it made a showing

> that the agreement was [affected] by fraud, undue influence, or overweening bargaining power; that enforcement would be unreasonable and unjust; or that proceedings in the contractual forum will be so gravely difficult and inconvenient that [the resisting party] will for all practical purposes be deprived of his day in court.[67]

1-48 Finally, it should be emphasized that *Mitsubishi* is concerned merely with interpretive presumptions; obviously it does not purport to take away Congress's right to determine what claims may be arbitrated. Had the Sherman Act itself included a provision excluding application of the FAA to antitrust actions, the question before the Court would have been an easy one. And Congress, of course, could so amend the Sherman Act if it wished.

1-49 Ultimately, therefore, the *Mitsubishi* decision cannot be understood by reference to a Manichean distinction between unregulated private rights and court-protected public rights. Instead, the decision presents a nuanced question of how to reconcile two statutory regimes: one that creates a privately enforceable but non-compulsory right to enforce antitrust claims and another that requires general enforcement of agreements to arbitrate private rights of action but neither distinguishes nor explicitly provides for the distinct status of mandatory rules.

---

[67] 473 U.S. at 632 (quoting *The Bremen,* 407 U.S. at 12, 15, 18) (internal quotations and citations not supplied) (alteration in original).

1-50 None of this is to say, of course, that there is no difference between a regime that allows parties to arbitrate mandatory rules and one that does not. But seen in its proper light, *Mitsubishi* does not so much reflect a sea change in the adjudication of public rights as it reflects an additional permutation in a landscape in which public rights have become partly privatized and private models of dispute resolution have received some degree of official sanction. The mere circumstance that *Mitsubishi* allows private arbitrators to adjudicate mandatory rules where the parties have given their pre-dispute consent does not ipso facto provide a compelling reason to reject that decision.

2. The Waiver Argument

1-51 *Mitsubishi's* critics have also focused on the consequences of ceding mandatory rules to arbitrators and have questioned whether arbitration of mandatory rules will damage the public interest by leading to under-enforcement of those rules. The question here boils down to one of arbitrator competence – can the arbitration process be trusted to vindicate mandatory rules? The *Mitsubishi* Court decisively

> reject[ed] the proposition that an arbitration panel will pose too great a danger of innate hostility to the constraints on business conduct that antitrust law imposes

and further

> decline[d] to indulge the presumption that the parties and arbitral body conducting a proceeding will be unable or unwilling to retain competent, conscientious, and impartial arbitrators.[68]

1-52 Others have not been so willing to place their trust in arbitrators. Critics have observed, for example, that "[t]he arbitrator is paid to consider the interests of the parties,"[69] and have maintained that, institutionally, arbitrators do not feel bound to follow the law.[70] The concern here is twofold: *first*, that arbitrators will ignore mandatory rules and yield unjust results in arbitrations involving such rules, and *second*, that this prospect will alter parties' incentives so as to cause them to enter into arbitration agreements in order effectively to waive the application of those nominally unwaivable rules.

---

[68] 473 U.S. at 634.
[69] Park, supra note 54, at 665-66.
[70] Ware, supra note 1, at 719-21.

1-53 The waiver argument has been developed most systematically as a rational choice argument. Eric Posner, for example, has argued that

> [i]f courts . . . enforce arbitration awards without subjecting them to de novo review, then arbitrators would be free to ignore mandatory rules if they wanted to. And arbitrators would want to ignore mandatory rules because they know that merchants, ex ante, prefer that their contracts be enforced as written and would prefer to pay for the services of arbitrators who enforce the contract rather than the mandatory rules that the contract may violate.[71]

Posner argues that this incentive can be corrected without forgoing the benefits of arbitration via a system that randomly subjects some, but not all, arbitral awards to de novo review.[72]

1-54 Andrew Guzman shows greater sensitivity to the mechanics of modern arbitration, in which the arbitrators are not actually selected until a dispute has already arisen, at which point the party looking to benefit from a mandatory rule will have the incentive to invoke it. He recognizes that any bias against mandatory rules must be filtered through the mechanism by which the parties arrange for the postdispute appointment of arbitrators. In modern international arbitration, that mechanism almost invariably provides for an arbitral institution to serve as an appointing authority to choose the tie-breaking arbitrator in the event that the parties or arbitrators appointed by them are unable to reach agreement on the selection.[73] In Guzman's view, the appointing authority will have an incentive to attract future business.[74] Guzman believes that these incentives can be corrected by laws that subject arbitrators to personal liability for ignoring mandatory rules.[75]

---

[71] Posner, supra note 7, at 650.

[72] *Ibid.* at 651-52. Posner also argues that *Mitsubishi* has proven effective because the very ambiguities of the decision have created incentives that are analogous to those that would exist under a system of random review. Although we share Posner's view that *Mitsubishi* does not appear to have resulted in underenforcement of mandatory rules, we are skeptical of this explanation. See infra note 85.

[73] Procedures for appointing arbitrators are generally provided in a set of procedural rules that the parties designate in their contract. Often those rules are promulgated by an arbitral institution such as the International Chamber of Commerce (ICC) or the American Arbitration Association (AAA), in which case the promulgating institution will generally be designated as the appointing authority. The commonly used UNCITRAL Rules provide for ad hoc arbitration with the Permanent Court of Arbitration in The Hague, The Netherlands serving as the appointing authority.

[74] Guzman, supra note 51 at 1302-07.

[75] *Ibid.* at 1316-34.

1-55 Before addressing the waiver argument, it is necessary to make the preliminary point that even if arbitrators are less likely than U.S. courts to enforce mandatory rules, that fact alone does not necessarily make *Mitsubishi* unpersuasive from a cost/benefit perspective. William Park has argued, for example, that a

> special rule of arbitrability for the international realm would be justified under a hierarchy of societal policies that take into account the peculiar need for neutrality in resolution of international contracts disputes

and notes that the question turns on

> the relative weights one gives to [the] competing considerations [of] proper enforcement of the law and neutrality of forum.[76]

In considering the costs of *Mitsubishi*, any such weighting must take account not merely of the risk of arbitrator bias, but also of the existence of other means by which the state may deter and punish mandatory rules violations. Arbitral awards, after all, are only binding inter se. To the extent that there were serious concerns about anticompetitive practices, there is nothing the arbitral tribunal in *Mitsubishi* could have done to prevent enforcement of the Sherman Act by the U.S. government or by injured third parties such as consumers. Moreover, one would have to balance the risk of arbitrator bias against the risk that courts enforcing mandatory rules may themselves be biased against foreign parties.

1-56 We are not in any case convinced that systemic under-enforcement of mandatory rules is the natural consequence of the *Mitsubishi* decision. In order to gauge the seriousness of these theoretical concerns, it is necessary once again to be absolutely clear about what is, and what is not, contemplated. In the first instance, the kind of bias that is contemplated here is distinct from bias in favor of or against a particular party. One can imagine, for instance, that a party with a greater bargaining power may try to select an arbitral mechanism designed to generally favor its litigation position, for example by securing a home field advantage. One might even see something of this phenomenon in the facts of the *Mitsubishi* case itself. Soler, the U.S. party, signed an agreement with a Japanese party that provided for arbitration in Japan under the rules of the Japan Commercial Arbitration Association. The Supreme Court noted in its opinion that the arbitrators selected to hear the case consisted of three Japanese lawyers ("one a former law school dean, another a former judge, and the third a practicing

---

[76] Park, supra note 54 at 667.

attorney with American legal training who has written on Japanese antitrust law.")[77] Without venturing to impugn the neutrality of those arbitrators or of the Japan Commercial Arbitration Association more generally, one may assume that the expectation of a home court advantage provided one reason why Mitsubishi preferred to arbitrate its dispute with Soler rather than submit to the jurisdiction of a U.S. federal court.

1-57 This risk of antiparty bias, of course, is not unique to the arbitral context. In fact it is the very desire to avoid the bias of domestic courts that has helped make arbitration such an attractive choice in international transactions. And for that very reason, the same economic considerations that would allegedly bias arbitration against mandatory rules should also secure the general neutrality of arbitration. Appointing authorities that seek to attract international business must be able to offer a neutral alternative to domestic courts and therefore have a general incentive to appoint fair and neutral arbitrators. There are therefore reasons to expect that a home field advantage in the arbitral context may be less meaningful than that which parties may expect, or at least hope for, before their own domestic courts.

1-58 In any event, the risk of a general antiparty bias is distinct from the question of mandatory rules. It presents a risk that arbitrators may be biased in favor of a particular party regardless of its legal position, not that they will have a fixed attitude toward mandatory rules outside of that context. The primary protection against such bias lies in norms requiring arbitrator neutrality and legal protections against adhesion contracts or other manifestations of improper bargaining power.

1-59 The bias anticipated by *Mitsubishi's* critics is of a much more specific nature. The proposition is that appointing authorities have an incentive to select otherwise neutral arbitrators who exhibit a particular bias against mandatory rules per se. Moreover, although both Posner and Guzman speak of an incentive to "ignore" mandatory rules, the problem they claim to identify will not exist if the bias of the arbitrators takes the form of an institutional aversion to hearing such claims. An arbitrator who views a mandatory rule as an irrelevant distraction to the primary contract claim may not obstruct the rule simply by ignoring it. Under the *Mitsubishi* standard, it is necessary for an arbitral tribunal to take cognizance of and actually decide a statutory claim before the U.S. courts will defer to the

---

[77] *Ibid.* at 634 n.18.

arbitrators' resolution of the claim. Thus, it must be the case that appointing authorities will choose arbitrators who will both take the step of entertaining claims based on mandatory rules and then reject those claims on the merits even if the record reveals them to be meritorious.

1-60 We are skeptical that this theory presents a credible picture of the world of international arbitration as it actually operates. It begins with a simple theoretical assumption – that in certain cases some parties at the time of contracting will have some unquantified incentive to avoid application of mandatory rules. But the mere fact that this may be the case does not yield the assumption that this impulse has sufficient weight to drive the economics of appointing authorities to the point that these institutions will exhibit systemic bias in favor of appointing arbitrators who will both entertain and deny meritorious mandatory rules claims, or that a steady supply of arbitrators exists who both fit this specific bill and meet the qualifications more generally demanded of arbitrators.

1-61 Without attempting a comprehensive defense of international arbitral practice, we find many reasons to expect that no such systemic bias taints the process of arbitrator selection. Fundamentally, the expectation of a pervasive but specifically tailored bias runs in the face of the more general demand for fair and neutral fora that has made international arbitration such an attractive option for so many parties. As the *Mitsubishi* Court itself both recognized and predicted, the expansion of arbitration into a dominant form of international dispute resolution has led to the diversification of the pool of arbitrators. The typical international arbitrator is not a narrowly focused trade specialist, but a legal professional who has achieved distinction in legal practice, and the pool includes retired judges, former government officials with experience in fields such as securities law enforcement, law professors specializing in both commercial law and public law fields such as public international law or human rights, accomplished private practitioners, and those who fit into several of the above categories. Parties who seek a fair and neutral adjudication desire persons of such caliber and experience, and one may expect such people to be moved by reputational interests and considerations of professional ethics that caution against misapplying mandatory rules for the purpose of attracting parties who wish to avoid those rules.

1-62 It also bears observing that the most common method of dispute resolution in international transactions – and particularly in transactions that involve substantial economic value – is arbitration by a three-arbitrator panel. This arrangement necessarily increases the cost of arbitration, and its popularity suggests that parties assign value to the predictability offered by a right to participate in post-dispute arbitral selection rather than consigning their fate to a single arbitrator selected by an appointing authority. A party who wishes to raise antitrust claims, for example, may select an arbitrator who has expertise in that area of law. It is exceedingly common for party-appointed arbitrators to agree on the selection of the presiding arbitrator, thus helping to ensure that the ability to address relevant mandatory rules will become a consideration in that selection as well. Moreover, in either event, the mechanism of a three-arbitrator panel provides a meaningful opportunity for a deliberative process in which the concerns of each party will be fully considered.

1-63 Although we cannot exclude out of hand the theoretical possibility that international arbitration of mandatory rules might lead to under-enforcement of those rules, we do not believe that the proposition can be established by reference to theoretical economic incentives alone. Instead, the attention of those concerned with *Mitsubishi's* consequences would be better focused on the actual experience of those invoking mandatory rules before arbitrators in the wake of that decision.

3. Arbitration of Mandatory Rules After Mitsubishi

1-64 Surprisingly, however, the debate over arbitration of mandatory rules remains theoretical despite what is now twenty years of experience in the post-*Mitsubishi* world. Although scholars continue to debate the risk of under-enforcement, we are unaware of any attempt to demonstrate that in two decades of international arbitration the *Mitsubishi* doctrine has actually resulted in under-enforcement of mandatory rules.

1-65 One ready way to test the impact of *Mitsubishi* on the enforcement of mandatory rules is to look at actual "second look" cases in which arbitrators have adjudicated a claim arising under a mandatory rule and the losing party has resisted enforcement of the award. As may be recalled, *Mitsubishi* did not itself involve a "second look," but simply the prospective issue of whether Soler was bound to bring its Sherman Act claims before the arbitral tribunal. It is here that we come across what may seem a stunning statistic. In the two decades since *Mitsubishi*, it appears that U.S. courts have decided only a single case in which a party has complained about an international tribunal's application of a statutory claim implicating a U.S. mandatory rule. That single case concerned an international tribunal's refusal to grant relief under the Sherman Act, and it reached the U.S. District Court for the Northern District of Illinois in 2002, a full seventeen years after the U.S. Supreme Court decided *Mitsubishi*.

1-66 That statistic is a surprising one given the debate on arbitral competence and neutrality that *Mitsubishi* occasioned. As recently as 1999, for example, Stephen Ware argued that *Mitsubishi* converted mandatory rules into default rules by effectively allowing parties to waive the protections of mandatory rules,[78] but as of that writing not a single U.S. decision reflected such a claim by an aggrieved party. One might be tempted to argue that the lack of relevant case law results directly from the strictness of *Mitsubishi* itself: if a U.S. court can do no more than verify that the arbitrators decided a mandatory rules question, what point is there in seeking to overturn a bad decision? But that argument is not convincing given the time that has elapsed and the debate (however unjustified) that has surrounded the decision. *Mitsubishi's* provision for enforcement-stage review consists of a single sentence of dictum in the divided opinion of a Court whose composition has subsequently changed, and much scholarly ink has subsequently been expended exploring the ambiguities of what exactly the Court contemplated. The U.S. court system is no stranger to novel claims, and *Mitsubishi* could easily have prompted cases testing the scope of the "second look."

1-67 The single case, *Abbott Laboratories v. Baxter International, Inc.*,[79] does not suggest that arbitrators will be poor stewards of U.S. public policy. The dispute in question focused on the actions of Baxter International, Inc., the licensor of process patents for the development of sevoflurane, the dominant anesthetic drug in the United States. Baxter's U.S. sub-licensee, Abbott Laboratories, initiated arbitration proceedings when Baxter commenced plans to compete against its licensees after acquiring a company (Ohmeda) that had developed an alternate process for producing sevoflurane. Invoking its status as a third-party beneficiary of Baxter's original license agreement with Maruishi Pharmaceutical Company, Abbott alleged that Baxter's actions violated certain exclusivity commitments set forth in the agreement. Baxter took the position that its action did not violate its contractual commitments and that any contrary

---

[78] Ware, supra note 1 at 710-12.

[79] 2002 U.S. Dist. LEXIS 5475 (N.D. Ill. Mar. 26, 2002), *aff'd*, 315 F.3d 829 (7th Cir. 2003), *reh'g en banc denied*, 325 F.3d 954 (7th Cir. 2003). Other cases in which the public policy defense of Article V(2) of the New York Convention has been raised have involved the analytically identical issue, but in the specific context the courts did not resolve the issue under the *Mitsubishi* rubric. See Donald Francis Donovan, "The Public Policy Defense to Recognition and Enforcement of Foreign Arbitral Awards in U.S. Courts" in *Global Reflections on International Law, Commerce and Dispute Resolution: Liber Amicorum in honour of Robert Briner* 242-44 (ICC Publishing 2005). These cases also provide no evidence of systematic underenforcement of mandatory rules.

interpretation would render the agreement unenforceable per se as an illegal market allocation. A multinational tribunal heard the case and agreed with Abbott, rejecting Baxter's contractual interpretation and its Sherman Act defense.[80]

1-68 Baxter then applied to the U.S. District Court for the Northern District of Illinois, seeking vacatur under the public policy exception to enforcement under Article V(2) of the New York Convention, and Abbott crossmoved to enforce the award. Although the Court cautioned that it owed great deference to the arbitrators' findings, it conducted what was effectively de novo review before issuing a decision that endorsed the arbitrators' findings.[81]

1-69 A divided panel of the U.S. Court of Appeals for the Seventh Circuit affirmed. In an opinion by Judge Easterbrook, the two-judge majority emphasized that *Mitsubishi* limited their review to confirming that the arbitral tribunal had "[taken] cognizance of the antitrust claims and actually decided them."[82] But they too endorsed the tribunal's rejection of the Sherman Act defense. Noting that "[w]hat relief the Antitrust Division [of the United States Department of Justice], the FTC [(Federal Trade Commission)] or a consumer would obtain is an interesting question," Judge Easterbrook's opinion emphasized that because Baxter's exclusivity commitment to Maruishi preceded its acquisition of Ohmeda, the antitrust issue, if any, arose from that acquisition, not the exclusivity commitment whose alleged anticompetitive effect hinged on the acquisition.[83] The opinion noted that if Baxter was truly concerned about anticompetitive effects, it was perfectly capable of divesting Ohmeda.[84]

1-70 What is one to make of the virtual absence of post hoc disputes challenging arbitral determinations of mandatory rules? Despite the concerns raised about the

---

[80] 2002 U.S. Dist. LEXIS 5475 at *12-16.

[81] The District Court opinion also includes a lengthy quotation from the arbitral award, which reflects the care with which the arbitrators themselves approached Baxter's invocation of the Sherman Act. *Ibid.* at *22-23.

[82] 315 F.3d 829, 832 (7th Cir. 2003).

[83] *Ibid.* at 832-33.

[84] *Ibid.* at 833. Judge Cudahy's dissent disagreed with the tribunal's contractual interpretation and application of the Sherman Act, and it rejected the majority's view that *Mitsubishi* precluded a more active role in vindicating the Sherman Act at the enforcement stage. *Ibid.* at 833-39 (Cudahy, J., dissenting). The fact that three out of the four federal judges who heard the case appeared to disagree with Baxter's case on the merits indicates that in this case at least the arbitral forum did not affect the outcome of that claim.

delegation of U.S. public policy to private arbitrators, the evidence suggests that U.S. mandatory rules remain a relatively marginal feature of present-day arbitration. To the extent that there was a substantial demand among parties to international transactions to waive the application of U.S. mandatory rules, and to the extent that arbitration was viewed as a means of achieving that waiver, one would have expected *Mitsubishi* to result in an increase of arbitration agreements designed specifically to remove enforcement of mandatory rules from the courts. The fact that the case law does not reveal any such trend suggests that one or both of the necessary preconditions have not been met. That fact in turn suggests that the economics of appointing authorities are not driven by a demand to avoid mandatory rules, which in turn suggests that appointing authorities do not have any particular incentive to select arbitrators who will underenforce those rules. In any event, the empirical evidence casts doubt upon the expectation of pervasive bias.[85]

1-71 Of course, even in a world where there is no systemic bias against enforcing mandatory rules, the *Mitsubishi* holding still creates the possibility, as with any arbitrable question, that an individual arbitral tribunal will get it wrong in a particular case and that courts will end up enforcing, without affording any opportunity for substantive appellate review, an arbitral award that rejects a meritorious claim arising under a mandatory rule. But that prospect, in our view, is far less troubling to the integrity of the international arbitral system. As long as there is no advance expectation of bias – in other words, if there is equal prospect in any particular case that a tribunal will over-enforce a mandatory rule – the potential for legal error should have limited effect on the parties' own bargaining.

---

[85] Posner has also noted the dearth of relevant second look case law and has suggested that the effect of the *Mitsubishi* decision itself may provide an explanation. See Posner, supra note 7 at 667-68. In his view, because *Mitsubishi* creates uncertainty as to how courts will react to under-enforcement of mandatory rules, arbitrators who wish to produce enforceable awards have an incentive to apply mandatory rules responsibly. Although we share Posner's view that the *Mitsubishi* regime appears to be working, we are skeptical that any ambiguity in the *Mitsubishi* decision is itself responsible for creating the necessary incentives. In the first instance, as already detailed, we do not believe that the *Mitsubishi* holding is in fact sufficiently ambiguous to provide a meaningful disincentive for an arbitrator who otherwise wishes to underenforce a mandatory rule. Although the decision has produced scholarly debate, arbitrators studying the decision have good reason to expect that their application of a mandatory rule will be upheld by a U.S. court whatever the outcome, as long as the arbitrators do not ignore the mandatory rule. In addition, even if Posner were right in theory, the disincentive he identifies cannot provide a satisfactory explanation of the lack of case law. The very ambiguity he identifies would create an incentive for parties to roll the dice and challenge arbitral determinations of mandatory rules even if those determinations were in fact responsible.

Parties will have no inducement to bargain away mandatory rules a priori, and the injured party should be able to reap the full value of a prospective mandatory rule claim in pre-litigation settlement negotiations.

1-72 Moreover, to the extent that instances of arbitral under-enforcement remain few in number, the prospect of government action to protect the public interest should be more meaningful. The Seventh Circuit noted the importance of third-party enforcement in Baxter, where it observed that

> [i]f the three-corner arrangement among Baxter, Maruishi, and Abbott really does offend the Sherman Act, then the United States, the FTC, or any purchaser of sevoflurane is free to sue and obtain relief.[86]

1-73 Hence, *Mitsubishi* has provided a clear public benefit. By enforcing agreements to arbitrate claims based on mandatory rules, courts have promoted the efficiencies of arbitration and saved the court system the burden and expense associated with a system that either requires separate, and duplicative, adjudications every time a party invokes a mandatory rule in an otherwise arbitrable dispute, or allows for de novo court review of arbitral determinations. At the same time, these efficiencies have been gained with no identifiable cost to the public interest.

IV. THE ARBITRATORS' PERSPECTIVE

1-74 We turn now to the perspective of an arbitrator asked to adjudicate a claim or defense alleging non-compliance with a mandatory rule. In the wake of the *Mitsubishi* decision, some argued that the principle given effect in that decision changed the nature of arbitration itself, requiring arbitrators to apply a distinct "mandatory rules method" that could lead to the enforcement of mandatory rules even in cases where the parties themselves had not agreed to arbitrate such claims. Writing in 1986, for example, Pierre Mayer urged the employment of such a method to confront a

---

[86] 315 F.3d at 832. We recognize that there may be instances in which third party enforcement will not provide a satisfactory protection. If a primary purpose of a mandatory rule is the protection of individuals (as might be the case, e.g., with antigambling laws and antidiscrimination laws) rather than collective interests such as efficient markets, the fact that other aggrieved parties could seek relief provides less comfort. And it may not be that government enforcement actions are available in all cases.

conflict between the will of the State having promulgated the mandatory rules of law, on the one hand, and, on the other hand, the will of the parties – from which indeed his authority is derived.[87]

And Marc Blessing has tellingly titled one of his articles on this topic "Mandatory Rules of Law versus Party Autonomy in International Arbitration."[88]

1-75 A number of commentators have proposed models for how the mandatory rules method should operate, but there appears to be no consensus favoring any particular test. Marc Blessing has set forth a set of six criteria that arbitrators should apply when considering whether to override the parties' choice of law to enforce a mandatory rule. These include such broad questions as whether the rule in question is "'application worthy', having regard to its financial or socio-economic goals and underlying policies, examined under a functional analysis," and whether the result "in view of all of the circumstances" qualifies as an "appropriate result."[89] Yves Derains has urged that where the parties have expressly excluded the application of a mandatory rule, an arbitral tribunal should apply the rule only where refusal to do so would violate "truly

---

[87] Pierre Mayer, "Mandatory rules of law in international arbitration", 2(4) *Arb. Int'l* 274, 276 (1986).

[88] Blessing, supra note 8.

[89] *Ibid.* at 32. Blessing's full list of the "six leading criteria" that should guide application of mandatory rules is:

(1) "The rule in question must be a norm of mandatory character."

(2) "The rule must be such as to impose itself irrespective of the applicable law."

(3) "The preconditions regarding the application (as per the particular mandatory rule) must be given–generally, the scope of mandatory rules must be construed narrowly . . . ."

(4) "There must be a close connection between the subject matter of the parties' contract and the jurisdiction area or State that had promulgated the mandatory rule or norm . . . 'Extra-territorial jurisdiction to impose economic sanctions has to be justified under the standard of international law.'"

(5) "The rule or norm as such must appear to be "application worthy", having regard to its financial or socio-economic goals and underlying policies, examined under a functional analysis, in particular:

– The nature of the values that aim to be protected by the norm, under the so-called 'shared-values-test.' Are these values of an essential character? Does the norm reflect a notion pertaining to a truly transnational public policy? Does it protect a fundamental principle or a universally recognized legal right?

– The impact which the application of the interested norm will have on the particular contractual relationship.

– [T]he legal effects of the norm (nullity, or partial nullity; *force majeure* exception), balancing all interests at stake."

(6) "The result must, in view of all the circumstances, qualify as an 'appropriate result'."

Ibid. at 31-32 (internal citations not supplied).

international public policy," and he includes within this category situations in which enforcement of a contract would violate the law of the place of performance.[90] Attempting to distill the work of several authors, Daniel Hochstrasser proposes that mandatory rules should be applied

> (a) [w]here the parties [have] chose[n] a special law with the sole purpose of circumventing or escaping mandatory rules of a legal system that would have applied to their agreement in the absence of this choice of law . . . . (b) Where the performance of the contract is affected by the invoked mandatory rules, and there is a close connection between the performance and the rules in question . . . . [and] (c) Where enforcement of the award would be doubtful or unlikely if the award does not take into consideration mandatory rules of the country where enforcement will be sought by the winning party.[91]

1-76 This type of approach has also gained some traction in international arbitral decisions. For example, an International Chamber of Commerce ("ICC") award from 1992

> accept[ed] the premise that there may be situations in which an international arbitral tribunal should admit the application of mandatory rules different from the law that the parties have chosen to govern their claims or relationships,

and further expressed a willingness to apply such laws provided that its own three-step test was met.[92]

---

[90] Yves Derains, Public Policy and the Law Applicable to the Dispute in International Arbitration, in *Comparative Arbitration Practice and Public Policy in Arbitration* 227, 251-52 (ICCA Congress Series No. 3, Pieter Sanders ed., 1986).

[91] Daniel Hochstrasser, "Choice of Law and 'Foreign' Mandatory Rules in International Arbitration", 11(1) *J. Int'l Arb.* 57, 85-86 (1994).

[92] Final Award in Case No. 6320 of 1992, XX YBCA 62, ¶ 153 (1992); see also Eric A. Schwartz, "The Domain of Arbitration and Issues of Arbitrability: The View from the ICC", 9 *ICSID Rev.: FILJ* 34 (1994) (discussing this award). The tribunal in that case specified that:

> 1) [T]he Tribunal must be satisfied that the mandatory rules different from the law that the parties have chosen to govern their claim or relationships must clearly be a "loi de police"
> . . . .
> 2) In the case of the mandatory law of a particular state, the thrust of the conditions for its extraterritorial application is that such state must have a strong and legitimate interest to justify the application of such a law in international arbitration.
> 3) Furthermore, if the respective law contains both public and civil (private) law rules, it must be shown that such state had a strong and legitimate interest to justifying the application of these civil (private) law rules in international arbitration.

1-77 The reasoning behind the mandatory rules method is broadly twofold. *First*, it expresses a concern that mandatory rules alter the duties of the arbitrator, who can no longer consider himself or herself simply a servant of the parties, but must also consider the broader public duty entrusted to arbitrators when courts cede their authority to enforce mandatory rules. Thus, for example, Blessing writes that

> under the US perspectives set on the basis of *Mitsubishi v. Soler* and the threat of the 'second-look doctrine', it is quite clear that an arbitral tribunal has a perceived duty, and not only a right, to examine the compatibility with US antitrust laws *ex officio*, wherever a matter could have anti-competitive effects within the United States.[93]

Writing earlier, Pierre Mayer struck a similar chord, maintaining that:

> The [*Mitsubishi*] decision is nonetheless of fundamental importance in that it demonstrates the connection between the issue of the right to apply mandatory rules and the obligation to do so. In holding that arbitrators have a right to apply such rules, the Supreme Court appears to presume that they are in some manner obliged to do so, which in turn makes it possible to trust them in this matter.[94]

1-78 The *second* concern is related, but focuses more specifically on the consequences to the arbitral system of not applying a mandatory rules method. By not proactively enforcing mandatory rules, it is argued, arbitrators make their determinations vulnerable to non-enforcement and thus violate their duty to render an enforceable award. Thus, Mayer writes,

> the arbitrator is pulled in different directions. He should seek to respect the contract and the intent of the parties, but at the same time be concerned with the efficacy of his award and the avoidance of annulment.[95]

Mayer links this concern not merely to the enforceability of a particular award, but to the health of the international arbitral system as a whole:

Ibid. ¶ 153. Applying this test, the tribunal refused to entertain a claim arising under the RICO Act on the ground that international principles of extraterritorial jurisdiction did not recognize a United States interest in a RICO claim by a foreign citizen residing outside the United States. The tribunal reached this conclusion without regard to whether U.S. courts applying U.S. extraterritoriality principles would have allowed the claim to go forward.

[93] Blessing, supra note 8, at 38.
[94] Mayer, supra note 87, at 279-80.
[95] *Ibid.* at 293.

One might imagine that in the *Mitsubishi* litigation the Japanese arbitrators, irrespective of the confidence the US Supreme court has reposed in them, decide that they ought after all simply to stick to the expressed will of the parties, apply Swiss law, and thus consider the contract to be perfectly valid whether or not the Sherman Act has been violated. What would then be the reaction of the Supreme Court, which was already divided in the *Mitsubishi* case, when it next has to face a similar case? The future of the US law depends on arbitrators' demonstration of their capacity correctly to apply mandatory rules of law.[96]

1-79 As with much surrounding the question of mandatory rules and arbitration, we believe that the risks to which this debate responds are more perceived than actual. Once the operative principles are clarified, there is less here than might be supposed. To the extent, however, that a unique mandatory rules method does have appeal to arbitrators, we would suggest that the method is both inconsistent with the *Mitsubishi* principle and potentially threatening to the very interests that the method seeks to protect.

1. Mandatory Rules and Arbitral Authority

1-80 To unpack this question, it is important to be clear about underlying concepts. The literature on mandatory rules too often assumes a binary framework, where the arbitrator must choose, on the one hand, between applying the mandatory rule, or honoring, on the other hand, the will of the parties. Thus, for example, Serge Lazareff, writes that

[t]here is a growing tendency of arbitrators to consider that they are exercising a judicial function that goes beyond the will of the parties, thus accepting more and more frequently the need to take account of laws other than the *lex contractus*.[97]

On one level, such statements might appear to present uncontroversial descriptions of the very prospect raised by the *Mitsubishi* decision, which contemplated

---

[96] *Ibid.* at 285; see also Hochstrasser, supra note 91, at 85:

"As far as the respect of national or transnational mandatory rules is concerned, it is important to point out that international arbitration finally depends on the goodwill of the States and their courts for the enforcement of arbitral awards. The standard reached under the New York Convention should not be put at risk by an attitude of disrespect toward national laws."

[97] Serge Lazareff, "Mandatory Extraterritorial Application of National Law", 11(2) *Arb. Int'l* 137, 142 (1995).

the application of the Sherman Act in the context of a dispute arising out of a contract governed by Swiss law. But much here depends on how exactly one defines the "lex contractus." Does the concept of "lex contractus" focus narrowly on causes of action and defenses that derive directly from the law governing the contract? Does it include foreign laws to which the law of the contract itself gives effect? Does it take account of the fact that modern arbitration agreements typically include dispute resolution clauses that are broader than their choice of law clauses?

1-81 It is instructive to consider some illustrative hypotheticals. Assume that two parties to an international transaction enter into a contract to be performed in Mexico. The contract contains a choice of law clause specifying that it is governed by New York law, and an arbitration clause that limits arbitral jurisdiction to breach-of-contract claims and thus by its terms excludes noncontractual causes of action. Even under such circumstances, there are numerous ways in which the contract as written could require the arbitrators to grapple with foreign mandatory laws simply by enforcing the parties' own contractual commitments.

1-82 For example, there is case law holding that New York courts applying New York law should refuse to enforce a contract that is otherwise unobjectionable under New York law if the contract violates the law of its place of performance and the parties entered into the contract with the intent to violate that foreign law.[98] Applying this principle in appropriate circumstances, New York law might deny enforcement of our hypothetical contract if the contract violated Mexican law.[99] By the same token, however, the negative implication of this same legal principle is that a contract should be enforced in some instances where it violates

---

[98] *Lehman Bros. Commercial Corp. v. Minmetals Int'l Non-Ferrous Metals Trading Co.*, 179 F. Supp.2d 118, 138 (S.D.N.Y. 2000).

[99] As Yves Derains has observed, the question may in theory be complex. Under a pure "subjectivist" theory of international contracts, an arbitrator might subordinate the choice of New York law to the parties' own agreement, making the choice of New York law effective only insofar as it does not contradict the parties' contractual commitments. Derains, supra note 90, at 235-36. If one accepts that the arbitral tribunal is bound by the will of the parties, then one must accept that the parties to this hypothetical contract are free, if they wish, to explicitly preclude the arbitrator from applying New York public policy which would invalidate the agreement. Derains proposes that arbitrators should require parties to specify if they wish to exclude from the applicable law those provisions which would render the contract void. *Ibid.* at 239. Of course, it will remain up to the enforcing jurisdiction to decide whether to enforce such an award pursuant to its own mandatory rules. And again, under the *Mitsubishi* approach, the enforcing jurisdiction will owe the tribunal no deference regarding mandatory rules that the arbitral tribunal did not take cognizance of and apply.

a foreign law. For example, if the parties had no idea at the time of contracting that their agreement violated Mexican law, or had reason to believe that it did not, or if it would have been unclear whether it did, New York law would mandate enforcement even if an illegality could be demonstrated.

1-83 Another example is the doctrine of *force majeure*. Like many jurisdictions, New York law implements the standard principle that a party's duty to perform a contract may be excused where performance has become impossible on account of some unanticipated event such as an act of god or a legal decree barring performance.[100] Provided that the necessary criteria are met, New York law might excuse a party from performing our hypothetical contract if, for example, the United Nations promulgated sanctions prohibiting the shipment of certain essential goods to Mexico. In this scenario, the foreign mandatory rule arises as a consideration that is relevant to the merits of the alleged excuse.[101] At the same time, however, the effect that the doctrine of *force majeure* gives to foreign mandatory rules is itself merely a default rule. New York law allows parties to allocate the risk of impossible performance however they wish, and the excuse of force majeure applies only when the parties have not done so.

1-84 Both of these examples illustrate instances in which foreign mandatory rules may come to bear on a contract governed by New York law. Even if one characterizes these examples as departures from the *lex contractus*, they do not require us to rethink the nature of arbitration. The relevance of foreign mandatory rules in this instance flows directly from the classical party-driven model of arbitration. It is the parties' own choice of substantive New York law that makes the foreign law relevant. Put another way, it may be said that substantive New York contract law itself already provides a mandatory rules method: the law specifies which mandatory rules may be relevant to enforcement of the contract and which circumstances may give rise to their application.

1-85 Although this may seem an elementary point, it is one that often gets lost in discussions of mandatory rules and international arbitration. Consider, for

---

[100] *407 East 61st Garage, Inc. v. Savoy Fifth Ave. Corp.*, 244 N.E.2d 37, 41 (N.Y. 1968).
[101] See, *e.g.*, *Fouchard Gaillard Goldman on International Arbitration* 849 (Emmanuel Gaillard & John Savage eds., Kluwer Law International 1999) (noting that "a law other than that governing the contract which prohibits the export of goods under the conditions set forth in the contract could be considered, under the law governing the contract, to be a *force majeure* event"); Derains, supra note 90, at 247-52 (distinguishing between "taking into consideration" and "application" of mandatory rules).

instance, the Swiss *Hilmarton/OTV* case, which has become something of a paradigmatic example in the mandatory rules debate, with one treatise describing it as a "clear application of the mandatory rules approach, under which the arbitrator felt entitled to give effect to the mandatory rules of a law other than that governing the contract."[102] In that instance, a sole arbitrator sitting in Geneva refused to enforce a contract governed by Swiss law but requiring performance in Algeria on the ground that the contract violated an Algerian prohibition on the use of intermediaries.[103] However, the arbitrator did not purport to override the parties' own choice of Swiss law. Instead, the arbitrator purported to give effect to that choice by ruling that Swiss law precluded enforcement of the contract on the ground that the Algerian illegality reflected "an affront to morality" forbidden by the Swiss Code of Obligations.[104] The Swiss Court of Appeal subsequently annulled the award on the ground that the arbitrator had misapplied Swiss law and that the result was arbitrary. The Court agreed with the arbitral tribunal that the central question concerned the effect of the Algerian prohibition under Swiss law:

> Hence, the issue in the present case is . . . knowing which conclusion must be drawn in Swiss law from the fact that said contract is contrary to an Algerian public law which forbids the use of intermediaries between the party seeking to obtain the contract and the authority awarding it.[105]

Although the Court accepted that the "parties undoubtedly intended to violate the Algerian law," it considered this fact in and of itself to be immaterial where the arbitrator did not make any finding of bribery or other corruption which would have offended Swiss law.[106] It noted that

> a contract is not illicit, and therefore null and void, only because it allows the parties to develop activities abroad which are prohibited by the local

---

[102] *Fouchard Gaillard Goldman*, supra note 101, at 854; see also Julian D M Lew, Loukas Mistelis and Stefan M Kröll, *Comparative International Commercial Arbitration* 422 (Kluwer Law International 2003) (same).

[103] Final Award in Case No. 5622 of 1988, XIX YBCA 105 (1994).

[104] *Ibid.* at 113-20. The provision at issue was Article 20(1) of the Swiss Code of Obligations, which provided that "a contract providing for an impossibility, having illegal contents or violating *bonos mores* is null and void." *Ibid.* at 110. The arbitral award's reliance on this provision is also reflected in *Fouchard Gaillard Goldman*'s account of the case. *Fouchard Gaillard Goldman*, supra note 101, at 854

[105] Tribunal Fédéral [Supreme Court], 17 April 1990, XIX YBCA 214, 217 (1994).

[106] *Ibid.* at 218-19.

law; only the violation of a Swiss legal provision is illicit according to Swiss law.[107]

The Swiss Supreme Court upheld the Court of Appeal decision, ruling that the annulment was justified under a Swiss standard limiting review of arbitral awards to "arbitrariness" rather than de novo merits review.[108] Fundamentally, therefore, the *Hilmarton* case did not require the application of a special mandatory rules method. The question instead was simply a standard question of substantive contract law arising under the very law that the parties themselves had chosen to govern the contract.[109]

1-86 Let us now complicate our hypothetical somewhat. Assume that our contract includes a broader arbitration clause, which commits the parties to arbitrate not only breach-of-contract claims, but also certain non-contractual claims, such as those arising under antitrust or securities laws, which relate to the transaction between the parties. At the same time, let us assume that the choice-of-law clause remains the same: it provides merely that the contract itself shall be governed by New York law. Thus, the contract contains a dispute resolution clause whose scope is broader than its choice-of-law clause.

1-87 The clauses contemplated by this hypothetical are standard. For example, the ICC recommends that all parties wishing to have recourse to ICC arbitration include the following standard clause in their contracts:

'All disputes arising out of or in connection with the present contract shall be finally settled under the Rules of Arbitration of the International Chamber of Commerce by one or more arbitrators appointed in accordance with the said Rules.'[110]

---

[107] XIX YBCA at 217 (1994).

[108] *Ibid.* at 220-22.

[109] Applicable conflicts-of-law rules can also require courts in particular jurisdictions to refer to mandatory rules arising under a law other than that otherwise applicable to the dispute. See, *e.g.*, Convention on the Law Applicable to Contractual Obligations, arts. 3, 7, June 19, 1980, 1605 U.N.T.S. 80, 19 I.L.M. 1492 (1980); Restatement (Second) of Conflict of Laws § 187(2)(b) (1989). An arbitral tribunal might interpret a contract to embrace the governing jurisdiction's choice-of-law rules in cases where the contract itself does not preclude such an interpretation. In this case, the application of mandatory rules by the arbitral tribunal would flow from the parties' own agreement rather than from an impulse to override the parties' autonomy.

[110] International Chamber of Commerce, "The standard ICC arbitration clause: Drafting the arbitration agreement", http://iccwbo.org/court/english/arbitration/model_clause.asp (last visited Jan. 22, 2006).

Such language, which provides for arbitration of disputes "arising out of or in connection with" the contract is precisely the kind of broad arbitration clause that the U.S. Supreme Court in *Mitsubishi* and other cases has interpreted to cover non-contractual claims.[111] At the same time, the ICC suggests that "it may also be desirable for the parties to stipulate in the arbitration clause itself . . . the law governing the contract."[112] Consistent with this phrasing, international contracts tend to specify the law "governing" the contract itself, not the law relating to all disputes "arising out of or in connection with" the contract.

1-88 In these circumstances, breach-of-contract claims would operate in the same way as in the previous hypothetical. An arbitrator honoring the parties' choice of law would decide the claim based on New York law except where New York contract law itself gives effect to a foreign law. But how about affirmative non-contractual claims, such as statutory antitrust or securities claims? The most reasonable conclusion would be that the parties have given the tribunal jurisdiction over any applicable antitrust claim that might otherwise be available to them. Thus, to the extent that U.S. law, Mexican law, or the law of a third jurisdiction, such as the European Community, might allow a party to bring a competition law claim that falls within the reach of the dispute resolution clause, the party should be free to bring any or all three claims before the arbitral tribunal.[113]

1-89 Although the consideration of three different and possibly conflicting, legal approaches to the same conduct would pose challenges, the claims would be ones that, under the *Mitsubishi* principle, the parties cannot waive. If the tribunal decided to entertain only the European Community and Mexican law claims,

---

[111] In *Mitsubishi*, for example, the arbitration clause that the Court construed to cover Soler's Sherman Act claims provided for arbitration of "[a]ll disputes, controversies or differences which may arise between [Mitsubishi] and [Soler] out of or in relation to" certain provisions of the agreement, "or for the breach thereof." 473 U.S at 617 (internal quotations not supplied).

[112] ICC, supra note 110.

[113] This approach is essentially the one adopted in ICC Case No. 4132, in which the tribunal determined that it could apply any applicable mandatory rules and considered applicable claims arising under both Korean and EEC law. Preliminary Award of September 22, 1983, Case No. 4132, X YBCA 49 (1985). As Derains notes,

> "[t]he process followed in this award consisted in placing the mandatory rules of the *lex contractus* on the same level as all the mandatory rules liable . . . to be applied to the parties' agreement. The fact that Korean mandatory rules belong to the *lex contractus* did not apparently confer on them any special grounds for being applied."

Derains, supra note 90, at 246.

Mitsubishi would leave the party free to bring the Sherman Act claim in U.S. courts.[114] And if parties are not free to limit the patchwork of overlapping mandatory claims that arise under the laws of various jurisdictions, why should they not be free to bring all of those claims before the same arbitrator? Under this scenario, the arbitration clause serves to consolidate these non-waivable claims, promoting efficiency and finality without introducing any complexity that does not already exist by virtue of the potentially overlapping mandatory rules. Here, the tribunal would need to assess each claim, including by determining whether each body of law would on its own terms apply to the challenged conduct.

1-90 Alternately, the tribunal might determine that the parties actually intended something narrower – for example that the choice of New York law should encompass both contract claims and other claims, or that the arbitrators should apply the same conflicts of law principles to non-contractual claims that they would have applied to contractual claims had the contract failed to specify a choice of law.[115]

1-91 In either case, the matter is a straightforward question of contractual interpretation. It is clear that the parties could choose to vest the arbitral tribunal with jurisdiction over as many overlapping mandatory rules claims as they wish. The question for the arbitrators is what authority the parties have granted, not whether they must look beyond that grant of authority to assume a "judicial" role. The inquiry, moreover, has nothing to do with the mandatory character of the norms in question.

1-92 Were the mandatory rules method concerned only with such basic questions of contractual interpretation, the debate would not be heated. For the reasons we have just discussed, arbitrators will often be justified in taking a broader approach to the application of mandatory rules underlying non-contractual claims than to the issue of what law governs a breach-of-contract claim. Just as a tribunal would be authorized to apply the law it found applicable to any claim falling within its jurisdiction as to which the parties had not specified a choice of

---

[114] For purposes of this hypothetical, we assume applicability of the basic antiwaiver principle endorsed by *Mitsubishi*, without inquiring whether exclusion of the Sherman Act might be justified on the ground that the European Community or Mexican law to be applied embodied analogous norms and provided adequate protection. See supra note 60 and accompanying text.

[115] Regarding different approaches that arbitrators may adopt to determining applicable contract law when the contract law itself is silent, see, for example, Blessing, supra note 8.

law, it would not need to employ a unique "mandatory rules method" to apply a mandatory rule to a claim based on that rule.

1-93 Hence, two things must be clear. *First*, because the contract can be read to include a broad grant of arbitral authority, the application of the mandatory rules method within that broad grant will serve to limit rather than expand the authority that the parties delegate to the arbitrators. Thus, the mandatory rules method becomes a form of arbitral docket control or prudential self-restraint, rather than a means of trespassing either the will of the parties or their legitimate expectations. In one instance, for example, an arbitral tribunal held that the parties had expressly submitted a claim arising under U.S. antiracketeering law to arbitration, but nevertheless refused to hear it after rendering it inadmissible pursuant to a mandatory rules analysis.[116] Of course, to the extent the tribunal does so limit its authority, courts following the *Mitsubishi* principle will allow the excluded claims to go forward should the aggrieved party seek to pursue them. The arbitrator may thus reasonably question how much is really gained from avoiding determination of such claims.[117] *Second*, the application of the mandatory rules method in this context operates as a form of default rule. If the mandatory rules at issue are arbitrable, then there is no reason why the parties could not have expressly delegated them to the tribunal either by pre-dispute or post-dispute consent. The mandatory rules method may thus operate as a gap filler where such clarity is lacking.

2. Application of Mandatory Rules Which Exceed the Parties' Agreement

1-94 Much of the literature on the mandatory rules method fails to distinguish between situations in which a contract has authorized the application of a foreign mandatory rule and those in which it has not.[118] We suspect that much of the

---

[116] Final Award in Case No. 6320 (ICC), XX YBCA 62-109 (1995).

[117] Presumably, moreover, that parties to commercial contracts prefer to have a clear sense, ex ante, of which mandatory rules may or may not apply in arbitration. An open-ended balancing test necessarily invites a degree of unpredictability that stands in tension with this desire.

[118] A notable exception is Yves Derains' consideration of arbitration and mandatory rules. After systematically discussing the different contexts in which the parties' agreement could justify the application of foreign mandatory rules, Derains argues that if the parties have specifically excluded such application, the arbitrator should honor that agreement unless "the mandatory rule excluded was considered to be contrary to truly international public policy." Derains, *supra* note 90, at 251. He appears to contemplate, however, a relatively expansive concept of international public policy. *Ibid.* at 251-52. Fouchard, Gaillard, and Goldman endorse international public policy as a more disciplined means of attaining the objectives of the mandatory rules method. *Fouchard Gaillard Goldman*, *supra* note 101, at 851-54. The role of international public policy

debate may actually focus on situations that do not really challenge the party-controlled model of arbitration. Our own review of the arbitral case law cited in the mandatory rules literature confirms others' conclusion that there are

> virtually no cases where the arbitrators have relied on the application of a mandatory rule to justify a decision other than that would have resulted from the application of the law chosen by the parties.[119]

The cases in question either reject the mandatory rules method, apply mandatory rules by virtue of the lex contractus, or otherwise reach a result consistent with the parties' agreement even if they acknowledge the theoretical possibility of applying mandatory rules outside the parties' agreement.[120]

1-95 By their own language, however, advocates of the mandatory rules method expressly contemplate the application of mandatory rules in situations where there is a conflict between such application and the parties' contract.[121] Such a conflict only exists in the narrowly defined setting in which an arbitrator deems the parties' agreement to exclude the application of a mandatory rule, but nevertheless determines that the rule should be applied. This is the issue raised by the specter of "prospective waiver" in the *Mitsubishi* case, in which the Court interpreted the parties' contract to require arbitration of Soler's claims, but questioned whether the contract allowed the application of the Sherman Act to those claims.[122]

– that is, a body of universal, fundamental norms that arbitrators are authorized or obligated to apply regardless the law chosen by the parties or otherwise applicable – in disputes subject to international arbitration is a distinct issue addressed separately by Pierre Mayer's contribution to this volume in chapter 2. While the concept enjoys broad acceptance, there remain, at a minimum, substantial issues as to the means by which the norms that qualify as international public policy might be identified and the source of the arbitrator's authority to apply them.

[119] *Fouchard Gaillard Goldman*, supra note 101, at 856-57. The only case cited to the contrary is *Hilmarton*, but that case does not implicate the mandatory rules method. See supra notes 102-108 and accompanying text.

[120] Of these decisions, only one appears to apply a mandatory rule which overrides the parties' agreement in part. In ICC Case No. 5946, a tribunal sitting in Switzerland awarded relief to the claimant but refused to include punitive damages owed under applicable U.S. law on account of their illegality under the law of the seat of arbitration. Final Award in ICC Case No. 5946 (ICC), XVI YBCA 97-118 (1991). That opinion has faced criticism from an advocate of the mandatory rules method on the ground that "it is not the duty of an arbitral tribunal to serve as the guardian of policing norms of the host State." Blessing, supra note 8, at 27 n.10.

[121] See supra notes 87- 88and accompanying text.

[122] Although the contract in that case did not explicitly exclude application of the U.S. Sherman Act, it provided that the agreement would be "governed by, and construed in all respects according to the law of the Swiss Confederation *as if entirely performed therein*." *Mitsubishi*, 473 U.S. at 637 n.19 (emphasis supplied).

1-96 Taking that precise hypothetical as a precondition for application of a distinct mandatory rules method, the method cannot be justified either as a legal matter or as a practical means of achieving the goals that advocates of the method identify. At the most basic legal level, the mandatory rules method must grapple with the fundamental question of the arbitrators' authority. Parties are not forced to arbitrate disputes. They sacrifice a judicial determination for an arbitral one only when they have agreed to do so. Both the nature and scope of the arbitrators' own jurisdiction derives from the parties' agreement, not from any obligation by the arbitrators to any particular forum.[123]

1-97 The notion that *Mitsubishi* somehow changed this calculus confuses the mandatory nature of the rules at issue with the wholly discretionary nature of arbitration itself. *Mitsubishi* provides an answer as to how mandatory rules and arbitration can coexist. It says that mandatory rules may be arbitrated but cannot, at the pre-dispute stage, be waived. The decision is hence indifferent to the question whether arbitrators enjoy jurisdiction to entertain particular claims invoking mandatory rules. Through the interaction of the "prospective waiver" doctrine and "second look" review, the *Mitsubishi* dicta uncouple the protection of mandatory rules from the arbitrator's jurisdictional decisions. Thus, while the *Mitsubishi* decision puts faith in the arbitral process with respect to the adjudication of mandatory rules, that faith is limited to the expectation that when parties submit mandatory rules to arbitration, the arbitral process will adjudicate those claims. Refusing to entertain mandatory rules claim will harm, if anything, the efficiency of the arbitral process, not the promulgating state's ability to ensure protection of its own mandatory rules.

1-98 This conclusion is reinforced by the sequence of the *Mitsubishi* Court's analysis. The Court first ruled that the parties had authorized the tribunal to adjudicate Soler's antitrust claims, and only because it determined that the parties had did the Court then consider whether they were bound by that choice.[124]

---

[123] New York Convention, supra note 5, art. V(1)(c) (enforcement may be refused where "[t]he award deals with a difference not contemplated by or not falling within the terms of the submission to arbitration, or it contains decisions on matters beyond the scope of the submission to arbitration"). The *Mitsubishi* Court recognized this point, observing that "[t]o be sure, the international arbitral tribunal owes no prior allegiance to the legal norms of particular states; hence, it has no direct obligation to vindicate their statutory dictates. The tribunal, however, is bound to effectuate the intentions of the parties." 473 U.S. at 636.

[124] See supra Part I(2).

Surely if the parties were entitled to limit the scope of their arbitration agreement so as to exclude the antitrust dispute entirely, they were also entitled to limit the tribunal's jurisdiction to certain kinds of antitrust claims – for example, those arising under Swiss law but not U.S. law.

1-99 But what of the arbitrators' concern to render an enforceable award? The concept of such a duty is well known to arbitration practitioners. Article 35 of the ICC Rules establishes, for example, the "General Rule" that

> [i]n all matters not expressly provided for in these Rules, the Court and the Arbitral Tribunal shall act in the spirit of these Rules and shall make every effort to make sure that the Award is enforceable at law.

As a general matter, it makes sense that arbitrators should be concerned with certain matters of enforceability. The patchwork of national laws and treaties that give effect to the international arbitral system generally does not regulate arbitrators directly, but instead sets forth the conditions under which arbitral proceedings and awards will be given legal effect and those under which they will not. Parties who resort to arbitration do so because they want arbitration to operate as an effective alternative to the court system, and for arbitral awards to provide that alternative they must be enforceable. This consideration has particular force with respect to the law of the country where the arbitration proceeding is located. The New York Convention gives special recognition to that such jurisdiction, providing that a State may refuse to enforce an international award that

> has been set aside or suspended by a competent authority of the country in which, or under the law of which, that award was made.[125]

1-100 As a general matter, therefore, it may be presumed that the parties wish the arbitrators to obey any particular procedures that are necessary to ensure confirmation and avoid annulment of the award under the law of the situs. To the extent that enforcement of the award in a different jurisdiction may be necessary to make effective an aggrieved party's remedy, the aggrieved party may wish to raise before the tribunal any particular enforceability requirements existing in that jurisdiction, and the arbitrators would do well to ensure compliance with such requirements to the extent that doing so entails actions (such as exercise of the arbitrator's typically broad procedural discretion) that fall within the parties' submission to arbitration. There is nothing controversial in that basic ideal. In

---

[125] New York Convention, supra note 5, art. V(1)(e).

fact, properly viewed, this duty is simply a manifestation of the party-controlled nature of arbitration.

1-101   It is a very different matter, however, to argue that this concern for enforceability might cause arbitrators to transgress the parties' own agreement. Such a strategy would seem particularly ill advised given that excess of jurisdiction is itself a basis to refuse enforceability of an award. Put another way, an agreement to limit the arbitrators' authority to apply a particular mandatory rule is also an agreement to reserve that rule for a national court that might apply it. And the New York Convention recognizes the interest of national courts in enforcing that agreement.

1-102   Another way to frame the issue is to consider who, institutionally, is best situated to protect the enforceability of a particular award. Basic procedural matters such as due process and equal treatment remain fundamentally within the control of the arbitrators. Parties will typically select an established set of procedural rules in their agreement, and they may set forth their own specific procedural requirements, but ultimately it is the arbitrators' responsibility to ensure fair proceedings. The question of substantive mandatory rules is different, however, not merely because parties have the legal authority to determine which mandatory rules do or do not fall within the submission to arbitration, but also because they are far better suited than arbitrators to make choice-of-law decisions in the manner best suited to protect the enforceability of the resulting arbitral award.

1-103   Consider the multi-jurisdictional character of award enforcement. Under the modern system of arbitration, arbitrators adjudicate the parties' legal claims and determine which, if any, remedies are appropriate. But arbitrators do not enforce their own awards. It is up to the parties either to comply with the award voluntarily or to seek enforcement in whichever jurisdiction they wish. A successful party will often have the opportunity to seek enforcement in several different jurisdictions – many of which may have no relevance to the dispute itself – where the losing party has assets. To do so, however, that party will have to bring the award to those countries' respective court systems, and each country will have its own mandatory rules that may affect the enforcement of the award. In order to facilitate this process, the parties are perfectly capable of structuring their original arbitration agreement in the manner best suited to ensure the arbitrability of those mandatory rules claims which are most likely to prove relevant at the enforcement stage. Indeed, under the regime of *Mitsubishi*, the parties should have an incentive to do so, because only by ensuring that the arbitral tribunal takes cognizance of and actually decides a claim arising under a mandatory rule can the parties avoid the prospect of having subsequently to litigate the mandatory rule in a U.S. court.

1-104 To the same extent that the parties are best situated to anticipate and provide for such contingencies, the arbitrators themselves are ill suited to do so. When exercising their mandate to adjudicate legal disputes, arbitrators may have little idea of which mandatory rules, if any, will ultimately prove relevant to the enforcement process. Any mandatory rules method that exceeds the parties' own submission to arbitration would therefore invite speculation and imprecision.

1-105 This problem is more complex in cases where a party may consider enforcement in different countries with different mandatory rules. Assume, for example, that an arbitrator rejects a breach-of-contract claim on the ground that the contract is illegal in the place of performance. By preemptively denying the claim, the arbitrator may well save the award from being refused enforcement in the place of performance. But this rejection will also prevent the claimant from obtaining relief in other countries that would not otherwise give any effect to the mandatory rule in question. If the parties have not authorized application of that mandatory rule, the result will be to reverse the merits of the case in the interest of preventing only partial unenforceability.

1-106 Of course, in the reverse scenario where the arbitrators do not apply the mandatory rule in question, the result may be to facilitate the parties' own avoidance of that rule. Some might perceive impropriety in this outcome, and justify the arbitrators' extraordinary intervention on that basis. But absent extraordinary circumstances, such as cases involving racial discrimination or criminal conduct in which an arbitrator could not enforce the parties' agreement without compromising his or her own integrity, the arbitrator has no warrant for acting outside the parties' agreement out of a concern that they are avoiding a mandatory rule. The very fact that different national courts may take different positions toward the enforceability of the same international contract highlights the fact that no single nation can rule the world of transnational commerce. In the event that arbitration were not an option, parties would always have the opportunity to pursue lawsuits in courts that recognize their claims and then to seek recognition of the resulting court judgment in the courts of other countries whose laws so allow – even if the courts of other third countries were not willing to provide such recognition. *Mitsubishi* tells us that parties may obligate themselves to bring certain claims before arbitrators rather than courts, but it does not purport to override limitations on national prescriptive or adjudicatory jurisdiction.

1-107 Ultimately, these complexities arising from the putative duty to ensure an enforceable award bring us back to the concern among U.S. commentators about whether arbitrators can be trusted to enforce mandatory rules. At first glance, the mandatory rules debate would appear to prove the *Mitsubishi* skeptics wrong, providing as it does an encouraging sign that arbitration practitioners are concerned about matters of justice that go behind the narrow interests of parties to arbitration agreements. But the ultimate question is whether a mandatory rules method rooted in the concern for issuing enforceable awards can truly provide an adequate means of protecting those rules.

1-108 Recall again the observation that there are

> virtually no cases where the arbitrators have relied on the application of a mandatory rule to justify a decision other than that would have resulted from the application of the law chosen by the parties.[126]

There could be many reasons for this circumstance, including the possibility that unmeritorious attempts to invoke mandatory rules outnumber meritorious ones. But it is also worth considering the incentives that the "award enforceability" approach to mandatory rules may create. The practice of using mandatory rules to gild the lily would present the enforcement-focused arbitrator with a no-lose situation. In the best case, the arbitrator may succeed in shoring up the award by limiting the legal avenues available to a party seeking to challenge the award. A court applying the *Mitsubishi* doctrine will defer to the arbitrator's application of the mandatory rule if it accepts that the arbitrator had jurisdiction to apply it. In the worst case, the court will refuse to recognize the preclusive effect of the mandatory rule determination and the arbitrators will remain in the same position they would have been had they never invoked the mandatory rule in the first instance: the arbitral award will remain effective subject to the proviso that the party resisting enforcement will be free to invoke any applicable mandatory rules in court.

1-109 Indeed, if the arbitrator were careful about how the mandatory rule applies (for example, if the arbitrator applied the rule in the alternative or assumed arguendo its application), a court might leave the arbitral decision

---

[126] *Fouchard Gaillard Goldman*, supra note 101, at 856-57.

untouched by simply interpreting it not to preclude judicial application of the mandatory rule. The situation would become more complicated, however, if the arbitrator applied a mandatory rule in a way that actually changed the outcome of the dispute. In the event that a court determined that the arbitrator lacked jurisdiction to apply the rule and that that circumstance constituted a ground to overturn the award, that action would constitute a much more direct rebuke.

1-110 Taken to its logical conclusion, this hypothetical would encourage the very thing that *Mitsubishi's* critics fear: an incentive to underenforce mandatory rules. While there is no evidence to suggest that such an incentive has crept into the world of international arbitration, arbitrators would still do best to focus on responsibly applying the law they believe applicable by virtue of the parties' agreement, regardless of the implications that agreement may have on the enforceability of an award, and even if that means that they must ignore otherwise applicable mandatory rules. In so doing, they will better serve the interests of the international arbitral system and, ultimately, the protections of the mandatory rules as well.

*Pierre Mayer**

CHAPTER 2

EFFECT OF INTERNATIONAL PUBLIC POLICY IN INTERNATIONAL ARBITRATION?

I. INTRODUCTION

2-1 It is first necessary to clear up the ambiguity of the expression: international public policy.

2-2 In civil law countries, the expression "ordre public international" means: the concept of public policy as applied in private international law. It is in fact the limited part of the public policy of a State which may constitute an obstacle to the application of a foreign law by the courts of that State, or to the recognition of a foreign judgment or arbitral award by such courts. It is in that sense that the expression is used in the "Resolution on public policy as a bar to the recognition of international arbitral awards" adopted in New Delhi in 2002 by the ILA (International Law Association).[1]

2-3 In a second sense, international public policy is the part of public policy which belongs to public international law. As an example, an embargo decreed as a sanction against a State by the Security Council of the United Nations[2] belongs to international public policy in that sense. To avoid any confusion with international public policy as a device used in private international law, it is sometimes called "truly international public policy".

---

* Professor at the University of Paris I (Panthéon-Sorbonne).
[1] The text of the Resolution can be found in the Report of the New Delhi Conference and in XXIX *YBCA* 339 (2004), with a presentation by Pierre Mayer and Audley Sheppard.
[2] Such as the ones adopted against Iraq in 1990 and 1991.

Loukas A. Mistelis and Julian D.M. Lew (eds), Pervasive Problems in International Arbitration, 61-69
© 2006 Kluwer Law International. Printed in the Netherlands

2-4 That leads me to distinguish truly international public policy from a third notion: that of transnational public policy, although unfortunately the two expressions are sometimes considered as synonymous. Transnational public policy in international arbitration is in fact the subject of my presentation, as I guess from the examples which are given as illustrations in the programme.

2-5 I shall successively consider:
- First, the notion of transnational public policy
- Secondly, its nature
- Thirdly, as a link with the subject addressed by Donald Donovan, the question whether, in a given case, an arbitrator should choose to rely on transnational public policy or rather to apply the mandatory rules of a State – the result being most often the same.

II. NOTION OF TRANSNATIONAL PUBLIC POLICY

2-6 "Transnational public policy" can be defined as the set of legal principles, not belonging to the law of a particular State, which may be relied upon by an arbitrator either as a bar to the enforcement of an international commercial contract, or, in a less direct manner, as an obstacle to the application of the State law normally applicable to such contract. The concept was introduced by Pierre Lalive in his famous report at ICCA in New York in 1986, and is now a classic.[3]

2-7 Indeed, transnational public policy is a necessary device in international arbitration. Since, unlike a court, an international arbitrator is not an organ of a State – even the State where he sits – it is neither easy nor satisfactory for him to rely on the public policy of any given State. He needs to have his own public policy.

2-8 On what is it based? A succinct answer to that question was given by the Institut de droit international at its session of Santiago de Compostela in 1989. A Resolution was adopted, pursuant to which

---

[3] Pierre Lalive, "Transnational (or Truly International) Public Policy and International Arbitration", in *Comparative Arbitration Practice and Public Policy in Arbitration*, ICCA Congress Series no 3 (1986), 257.

in no case shall an arbitrator violate principles of international public policy as to which a broad consensus has emerged in the international community.[4]

2-9 Evidence of such a consensus will most often result from a scrutiny of the legal systems of the various States, or from the existence of one or more international treaties. A typical example of the way arbitrators reason is the famous award rendered by Judge Lagergren in a case in which a party claimed the payment of a commission, which in the circumstances clearly appeared to have been promised as a reward for acts of corruption. Although the defendant only raised objections based on the interpretation of the contract, the arbitrator invoked transnational public policy to justify its refusal to even enter into the merits of the case:

> Such corruption is an international evil; it is contrary to good morals and to an international public policy common to the community of nations.[5]

2-10 Other principles often cited by authors are those which condemn:
- racial or religious discrimination
- drug trafficking
- terrorism
- trade in stolen art objects
- traffic in human organs.

2-11 The notion of transnational public policy thus appears relatively clear; its nature is more ambiguous.

III. NATURE OF TRANSNATIONAL PUBLIC POLICY

1. Proposed Analysis

2-12 Transnational public policy performs the same function as State public policy or truly international public policy: it eliminates the agreements, rules or decisions that would contravene certain fundamental values or interests. But does

---

[4] The text of the Resolution can be found in 79 *Revue critique de droit international privé* 191 (1990).

[5] Award rendered in ICC case no. 1110, *Argentine engineer v. British company*, 3 Arb Int 282 (1987). It has been partially published by Julian D M Lew, *Applicable Law in International Commercial Arbitration* (Oceana 1978), p 553. See also ICC case no 1110, ibid.

it have the same nature? When we say, for instance, French public policy, or English public policy, we refer to a component of a given legal system. That legal system imposes on its subjects the duty to comply with the principles and rules on which it confers a public policy character, and in case of non-compliance it imposes on its courts the duty to restore a situation that will be in accordance with these principles and rules. Similarly, truly international public policy is a part of international law, the part which even an agreement between two States may not violate. Can the same be said of transnational public policy? Is there a legal system, distinct from the States and from international law, that imposes on its subjects the duty to respect the principles and rules on which it confers a public policy character?

2-13 Such a legal system has been said to exist. One of its finders, or inventors, Professor Berthold Goldman, has given it the name of *lex mercatoria*.[6] Others prefer to call it new law merchant, or transnational law, although this last expression has also been given other meanings, notably by Professor Philip Jessup.[7] *Lex mercatoria* would be the legal system spontaneously emerging from the society of international merchants, the so-called *societas mercatorum: ubi societas, ibi jus*. And transnational public policy would be the part of the *lex mercatoria* presenting the characters of public policy.[8]

2-14 It is important to decide whether transnational public policy is, or is not, a part of a legal system, because its nature will not be exactly the same.

2-15 I personally do not believe that a legal system corresponding to the definition of *lex mercatoria* exists. Since this is not the time and place for a demonstration, I shall just mention briefly the main reason why I think that *lex mercatoria* may well be the name given to a set of legal rules, but does not constitute a legal system.

2-16 A legal system is formed not only of rules, but, even more importantly, of judges and of organs exercising a power of coercion. *Lex mercatoria* lacks both.

---

[6] Berthold Goldman, "Frontières du droit et *lex mercatoria*", (1964) *Archives de philosophie du droit*, 177.

[7] See Philip Jessup, *Transnational Law* (Yale University Press 1956).

[8] Lalive, supra note 2; L Matray, "Arbitrage et ordre public transnational", in J Schultz and AJ van den Berg (eds), *The Art of Arbitration, Liber Amicorum Pieter Sanders* (Kluwer Law and Taxation 1982) p. 241.

In particular, contrary to what has been suggested by some authors,[9] arbitrators are not empowered to adjudicate disputes by the society of merchants and do not render their awards in the name of that society: they receive their powers only from the parties in the particular dispute; and only State courts and State organs of coercion are able to enforce arbitral awards. It is even doubtful that there is a society of international merchants; it requires more than doing business together to form a society.

2-17 Now, even if there was a society of international merchants, could the principles known as transnational public policy emanate from that society? This would be surprising, since what these principles accomplish is mainly to limit the freedom of trade, which is not what merchants normally wish to do. If we take for instance the prohibition of the traffic of illicit drugs, there are on the one hand those who are involved in such trafficking, who do not want it to be limited, and on the other hand those whose activities are totally different, who simply do not care; or if they do, it is as ordinary citizens, not as merchants.

2-18 The prohibition, as an element of transnational public policy, therefore rests on the common feelings of ordinary citizens, inscribed in the legislation of a majority of States, and/or in international treaties drafted and signed by them. That does not make it part of a legal system which would be distinct both from the States and from international law.

2-19 What is transnational public policy then? And since it is not a set of legal principles having a binding force, resting on a legal system, where does its power to deprive a contract of its binding force, or to exclude the law chosen by the parties, come from? What justifies that an arbitrator, who is supposed to order the parties to abide by the terms of their agreement, refuses to do so on the ground that these terms violate a principle which he declares to be part of transnational public policy?

2-20 There is in my opinion only one possible answer to such question, although it may seem disappointing: it is his position as an arbitrator that gives him the freedom to invoke the principles which he considers to be worthy of being respected. Transnational public policy is not imposed *on* the arbitrator, it is

---

[9] See, for example, Philippe Fouchard, *L'arbitrage commercial international* (Dalloz 1965), 403, according to whom arbitrators and arbitral institutions are the "veritable prevoir jurisdictionnel de [la] société internationale des commerçants".

imposed *by* the arbitrator, by virtue of the powers conferred on him by the parties.

2-21 Let me immediately qualify this statement. I am not saying that the arbitrator is at liberty to do anything he pleases. He should act reasonably, he should defend, and defend only, those principles which are considered as inviolable by the community of men, or by a majority of States having enacted legislation or entered into treaties in order to protect them. That is his duty, it being observed that it is not a legal duty since it is not sanctioned as such; it is a professional, and to some extent a moral, duty.[10]

2. Consequences of the Proposed Analysis

2-22 This approach leads to slightly different results from those to which one is led if one considers transnational public policy as an objective element of a transnational legal order. In the approach which I favour, the arbitrator's duty is less strictly defined. He enjoys a certain degree of liberty in his assessment of what is tolerable and what is not.

2-23 When one mentions the necessity of a consensus between States, how broad must the consensus be? It is for the arbitrator to decide. When one insists that, to be part of transnational public policy, a principle must be of paramount importance, who assesses the importance of a given principle? It can only be the arbitrator. There is no absolute truth: one arbitrator may consider that a certain principle, which is shared by a majority of States, but rejected by an important minority, does not deserve to be upheld, to the detriment of the party who claims that the contract must be performed. Another arbitrator may take the opposite view. Their respective moral and even religious convictions play a role.

2-24 There is a famous case which illustrates that rather clearly: the case of the ship "Le Créole". It was a slave ship which carried slaves belonging to American owners. The slaves revolted while the ship was at sea, and sailed it to the Bahamas. When they arrived, the English authorities set them free, slavery having been abolished in England. The United States espoused the claim of their nationals, and a mixed arbitral commission had to decide whether England, by setting the slaves free, had violated international law.

---

[10] See Pierre Mayer, "La règle morale dans l'arbitrage international", in *Etudes offertes à Pierre Bellet*, Litec, p 379.

2-25 The award was rendered in 1855. It reads:

> I do not need to cite authorities to demonstrate that slavery, although odious and contrary to principles of justice and humanity, can be established by the laws of a country; and that, having been so established in several countries, it cannot be against the law of nations.[11]

2-26 The award, deciding a case between two States in accordance with international law, may have been correct at the time. But suppose the dispute had been brought before you, as an arbitrator, by the owners claiming that their title be recognised and the slaves returned to them, would you, even at the time, have counted how many States had established slavery, how many ignored the institution and how many condemned it? I suppose not. You would have relied on the fact that slavery is "odious and contrary to principles of justice and humanity", because you would have shared these principles.

2-27 Transnational public policy is not a definite part of a legal system, which the arbitrator would have the duty to uphold; it is a device which allows the arbitrator to refuse to enforce a contract, or to apply a law, which contravenes values which he, in accordance with a view shared by the community of men and endorsed by legislators (national or international), deems to be essential.

IV. CHOICE BETWEEN RELIANCE ON TRANSNATIONAL PUBLIC POLICY AND APPLICATION OF MANDATORY STATE RULES

2-28 Since transnational public policy must reflect a broad consensus between the States, in most cases it will not differ from the rules which are to be found in the applicable State law. Is it then preferable to apply the mandatory rules of the State, or to invoke transnational public policy?

2-29 I shall distinguish two situations, depending on whether the mandatory State rule is present in the *lex contractus*, or is only present, as a *loi de police*, in the law of another State, not chosen as *lex contractus* by the parties.

2-30 In the first situation I do not see why the arbitrator would not simply apply the *lex contractus*. A precise rule is preferable to a vague principle. In addition, if

---

[11] *Recueil des arbitrages internationaux,* edited by A de Lapradelle and N. Politis, vol 1, (Paris, Les Editions Internationales 1954-1957) p. 686.

the *lex contractus* has been chosen by the parties it would even be strange not to apply it without a major reason.

2-31 In the second situation it is more difficult to choose. The choice is between reliance on transnational public policy on the one hand, and on the other hand the *méthode des lois de police*, consisting of the application of a law other than the *lex contractus*, based on its mandatory character and on its close connection with the situation.[12]

2-32 The second reasoning was adopted in an ICC arbitration award in 1989. A contract had been concluded between a Hungarian company and a foreign company, for the collection and sale by the first party to the second, of certain glands to be taken from dead human bodies in Hungary. The contract was subject to Swiss law. It was argued by the buyer that the contract violated the principle of the integrity of the human body. The arbitral tribunal checked whether under Hungarian law – as the law of the territory – such trade was licit or not; it found that it was licit.[13]

2-33 If the tribunal had chosen to rely on transnational public policy, it would not have found a precise answer to the problem because the scope of the prohibition of the trade of human organs varies: in some countries the prohibition is absolute, while in other countries it depends on whether there is a payment, or even on who pays whom. It is preferable to apply the precise rules of the State concerned, rather than a vague principle which is not applied in the same manner in the various countries.

2-34 The same can be said of the prohibition of corruption. Where there is a clear act of corruption, which is proven, the easy way, it is true, is to apply the transnational public policy principle. But the limit is not always clear between what is a licit commission and what is corruption. For instance in some countries one has to distinguish between innocent "facilitating payments" and corruption. Equally since it is most often impossible to prove the existence of corruption, there are sometimes legal provisions which prohibit the payment of any commission, based on a presumption of corruption. Such technical rules cannot

---

[12] See Pierre Mayer, "Mandatory Rules of Law in International Arbitration", 2(4) *Arb Int* 274 (1986); Christophe Seraglini, *Lois de police et justice arbitrale internationale*, (Dalloz 2001).

[13] ICC Award no 5617, extracts in 121 *Journal du droit international (Clunet)* 1041 (1994).

be part of a transnational principle; however, it may be justified to apply them if they serve legitimate State interests.

2-35 Transnational public policy is a particularly convenient notion when the public policy principle is universally recognised, and where, at the same time, there is no doubt that it has been violated. When it is not universally recognised, much depends on the subjective views of the arbitrator; that cannot be avoided. Also, where the exact scope of the principle is uncertain, other mechanisms may have to be preferred. Transnational public policy therefore undoubtedly appears as one, but only one, of the devices which the international arbitrator may use to protect values which the parties are not allowed to ignore.

*Catherine Kessedjian**

CHAPTER 3

DETERMINATION AND APPLICATION OF RELEVANT NATIONAL AND INTERNATIONAL LAW AND RULES

I. INTRODUCTION

3-1 It is very difficult to be original on a subject such as the one which the editors asked us to study. Very important studies have already been published[1] and most of them are still relevant today. Some important developments have established themselves which do not seem to be challenged. Having said that, we are going to present what we consider to be the main issues still pending, with the following caveat.

3-2 We are not going to tackle the issues of mandatory laws and public policy, since other chapters of this book have dealt with them.[2] However, public policy always lurks around, particularly in non contractual matters. Nonetheless, the assumption of this chapter places the discussion within the ambit of party autonomy, *i.e.* the freedom left to the parties by the public policy of the States which may have an interest in the activity at stake.[3]

3-3 A second assumption is also important to bear in mind: we will consider that the parties to the dispute are professionals and have chosen to go to arbitration "*en connaissance de cause*" or, at least, that they should have known what it meant. It is an important assumption even though international trade in the 21st

---

*   Professor, University Panthéon-Assas Paris II.
[1] See the bibliography published by Jean-François Poudret et Sébastien Besson, *Droit comparé de l'arbitrage international* (Bruylant, LGDJ & Schulthess 2002) Chapter 7, 603-604.
[2] See Chapter 1 by Donovan and Greenawalt and Chapter 2 by Mayer.
[3] This limits considerably the interest of the discussion, for most of the difficult issues are nowadays left to public policy. It is becoming more common to see the traditional conflict of laws replaced by a conflict of mandatory norms or of public policies.

century is not what it was in the middle of the 20th century. Then, it was operated mainly by large multinational corporations. Today, a great number of small and medium size corporations are also participating in transnational economic activities. This factor should be kept in mind by lawyers particularly when it comes to the definition of applicable law or rules.

3-4 We are excluding *ex aequo et bono* (*amiable composition*) arbitration agreements since, an award rendered *ex aequo et bono* is based on something other than law or rules *stricto sensu*.

3-5 We will not study in depth the matter of *dépeçage* since we consider that this is a common sense issue, *i.e.* an issue which needs to be resolved on a case-by-case basis. *Dépeçage* should be allowed where it makes sense, where the activities in dispute, or the issue at stake, are clearly severable and fall within the ambit of different legal systems or sets of rules, where it allows better justice to be done.

3-6 Traditionally, we would have dealt only with contractual matters. However, more often than in the past, arbitral tribunals now have to deal with non-contractual issues. This trend was anticipated by the negotiators of the New York Convention of 1958 which applies equally to awards rendered in contractual and non contractual matters.[4] Hence, the matter of applicable law has become more complex in those cases. Indeed, different reasoning must be applied in contractual and non contractual cases. In addition, some time should be devoted to investment disputes as these disputes leading to arbitration grow every day.

II. *ETAT DES LIEUX* (INVENTORY)

3-7 In contractual matters we have a multitude of different norms:[5] international treaties, national laws, anational instruments (such as the UNIDROIT Principles[6] or the Principles of European Contract Law[7]), to name only a few. These "instruments" are usually grouped under the generic term of "rules" which also

---

[4] See Article I(1) and *a fortiori* Article I(3)

[5] We use the generic term "norm" to encompass laws, rules and other types of juridical norms. See also Julian Lew, Loukas Mistelis and Stefan Kröll, *Comparative International Commercial Arbitration* (Kluwer Law International 2003), Chapter 18.

[6] On the UNIDROIT Principles see www.unidroit.org and www.unilex.info.

[7] On the PECL see Hugh Beale and Ole Lando, *Principles of European Contract Law* (Kluwer Law International 1999). See also http://www.cisg.law.pace.edu/cisg/text/peclintro.html.

cover any number of anational norms, transnational law, *lex mercatoria,* and the like. At least two exceptions may be pointed to here: (1) Section 46 of the English Arbitration Act 1996 speaks of "other considerations" and does not use the word "rules". Whether that expression also covers such anational norms as mentioned earlier is arguable, although the majority of the doctrine seems to have accepted such an interpretation.[8] (2) The 1999 Swedish Arbitration Act does not contain any provision on the law applicable to the merits of the case. No guidance may be inferred from that law.

3-8 In non-contractual matters, we may have some international treaties (particularly, if the arbitral tribunal has to deal with environmental matters), but mostly we have national laws but, as far as we know, no anational instrument. However, in competition matters, apart from the public law aspect, tort principles may be applied. Hence, there may be a need for the tribunal to look at instruments issued by the International Competition Network which could be classified as "grey literature" but may have an important influence if the tribunal tries to ascertain some cross-border convergence in competition matters. In the telecommunication and internet area, there may be similar groups which issue some standards and practices which may be relevant.[9]

3-9 In investment disputes, there are some aspects which are contractual and some which are not. But those which are not contractual are not automatically delictual or tort issues. They may be of a different nature, specific to investment law.[10] This would need a more lengthy development than what the scope of this chapter allows, but we wanted just to signal the issue.

---

[8] See Alan Redfern & Martin Hunter, *Law and Practice of International Commercial Arbitration* (4th edition with Nigel Blackaby and Constantine Partasides, Sweet and Maxwell 2004), 2-2 and page 126; Michael Mustill & Stewart Boyd, *Commercial Arbitration 2001 Companion*, (2nd edition, Butterworths 2001) 50; Claude Reymond, "L'Arbitration Act 1996: convergence et originalité", *Rev Arb* 1997, 45, at 63; Poudret & Besson, supra note 1, 609-610.

[9] This could be in line with the concept of transnational law as understood by Klaus Peter Berger:

> Transnational law is based on the functional legal comparison, a methodology that tends to look behind the dogmatic differences of domestic legal systems by distilling common legal values and concepts out of seemingly different domestic legal rules,

in: *The Practice of Transnational Law* (Kluwer Law International, 2001) p 108.

[10] And indeed several pertain to treaty interpretation. See Chapter 13 by Kaufmann-Kohler and Chapter 12 by Weiniger.

III. HIERARCHY?

3-10 The question of hierarchy appears mainly when the parties have not expressed any choice of law and the arbitral tribunal is faced with the duty to define which law or rules it will apply to the merits of the case. Speaking of a hierarchy of norms is taking side on the philosophical debate around the role of States in a global economy as appeared quite clearly during the conference which gathered friends, colleagues and students of the late Philippe Fouchard, in Paris, on 11 March 2005.[11] Some argue that there is no need for an *a priori* hierarchy and plead only for a pragmatic approach, on a case by case basis.

Those who plead for such an approach claim that, in a globalised world, juridical territorialism is an absurdity. Hence, transnational economic activities can only be regulated by global norms, "a-cultural norms", specifically crafted for them by the operators and not the States. Their position is not new and, in ancient times, has already existed. When the Roman Empire was destroyed by the barbarian invasions, Roman law and Roman judges disappeared and the only way to solve dispute was left to arbitration.[12] It is a similar phenomenon we are witnessing today.

3-11 In order to justify, legally speaking, their position, they might rely on the fact that a number of arbitration laws and rules provide that the arbitrators may apply "rules of law" and not only "law", meaning certain juridical norms, applicable to transnational commercial activities, which do not stem from a State. This trend is well established and is a sign of what could be defined as the "denationalisation of arbitration".[13] But there are still a number of laws which do not allow such a reasoning and expressly direct arbitrators to apply a "law", meaning a national legal system. This is the case of Germany, for example,[14] This is also the case of the Rome (EC) Convention of 1980 on Law Applicable to Contractual Obligations and for a number of international instruments particularly those emanating from UNCITRAL.

---

[11] The reports are published as a special issue of the *Revue de l'arbitrage* 2005 no 2. A critical summary is published in volume 7-2 of the *International Law Forum*.

[12] François Terré, "L'arbitrage, essence du juridique", in: *Liber Amicorum Claude Reymond – Autour de l'arbitrage* (Litec, 2004) 309, at 310.

[13] Whether these a-national norms are called "lex mercatoria" or not does not really matter. We consider the expression as being so ideologically loaded that we prefer not to use it. See also Lew/Mistelis/Kröll, supra note 5, at paras. 18-46 et seq.

[14] Section 1051 al. 2 of the ZPO.

3-12 To say that, however, does not automatically entail that there is no need for any hierarchy among those norms. We, for one, are of the opinion that some hierarchy must be established *in abstracto*. Indeed, the different norms which may be of use to an arbitral tribunal in reaching a decision do not have the same nature, the same value. It cannot seriously be disputed that an international convention does not have the same nature as a trade usage or an ICC codified practice or national law. Trying to establish a hierarchy is a guarantee of some legal security and certainty in a field which, from talking to the "clients",[15] seems to lack so much of that. This is particularly crucial in cases where the parties have not been able to negotiate and adopt a choice of law clause in their contract. This is still not that infrequent[16] as transnational economic activities are more often conducted by small and medium size undertakings which do not necessarily have their deals reviewed by a lawyer before signature.[17] The only conclusion one may draw from the fact that the parties to a contract have not expressed a choice of law is that, either they forgot about it, or they disagreed about it. We cannot agree with those who conclude from the parties' silence that they wanted to have their agreement regulated by a-national norms or general principles or any transnational law or even, for that matter, an international convention which is not *per se* applicable to the case and is not part of *jus cogens*.

3-13 Since we are within the scope of freedom of contract, the agreement of the parties must first be applied. This is a commonplace, and is provided for by all arbitral rules and laws around the world. Whether the tribunal may reach a solution by the sole interpretation of the contract and without resorting to any external norm, is very seldom in practice and will only call our attention briefly later on. If the parties have expressed a choice, their choice should be respected by the Tribunal and interpreted to the fullest extent possible. Party autonomy goes beyond the contractual agreement of the party on the technical aspects of their relations. It also encompasses any agreement (express and clear) on the application of legal norms, for example, an international convention, as long as that convention may be applied by the mere will of the parties (see, for example,

---

[15] We call "clients" the corporations who use the arbitral process for their disputes. Contrary to what is sometimes argued, arbitration must be approached from their point of view, and not that of the lawyers who help them.

[16] ICC statistics show that it remains at around 20% of their case load. In addition, it may be the case that the choice of law clause does not cover all issues.

[17] In our view, this does not minimise the influence of the presumption of professionalism mentioned at the outset of this chapter. We consider that an undertaking dealing on the international plane must be considered as a professional even though it may not use all the means to protect its interests.

the Vienna Convention on Contracts for the International Sale of Goods of 1980) beyond its own scope of application as defined in the convention itself. Hence, the will of the parties may well extend the scope of application of a convention, as long as that convention is of such a nature that allows this extension.

3-14 The same is true if the parties have clearly chosen to place their agreement under the umbrella of anational norms whatever they may call them.[18] If, for example, their choice of law clause mentioned "transnational law" without more, they are taking the risk that the tribunal would equate that expression with norms found in arbitral practice (insofar as this may be ascertained) or norms such as the UNIDROIT Principles or the European Principles of Contract Law. It is very difficult to know what the actual business practice in this regard is.[19] There are some indications in the study conducted by Klaus Peter Berger and the Center for Transnational Law (CENTRAL),[20] but we are lacking more precise empirical study,[21] particularly studies which do not include arbitrators.[22] The CENTRAL enquiry seems to justify that some hierarchy be established between norms, in view of the fact that some of the persons who answered the enquiry indicated that, if they did use some kind of "transnational law", it was *in conjunction with*, but *not in lieu of*, domestic law,[23] either to supplement it or to interpret it.[24]

3-15 In the absence of a clear choice by the parties, the absence of any obligation by the arbitral tribunal to apply an international treaty or convention (apart from

---

[18] This is accepted by most arbitration laws and rules apart from the 1961 European Convention and the UNCITRAL Rules (Article 33) which, in this respect, are outdated. See very useful chart established by Poudret & Besson, supra note 1, at 615.

[19] In that respect, one could comment that some papers delivered at international conferences entitled "contract practice" are speculations by the author, sometimes from model contracts (ICC or other) and not based on an analysis of actual contracts. See for example, Prof. Fabio Bortolotti's paper for the UNIDROIT/ICC Joint Seminar, Paris, 10 December 2004.

[20] See supra note 9, at 91-113 and chart D-01 at 159.

[21] Berger indicates that the CENTRAL enquiry "does not purport to be a representative one" (at p. 96). Indeed, as always in this kind of enquiry, only 29.6% of the questionnaires were returned (at p. 100) but a smaller number was really useful i.e. 23.4%. The result of the enquiry must also be nuanced by the fact that a fairly large number of responses came from arbitrators who are more familiar with the concept of "transnational law" (at p. 104).

[22] An interesting additional information may be found in the statistical chart published by the ICC (*ICC Bulletin* 2004-1, 13) which shows that, in the great majority of cases when the parties have made a choice, they have opted for a domestic law.

[23] Supra note 9, at p. 107.

[24] In theory, it is questionable whether such a role can be given to transnational norms. But we will not discuss this issue here because we would also have to discuss the neat concept of "internationally useful construction" of domestic law.

those forming *jus cogens*,[25] those specific to investment law in case of an investment arbitration, and, perhaps, some well established general principles of law) leads us to conclude that the tribunal should first find the applicable national law. It is only if the country, whose law is identified as applicable to the matter, is a Party to a particular treaty or convention, that the arbitral tribunal would be entitled to apply such treaty or convention. The reasoning justifying such a conclusion is that, in the absence of a clear choice to the contrary, the parties should have known that the application of a national body of law may encompass international norms which are part of that country's system.[26]

3-16 What is the place of the UNIDROIT Principles or the European Principles of Contract Law when the parties have remained silent[27] as far as their potential application? One way of reasoning would be to look to the applicable law to find out what role these Principles could play within that system. The chances are that such a question cannot be answered since, except for the case of Panama,[28] the national laws are silent on this issue, and the question is seldom asked to the courts so that there is little or no case law yet developed in domestic courts.[29] Another path would be to simply "apply" the preamble of each of those documents which defines the cases in which they were meant to be applied.[30] Of course, one may question whether the bodies which prepared and adopted such documents had the authority or the power to define for themselves which those

---

[25] With all the difficulties inherent in a notion which is still debated in public international law circles. Sometimes the UN Charter is said to embody international public policy and, as such, is to be applied by arbitrators (see, for example, Alain Prujiner, comment under CA Québec 31 mars 2003, *Air France v. Lybian Airlines, Rev arb*, 2003, p.1365-95.

[26] This is true whatever the way in which international law is rendered applicable by that country's system, i.e. whether that system is a monist or a dualist one.

[27] As explained above, what may be deduced from the silence of the parties is a difficult question. In our view nothing much may be deduced apart from the fact that they could not agree on any applicable law or rules.

[28] Decreto-Ley No. 5 du 8 juillet 1999, portant Loi d'arbitrage, mediation et conciliation, Articulo 27.

> El tribunal apreciará las estipulaciones del contrato para la aplicación del Derecho que gobierna la relación contractual, y tendrá en cuenta los usos y prácticas mercantiles y los principios de los contratos de comercio internacional de UNIDROIT.

[29] As far as we know there is one French decision which used "les principes relatifs aux contrats du commerce international" after having refused to enforce an arbitration clause (CA Grenoble, 24 January 1996, *Rev. Arb.* 1997, p. 87, chronique Y. Derains). This decision remains isolated.

[30] Note that the Preamble of the UNIDROIT Principles has been changed in the 2004 edition to provide now that the principles may be applied when the parties have not chosen any law to govern their contract and also that they may be used to interpret or supplement domestic law.

cases are. But this question may be too theoretical, particularly in a world where juridical pluralism seems to be widely accepted and at a time when these instruments have been around for many years and widely publicised, discussed and commented upon, so much so that it can no longer be said that parties to an arbitration agreement could be unaware of them. Could we say that these Principles, at least the UNIDROIT Principles, are to be equated to the new "transnational commercial law"? There is little doubt that arbitrators, favourable to such a concept and who do not like to revert to a specific national law (for many different reasons) and do not want to use the expression "lex mercatoria" which is often considered as "too loaded", would find it easy to refer to the UNIDROIT Principles.[31] Whether that is good or bad reasoning is a different matter. One aspect remains clear, however, UNIDROIT Principles are unfit for any other matters than contracts. Hence, the rules they propose may not be extended beyond purely contractual matters.

3-17 Let us turn now to the role of usages. Many arbitration rules and laws specify that "in all cases, the arbitral tribunal applies the trade usages" (see for example, the ICC Arbitration Rules). No specific definition of that concept is given. But it is easy to see that because they are "trade usages" they can only designate professional, technical usages and probably not legal usages. Hence this is not helpful for our concern about application of rules of law. We are aware that a number of doctrinal works or arbitral awards have interpreted the notion of usages widely to include general principles of law.[32] We consider that this is not a useful way of reasoning as it adds more uncertainty to the matter, by mixing up concepts, than it brings clarity, security and efficiency. The same is true when equating trade usages with model contracts. Indeed, if the parties have taken the model contract as such without changing a word, saying that they have applied a "trade usage" is not helpful because the model contract has become the parties' contract. It is only if the model contract has been amply commented upon, interpreted and applied to concrete reported cases that we might infer from the parties' choice that they intended to incorporate into their choice all of those comments. This could happen in very specialised branches of activities (trade of fresh fruits, transport of ore and the like). If, on the contrary, the parties have departed from the model contract, the above construction fails to be convincing

---

[31] See the very clever and subtle explanation given by Berger, supra note 9, at 106-107.

[32] For example, Eric Loquin, "La réalité des usages du commerce international", *Rev Int Dr Eco* 1989, p 163 and *L'application de règles anationales dans l'arbitrage commercial international, in l'apport de la jurisprudence arbitrale,* ICC Publication no 440-1, 1986, p. 67. The author repeated the same position in his report in honour of Philippe Fouchard on 11 March 2005.

as the parties have shown that they disagree, at least partly, with the model contract. Then the only way to get around the difficulty is to use *dépeçage* and find out the applicable law for those aspects of the model contract which the parties have departed from.

3-18 The issue of hierarchy takes an interesting turn in the area of State contracts (*contrats d'Etat*). Within the context of ICSID arbitration, article 42(1) contains a tension between the nationalisation and the transnationalisation of the dispute.[33] This is the case only where the parties have not chosen the applicable rules of law. Indeed, the second sentence of article 42(1) provides:

> "In the absence of such agreement [on the choice of law], the Tribunal shall apply the law of the Contracting State party to the dispute (including its rules on the conflict of laws) and such rules of international law as may be applicable".

3-19 The first question is what is the meaning of "international law". Should it be interpreted in the narrow sense, *i.e.* law made by States whether bilaterally or multilaterally or could it include anational norms? The first interpretation is certainly what the negotiators had in mind when drafting that provision.[34] However, this does not mean that the Convention may not be interpreted with 21st century concepts if it can be said that the concept of "international law" nowadays also encompasses anational norms.[35]

3-20 The second question is what is the role of international law in relation to the law of the Contracting State party to the dispute? Is it to supplement that law, to make sure that law is not contrary to international law, to interpret that law, to replace that law, or all four? As suggested by Silva Romero when he speaks of "moderate internationalisation", the truth probably lies in a fair equilibrium between the domestic law of the State and international law. It is comforting to

---

[33] These terms are inspired by a very interesting article by Eduardo Silva Romero, "La dialectique de l'arbitrage international impliquant des parties étatiques – Observations sur le droit applicable dans l'arbitrage des contrats d'Etat", *ICC Bulletin* 2004, p. 86. Mr. Romero speaks of "internationalisation" while we prefer the term "transnationalisation" which, in our view, better describes the current phenomenon.

[34] See Christoph Schreuer, *ICSID Convention* (Cambridge 2001) chapter devoted to Article 42, and a number of ICSID awards. See also, Christoph Schreuer, "Failure to Apply the Governing Law in International Investment Arbitration", 7 *Austrian Review of Int'l and European Law* 147-195 (2002)

[35] This is what the private party to the dispute asked the arbitral Tribunal to do in ICC cases no 7110 and no 9474 both cited by Silva Romero, supra note 33, p. 95, footnote 46.

see that at least in one ICC award,[36] the arbitral tribunal applied the domestic law of the State and confirmed the soundness of its decision by finding an identical solution in the UNIDROIT Principles, in other words not applying the Principles but deriving inspiration from them.

3-21 The third question relates to the meaning of the parenthesis "(including its rules on the conflict of laws)". These few words clearly show, first, that the States negotiating the ICSID Convention knew they were dealing with something else than contract. Indeed, it is universally accepted[37] in contractual matters that the theory called *"renvoi"* should not be applied as the parties must have had in mind the substantive law of the legal system applicable and not its conflict of laws rules. Secondly, by allowing the play of conflict of law rules in investment matters, the negotiators had a clear view on what is known as "co-ordination of legal systems". Indeed, if the legal system of the State in dispute does not consider that its own law is applicable to the matter but differs to another law, it is much better to apply that other law than to force arbitrarily the application of a norm that is not "interested" in regulating the matter. By looking at the connecting factor at the heart of the conflict of laws rule, one knows the kind of hypothetical cases which the applicable law anticipated to regulate. Outside this scope, there is no reason to force the application of that law. One could take the example of labour law dispute. It is often the case that labour relations between the foreign investor and its employees in the host State will be regulated by the domestic law of that State. However, the conflict of laws included in the host State's labour law may provide for some matters to be regulated by the law chosen by the parties in the contract of employment. If the dispute between the investor and the host State relates to the matters regulated by the employment contract, then Article 42 of the ICSID Convention allows the tribunal to apply the law chosen in that contract instead of the domestic substantive law of the host State, under the condition – as always – that those domestic substantive norms are not considered as public policy.

---

[36] Case no. 7365, *ICC Bulletin*, 2004, pp 117-118.

[37] At the time of the ICSID negotiations, among the small number of countries who apply *renvoi* in general, there may have been only one (Austria) which applied the theory in contractual matters. That country has now changed its system. See also Article 15 of the Rome Convention on the law applicable to contractual obligations.

IV. ROLE OF CONFLICT OF LAWS

3-22 In contractual matters, it is now widely accepted that arbitral tribunals are free to define the applicable law without resorting to any specific conflict of law rule. In fact, it is possible to argue that a special conflict of law rule has been developed by arbitration practice, called *"voie directe"*, by which the tribunal finds out with which legal system the contract (or the activity in the case of a complex set of contracts) which led to the dispute has the most significant relation.[38] Some arbitral tribunals may find it necessary to complement their initial reasoning by using a conflict of law rule they find in a convention such as the Rome Convention of 1980. But nothing obliges them to do so. This is a consequence of the denationalisation of arbitration mentioned earlier, exemplified by the fact that the arbitral tribunal has no "seat", hence it is not a "forum" in the legal meaning of the word even if there is a "place of arbitration".[39]

3-23 Can the conflict of laws analysis lead the tribunal to apply the UNIDROIT Principles? Some Tribunals have said so. This is the case of an award rendered in 2001 under the auspices of the Arbitration Institute of the Stockholm Chamber of Commerce.[40] Apparently, the Tribunal used the *"voie directe"* method but also came to such a conclusion from an additional analysis based on the Rome Convention. As far as this latter analysis is concerned, it is a misguided interpretation of what the Rome Convention provides[41]. Indeed, that Convention only contemplates national laws and not any rule of law. Only if the national law applicable by virtue of the Rome Convention conflict rules accepts that some other rules of law may be applied to the matter, is the Tribunal entitled to look at other rules than the national law. Otherwise, the Rome Convention cannot, by itself, lead to the application of rules such as the UNIDROIT Principles[42].

---

[38] This is different from saying that the tribunal must apply the most appropriate rule.

[39] The role and function of the "place of arbitration" have changed over the years. Nowadays, it is mainly formal (to determine the recourse against the award) and may still be important for public policy purposes. But Poudret & Besson argue with conviction that the applicable law analysis arbitral tribunals are allowed to make is defined in the *lex arbitrii* which depends upon the place of arbitration (supra note 1, p 608).

[40] Case no 117/1999, *Stockholm Arbitration Report* 2002, pp 59-65 and the comment by Loukas Mistelis, *Unif L Rev* 2003, pp 631-640.

[41] This will not change with the proposal of Regulation which will replace the Rome Convention (Com (2005) 650 final 15.12.2005). Indeed, if the new Article 3 allows parties to a contract to choose non-state law as the applicable law to their contract, there is no equivalent rule when the parties have remain silent.

[42] See the Report on the Convention on the law applicable to contractual obligations by Mario Giuliano and Paul Lagarde Professor, EEC Official Journal no C 282, 31 October 1980 0001 –

3-24 What if the Tribunal has used the *voie directe*? Could it consider that the most appropriate rules are the UNIDROIT Principles or another equivalent norm? The answer to that question depends on one's conception of the role of the arbitral tribunal in the absence of a choice of law made by the parties. If the role is to find the supposed "will of the parties", then the *voie directe* can only lead to the application of norms which were known at the time when the parties concluded their agreement. Then comes the debate over the question: when is a norm sufficiently known? It is fair to say that in 2005, the UNIDROIT Principles 1994 are sufficiently known. How long should we wait in the case of the 2004 version? The answer will obviously differ from one tribunal to the other. If the role of the tribunal is to find the rules with which the contract or the activity at stake (assuming there are more than one contract) have the most significant link, it may be risky to find such link with rules of the so-called *lex mercatoria* or the UNIDROIT principles. If, on the contrary, the goal is to find the objectively most appropriate rule, then *lex mercatoria* or the UNIDROIT principles could come into play. Whether this conclusion could be foreseen by the parties would depend on the wording of the arbitration rules chosen by them. ICC Rules of Arbitration, Article 17(1), would certainly help such an analysis.[43] Indeed, it may be said that by choosing an ICC Arbitration, the parties have chosen Article 17 of the ICC Rules and have taken the risk that the arbitral tribunal interpret that text in the most liberal way.

3-25 As far as non contractual relations are concerned, even though it is proposed to allow a large place to party autonomy, it is more doubtful that it can play the same role as in contractual matters. The first difference lies in the fact that if there is a choice of law agreed by the parties, it can only be made *a posteriori* once the tort has been committed. The second difference, in our view one of great importance, is triggered by the fact that a tort may have an impact on many more people than the parties themselves. Hence, the potential influence of the award is greater than a purely *inter partes* decision. This is not to say that the award will have a *res judicata* effect against a non-party. But it may be used in subsequent/parallel proceedings (whether arbitral or judicial in domestic courts) and eventually be contradicted.

0050. Whether this will be changed in the future European Regulation aimed at replacing the Rome Convention is unclear at this stage.

[43] Whether this very liberal wording, frees the arbitral tribunal from the question of the application in time of the rules it finds the most appropriate, will be studied later.

V. A SPECIAL NOTE ON THE INTERPRETATION OF THE CONTRACT

3-26 If the parties' agreement itself is the object of interpretation, does the arbitral tribunal need to search for the applicable law first and then find in that law the principles of interpretation? On the contrary, is this a matter of general principles of interpretation as codified in the law of Treaties for example?[44] As it is well known, the Rome Convention (Article 10) provides that the interpretation of the contract must be made by the applicable law[45]. We consider that it would be easier to avoid looking at the applicable law so that solving the litigation would not be complicated if it can be done via only the interpretation of the contract.

VI. HOW TO ASCERTAIN THE CONTENT OF THE APPLICABLE LAW?

3-27 A special mention is necessary for the English Arbitration Act of 1996 and its Section 45. It is a form of "*juge d'appui*" for the applicable law, as far as English law is concerned (Section 82). As far as we know, it is a unique provision which does not exist, as such, in any other arbitration laws.[46] The conditions for its application make it difficult to work in practice. Indeed, the application to the judge will only be possible if it has been accepted by all parties to the arbitral proceedings or is made with the permission of the arbitral tribunal and the court. The court must be satisfied that the determination of the question is likely to produce substantial savings in costs and the application was made without delay. These drastic conditions are obviously intended to avoid delaying tactics by one of the parties to the arbitral proceedings.

3-28 The peculiarity of Section 45 of the English Act is that it could allow the arbitral tribunal to refer a preliminary question of EC Law to the European Court of Justice via the judge. Indeed, we all know that, for good reasons, the ECJ has so far always refused to hear preliminary questions coming from arbitrators.[47] It is true that the wording used by Article 234 of the EC Treaty is quite precise and

---

[44] Silvia Ferreri, "Le juge national et l'interprétation des contrats internationaux", *Revue int de droit comparé*, 2001, pp. 29-60.

[45] This provision is unchanged in the proposed Regulation.

[46] Section 1050 of the German ZPO deals with obtaining proof and its application to ascertain the content of the applicable law is questionable. The same is true with Section 589(1) of the Austrian Code of Civil Procedure.

[47] See more recently *Denuit v. Transorient Mosaïque Voyages & Culture SA*, Case C-125/04, 27 January 2005.

covers only domestic courts of the Member States[48]. Some have interpreted the provision and its interpretation by the ECJ to limit preliminary questions only to a court seized of a substantive question which it has to decide itself.[49] This interpretation seems to be a departure from the clear language of Article 234 of the EC Treaty which speaks of a preliminary question which is necessary to "enable it to give judgement", and not of a question necessary to "solve the dispute on the merits".

3-29 The Netherlands Code of Civil Procedure Article 1044 provides for the help of the Court of First Instance in The Hague to secure information on foreign law as is made possible by the London Convention of 7 June 1968.[50] One might argue that even in absence of such an explicit provision, the *"juge d'appui"* could do so as long as he is located in a country which is a Party to the London Convention. However, as a practical matter, an arbitral tribunal may find it preferable not to have recourse to such a possibility as it may be quite cumbersome and take a long time. In addition, only rarely the explanations given by the parties are insufficient to ascertain the content of the applicable law. In addition, this provision cannot be used to ascertain the content of EC Law via a preliminary question to the ECJ because the EC is not a Party to the London Convention.

3-30 Also worth mentioning here is a recent decision by the Italian Constitutional Court allowing arbitral tribunals which must apply Italian law to refer a preliminary question to the Court if the constitutionality of the law applicable to the case is in question.[51]

3-31 What about the so-called *lacuna* in the applicable law? It is fashionable to say that some systems of law may lack rules for sophisticated, modern, economic

---

[48] Despite the reform of the EC judicial system by the Nice Treaty, the wording of Article 234 has not been changed. Equally, Article III-369 of the proposed Constitution has not changed the wording relevant here, though it adapts the text to other modifications included in the Constitution.

[49] This is the analysis of Christoph Liebscher, *The Healthy Award* (Kluwer Law International 2003) pp.38-39 citing Holto, 22 January 2002 in which the ECJ states "[only a tribunal which] is called upon to give judgment in proceedings intended to lead to a decision of a judicial nature" may make a reference. However, there is little doubt that a court asked by an arbitral tribunal to pass a judgment on the applicable law is rendering a judicial decision. There is also little doubt that an arbitral tribunal is also rendering a judicial decision.

[50] European Convention of 7 June 1968 on Information on Foreign Law.

[51] 22 November 2001, Translation of the decision into French in *Rev Arb*, 2002, p 185, note D. Borghesi.

or financial activities. On the contrary, it may also be said that any system of law contains enough general rules from which to derive a solution, even though a detailed rule has not yet been developed for a specific relation or activity. This is the case, for example, with the *bona fide* principle which may allow overcome the absence of a hardship principle in domestic law.

VII. EVOLUTION OF THE APPLICABLE LAW OVER TIME

3-32 This is an old issue which is always current, not only with regard to national laws but also anational norms as is exemplified by the recent amended and supplemented second edition of the UNIDROIT Principles.

3-33 In contract matters, we are of the opinion that the applicable law or rule is the law or rule as it stands at the time the contract was formed. This is the usual rule in contract matters[52]. The only exception would be if the new rule has become one of a mandatory nature. In tort, we should apply the law as it stands at the time the tort was committed.

VIII. EXTENT TO WHICH A JUDGE MAY CONTROL THE APPLICATION OF THE LAW OR RULES BY THE ARBITRAL TRIBUNAL

3-34 Most arbitration laws do not allow such a control as it would come too close to a "*révision au fond*" which is usually prohibited. In the United States, the Federal Arbitration Act does not provide for such a control but one has been judicially crafted, called the "manifest disregard of the law". Some courts have interpreted that expression to mean: "wilful inattentiveness to the governing law". In other words, it will be rarely applied as it requires more than an error or misunderstanding of the law, but a finding that the record shows the arbitrators knew the law and explicitly disregarded it.[53]

3-35 Whether the reasoning (*motivation*) of the award is relevant or not is not open to verification by the judge in most systems as it is under French law.[54] Under French law, even if the award contains a contradiction between two sets of

---

[52] Article 17 of the Rome Convention (provision unchanged in the proposed Regulation).
[53] See for example, *Bowen v. Amoco Pipeline Company*, 254 F 3rd 925 (10th Cir, 2001).
[54] Paris, 1st chamber C., 27 June 2002, *Rev Arb* 2003, p 427, note Cécile Legros.

reasons, this is not a ground for the judge to void the award or refuse enforcement.[55]

3-36 In at least four countries (France[56], The Netherlands,[57] the United States[58] and Sweden[59]), the award may be voided or the *exequatur* refused if the arbitral tribunal violated the terms of its mission. Could one use the violation of its mission by the arbitral tribunal as a ground to ask the judge to review the way the tribunal has applied the applicable norms? Could we say, for example, that if the parties have chosen French law and the tribunal's application of that law is wrong, the tribunal has violated the terms of reference? But if the argument is based on the violation of the will of the parties, the conclusion to this question would be different depending whether the parties had agreed on the applicable law or not. Is this tenable? In fact, there is almost no case law on this issue. Under French law, even if this ground for annulment is often invoked by the parties, it is seldom accepted by the courts.[60] However, Fouchard Gaillard and Goldman accept the idea that if the tribunal has applied Japanese law instead of the English law chosen by the parties, the award could be voided or enforcement refused for violation of the scope of its mission.[61] Same question if the tribunal has applied the UNIDROIT Principles or general principles of transnational economic law. Are judges in one country better placed than arbitrators to say what those norms are, and which is the "right" outcome of the dispute? Justice is always relative. We all know that judicial truth is not The Truth.

3-37 Those laws which allow a revision of the way the law has been applied by the arbitral tribunal, usually impose a set of conditions which makes the appeal more difficult. For example, the English Arbitration Act 1996, Section 69 provides that all parties must agree on such an appeal and it must be authorised by the judge. A number of other conditions concerning the merits of the appeal

---

[55] Civ 1, 14 June 2000, CA Paris 16 November 2000 and 28 June 2001, *Rev Arb* 2001, 729, note approbative H Lécuyer; Civ. 1, 11 may 1999, *Rev Arb* 1999, p 810, note E Gaillard.

[56] Article 1502(3).

[57] Article 1704 al.2 lit. d.

[58] 9 U.S.C. §10(a)(4).

[59] Article 34(2).

[60] S Crépin, *Les sentences arbitrales devant le juge français – Pratique de l'exécution et du contrôle judiciaire depuis les réformes de 1980-1981* (LGDJ, 1995), para 371.

[61] *Traité de l'arbitrage commercial international* (Litec 1996), para 1637. The Paris Court of Appeals refused to void an award in which the tribunal had taken French law as guidance for the application of Egyptian law since, as the tribunal noted, Egyptian law was inspired by French law (Paris, 10 March 1988, *Rev Arb* 1989, p 269, note Fouchard).

must also be met. In addition, if the parties have agreed that the award is not to be reasoned, they are considered to have waived their right to appeal on a point of law. As for Section 45, Section 69 applies only if the point of law refers to English law and the parties are allowed to opt out of the application of Section 69 altogether.

3-38 A special mention should be made of a decision of the Swiss Federal Court[62] which allows the court to review the law applicable to the assignment of a contract since that question was preliminary to the validity and existence of the assignment of the arbitral clause. In this case, the review of the law is a preliminary question necessary to determine the arbitral tribunal's competence and not to decide the matter on the merits. This decision does not contradict the general prohibition of review on the merits (including the law applicable to the merits) known under the Swiss Private International Law Act.

3-39 If the arbitral tribunal has applied a law which has not been invoked by either of the parties and there has not been an opportunity for both parties to express their views on the point, the award could be voided or the enforcement refused for violation of due process.[63]

3-40 The almost entire absence of any control *a posteriori* by a judge of the way the tribunal has applied the law or the rules deemed applicable to the case shows how crucial it is for the parties' security that the arbitral tribunal does a good job in choosing the law or the rules applicable to the merits of the case and applying them.

3-41 With that aim, we venture to propose a method[64] which, hopefully, should safeguard the award against annulment or refusal of enforcement, along the following lines:

1. In any case, whether or not the parties have incorporated a choice of law clause in their agreement, the tribunal should apply the contract in its

---

[62] 16 October 2001, *Automobiles Peugeot c/ Omega Plus*, Rev Arb 2002, p 753, note P-Y Tschanz.

[63] Catherine Kessedjian,"Principe de la contradiction et arbitrage", *Rev Arb* 1995 381; *Fouchard Gaillard Goldman on International Arbitration* (E. Gaillard & J. Savage eds, Kluwer Law International 1999) at para 1639; Poudret & Besson, supra note 1, at p 784, note 213.

[64] Compare with the method proposed by Lew/Mistelis/Kröll, supra note 5, Chapter 17 *in fine*, p 437.

entirety, and, where pertinent, any trade usage which the parties knew or should have known.

2. If the parties have made a choice, the tribunal should respect that choice unless the result would be contrary to the mandatory rules or public policy of the host State (in case of investment disputes), the place of arbitration[65] and of the country in which the award is likely to be enforced.[66]

3. In the absence of a choice by the parties,
3.1. the tribunal should look at any international law norm which is applicable under its own scope of application (this is particularly important in investment arbitration);
3.2. if the issues at stake cannot be resolved by the norms defined in 2.1. above, the tribunal should look at the *lex arbitrii* to determine the method they should follow to define the applicable law, (i.e. essentially, either through the *voie directe* or through a conflict of laws rule they find appropriate[67]).
3.3. in appropriate cases, the tribunal should verify that the applicable law is not contrary to *jus cogens* or widely accepted general principles of international law.
3.4. in any case, the tribunal should also try to find support for its decision in widely accepted anational norms which the parties knew or should have known.

---

[65] The place of arbitration is important *de lege lata* because the award may be open to a recourse for violation of mandatory rules or public policy. This role is now contested by some members of doctrine (see presentation by Jean-Baptiste Racine on 11 March 2005).

[66] We know this is not easy to define.

[67] In our view, the *voie directe* is a conflict of laws rule. Hence, the tribunal should always use the *voie directe* even when the *lex arbitrii* says that it should look at the most appropriate conflict of laws rule. As a result, we find question 3 in Lew/Mistelis/Kröll, supra note 5, too complicated.

*V V Veeder QC**

CHAPTER 4

THE TRANSPARENCY OF INTERNATIONAL ARBITRATION: PROCESS AND SUBSTANCE

I. INTRODUCTION: ARBITRAL CONFIDENTIALITY IN RELATED COURT PROCEEDINGS

4-1 Much has been written about the confidentiality and privacy of arbitration proceedings from *Esso* (1995)[1] via *Bulbank* (2000)[2] to *Aegis* (2003);[3] but, until recently, almost nothing has been said about the secrecy of court proceedings relating to a confidential arbitration or confidential award.

4-2 Whereas by their arbitration agreements parties may expressly agree to differing degrees of secrecy in relation to their own arbitration, no similar agreement is usually made in relation to court proceedings ancillary to that arbitration; no institutional or other arbitration rules, to my knowledge, currently provide expressly for the secrecy of such court proceedings, still less the express waiver of any legal right to a public court hearing otherwise enjoyed by a party;[4]

---

*   Essex Court Chambers; General Editor "Arbitration International"; Visiting Professor on Investment Arbitration, King's College, University of London.
[1]   *Esso Australia Resources Ltd and others v. The Hon Sidney James Plowman, The Minister for Energy and Minerals and others*, 10 Commonwealth Law Reports 183 (1995). See also expert reports by Bond, Boyd, Lew and Smit in 11 *Arb Int* 231 (1995).
[2]   Supreme Court, 27 October 2000, *Bulgarian Foreign Trade Bank Ltd v. AI Trade Finance Inc*, 15(11) Mealey's IAR B 1 (2000), 13(1) WTAM 147 (2001).
[3]   *Associated Electric & Gas Insurance Services Ltd v. European Reinsurance of Zurich* [2003] UKPC 11, [2003] 1 WLR 1041.
[4]   For example, Article 25(4) of the UNCITRAL Arbitration Rules provides that the arbitration hearings shall be held "in camera"; and by Article 32(5), the award "may be made public only with the consent of both parties". The broadest institutional rules on the confidentiality of arbitration, Article 30 of the LCIA Rules and Articles 73-76 of the WIPO Arbitration Rules, are

and of course, in any event, such court proceedings are rarely consensual. In non-arbitration proceedings in court, subject only to specific exceptions, state courts do not usually sit in secret, delivering secret judgments and making secret orders. Such secrecy is the historical hallmark of absolute tyranny; and its despotic attractions remain self-evident. Hence Article 6(1) of the European Convention on Human Rights is designed to protect the citizen from secret justice by requiring "a fair and public hearing".

4-3 A quarter of a century ago, in its report on the *Axen* case (1981), the European Commission on Human Rights explained the rationale for Article 6:

> [...] the public nature of the proceedings helps to ensure a fair trial by protecting the litigant against arbitrary decisions and enabling society to control the administration of justice ... Combined with the public pronouncement of the judgment, the public nature of hearings serves to ensure that the public is duly informed, notably by the press, and that the legal process is publicly observable. It should consequently contribute to ensuring confidence in the administration of justice.[5]

4-4 That rationale has since been applied time and time again by the European Court of Human Rights, most authoritatively in *Werner v. Austria* (1997) where the Court described the visible and public administration of justice as the guarantee of a fair trial "which is one of fundamental principles of any democratic society".[6] This publicity is even more important for the court judgment than for the court hearing itself.

4-5 In a legal system based on judicial precedent, the rationale can be extended to the need to develop the law by judicial reasoning and to allow legal practitioners to practise their profession with access to published law reports. In English legal proceedings, the English judge takes the law from the practitioners in the case; and he has no law clerk nor even sufficient time to conduct any significant legal research by himself. As Lord Justice Denning said in one of his early judgments: it was

---

either silent on the confidentiality of legal proceedings ancillary to the arbitration or merely limit disclosure to the extent necessary in connection with court proceedings on the award.

[5]   Commission Report of 14 December 1981, B.57 (1982-1983).

[6]   *Werner v. Austria* (1997) 26 EHHR 310.

unfortunate that the principle I have enunciated was not drawn to the attention of the court in [an earlier judgment of the Court of Appeal], but that was my fault because I was counsel in the case.[7]

Without publicly reported reasoned judgments available to practitioners, the English legal system could not work as it does, the common law and statutory interpretation could not develop as it has; no useful textbooks could be written; and law schools would eventually fall silent, even Queen Mary College.

II. ESTABLISHED CONFIDENTIALITY

4-6 Until recently, only three jurisdictions had addressed expressly the confidentiality of the arbitral process in court proceedings ancillary to the arbitration. The first was France, in *Aita v. Oijeh* (1986).[8] The losing party to an English arbitration there challenged the award, which had been made by Lord Wilberforce in London, before the Paris Cour d'appel. The French Court rejected the challenge because it was legally hopeless to try to set aside under the new 1981 Decree an award made outside France; but more significantly, the Court ordered the applicant to pay significant costs (200,000 FFrs) for having in bad faith caused in court a public debate on matters which should have remained confidential between the parties. Where applications to set aside an award are made without bad faith or abuse of process, the court judgment and award in France become public documents, as Dr Crépin's archival work has demonstrated.[9]

4-7 The second was Bermuda. In enacting the UNCITRAL Model Law in the Bermuda International Conciliation and Arbitration Act 1993, the Bermudan legislator added two important provisions: Section 45 provided that, subject to the Bermuda Constitution, proceedings in any Bermudan court under the 1993 Act shall be heard otherwise than in open court on the application of any party to the proceedings; and Section 46 contained a detailed code imposing restrictions on the reporting of court proceedings not so heard in open court. Under this statutory scheme, there is no judicial discretion to hold a hearing in open court; and only a limited discretion to direct that any information from a private hearing

---

[7] *Cassidy v. Minister of Health* [1951] 2 KB 343, 363, referring to *Gold's Case* [1942] 2 KB 293 (cited in Pannick, *Judges* (1987), p 209).

[8] *Aita v. Oijeh*, Cour d'appel de Paris, 18 February 1986, *Dalloz Jur* 1987, 339 and *Rev Arb* 1986, 583, note Flécheux, *Dalloz Jur* 1987, 339 and note Gaillard, *Dalloz Chron* 197.153, 155. (Professor Emmanuel Gaillard was Counsel for the successful respondent in this case).

[9] Sophie Crépin, *Les sentences arbitrales devant le juge français: pratique de l'exécution et du contrôle judiciaire depuis les réformes de 1980-1981* (Paris, 1995).

can be published. There is, however, a judicial discretion to permit the publication of a judgment "of major legal interest" in law reports and professional publications, subject (on a party's application) to the removal of names and other details of the case and a delay in publication, not to exceed ten years.

4-8 One of the factors which led to this legislation was the enforcement in Bermuda of a Soviet award made "in camera" by the Foreign Trade Arbitration Commission in *SNE v. Joc Oil* (1984). Under earlier legislation enacting the 1958 New York Arbitration Convention, the Bermuda court proceedings were held in public; and the court file, including the Russian original text of the confidential award, remained publicly available in the archives of the Bermuda Supreme Court. This led directly to its publication (*inter alia*) in the *ICCA Yearbook*.[10] What was thereby lost in confidentiality was subsequently gained by English jurisprudence: the Bermuda Court of Appeal's judgment and the FTAC award led significantly to the English Court of Appeal's decision in *Harbour v. Kansa*, re-stating the modern English rule on the separability of the arbitration clause, which is now codified in Section 7 of the English Arbitration Act 1996.[11]

4-9 The third was a case in New Zealand. In *TV New Zealand* (2000)[12] a confidential award made in New Zealand was subjected to court proceedings in New Zealand. The award dealt, apparently, with the private life of a well-known public figure in highly embarrassing personal detail (although his company was the successful party in the arbitration). The award was challenged by the losing party under New Zealand's arbitration legislation apparently in good faith, without any abuse of process. Of course, the press were eagerly awaiting the public unveiling of this award in these court proceedings. However, the public figure did not wish his private life to be publicly unveiled; and the New Zealand Court had therefore to weigh the award's confidential status under Section 14 of the New Zealand Arbitration Act 1996[13] with New Zealand's constitutional

---

[10] *Sojuznefteexport (SNE) v. Joc Oil Ltd*, (1990) XV YBCA 384 (Bermuda Court of Appeal, 7 July 1989); (1993) XVIII YBCA 92 (FTAC Award in English translation; 1984. The original Russian text remains unpublished).

[11] *Harbour Assurance Co Ltd v. Kansa General International Insurance Co Ltd* [1993] 1 Lloyd's Rep 455, [1993] QB 701, per Hoffmann LJ at p. 723F.

[12] *Television New Zealand Ltd v. Langley Productions Ltd* [2000] 2 NZLR 250; note D. Williams (2000) NZLR 61.

[13] Section 14 [entitled: Disclosure of Information Relating to Arbitral Proceedings and Awards Prohibited] provides:

requirement for a public court hearing. Balancing these two conflicting texts, the learned Judge decided in favour of a public hearing; and the confidential award then became publicly available to the press. Curiously, the challenging party then discontinued its court application.

4-10 These French and New Zealand cases illustrate different aspects of the same problem, without offering any effective solution approaching the Bermudan legislation.

III. CONFIDENTIALITY AND ENGLISH LAW

4-11 To these three jurisdictions addressing the issue a fourth has recently been added. In *Bankers Trust (2005)*,[14] relating to an award made in London by a Swedish sole arbitrator, the English Court of Appeal had to consider the question whether and, if so, to what extent English court proceedings challenging the award were secret. The leading judgment was delivered by Lord Justice Mance (as he then was), who before his appointment to the English bench was a prominent arbitration practitioner and commercial arbitrator; and, thankfully, this important judgment was not delivered in secret. It merits the widest attention, together with the judgment of the Commercial Court (Mr Justice Cooke), which was upheld on significantly different grounds.

4-12 The case concerned a contractual dispute between two entities of the City of Moscow and two commercial bankers, under Russian substantive law. The arbitration took place by express agreement under the UNCITRAL Rules; and accordingly the arbitration hearings were held "in camera"; and in the absence of all parties' consent otherwise, the award remained confidential and unpublished. The bankers then challenged the award under Section 68 of the English Arbitration Act 1996 in the English Court, on the basis that the arbitrator had

---

(1) Subject to subsection (2), an arbitration agreement, unless otherwise agreed by the parties, is deemed to provide that the parties shall not publish, disclose, or communicate any information relating to arbitral proceedings under the agreement or to an award made in those proceedings.

(2) Nothing in subsection (1) prevents the publication, disclosure, or communication of information referred to in that subsection-

    (a) If the publication, disclosure, or communication is contemplated by this Act; or
    (b) To a professional or other adviser of any of the parties.

[14] *Department of Economics, Policy & Development of the City of Moscow & another v. Bankers Trust and another* [2005] QB 207, on appeal from the Commercial Court [2003] 1 WLR 2885 (Cooke J).

committed a "serious procedural irregularity" affecting the award. It was alleged that the arbitrator had failed to act fairly and impartially in accordance with the mandatory requirements of Section 33 of the 1996, to comply with the requirements as to the form of the award and to decide all issues put to him, thereby frustrating the object of the arbitration (namely the fair resolution of the parties' dispute). It was accepted that the bankers made their challenge to the award in good faith; and their applications were heard by the Commercial Court "in private". The arbitrator was a nominal party to those proceedings but not present or there legally represented. In March 2003 after a hearing lasting five days, Mr Justice Cooke in a reasoned judgment dismissed the applications. The issue then arose as to whether this first judgment was public or secret.

4-13 The bankers wanted this judgment to be secret, limited only to the disputing parties. The City of Moscow wanted the judgment to be public. As recorded in the later judgments, its "expressed reason" for wishing publication was a desire to demonstrate to the international financial markets or investment community generally that the arbitration award, deciding that the City of Moscow had not committed any financial default, had been the subject of a detailed and careful scrutiny by the English Commercial Court which had rejected all attacks upon the award.[15] Its *unexpressed* reason was possibly to achieve indirectly what it could not achieve directly, namely the public dissemination of the award's reasons which may have been quoted, extensively, in Mr Justice Cooke's first judgment.[16] It seems unlikely that Moscow's tax-payers would be equally interested in the interpretation of Section 68 of the English Arbitration Act 1996 on "serious procedural irregularity". It also appears that the City of Moscow's desire for publicity post-dated the first judgment: it had not earlier requested the court hearing to be held in public; it had made no earlier application that this first judgment should be delivered in public, even in an edited form; and it had even sought a specific order from the arbitrator confirming the confidentiality of the arbitration, given that the arbitration raised "highly sensitive political issues so far as Moscow itself was concerned".[17] Mr Justice Cooke concluded that the City

---

[15] As described by the Lord Justice Mance, see paragraph 6 at page 214C of the law report.

[16] See Cooke J's second judgment, paragraph 44 at p 2897 of the law report.

[17] See Cooke J's second judgment, paragraphs 27 & 28 at p 2893 of the law report. In sensitive commercial litigation, the English Court can readily "edit" its public judgment: for example, see the remarkable judgment of Mustill J in *Spinneys v. Royal Insurance* [1980] 1 Lloyd's Rep 406, a case involving Lebanon's civil strife, where on the parties' request the learned judge refrained from citing the names of the many witnesses whose lives could be endangered from undue publicity (although this trial took place in public). Using its powers to hear cases in camera, the Commercial Court and Court of Appeal have heard appeals from awards stated in the form of a

of Moscow had provided no good reason for requiring publication of his first judgment[18]. If hard cases make bad law, bad cases can make for interesting law.

4-14 This dispute over secrecy was fully argued by the parties at a later court hearing, also held in private; and in June 2003, Mr Justice Cooke delivered a second reasoned judgment that his first judgment was secret. This second judgment, however, was public and not secret. He decided that the privacy of an English arbitration and the confidential status of an English award did not automatically transfer to an English court hearing on a challenge to that award under the 1996 Act; but nonetheless, applying his judicial discretion under the relevant English Civil Procedural Rules (CPR r 62.10),[19] he decided that his first judgment should be known only to the disputing parties. He also decided that the result of the first judgment as formally recorded in the Court's order, "like the result of the arbitration" could be published by any party. The Court's order is therefore publicly known; but the reasoned first judgment itself remains unavailable to the public; and, perhaps surprisingly, for a long time its terms were not even made available to the arbitrator whose conduct of the arbitration and award had been so thoroughly vindicated by Mr Justice Cooke.[20] Less surprisingly, given the powers of the English Court for contempt of its orders, this first judgment has not become available in *samizdat*, not even in *Mealey's* published in the USA; and it remains tantalizingly secret still.

4-15 In the Court of Appeal, Lord Justice Mance identified a "spectrum" of confidentiality. At one end was the confidential arbitration; in the middle was the court hearing on the arbitration application under Section 68 of the 1996 Act; and

---

special case (where lives were at risk from publicity); and more recently, part of the *AEGIS* appeal in the Privy Council, supra note 3, was heard under non-reporting restrictions, given that the issue was whether or not the award was confidential (see also reference below).

[18] See Cooke J's second judgment, paragraph 45, at p 2898 of the law report.

[19] CPR r. 62.10 (for full citation, see footnote 31 below):

> (1) The Court may order that an arbitration claim be heard either in public or private ... (3) Subject to any order made under paragraph (1) ... (b) all other arbitration claims will be heard in private.

[20] By accident, however, certain members of the public attended part of the court hearing; and by another accident the Commercial Court made this first judgment publicly available as a result of which the full text was published in good faith on Lawtel's web-site (the judgment was not itself marked "private"), with a separate summary issued to its 15,000 or so subscribers. (Lawtel is an electronic on-line library for legal practitioners). The latter error was soon corrected upon Bankers Trust's urgent protest; but Lawtel's brief summary was allowed to remain in circulation by the Court of Appeal (from which it appears that this first judgment may be of general importance to the interpretation and application of Section 68 of the English 1996 Act, including the scope of an arbitrator's duty to give "reasons" in his award).

at the other end was the Court's formal order following its reasoned judgment. A formal order could be public: its bare recital that an application had been granted or dismissed (with costs) could disclose little or nothing. A reasoned judgment might well disclose much about a confidential award or arbitration; but, in the learned Judge's words:

> there could be no question of withholding publication of reasoned judgments on a blanket basis out of a generalised, and in my view, unfounded, concern that their publication would upset the confidence of the business community in English arbitration.[21]

The decision to permit or withhold publication of a judgment would therefore depend upon the discretion of the Court, fitted to the particular case-at-hand; and as regards CPR 62.10, the learned Judge significantly referred to the rule as a "starting-point" only, and expressly not as a "presumption".[22]

4-16 In the end, Lord Justice Mance decided against publication of the first judgment, concluding:

> Here the parties agreed contractually on a confidential alternative to litigation. The Arbitration Act 1996 and the CPR allow access to the court in the public interest, in order to support fundamental principles of fairness governing arbitration. It cannot be a breach of UNCITRAL Rules to invoke the court's supervisory jurisdiction. It could serve as an inappropriate deterrent to such access if the making of such an application were to dispose a court to order, at the instance of a party, a public hearing or judgment in circumstances when the sensitivity and confidentiality of the subject matter would otherwise point in an opposite direction.[23]

4-17 In his concurring judgment, Sir Andrew Morritt VC also referred to this same spectrum, concluding:

> Plainly not all the arbitration claims referred to in CPR r 62.10(3)(b) need to be treated as confidential. And those that do will vary in the extent to which they should be treated and the method by which to do so.[24]

---

[21] Supra note 14, at para 41.
[22] *Ibid*, at para 42.
[23] *Ibid*, at para 47.
[24] *Ibid*, at para 56.

4-18 These appellate judgments repay quiet study; and there is time here only to select two points. The first arises from the change in English legal terminology from court hearings "in chambers" to court hearings "in private" under the CPR, which was effected in 2002 under Lord Woolf's reforms enacted by the Civil Procedure Act 1997. Under the old pre-Woolf rules, the phrase "in chambers" did not refer to a secret hearing "in camera", but rather to the practice that such chambers' hearings could be heard in the judge's room rather than a court-room.[25] In the Commercial Court, however, arbitration hearings "in chambers" usually took place in the same court-room as a public hearing.

4-19 Under Lord Woolf's reforms to civil procedure, the use of all Latin tags being considered antiquated, the phrase "in camera" disappeared; and the new CPR introduced in 2002 the more limited concepts of a "public" hearing and a "private" hearing which was secret. Many commentators wrongly assumed that the new phrase "in private" in the CPR was to be equated with the old phrase "in chambers", without attracting the attributes of a secret hearing formerly "in camera". It is well settled, however, both before and after the CPR, that generally a judgment delivered in a court hearing in chambers or in private does not thereby automatically acquire a secret status; and even the exclusion of the public or the press at a private hearing does not generally amount to a ban on the later publication of what took place at that hearing. As Mr Justice Cooke decided, the general position, apart from arbitration, is that a court judgment "is open to the world unless the court should decide otherwise".[26] However, arbitration is placed in a special category under the CPR.

4-20 As recited by Lord Justice Mance's judgment, it was the practice before the 1996 Arbitration Act, under the old RSC Order 73, to hear applications challenging an award in public. As a result, the law reports contain many judgments on such arbitral challenges; and they still fill many footnotes in *Mustill & Boyd, Merkin* and *Russell*. Generally, even judgments delivered in chambers could be released by the judge into the public domain, notwithstanding the joint protests of the parties, if the judge thought the judgment raised a point of law of general public importance. There are many reported judgments under the old 1950-1979 Acts which fell into this category. In the days before Queen Mary's School of International Arbitration existed, when no law school taught the law

---

[25] *Hodgson v. Imperial Tobacco* [1998] 1 WLR 1056. For court hearings "in chambers", see *Scott v. Scott* [1913] AC 417, at pp 436-437, 443, 445-446, 453, 476-477.
[26] The second judgment, paragraph 15 at page 2889 of the law report.

and practice of English arbitration, that judicial practice was the way which allowed many of us to learn about English arbitration. Moreover, in the Commercial Court, every Friday morning, there would be crammed before the Commercial Judge a mass of Junior Counsel, Solicitors and Solicitors' Managing Clerks, all awaiting their turn to make their applications in chambers. In the meantime, each had to listen and learn from the earlier applications. It was there, whilst waiting, that we heard the young Mustills, Binghams, Savilles and the much-missed Brian Davenport argue the finer points of English arbitration law; and it was that same practice which allowed the Commercial Judge and practitioners to keep the pulse of London Arbitration. All this took place "in chambers"; it was far from secret; and it was a very good arbitration school.

4-21 The question is whether the regime under the 1996 Act was intended to be different from its statutory predecessors. When it was brought into effect in January 1997, the 1996 Act was accompanied by a new Order 73 of the Rules of the Supreme Court, the predecessor to the later CPR. This new Order 73 provided, in the language of the earlier rules, that court applications under the 1996 Act would ordinarily be heard "in chambers"; and in a formal statement by the Commercial Judge in January 1997, delivered in public, it was noted that special arrangements would be required to publicise court decisions on the 1996 Act amongst judges and practitioners to facilitate "consistency of approach".[27] The school of arbitration, in one form or another, would continue through publicity. As recited in Lord Justice Mance's judgment, however, the full implications of a court hearing "in chambers" remained relatively unexplored in 1997 (para. 18). The present CPR was introduced by the Rule Committee after consultations in 2001, including the Commercial Court Users' Committee. It was a very English form of consultation; and few can therefore remember being consulted; or if they were, whether the implications of the rule change were fully brought to their conscious understanding. There is always a danger for the user and practitioner in changing procedural rules; and the CPR changes very often. All this explains why many practitioners read Mr Justice Cooke's second judgment with surprise and dismay: it seemed to put off forever the third edition of *Mustill & Boyd* and make it increasingly difficult for practitioners to advise on the application of the 1996 Act if important judgments on the 1996 Act were now predominantly to be delivered in secret.

---

[27] Practice Note (Arbitration: New Procedure) [1997] 1 WLR 391, per Colman J.

4-22 It is fair to add that a careful reading of Lord Justice Mance's judgment can assuage many of these fears. But not all. How can the Rule Committee consider making such important substantive changes to the law and practice of English arbitration, without the same kind of genuine consultation which preceded the 1996 Act in regard to the confidentiality and privacy of the arbitral process? In the quotation from Bentham cited by Lord Justice Mance,[28] taken from Lord Shaw's speech in *Scott v. Scott* (1913):[29]

> Publicity is the very soul of justice ... it keeps the judge himself while trying under trial;

to which Lord Shaw wisely added:

> [...] there is no greater danger of usurpation than that which proceeds little by little, under cover of rules of procedure, and at the instance of judges themselves.

4-23 It cannot be assumed that English legal practitioners are sufficiently astute or informed to detect always the effects of minor changes in the wording of the CPR; and it ought not to take Lord Justice Mance to rescue London Arbitration from such effects.

4-24 The second point is whether English arbitration proceedings and awards are implicitly so confidential under English law; and, if so, whether they should be. Lord Justice Mance started his judgment with a statement of broad principle:

> Among features long assumed to be implicit in the parties' choice to arbitrate in England are privacy and confidentiality.

This generalisation was irrelevant to the case, given the parties' express agreement to the UNCITRAL Rules; and it is somewhat controversial as an unqualified statement of English law. The first hint that an arbitration hearing was generally "confidential" under English law, as opposed to being merely "private", came with Mr Justice Leggatt's judgment in *The Eastern Saga* (1984), twenty years ago; and the recent decision of the Privy Council in *Aegis* (2003) suggests there may exist an important distinction between confidentiality and privacy, with only the latter providing the general principle implicit under

[28] Paragraph 15 at pp 217-218 of the law report.
[29] [1913] AC 417.

English law.[30] There may also be an important distinction between the privacy of the arbitration hearing (including the arbitral deliberations) and the status of the arbitration award.

4-25 As a result of this attribution of confidentiality, confirmed by the CPR, both Mr Justice Cooke and the Court of Appeal treated arbitration applications as a special hybrid category. Under the CPR, court applications under Section 68 fall to one side; and court judgment under Section 69 of the 1996 Act, on appeals from an award on questions of English substantive law, fall to the other side of this category: CPR Rule 62.10(3)[31] imports a different rule that such hearings will be heard "in public", subject to an order otherwise. Both are only "starting-points" and not fixed rules or even a presumption. The most important aspect of Lord Justice Mance's judgments, therefore, is that all these questions eventually turn not upon any absolute rule applicable to a uniform special category applicable to all arbitrations but upon a judicial discretion whether or not to apply the rule or its exception in any particular case, depending upon its own individual circumstances. Moreover, the recent practice of the Commercial Court confirms that the *Bankers' Trust* case, contrary to initial fears, has not led to a judicial reaction against publicity for important judgments on the law and practice of arbitration. English arbitration has not become a state secret.

4-26 A pragmatic balance has to be struck; but publicity, or transparency, remains essential to the working of the 1996 Act and more generally to the public acceptance of arbitration.

---

[30] *Oxford Shipping Company Limited v. Nippon Yusen Kaisha (The Eastern Saga)* [1984] 2 Lloyd's Rep 373; *Associated Electric & Gas Insurance Services Ltd (AEGIS) v. European Reinsurance of Zurich* [2003] UKPC 11, [2003] 1 WLR 1041 (PC), per Lord Hobhouse.

[31] This rule provides:

(1) The court may order that an arbitration claim be heard either in public or in private.
(2) Rule 39.2 does not apply.
(3) Subject to any order made under paragraph (1) –
(a)   the determination of –
    (i) a preliminary point of law under section 45 of the 1996 Act; or
        (ii)   an appeal under section 69 of the 1996 Act on a question of law arising out of an award,
will be heard in public; and
(b) all other arbitration claims will be heard in private.
(4) Paragraph (3)(a) does not apply to –
(a) the preliminary question of whether the court is satisfied of the matters set out in section 45(2)(b); or
(b) an application for permission to appeal under section 69(2)(b).

4-27 At one extreme, arbitration is sometimes seen as so private, so unaccountable, so suspicious to third parties, practitioners, regulators and other state agencies, that only full publicity can demonstrate how it really works. But with full publicity, other parties may turn away from arbitration completely; or at least from those jurisdictions which do not respect a reasonable amount of privacy agreed by the parties. At the other extreme, the lack of all confidentiality in court may lead certain commercial parties to establish a private and confidential appellate process, separate from state courts. But strict privacy at this appellate level could lead increasingly to the atrophy of arbitration law. In the middle lies the compromise suggested by the Bermudan legislation and so carefully analysed by Lord Justice Mance. It is reflected elsewhere by the practice of "anonymisation" in Germany and Switzerland, whereby reported judgments have names and identifying details removed from the law report of the court proceedings on an arbitration award[32]; and both in Norway and more recently in New Zealand, legislative proposals have been made to strike a new balance between public justice and private confidentiality for arbitration parties.[33]

IV. CONCLUSION

4-28 In conclusion, we do need a new "spectrum" which is sufficiently flexible to cater for all horses for all courses. For some arbitrations, even the existence of the dispute will be strictly confidential. For others, the full award can be a public document. Whilst a successful party should not have its confidential secrets disclosed in court proceedings, it is also essential that arbitration law develops publicly with legal reasoning by state judges, for the ultimate benefit of all arbitration users themselves. The world of arbitration would be much the poorer, for example, without *Tobler v. Blaser,*[34] *Gosset*[35] and the *BGH Decision of 27*

---

[32] An excellent analysis on the "anonymisation" of German judgments may be found at: http://www.jurpc.de/aufsatz/20040073.htm.

[33] See Clause 14F et seq of the New Zealand Law Commission's proposed Arbitration Amendment Bill 2004, whereby the Court may derogate from the general principle of public court proceedings on the application of any party and

> only if the Court is satisfied that the public interest in having the proceedings conducted in public is outweighed by the interests of any party o the proceedings in having the whole or any part of the proceedings conducted in private.

[34] Swiss Federal Supreme Court, *Tobler v. Blaser,* BGE 59 I 177 (on separability).

[35] Cour de cassation, 7 May 1963, *Ets Raymond Gosset v. Carapelli*, 91 Clunet 82 (1964), Dalloz (1963) p. 545, with note J. Robert. (on separability).

February 1970[36] from Switzerland, France and Germany on the legal autonomy of the arbitration clause from the substantive contract in which it is embedded; and without the public judgments in *Bankers Trust,* so too would English law. If the position were ever to change significantly in the future, the next anniversaries of the School of International Arbitration would probably, of necessity, be much less interesting and much, much shorter.

---

[36] BGH Decision of 27.2.1970 – VII ZR 68/68(2) OLG Cologne, translation in English (1990) 6 *Arb Int* 79, with notes by Schlosser and Boyd.

*Dr Klaus Sachs**

CHAPTER 5

TIME AND MONEY: COST CONTROL AND EFFECTIVE CASE MANAGEMENT

I. INTRODUCTION

5-1 The question that the organizers of this 20th Anniversary Conference have asked me to address is *"whether arbitration is still inexpensive"* – that is a quite provocative way to put the question and a cynical mind could be tempted to reply: *"Poser la question c'est d'y répondre"*, and leave it at that. However, the subject of the growing costs of arbitration proceedings is too much of a concern to the users of arbitration services to be cynical. It deserves a closer review and discussion.[1]

5-2 No, international commercial arbitration today is not inexpensive. But has it ever been? Is it expensive compared to the costs of bringing the same claim before the state courts? Is it expensive in relation to the sums in dispute? Are the arbitrators' or the lawyers' fees, or both, the source of the complaints? Are there ways of reducing the costs without running the risk to seriously affect the fairness in the process? How can effective case management contribute to control the costs? These are some of the issues raised by the topic I have been asked to address and, since I am a lawyer with a German legal background, you will understand that I shall deal with these issues more from a civil law perspective.

---

[*] Partner, CMS Hasche Sigle, Munich.
[1] See, for example, Michael Schneider, "Lean Arbitration: Cost Control and Efficiency Through Progressive Identification of Issues and Separate Pricing of Arbitration Services", 10(2) *Arb Int* 119 (1994); Mauro Rubino-Sammartano: "Is Arbitration to be just a Luxury Clinic?", 7(3) *J Int'l Arb* 25 (1990).

Loukas A. Mistelis and Julian D.M. Lew (eds), Pervasive Problems in International Arbitration, 103-115
© 2006 Kluwer Law International. Printed in the Netherlands

II. THE COSTS OF ARBITRATION

1. The Cost Structure of Arbitration

5-3 For the purpose of our discussion, it is important to understand the cost structure of arbitration, *i.e.*, how the costs of arbitration are composed and how they are calculated. Usually, the term "cost of arbitration" is understood in a broad sense, covering on the one hand the procedural costs and on the other hand the costs of the parties.[2]

5-4 The principal cost items of the proceeding are
- (i) the arbitrators' fees and expenses in conducting the proceedings and
- (ii) in institutional arbitration, the costs and fees of the arbitration institution.

5-5 The costs of the parties mainly comprise
- (i) the lawyers' fees and expenses,
- (ii) the fees and expenses of party-nominated experts or expert witnesses and
- (iii) the parties' internal and non-productive costs, such as the services of in-house counsel and the diversion of management time.

2. The Various Methods of Calculating the Arbitrators' Fees

5-6 Looking first at the arbitrators' fees as the most important element of the procedural costs, one can note that the methods of calculating such fees vary quite considerably depending on whether the proceedings are administered by an institution, and if so, by which one, or whether they are non-institutional, *i.e.*, *ad hoc* proceedings.

---

[2] See Christian Bühring-Uhle, *Arbitration and Mediation in International Business, Designing Procedures for Effective Conflict Management*, (Kluwer Law International 1996), p 113; Julian D M Lew / Loukas Mistelis / Stefan Kröll, *Comparative International Commercial Arbitration* (Kluwer Law International 2003), paras 25-78 – 25-86.

(a) Institutional Arbitration

5-7 In institutional arbitration, the arbitration and the administrative fees are determined pursuant to the cost provisions of the relevant institutional rules. Comparing those provisions of the various well-known arbitration institutions, one finds that the calculation methods for calculating arbitrator fees can be quite antagonistic. One extreme is the method based on the value in dispute, *i.e.*, *ad valorem* compensation, which does not take account of the time worked on the case, and the other extreme is a calculation system based on periodic or daily fees, regardless of the value in dispute.

5-8 For instance, a typical *ad valorem* compensation method is the one employed by the German Arbitration Institution, DIS.[3] Thus, section 40(1) of the DIS Rules provides that the arbitrators' fees shall be fixed by reference to the amount in dispute without any further criteria. Until recently the only exception to this rule was if proceedings are terminated prematurely, i.e., by way of settlement. In such a case the tribunal may at its discretion reduce the fees in accordance with the progress of the proceedings (section 40(7) of the DIS Rules). In practice, this is commonly done, and the reduction rate normally ranges between 20 and 80 % depending on how far the proceedings had advanced before they were terminated. A similar *ad valorem* method is practiced by the Vienna Arbitral Centre (see Article 24 of the Vienna Rules). Such value-based calculation is certainly a rather rigid method and has its roots in the equally *ad valorem* based court and lawyer fees in certain civil law countries. However, it has the advantage that the arbitrators' fees are predictable – which gives comfort to the parties.

5-9 Interestingly, to make the system more flexible, the German Arbitration Institution as of 1 January 2005 amended its Rules by stipulating that the arbitrators' fees may be increased by up to 50 % of the regular amount depending on the legal or factual complexity of the case (Appendix to section 40(5), point 13, DIS-Rules). Similarly, the recently revised Vienna Rules provide that the arbitrators' fees may be increased up to 1/6 of the regular amount (Article 24(6) Vienna Rules).[4]

---

[3] Deutsche Institution für Schiedsgerichtsbarkeit, http://www.dis-arb.de/.
[4] International Arbitral Center of the Austrian Federal Economic Chamber, also known as the Vienna International Arbitration Centre (VIAC), http://www.wk.or.at/arbitration/.

5-10 As the other extreme, a purely time-based system, for instance, is employed by ICSID. According to the current Schedule of Fees as of 8 March 2004, ICSID has fixed a *per diem* of US$ 2,400 without any regard to the sums in dispute or applying other criteria.[5]

5-11 Most other well-known institutions, however, combine the two methods, either by primarily calculating the fees as a percentage of the sum in dispute within a certain range of a minimum and a maximum fee, the exact fee being determined by other valuation criteria, or by primarily calculating them on the basis of the time spent but fixing the exact amount having due regard to other circumstances of the case.

5-12 For instance, the ICC system primarily fixes the fees in accordance with a fee scale setting forth the minimum and the maximum arbitrators' fees by reference to the sum in dispute. However, pursuant to Article 2(2) of Appendix III to the ICC Rules of Arbitration,[6] the Court shall also take into consideration

[the] diligence of the arbitration, the time spent, the rapidity of the proceedings, and the complexity of the dispute

so as to arrive at a figure within the limits of the fee scale, or even at a figure higher or lower than those limits.

5-13 For the purpose of this discussion it is particularly interesting to note that in ICC proceedings the diligence of the arbitration is one important criterion. Indeed, according to the *"Guide to the New ICC Rules of Arbitration"* by Yves Derains and Eric A. Schwarz, the diligence of the arbitration

… [i]s probably the single most important factor that is likely to affect the Court's decision on fees. Although the rapidity of the proceedings obviously depends on a number of different factors, some of which are beyond the arbitrators' control, arbitrators are normally rewarded by the Court when they are perceived as performing their functions with expedition and efficiency. Conversely, an arbitrator's remuneration may suffer for lack of diligence.[7]

---

[5] International Centre for the Settlement of Investment Disputes, http://worldbank.org/icsid.

[6] Available at http://www.iccwbo.org/court/english/arbitration/rules.asp.

[7] Yves Derains / Eric A Schwarz, *Guide to the New ICC Rules of Arbitration* (Kluwer Law International, 1998), p 330.

5-14 Thus, the policy – but unfortunately not always the practice – of the ICC Court is to reward the arbitrators for their efficient case management by increasing their fees. And it is rather clear that, on balance, such policy is ultimately to the benefit of the parties since an efficient case management reduces the duration of the proceedings and, by way of consequence, the lawyers' fees.

5-15 A further advantage of a system such as the one employed by the ICC is that it avoids any temptation by the arbitrators to drag out the proceedings in order to increase their fees. It is interesting to note in this connection that the length of hearings in ICC cases is, as a general rule, considerably shorter than in an arbitration where the arbitrators are primarily paid based on time worked. Indeed, it is in my experience extremely rare that main hearings in ICC cases last longer than one week, whereas two to six or even more-week hearings are quite customary in common law proceedings where the time-based system prevails. It seems to me that this remarkable difference can not only be explained, as it often is, by the fact that traditional common law style arbitration is generally more time-consuming than civil law arbitration, but also, and not as the least factor, by the different methods of calculating the arbitrators' fees.

5-16 A similar system combining an *ad valorem* method with other criteria is put into practice by the new Swiss Rules of International Arbitration which came into force on the 1st of January 2004, harmonizing and replacing the former rules of international arbitration of the various local Chambers of Commerce and Industry in Switzerland.[8] Thus, Article 39 of the new Swiss Rules provides that the fees

> shall be reasonable in amount, taking into account the amount in dispute, the complexity of the subject-matter, the time spent by the arbitrators and other relevant circumstances of the case.

Following these principles the exact fee shall then be determined in conformity within the fee scale contained in the Schedule of the Costs of Arbitration, the system of which is similar to that of the ICC Appendix III.

5-17 By contrast, the methods employed by the LCIA and AAA are primarily based on time worked. According to the LCIA Schedule of Arbitrators Fees and Costs effective 1 June 2003, the tribunal's fees shall be calculated by reference to

---

[8]   See http://www.swissarbitration.ch.

the work done by its members in connection with the case at hourly fees within the range of £150 to £350.[9] The exact rate depends on

> "the particular circumstances of the case, including its complexity and the special qualifications of the arbitrators".

A similar mainly time-based compensation system is practiced by the AAA.[10]

(b)   UNCITRAL Arbitration Rules 1976 and ad hoc Arbitration

5-18 In non-institutional, *i.e.*, *ad hoc* arbitration proceedings, there are no firm rules as to how to calculate the arbitrators' fees. In cases where the parties have referred to the UNCITRAL Arbitration Rules 1976,[11] Article 39(1) provides that

> the fees [of the arbitrators] shall be reasonable in amount taking into account the amount in dispute, the complexity of the subject-matter, the time spent by the arbitrators and any other relevant circumstances of the case.

5-19 Article 39(2) of the UNCITRAL Arbitration Rules further provides that if an appointing authority has been agreed upon or designated by the Secretary General of the Permanent Court of Arbitration at The Hague, the arbitral tribunal in fixing its fees, if it considers appropriate, shall take into account the schedule of fees of such institution – for instance, the ICC Rules when the ICC Court is the appropriate authority.

5-20 In *ad hoc* cases which do not follow the UNCITRAL Arbitration Rules 1976, the fees for the arbitrators in common law countries are customarily calculated on the basis of hourly or daily fees. In arbitration proceedings between parties coming from civil law countries, the arbitrators' fees are in most cases calculated by reference to the fee schedule of an institution, and, more rarely, as a percentage of the value in dispute. For instance, in the most prominent current German arbitration case, *Federal Government v. Toll Collect*, which is an *ad hoc* case concerning claims by the Federal Government in the amount of 4.2 billion Euro, the fees of the arbitrators are reported to have been fixed at a lump-sum amount in the range of 1 to 2 million Euro each.

---

[9]   See http://www.lcia.org/ARB_folder/arb_english_main.htm#schedule.
[10]   See http://www.adr.org/sp.asp?id=22090.
[11]   See http://www.uncitral.org/uncitral/en/uncitral_texts/arbitration/1976Arbitration_rules.html.

5-21 As we all know, daily and hourly arbitrators' fees can be quite substantial. For example, a sitting fee of £3,500 for a hearing day of 7 to 8 hours is not unusual for a London-based *ad hoc* tribunal. Thus, a two-week hearing can easily result in arbitrators' fees of more than £ 100,000.

5-22 A particular feature of the English practice – and very rarely practiced on the European continent – is to provide for cancellation fees in case the parties cancel the hearings.[12] The exact amount of such cancellation fees then depends on how early or late the hearing is cancelled.

(c) The Administrative Fees

5-23 In addition to the arbitrators' fees, parties to institutional arbitration proceedings have to pay the fees of the institution. Again, the method of calculating the administrative fees depends on the rules of the institution in question and, similarly to the compensation of the arbitrators, whether the compensation method is based on time worked or on the value in dispute. Most institutional rules provide for one upper limit of their fees. For example, at the ICC, the maximum administrative fee is US$ 88,800, which corresponds to an amount in dispute of US$ 80 million or more. Under the new Swiss Rules, the maximum fee is SF 50,000 which is reached if the amount in dispute exceeds SF 100 million.[13]

5-24 Obviously, in *ad hoc* arbitration there are no administrative fees (except for rather marginal fees if an institution intervenes as appointing authority), and for that reason parties are often tempted to agree on *ad hoc* rather than institutional arbitration. However, one should never forget that the availability of a competent institution may be a valuable support for the proceedings, particularly when the courts of the place of arbitration do not provide the services of the institution, such as appointment of arbitrators, decisions on their challenge and other assistance in the procedure.[14]

(d) The Comparison between the Different Calculation Methods

5-25 Leaving the administrative fees aside, the different ways to calculate the cost of the tribunal lead to different results. Even among those institutions which

---

[12] See, e.g., the discussion in *K/S Norjarl A/S v. Hyundai Heavy Industries Ltd* [1992] 1 QB 863.
[13] Under the DIS Rules the maximum is EUR 25,000, under the SCC Rules EUR 60,000.
[14] Schneider, supra note 1, at p 119; See also William Slate II, "International Arbitration: Do Institutions Make a Difference?" 31 *Wake Forest Law Review* 41 (1996).

provide for a primarily value-based compensation, the differences are quite significant as illustrated in the following chart:

Value in dispute	FEES				
	ICC €1 = USD1.30 (average fee)	DIS	Swiss Rules €1 = 1.55CHF (average fee)	SCC	Austrian Rules
€ 1 million	86.029,30	64,185.00	105,832.00	60,500.00	66,250.00
€ 5 million	171.904,00	146,685.00	208,335.00	126,500.00	136,250.00
€ 10 million	209.036,00	196,185.00	282,499.00	169,400.00	186,250.00
€ 50 million	341.686,00	328,185.00	441,182.00	226,600.00	311,250.00
€ 100 million	423.370,00	427,185.00	538,119.00	273,900.00	436,250.00

5-26 This chart shows that the tribunal's fees under the SCC Rules[15] are the lowest and those under the Swiss Rules the most expensive. The fees under the ICC, DIS and Austrian Rules range between the two, with amounts quite similar among themselves – which is due to the fact that both the DIS and the Austrian institution recently brought their fees in line with the average ICC fees.

5-27 Obviously, it is difficult to compare the fees of these institutions – where the fees or at least the range within which they will be fixed is predictable as a function of the value in dispute – to those of proceedings in which the tribunal's costs are calculated – exclusively or primarily – based on time and therefore depend on the conduct of the proceedings in the given case. But, in general, one can say that a time-based system tends to be more costly than a value-based one in cases where the amount in dispute is relatively low, *i.e.*, in the range of 1 to 10 million Euro, whereas it tends to be less expensive in cases where the claims are larger. The reason for this is that, as a rule, the duration of the proceedings does not depend on the value of the dispute. Thus, unless the parties and the tribunal agree on an expedited procedure, a hearing will not be reduced from two weeks to one or two days just for the reason that the claims are relatively small.

(e) The Cost of Legal Representation

5-28 Let me now turn to the lawyers' fees which obviously are the main element of the parties' cost. The internationally established practice today is to calculate

---

[15] See http://www.sccinstitute.com/uk/home/ (Arbitration Institute of the Stockholm Chamber of Commerce).

the lawyers' fees as a function of the time spent whatever the sums in dispute. This used to be different for instance in Germany where the lawyers' fees used to be calculated purely on the basis of the amount in dispute. But even in Germany the time-based calculation, at least in international cases, is today the rule. And this method very simply means: the longer the procedure, the more work done; and the larger the legal team assigned to it, the more expensive the lawyers' fees become.

5-29 Arbitration practice shows that the cost of legal representation can indeed be very substantial.[16] Let me give you a few examples from some recent ICC cases of which I have knowledge:

Amount in dispute *	Total fees of Arbitrators	Total fees of Counsel to Parties	share of Arbitrators' fees on total fees
USD 218,836,536	USD 624,800	USD 4,294,631	13% USD 4,919,431
USD 59,148,553	USD 404,790	USD 4,288,926	8.6% USD 4,693,716
USD 12,598,548	USD 225,313	USD 1,874,472	10.7% USD 2,099,785
USD 40,520,624	USD 126,722	USD 2,116,365	5.6% USD 2,243,087
USD 50,328,666	USD 650,000	USD 2,506,988	20.6% USD 3,156,988

*   Conversion rates to USD at the date of issuance of award

5-30 If compared to the considerable amounts in dispute, counsel fees in such amounts seem less remarkable; in absolute terms, they are impressive. If you break down such sums to the number of hours billed, you can see the legal machinery behind such cases, involving the services of several expensive senior partners and counsel and whole troops of younger partners, senior and junior associates, junior counsel, paralegals and other assistants.

5-31 There are cases where the cost of legal representation seems to be out of proportion with the subject matter or the economic value of the dispute. Thus, I have experienced a jurisdiction dispute in which the total cost of legal

---

[16] Michael Bühler, "Awarding Costs in International Commercial Arbitration: an Overview", *ASA Bulletin* 2/2004, p 249.

representation – at such early stage – was close to US$ 1 million. And I know about a case between a German supplier and its distributor from Lebanon where the claim by the Lebanon distributor was about 1.5 million Euro, and the lawyers' fees at the end amounted to 350,000 Euro for Claimant and 200,000 Euro for Respondent.

5-32 It is further interesting to note that the relative importance of the costs of the tribunal compared to the total cost of the proceeding is not insignificant, but clearly the tribunal's cost represent the lower share. For instance, according to a study undertaken by a well-known Swiss arbitrator, in ICC practice, the share of the tribunal's cost of the total cost of the proceeding nowadays is in the range of 10 %. What is particularly interesting in this study is that still 10 years ago such share was two times higher, *i.e.*, 20 %, which suggests that the growing costliness of arbitration is much more the result of lawyers' fees becoming more and more expensive, than of the one of increasing arbitrators' and institutional costs.

III.   THE REASONS FOR THE INCREASING COST OF ARBITRATION

5-33 Arbitration certainly has never been inexpensive, but lawyers' fees of the magnitude just described would have been unthinkable some 20 years ago. So what has happened?

5-34 On the one hand, one can observe that the more international arbitration has become the principal means of dispute resolution in international business, the more it has been transformed from a rather informal proceeding to a judicial procedure which resembles more and more traditional litigation. At least this is the civil law perspective. The times have long gone by when arbitration was conceived as a true alternative to resolve commercial disputes among peers. For instance, arbitration clauses which give the tribunal the powers of an *amiable compositeur* or to decide *ex aequo et bono* have practically disappeared.[17]

5-35 On the other hand, it is probably true that the subject matters in dispute over the years have become more complex, both in technical and legal terms. Often the amounts at stake are enormous, and quite naturally, each party wants to win its case. Parties are aware that there is no appeal on the merits. So they know that unlike litigation there is only one round to fight, and they want to present their claim and their defence, respectively, in the best possible way. It is sometimes

---

[17]   See, e.g., Article 17(3) ICC Rules.

said that for that reason cost considerations are of secondary importance. This may be true for very large cases and very large companies, but most certainly not for the vast majority of arbitration cases where, for instance, according to the statistics of the ICC, the claims range between half a million and 10 million Euro, and where the parties often are mid-sized companies.

IV. How to Control and Reduce the Cost of Arbitration

5-36 Now, are the lawyers or the arbitrators responsible for the problem? On the one hand, it is true that many of the disputes that are nowadays brought before arbitral tribunals are much more complex both in terms of law and facts than they were some decades ago. Often tons of documents and huge amounts of information have to be analysed for preparing the case. Dozens of witnesses have to be interviewed, expert witnesses have to be consulted, extensive legal research has to be done and comprehensive submissions have to be prepared. All this can only be achieved if the law firms work in teams, and there are certainly cases which are so complex that they justify a larger team of lawyers.

5-37 On the other hand, one can also observe that parties' counsel spend more and more often much energy and time on fierce battles on procedural issues: they challenge the jurisdiction of the tribunal; they claim the extension of the arbitration clause to a non-signatory party; they make challenges against an arbitrator; they introduce requests for various interim relief; they request the production of documents; they file applications for the exclusion from the file of privileged documents; they submit applications for security for costs; and so forth. In some cases, these actions may be legitimate for the proper defence of the case, but often they are used as tactical manoeuvres. Whatever the motives, these procedural battles resemble more and more traditional litigation and are a serious challenge to the smooth conduct of arbitration proceedings.

5-38 When Dr Robert Briner, at the time Chairman of the ICC Court of Arbitration, was asked at an ASA Symposium in Basel in January 2005 what he thought about the problem, he stated that, in the ICC's experience, the long delays and the resulting increase of costs in arbitration were rather caused by parties' counsel, not so much by the arbitrators. He criticized that often procedural issues were due to bad contract drafting; that much of the delay and high costs about which parties complain are in fact due to actions of their own counsel; he also recommended that parties should give precise instructions to counsel; and in house counsel should be present when the procedural timetable or other procedural issues are discussed.

5-39 These comments by Dr. Briner are certainly interesting. But one should not only blame parties' counsel. There is also quite a lot that arbitrators can achieve to control and reduce the cost of arbitration by a pro-active conduct of the proceedings and in interaction with parties' counsel.

5-40 Thus, the tribunal should quickly eliminate peripheral issues, particularly on the procedural level, wherever possible and focus on the essence of the dispute.

5-41 The tribunal should also more often consider the bifurcation of the proceedings – in a first phase dealing with the merits of the case and a second one, if any, dealing with the quantum. Preparatory hearings shall be used to discuss and determine with counsel the factual and legal issues which in the tribunal's preliminary assessment are of particular importance. My personal experience shows that such initiatives by the tribunal are generally well received, particularly when the parties, or their representatives, are present at such preparatory hearings.

5-42 Witness conferencing, especially among technical or expert witnesses, may also be used as a tool to reduce the length of the hearing and to focus on the crucial issues in dispute. Obviously, witness conferencing requires the arbitrators to familiarize themselves with the file in detail before such conference hearing because they have to take the lead in such conferences. But this is a task which parties are entitled to expect from the tribunal in any event.

5-43 Last, but not least, consideration should be given to the question whether arbitrators should not more openly encourage parties to settle their dispute where a settlement would appear to be in the interest of all the parties. In many jurisdictions, such as my own, Switzerland and Austria, the participants in arbitration clearly regard the facilitation by the tribunal of voluntary settlements as one of the primary goals of arbitration, and indeed the vast majority of the cases is terminated through amicable settlement.

5-44 Whether such approach is suitable at all, and at which point in time, depends on the circumstances of the case. In making this proposal, I am perfectly aware that common law practice looks critically at the tribunal engaging itself in settlement discussions. But it seems to me that, whatever the differences in legal culture, one should not *a priori* exclude such initiatives but should inquire with the parties, at a given moment, whether they would be interested in the tribunal taking such initiatives. In my experience, more often than not that is the case – even with parties coming from common law jurisdictions.

V. CONCLUSION

5-45 As a conclusion, let me say that the change of the size and complexity of the disputes that are nowadays brought before international arbitral tribunals has also changed the characteristics of arbitral proceedings. They have become more and more similar to litigation, and by that I mean common law style litigation, and thereby very costly. The complaints that we hear should be taken seriously. Both, counsel and arbitrators, can and should contribute to avoid excessive cost by ensuring an efficient case management and focusing on the relevant issues. It would be regrettable if parties, particular in mid-sized companies, would tend away from arbitration because they fear that they can not afford it any more.

PART II

NATIONAL AND INTERNATIONAL REGULATION
OF INTERNATIONAL ARBITRATION

*Henri Alvarez**

CHAPTER 6

AUTONOMY OF INTERNATIONAL ARBITRATION PROCESS

I. INTRODUCTION

6-1 For some time, it has been accepted that the international commercial arbitration process enjoys substantial autonomy and is insulated to a large extent from the application of national laws and court control. This autonomy and the procedural flexibility it permits have generally been seen as a significant advantage of international commercial arbitration and to have contributed to the widespread use of arbitration in the resolution of international disputes. In light of the extensive use of international commercial arbitration and its significant degree of autonomy, one may legitimately ask whether an autonomous set of international procedural rules has emerged and, if so, the extent to which international rules or national laws restrict or affect any such international procedural rules.

6-2 While a number of general principles, practices and tendencies have emerged, we are still some way from being able to say that there is an autonomous set of international procedural rules or a consistent international arbitration practice. Beyond general principles and practices, there remains a wide diversity of more specific practice and procedures in international commercial arbitration, which reflects the diversity of the parties and disputes submitted to arbitration and the counsel and arbitrators appointed to present and resolve these disputes. Further, despite some general harmonisation of national laws, substantial differences remain both in respect of the content of these laws and the manner in which they are interpreted and applied by national courts. Finally, there are a

* Fasken Martineau DuMoulin LLP, Vancouver, B.C., Adjunct Professor at the Faculty of Law, University of British Columbia.

Loukas A. Mistelis and Julian D.M. Lew (eds), Pervasive Problems in International Arbitration, 119-139
© 2006 Kluwer Law International. Printed in the Netherlands

number of aspects of arbitral procedure which have yet to receive much, if any, attention from arbitrators and parties on the one hand and national laws and courts on the other. These promise to raise new, challenging issues. A thorough review of the current state of international arbitral process, if achievable, would greatly exceed the scope of this paper. Rather, my purpose is to examine a number of emerging issues or potential problems in the areas of procedure, nomination and appointment of arbitrator, separability of the arbitration agreement and "Kompetenz-Kompetenz", and standards in respect of expert evidence.

II. INTERNATIONAL ARBITRATION PROCEDURE

6-3   The general structure or framework which gives rise to the autonomy of arbitral process and, more specifically, procedure, is built on the base of the New York Convention[1]. Article V of the Convention limits the procedural grounds for refusing recognition or enforcement of a foreign arbitral award to the following:

Article V
1. Recognition and enforcement of the award may be refused, at the request of the party against whom it is invoked, only if that party furnishes to the competent authority where the recognition and enforcement is sought, proof that:
[…]
(b)   the party against whom the award is invoked was not given proper notice of the appointment of the arbitrator or of the arbitration proceedings or was otherwise unable to present his case; or
[…]
(d)   the composition of the arbitral authority or the arbitral procedure was not in accordance with the agreement of the parties, or, failing such agreement, was not in accordance with the law of the country where the arbitration took place;
[…]
2. Recognition and enforcement of an arbitral award may also be refused if the competent authority in the country where the recognition and enforcement is sought finds that:
[…]

---

[1]   This is the familiar name applied to the United Nations Convention on the Recognition and Enforcement of Foreign Arbitral Awards (New York, 10 June 1958).

(b)   the recognition or enforcement of the award would be contrary to the public policy of that country.

6-4   These grounds, as well as the other grounds in Article V of the Convention, have been adopted by the UNCITRAL Model Law on International Commercial Arbitration and national laws influenced by it, as well as many modern arbitration statutes more generally.   The Model Law contains two general principles regarding the question of arbitral procedure:

Article 18 – Equal Treatment of Parties
The parties shall be treated with equality and each party shall be given a full opportunity of presenting his case.

Article 19 – Determination of rules of procedure
1. Subject to the provisions of this Law, the parties are free to agree on the procedure to be followed by the arbitral tribunal in conducting the proceedings.
2. Failing such agreement, the arbitral tribunal may, subject to the provisions of this Law, conduct the arbitration in such manner as it considers appropriate. The power conferred upon the arbitral tribunal includes the power to determine the admissibility, relevance, materiality and weight of any evidence.

6-5   In its Article 5, the Model Law also limits court intervention in the arbitral process except where expressly provided in the Law.

6-6   The resulting general structure, widely adopted to varying extents, is intended to give broad autonomy to the parties to agree on arbitral procedure. This freedom is subject to certain limited mandatory provisions which require a particular standard of treatment of the parties and includes the opportunity to present their respective cases.   In the absence of agreement by the parties, broad discretion is granted to the arbitral tribunal to determine the arbitral procedure either indirectly by way of the institutional rules adopted or directly in the case of *ad hoc* arbitration.

6-7   Attempts have been made to identify the fundamental, mandatory principles which limit the scope of autonomy of the parties or discretion of the arbitral tribunal in respect of procedural matters. For example, the notion of international procedural public policy has been adopted and developed by the International

Law Association and a number of authors.[2] Others have addressed the question as an aspect of the duty to arbitrate in good faith and to ensure a general notion of procedural fairness, good faith[3], or "due process".[4]

6-8 However, the applicable standards in respect of the fundamental principles of treatment of the parties and the opportunity to present one's case are articulated differently in national laws and arbitral rules. For example:

Treatment of the parties:
- "The parties shall be treated with equality" (Model Law, Article 18)
- "The tribunal shall act fairly and impartially as between the parties" (English Arbitration Act 1996, Section 33(1)(a))
- Due process ("*principe de la contradiction*", said to include equality of the parties) (French new Code of Civil Procedure, Articles 1460, 1502)
- "The arbitral tribunal shall assure equal treatment of the parties" (Swiss Private International Law Act, Article 182)
- "The arbitral tribunal shall act fairly and impartially" (ICC Rules, Article 15(2))
- "Treated with equality" (AAA – International Arbitration Rules)
- "Act fairly and impartially as between all parties" (LCIA Rules, Article 14.1)
- "Provided that the parties are treated with equality" (UNCITRAL Arbitration Rules, Article 15(1)).

Opportunity to present one's case:
- "A full opportunity of presenting his case" (UNCITRAL Model Law, Article 18)
- "A reasonable opportunity of putting his case and dealing with that of his opponent" (English Arbitration Act 1996, Section 33(1)(a))

---

[2] See Audley Sheppard, "Interim ILA Report on Public Policy as a Bar to Enforcement of International Arbitration Awards", and Pierre Mayer and Audley Sheppard, "Final ILA Report on Public Policy as a Bar to Enforcement of International Arbitral Awards", 19 *Arb Int* 217, 249 (2003). See also Fernando Mantilla-Serrano, "Towards a Transnational Procedural Public Policy", 20 *Arb Int* 333 (2004).

[3] See VV Veeder, "The Lawyer's Duty to Arbitrate in Good Faith", The 2001 Goff Lecture, 18 *Arb Int* 431 (2002).

[4] See Gabrielle Kaufmann-Kohler, "Globalization of Arbitral Procedure", 36 *Vanderbilt Journal of Transnational Law* 1313 (2003); Julian Lew Loukas Mistelis and Stefan Kröll, *Comparative International Commercial Arbitration* (Kluwer Law International 2003) paras 21-14 – 21-18.

- "Due process" (*principe de la contradiction*, including equality of the parties) (French New Code of Civil Procedure, Articles 1460, 1502)
- "The arbitral tribunal shall assure … the right of the parties to be heard in an adversarial procedure" ("*en procédure contradictoire*", Swiss Private International Law Act, Article 182(3))
- "A reasonable opportunity to present its case" (ICC Rules, Article 15(2))
- "A fair opportunity to present its case" (AAA International Arbitration Rules, Article 16)
- "A reasonable opportunity of putting its case and dealing with that of its opponent" (LCIA Arbitration Rules, Article 14.1)
- "A full opportunity of presenting its case" (UNCITRAL Arbitration Rules, Article 15(1))

6-9 While these laws and arbitral rules have the same general goals, there are distinctions which may give rise to divergent interpretations by different arbitrators and courts. Further, each of these standards leaves substantial discretion to the arbitral tribunal whose understanding and exercise of that discretion may vary significantly depending on the particular tribunal's composition.

6-10 Assessment of the appropriate standard and its application to the specific circumstances by the arbitral tribunal will depend very much on the choice of the parties in selecting their legal representatives, the members of the arbitral tribunal and the place of arbitration. For example, the expectations of the parties with respect to procedural fairness are usually those of the counsel representing them. In the absence of specific international rules dealing with questions such as document disclosure, privilege, conflicts of interest and witness preparation, counsel will often rely on the legal and ethical rules with which they are familiar. This will be so even in the case of counsel highly experienced in international commercial arbitration. As a result, the positions advanced on behalf of the parties will often reflect the background and experience of counsel. Further, the assessment of the positions of the parties and the standard for procedural fairness adopted will also depend upon the legal background of the members of the arbitral tribunal in the absence of specific, detailed rules. Thus, an arbitral tribunal's appreciation of procedural fairness and an alleged violation of the same may depend very much on the composition of the tribunal itself. In these circumstances, it is hard to speak of a set of procedural rules or of consistent international practice.

6-11 Assessment of compliance with the applicable standard of treatment of the parties will also be relevant for the courts at the seat of arbitration or at the place of enforcement of the award. For example, the courts at the place of arbitration may find a breach of public policy where an award is procured by fraud or by other conduct that breaches procedural public policy. The English Commercial Court's decision in *Profilati Italia SRL v. Paine Webber Inc* suggested that deliberate withholding of a document from production in an international commercial arbitration could be contrary to public policy under Section 68 of the Arbitration Act 1996.[5] Such a possible conclusion, however, would depend on the scope of document production ordered by the arbitral tribunal which, in turn, would depend on some of the factors discussed above.

6-12 Examples of where differences in practice, and in appreciation of the fundamental standard for the treatment of the parties and the opportunity for them to present their respective cases, could arise include the following:

Document Production
- The scope or extent of document production granted by the tribunal.
- The timing of document production. Should this occur at the outset and before submission of the parties' full cases? Or during/after presentation of the parties' pleadings and witness statements?
- The treatment of privilege or professional obligations of confidentiality (considered to be of a public policy nature in many jurisdictions).
- The response to a failure to comply with orders for production of documents.
- The status and permitted use of an opponent's documents that have been obtained improperly (what limits, if any, apply?).

The Preparation of Factual Witness Statements
- While there is a general trend to use written witness statements and to proceed to cross-examination and re-examination at the oral hearing, substantial differences remain as to how and by whom witness statements are prepared.
- Interviewing of witnesses by party representatives?

---

[5] *Profilati Italia SRL v. Paine Webber Inc*, [2001] 1 Lloyd's Rep 715, as quoted in Veeder, supra note 3, pp. 442-443.

- The scope of questioning by the tribunal and cross-examination may vary considerably depending on the identity of counsel and the composition of the arbitral tribunal.

The Role of Expert Witnesses
- Absent agreement of the parties, the use of party-appointed or tribunal-appointed experts will be in the discretion of the arbitral tribunal. Each requires careful handling to ensure fairness between the parties.
- Independence of the expert, whether tribunal or party-appointed.
- Admissibility/Scope/utility of the expert's opinion and respect for the tribunal's decision-making mandate.
- Preparation of the expert's report and disclosure by the expert.

6-13 While there are some general trends with respect to the procedure in respect of these matters, the determination of disputes will depend very much on counsel and the composition of the arbitral tribunal.

6-14 One promising, positive development is the IBA Rules on the Taking of Evidence in International Commercial Arbitration which address a number of basic points, including document production (Articles 3 and 9); witnesses of fact (Article 4); and expert witnesses (Articles 5 and 6). These rules are very general in nature and remain subject to vagaries of interpretation and application by different tribunals. The IBA Rules suggest a starting point, but a consistent and predictable standard of evidentiary procedure has not yet been achieved.[6]

6-15 An emerging issue is the role of ethical standards for counsel and their applicability in international commercial arbitrations. To date, this topic has received relatively little attention.[7] While many international arbitral tribunals may

---

[6] It should be noted that the development of guidelines and rules has not been without controversy. For example, the UNICTRAL Notes on Organizing Arbitral Proceedings (1993 / 1996) originally conceived as "guidelines", gave rise to heated debate. For the text of the Notes see Report of the United Nations Commission on International Trade Law on the work of its 29th session, Official Records of the General Assembly, Fifty-first Session, Supplement No 17 (A/51/17) (reproduced in UNCITRAL Yearbook, vol. XXVII: 1996). For the relevant debate see, e.g.: Pierre-Yves Gunter, "Transnational Rules and the Taking of Evidence" in Emmanuel Gaillard (ed), *Towards a Uniform International Arbitration Law* (Juris 2005), pp. 129-161.

[7] Among the few articles on this topic see: Jan Paulsson, "Standards of Conduct for Counsel in International Arbitration", 3 *Am Rev Int'l Arb* 214 (1992); Veeder, supra note 3; Peter C Thomas, "Disqualifying Lawyers in Arbitrations: Do the Arbitrators Play any Proper Role?", 1

be of the view that it is not their task to apply the ethical rules applicable to counsel in their home jurisdictions, or even, those standards in effect at the place of arbitration, this may not be the view of the courts of the place of arbitration. For example, in New York State, there are decisions in which the courts have held that compliance with local ethical standards is a matter of public policy which may require the granting of an injunction to stay arbitration pending a determination of the issue.

6-16 Further, the ethical standards applicable to counsel in their home jurisdiction may govern, and consequently affect, their conduct in an international commercial arbitration held in another State.[8] The same ethical standards may not apply to opposing counsel and may not be known to the arbitral tribunal. In addition, a party's expectations, and those of its counsel, with respect to appropriate conduct in regard of the various aspects of arbitral procedure may well be informed by their understanding such ethical rules. As a result, ethical rules may indirectly impact the procedure and the fairness of the arbitral procedure.

6-17 For example, ethical rules in respect of privilege or professional obligations of confidentiality, treatment of privileged or confidential documents of the other party when disclosed inadvertently or outside the document production process, and conflicts of interest by counsel may raise difficult questions of basic procedural fairness and affect the enforceability of the award. Unfortunately, there are very few, if any, international rules on ethical conduct which apply in international arbitration. In the absence of these, parties and arbitrators may be left in some uncertainty as to the applicable standard and the possible effect on the procedural fairness of the arbitration.[9]

Am Rev Int'l Arb 562 (1990); Catherine Rogers, "Fit and Function in Legal Ethics: Developing a Code of Conduct for International Arbitration", 23 *Michigan J Int'l L* 241 (2002); Catherine Rogers, "Context and Institutional Structure in Attorney Regulation: Constructing an Enforcement Regime for International Arbitration", 39 *Stanford J Int'l L* 1 (2003).

[8] See, e.g., the discussion of EU Directive 98/5/EC of February 16, 1998 discussed in Veeder, supra, footnote 3, pp 431-433.

[9] For example, different arbitral tribunals have reached opposite conclusions depending on whether or not specific ethical standards were applicable. In one ICC arbitration, the tribunal declined to apply the code of ethics of a bar association "in the context of an international arbitration proceeding" where an application was made to disqualify counsel for the respondents where that counsel had previously provided to one of the claimants advice relating to the investment in dispute in the arbitration. One of the defences raised by the respondents related directly to advice previously given by their counsel to one of the claimants. That claimant applied to have counsel for the respondents disqualified on the basis of the provisions of the civil and criminal codes as well as the conflicts of interest provisions of the code of ethics of the home State of the respondents and of their counsel. The tribunal found that the request to

6-18 The freedom accorded to parties to agree on procedure and the broad discretion left to arbitrators to determine the procedure in the absence of agreement of the parties leaves a significant amount of uncertainty as to the specific rules or principles a tribunal will apply. Unless the handling of these issues is discussed and settled by the tribunal and the parties at the outset, considerable uncertainty and possible unfairness may result.

6-19 While we have seen the development of a number of general principles, some harmonization of national laws and the promising emergence of private codifications or rules on certain aspects of international arbitration procedure, it is still too early to conclude that we have today a set of procedural rules or a consistent international arbitration practice.

III. NOMINATION AND APPOINTMENT OF ARBITRATORS

6-20 As in the case of procedure, the parties to an international commercial arbitration generally have broad autonomy to select and agree upon the members of the arbitral tribunal or the method of appointment of the tribunal. Failing agreement by the parties on the constitution of the tribunal, a default mechanism is generally provided by national arbitration laws. In many countries, in the absence of the adoption of institutional rules, the function of nominating arbitrators is assumed by the courts. However, in certain countries, the law provides for the appointment of the arbitral tribunal by arbitral institutions even where the parties have not agreed to institutional arbitration.[10]

6-21 There is a general tendency to permit the parties a broad choice as to who may serve as an arbitrator.[11] The previous aversion to naming a sole arbitrator or presiding arbitrator from the country of one of the parties has diminished. For example, the Model Law provides, in relevant part, as follows:

---

exclude counsel was not within the scope of the arbitration clause and should be the subject of separate, domestic proceedings. In addition, among other grounds, the tribunal expressed doubts as to the application of the code of ethics of a domestic private bar association in the proceedings before it. On the other hand, in a different case sited in New York, another tribunal had little hesitation in applying the local code of ethics in dismissing an application to exclude counsel. See Horacio Grigera Naón, "Choice of Law Problems in International Commercial Arbitration", *RCADI* vol 289 (2001) at 157-161.

[10] See, for example, Colombia, Ecuador, El Salvador, Honduras and Panama.

[11] Certain restrictions still exist in countries such as Costa Rica where arbitrators serving in arbitrations with a seat in Costa Rica must be lawyers and members of the local national bar. Until recently, the situation was the same in Chile. In a number of other Latin American countries, arbitrators serving in "*arbitrajes de derecho*" must be lawyers.

Article 11: Appointment of arbitrators
1. No person shall be precluded by reason of his nationality from acting as an arbitrator, unless otherwise agreed by the parties.

...

5. A decision on a matter entrusted by paragraph (3) or (4) of this article to the court or other authority specified in article 6 shall be subject to no appeal. The court of other authority, in appointing an arbitrator, shall have due regard to any qualifications required of the arbitrator by the agreement of the parties and to such considerations as are likely to secure the appointment of an independent and impartial arbitrator and, in the case of a sole or third arbitrator, shall take into account as well the advisability of appointing an arbitrator of a nationality other than those of the parties.

Nevertheless, certain rules maintain limitations based on nationality of arbitrators.[12]

6-22 Lack of independence or impartiality is generally considered a ground for setting aside or refusing to enforce an arbitral award. In many countries, lack of independence or impartiality is considered an aspect of public policy which may give rise to challenge of an arbitrator during the course of the arbitral proceedings. In countries adopting the Model Law, as well as in a number of others, unsuccessful challenges before the arbitral tribunal or the administering institution may be submitted to the courts during the arbitral proceedings. Some other arbitral regimes only permit challenges after the issuance of the award, either by way of an application to set aside or as a ground for resisting enforcement.

6-23 The relevant Model Law provisions addressing the grounds and procedure for challenging an arbitrator are Articles 12 and 13:

Article 12 – Grounds for challenge
1. When a person is approached in connection with his possible appointment as an arbitrator, he shall disclose any circumstances likely to give rise to *justifiable doubts as to his impartiality or independence.* An arbitrator, from the time of his appointment and throughout the arbitral proceedings, shall

---

[12] E.g., ICSID, the LCIA and the ICC where the appointment of a sole or presiding arbitrator is concerned. Nevertheless, in practice, even where the applicable rules do not expressly prohibit the nomination of a sole or presiding arbitrator of the same nationality as one of the parties, the general practice appears to be to avoid such a nomination.

without delay disclose any such circumstances to the parties unless they have already been informed of them by him.

2. An arbitrator may be challenged only if circumstances exist that give rise to *justifiable doubts as to his impartiality or independence*, or if he does not possess qualifications agreed to by the parties. A party may challenge an arbitrator appointed by him, or in whose appointment he has participated, only for reasons of which he becomes aware after the appointment has been made. [Emphasis added]

Article 13 – Challenge procedure
1. The parties are free to agree on a procedure for challenging an arbitrator, subject to the provisions of paragraph (3) of this article.
2. Failing such agreement, a party which intends to challenge an arbitrator shall, within fifteen days after becoming aware of the constitution of the arbitral tribunal or after becoming aware of any circumstance referred to in article 12(2), send a written statement of the reasons for the challenge to the arbitral tribunal. Unless the challenged arbitrator withdraws from his office or the other party agrees to the challenge, the arbitral tribunal shall decide on the challenge.
3. If a challenge under any procedure agreed upon by the parties or under the procedure of paragraph (2) of this article is not successful, the challenging party may request, within thirty days after having received notice of the decision rejecting the challenge, the court or other authority specified in article 6 to decide on the challenge, which decision shall be subject to no appeal; while such a request is pending, the arbitral tribunal, including the challenged arbitrator, may continue the arbitral proceedings and make an award.

6-24 There has been growing adoption of the test of "justifiable doubts" as to an arbitrator's impartiality or independence in statutes dealing with international commercial arbitration.[13]

6-25 However, the articulation of a "justifiable doubts" test is new to common law countries which continue to apply a standard based on "bias" or an "apprehension of bias". Further, the bias test is articulated differently and applied differently by the courts in various common law countries. For example, the

---

[13] Note that the test under the English Arbitration Act 1996 is "justifiable doubts as to his impartiality" (Section 24(1)(a)). In the United States, the test articulated in the Federal Arbitration Act 1925 is "evident partiality or corruption".

Canadian test is a reasonable apprehension of bias. In Australia the test is one of "real possibility" of bias, in England the test is a "real danger" of bias and in the United States the test is "evident partiality".

6-26 The disparity between the standards applied by the courts in determining bias or independence and impartiality presents a substantial challenge to a uniform rule or consistent practice in respect of this aspect of the nomination of arbitrators.[14] This is further complicated by the different practices of arbitral institutions in appointing arbitrators and dealing with challenges. Unfortunately, the decisions of arbitral institutions on challenges are not published and, as a result, little guidance can be obtained from them.

6-27 As a result, there is no single international standard or rule governing the independence and impartiality of arbitrators and different criteria may apply depending on whether the question is addressed by the arbitral tribunal, an arbitral institution or a national court. While there is a general understanding that arbitrators must be both independent and impartial, significant differences remain in how the precise standards to achieve this goal are articulated and applied. This may give rise to uncertainty on behalf of arbitrators in determining whether they can accept an appointment and on behalf of parties seeking to appoint arbitrators or to confirm the independence and impartiality of arbitrators nominated by their opponents or appointed as sole or presiding arbitrators.

6-28 One recent attempt to begin to address this challenge is the IBA Guidelines on Conflicts of Interest in International Arbitration. The Guidelines reflect the best current international practice and are intended to promote clarity and uniformity in questions of conflicts of interest and disclosure in international

---

[14] The disparity in standards is not restricted to common law jurisdictions. For a discussion of the different tests and the standards for arbitrator independence and impartiality more generally, see: Background Information on the IBA Guidelines on Conflicts of Interest in International Arbitration and The IBA Guidelines on Conflicts of Interest in International Arbitration, available on the IBA website at http://www.ibanet.org/images/downloads/guidelines%20text.pdf and also http://www.ibanet.org/images/downloads/Background%20Information.pdf. Another difficult aspect of the question of independence and impartiality is the assimilation of the standard for arbitrators to that for judges. This is the case in a number of jurisdictions such as Australia, Canada, England, France, Mexico, The Netherlands, New Zealand, Singapore, Switzerland and the United States. On the other hand, the standard in Sweden appears to be slightly stricter in the case of the standard applicable to arbitrators as opposed to judges. In Germany, the standard of impartiality and independence is said to be more stringent for judges than for arbitrators. In addition, in certain countries, a distinction still remains between the standard applicable to a sole or presiding arbitrator and party-appointed arbitrators.

arbitration. Although the guidelines expressly recognize that they are not legal provisions and do not override any applicable national law or arbitral rules chosen by the parties, the hope is that they will find general acceptance in the international arbitration community and thereby assist in the development of a consistent practice or standard.[15] Of course, this can only be a first step since the Guidelines have necessarily been drafted at a general level. Greater consistency and uniformity in decision-making on questions of independence and impartiality, continued study and better knowledge of decisions on challenges both by arbitral institutions and courts will be required to progress the effort commenced by the IBA.[16] As an important continuation of its efforts, the Arbitration Committee of the Dispute Resolution Section of the IBA has established a task force to monitor and review the use and application of the Guidelines and decisions on challenges to arbitrators.

IV. SEPARABILITY AND KOMPETENZ-KOMPETENZ – DIFFERENT APPROACHES TO THESE QUESTIONS AND LIMITS

6-29 The principles of separability and Kompetenz-Kompetenz have been broadly adopted in modern national laws and arbitral rules. Together, they have been referred to as the conceptual cornerstones of international arbitration as an autonomous form of international dispute resolution.[17] While these principles are generally adopted in national laws and accepted by national courts, the manner in which they have been implemented and are applied by the courts may vary considerably.[18]

---

[15] See the Introduction to the IBA Guidelines on Conflicts of Interest in International Arbitration.

[16] In this regard, see the comments of Jan Paulsson, "Ethics and Codes of Conduct for a Multi-Disciplinary Institute", 70 *Arbitration* 1993 at pp 119-200 (2004).

[17] See Laurence Craig, William Park & Jan Paulsson, *The International Chamber of Commerce Arbitration* (3rd edition, Oceana and ICC Publishing 2000), Section 5.04. See also Robert H Smit, "Separability and Kompetenz-Kompetenz in International Arbitration: *Ex Nihilo Nihil Fit*? Or Can Something Indeed Come from Nothing?", 13 *AmRevInt'lArb* 19 (2002) and the sources cited therein. Also, Lew, Mistelis, Kröll, *Comparative International Commercial Arbitration* (2003), pp. 99-106, 332-339.

[18] See, e.g., Jean-François Poudret and Sebastien Besson, *Droit comparé de l'arbitrage international* (Schulthess *et al* 2002), pp. 133-150, 406-481. The United States is an example of a different approach to these principles, and particularly that of Kompetenz-Kompetenz, despite the general pro-arbitration bias in US law. See Smit, supra note 17 and the recent interesting decisions in *Glazer v. Lehman Brothers, Inc*, Nos 03-4312/4415 (6th Cir. 2005); *Howsam v. Dean Witter Reynolds, Inc*, 537 US 779 (2002); *Green Tree Financial Corp v. Bazzle*, 539 US 444 (2003); *Pacificare Health Systems, Inc. v. Book*, 538 US 401 (2003).

6-30 An area in which the determination of an arbitral tribunal's jurisdiction over its own jurisdiction has recently given rise to differing reactions from State courts is where arbitrators have extended the application of arbitration clauses to non-signatories. Recent decisions in Canada, England, the United States, Switzerland and France reflect a broad range of approaches.

6-31 In a recent, surprising decision, the British Columbia Court of Appeal has refused to enforce an arbitral award rendered in California on the basis that it was made against an individual person who had not signed an arbitration agreement.[19] This case involved an individual who had signed an arbitration agreement on behalf of a Canadian company. The other party to the agreement was a California firm. A dispute subsequently emerged between the Canadian company and the California firm, and an arbitration took place in California.

6-32 During the arbitration, the arbitrator ruled that the individual, F, was a proper party to the arbitration proceedings and should be held personably liable for any debts of the corporation that might ultimately be imposed and be jointly liable to pay any costs awarded, even though he was not a named party to the arbitration agreement and had not signed the contract in which the arbitration agreement was contained in his individual capacity. The California firm was awarded $94,828.26 in the arbitration. The California firm then tried to enforce the award in British Columbia against both the Canadian company and F.

6-33 The British Columbia court of first instance refused to enforce the award against F on the grounds that he was not a party to the arbitration agreement. The court held that for the purposes of enforcement of an arbitral award, the parties against whom the award may be enforced are those who are signatories to the arbitration agreement "in writing" and not persons procedurally added involuntarily as parties during the course of the arbitration. As F was not a named party to the contract and had not signed the contract in his personal capacity, he was not a party to the arbitration agreement contained in the contract and the award could not be enforced against him. The court also held that the award was not enforceable against F personally since the claim against him for personal liability could not properly have been the subject of arbitration under the agreement in question since F was not a party to it. Accordingly, the court exercised its discretion and refused enforcement pursuant to Article V(2)(a) of the *Foreign Arbitral Awards Act* (which implements the New York Convention in British

---

[19] *Javor v Francoeur*, [2004] BCJ No. 448, 2004 BCCA 134.

Columbia) and Section 36(1)(b)(i) of the British Columbia *International Commercial Arbitration Act* (which implements the Model Law).

The court declined to rule on the objection that enforcement of the arbitral award against F would be contrary to public policy on the basis that the personal liability of a company representative for a corporate obligation on the alter-ego theory could only be decided by a court of law. It appears that the court declined to consider this question on the basis that it had insufficient evidence to gauge the strength of the evidence led before the arbitrator which resulted in the finding that F was the alter-ego of the Canadian company.

6-34 A unanimous Court of Appeal upheld the lower court's decision in a very brief judgment. However, one of the judges qualified the Court of Appeal's decision in the following statement:

> ¶7… I would add that there is a general principle that courts should respect and enforce arbitral awards and comment that this result does not derogate from this principle. There is room in British Columbia for refusing to enforce an award where the subject matter in the dispute is not capable of settlement by arbitration under the law of British Columbia and that this is one of those rare cases which in my view…fits within the narrow exception to the enforcement of arbitral awards.

6-35 Unfortunately, neither court appears to have considered the question of deference to the arbitrators' findings of fact and legal conclusions in holding that F was the alter-ego of the Canadian company and, as such, was a proper party to the arbitration agreement. Further, it appears that both courts failed to recognize the distinction between the question of the interpretation of an arbitration agreement and the proper parties to it and the question of whether the subject matter of a dispute is objectively arbitrable. This is one of the very rare examples of refusal of enforcement of a foreign or international award in Canada.

6-36 In *Peterson Farms Inc.*,[20] the English Commercial Court set aside an arbitral award rendered in London in which the "group of companies" doctrine had been applied to grant damages to entities of the C & M Farming Ltd group which were not named as parties to the sales agreement which contained an ICC arbitration clause. The law applicable to the sales agreement were the laws of Arkansas, USA and the place of arbitration was London. In its decision, the court held that a challenge to jurisdiction under Section 67 of the *Arbitration Act 1996* was by

---

[20] *Peterson Farms Inc v. C & M Farming Ltd* [2004] All ER (D) 50; (2004) EWHC 121 (Comm).

way of a full hearing and that the relevant question was not whether the arbitral tribunal had been entitled to reach the decision to which it came, but whether it was correct in doing so. According to the Court, the ultimate arbiter of jurisdiction is not the arbitral tribunal itself.

6-37 In its award, the arbitral tribunal held as follows:

86. The tribunal does not accept Peterson's arguments. Under the doctrine of separability, an arbitration agreement is separable and autonomous from the underlying contract in which it appears. The autonomy of arbitration agreements has become a universal principle in the realm of international commercial arbitration. A corollary to the separability doctrine is that the law applicable to the arbitration agreement may differ from the law applicable to both the substance of the contract underlying the dispute and to the arbitral proceedings themselves. The right of C & M to make claims for the C & M Group is a question of an interpretation of the arbitration agreement contained in the Agreement, including the intention of the parties. In the absence of any choice of law made by the parties with regard to the arbitration agreement itself, this tribunal will determine this question in accordance with the common intent of the parties...

93. The tribunal does not consider that it is legally precluded from considering C & M's damages claims to cover and embrace the damages of all C & M Group companies. The group of companies doctrine provides that an arbitration agreement signed by one company in a group of companies entitles (or obligates) affiliate non-signatory companies, if the circumstances surrounding the negotiation, execution and termination of the agreement show that the mutual intention of all the parties was to bind the non-signatories. Following the *Dow Chemical* decision and ICC Case Nos. 2375 and 5103, the tribunal recognized that because a group of companies constitute the same "economic reality" one company in the group can bind the other members to an agreement if such a result conforms to the mutual intentions of all the parties and reflects the good usage of international commerce. This tribunal considers that such circumstances are present in this case.

100. In summary, the record of correspondence between the parties and internal documents of Peterson, the preliminary documents exchanged between the parties, and the general nature of the poultry business demonstrate that Peterson intended to enter into and perform under a contract with all the entities forming the C & M Group of companies. Peterson knew that it was contracting with a group as a whole and that its product would be

used in an integrated operation that involved all members of the C & M Group. The tribunal considers that C & M is fully entitled to claim all damages suffered by the C & M Group and arising out of the contractual relationship with Peterson.[21]

6-38 The Court found that the tribunal's approach was seriously flawed in law. The Court stated that the issue raised a question of interpretation of the agreement between the parties and that such questions were expressly subject to Arkansas' law pursuant to the terms of the agreement. The identification of the parties to an agreement is a question of substantive and not procedural law. The Court held that there was no basis for the arbitral tribunal to apply any other law and that no other law could properly be derived from "the common intent of the parties". The common intention of the parties was expressed in the agreement: both Arkansas and English law. The "law" the tribunal derived from its approach was not the proper law of the agreement nor the law of the place of arbitration but, in effect, the group of companies doctrine itself.[22] The court went on to find that the parties had agreed that with respect to the group of companies doctrine Arkansas law was the same as English law and the group of companies doctrine was not recognized in English law.[23]

6-39 The decision of the US Court of Appeals for the Fifth Circuit in *Bridas S.A.P.I.C. v. Government of Turkmenistan, et al.*[24] offers another recent interesting example of the court's treatment of an arbitral tribunal's finding on its own jurisdiction. In that case, Bridas was involved in oil exploration in Turkmenistan. It entered into a joint venture agreement ("JVA") with Turkmeneft, a production association formed and owned by the Turkmeni Government. The JVA provided for ICC Arbitration and was governed by English law.

6-40 The Government ordered the suspension of the JVA work and prohibited Bridas from importing or exporting within its territory. Bridas commenced an arbitration against both Turkmeneft and the Government, which objected that it was not a proper party. The majority of the arbitral tribunal ruled to the contrary and held that the Government was bound to arbitrate the dispute with Bridas because it had not taken any steps to extricate itself from the proceedings and,

---

[21] [2004] EWHC 121 at pp 8-9.
[22] On this issue see generally Chapter 14 below.
[23] Supra note 21, paras 47 and 62. The court set aside that part of the award which awarded payment of losses suffered by C & M Group members which were not party to the arbitration.
[24] 345 F.3d 347, 2003 US App. Lexis 18612 (5th Cir. Tex. 2003), *certiorari* denied March 22, 2004, 124 S. Ct. 1660.

significantly, there were a number of commitments in the JVA that only the Government could give or fulfil. The tribunal eventually issued an award on the merits in favour of Bridas against both Turkmeneft and the Government.

6-41 Bridas initiated a suit in Texas District Court (the seat of arbitration) seeking to confirm the award. The Government renewed its objections as to jurisdiction and sought an order refusing confirmation and vacating the award. The District Court, finding a lack of "clear and unmistakeable" evidence that the parties intended an arbitrator to decide the matter of jurisdiction, held that the courts ought to decide the jurisdictional issue pursuant to the Supreme Court's decision in *First Options*.[25] It conducted an independent review of the status of the Government and concluded that it was a proper party, both by principles of agency and estoppel.

6-42 On appeal, the Circuit Court reviewed the district court's findings of law *de novo*. It considered the issue of the identity of proper parties to depend on the intention of the parties. The "four corners" of the JVA did not reveal such an intention and the government did not sign the JVA nor was it a defined party to it. The Court therefore undertook a secondary analysis and examined six recognized theories for binding a non-signatory to an arbitration agreement: (1) incorporation by reference; (2) assumption; (3) agency; (4) veil-piercing/alter ego; (5) estoppel; and (6) third-party beneficiary. Bridas admitted that the first two theories had no application. Agency was not accepted by the Court. The Court placed an onus on Bridas, as a sophisticated commercial enterprise, to express its understanding that the Government was signing as an agent and its intention that it be bound as such, within the written agreement. Estoppel was held to be inappropriate in circumstances where the non-signatory had not relied on the agreement containing the arbitration clause (whose applicability it subsequently chose to deny) to commence an action in the courts against a signatory. The argument based on third-party beneficiary failed for the same reasons as estoppel.

6-43 Although the District Court held that the Government was not the alter ego of Turkmeneft, the Circuit Court found that the District Court had failed to fully assess the issue. Accordingly, it remanded the determination of this issue to the District Court with a lengthy list of factors, including a number specific to sovereign governments, for the District Court to consider in its review.

---

[25] *First Options of Chicago, Inc v. Kaplan*, 514 US 938.

6-44 The approach taken by the courts in the cases set out above can be contrasted with that of courts in other jurisdictions such as Switzerland and France. For example, in a recent decision, *X Sal Y Sal et A v. Z Sarl*,[26] the Swiss Tribunal Fédéral held that it was not appropriate to impose excessively strict requirements of formal validity in respect of the extension of the application of an arbitration clause to a third party.

6-45 Although the formal requirements of Article 178(1) of the Swiss Private International Law Act (which requires a written form to prove the existence of the agreement) apply to the agreement by which the initial parties expressed their will to submit to arbitration, this decision confirms that the scope of the parties is not restricted only to those named in the written agreement. According to the Tribunal Fédéral, the proper inquiry seeks to identify the intended parties to the agreement. If a party is not specifically referred to in the agreement, the question to be asked is whether a person nevertheless falls within its scope of application *ratione personae*.[27] The Tribunal also held that the parties had expanded the scope of the applicable law by choosing the ICC Rules of Arbitration which require the arbitral tribunal to take account of the contractual provisions and the relevant trade usages.[28]

6-46 Certain French case law goes further. For example, the Paris Court of Appeals has held that:

> An arbitration clause in an international contract has a validity and an effectiveness of its own, such that the clause must be extended to parties directly implicated in the performance of the contract and in any disputes arising out of the contract, provided that it has been established that their respective situations and activities raise the presumption that they were aware of the existence and scope of the arbitration clause, and irrespective of the fact that they did not sign the contract containing the arbitration agreement.[29]

---

[26] Of October 16, 2003 reported in the *Rev Arb* 2004, No 3 at pp. 696-707 and commentary by Laurent Lévy and Blaise Stucki at pp 707-718.

[27] These are questions of substance, and not form, which the Swiss federal tribunal went on to interpret in a liberal manner.

[28] Supra note 26, at 706.

[29] *Korsnas Marma v. Durand-Auzis*, 1989 *Rev Arb* 691 as cited and commented in *Fouchard Gaillard Goldman on International Commercial Arbitration*, Emmanuel Gaillard and John Savage eds, (Kluwer Law International 1999) at pp 288-289. See also the other decisions cited by the authors. See also Poudret and Besson, supra, note 18, pp 229-232.

6-47 These few examples demonstrate a widely differing approach to the treatment of non-signatories as an aspect of the arbitral tribunal's determination of its own jurisdiction. While there is general agreement that the question should be determined by the arbitral tribunal in the first instance,[30] there is a wide variety of approaches taken by national courts reviewing such jurisdictional decisions. Again, this illustrates the acceptance of certain general principles or approaches which are subject to wide variation when one descends to the level of specific application of those principles.

V. STANDARDS IN RESPECT OF EXPERT EVIDENCE

6-48 As in the case of procedure more generally, the use of experts in international commercial arbitration has given rise to some general principles or practices. These include the requirement that party-appointed experts meet and consult before a hearing and prepare a joint report and hearing expert witnesses "in confrontation" or, in other words, at the same time or consecutively and to have them both available for questioning by the tribunal simultaneously. These practices, with proper preparation, can be very beneficial and contribute to the efficiency and effectiveness of an arbitration. Further, the use of tribunal-appointed experts, unfamiliar to the common law world, is not unusual and certain general practices surrounding their role have developed. A number of these general practices or tendencies are addressed in the IBA Rules on the Taking of Evidence in International Commercial Arbitration.

6-49 However, these are, again, general rules and a number of important specific aspects of the expert evidence, whether party-appointed or tribunal-appointed, remain to be determined on a case-by-case basis. Often, these points may never be addressed or may only be considered once a problem has arisen and it is too late. Among these issues are the following:

- The independence of the expert and its significance with respect to the admissibility and weight of the expert's evidence.
- The permissible scope of expert evidence – Should experts opine on how the arbitral tribunal should actually decide? This is generally regulated in detail by national laws, yet receives little attention in international commercial arbitration.
- The qualifications of the expert and his standing to give opinion evidence.

---

[30] Except in the United States.

- Disclosure of documents and information considered by the expert.
- The preparation of the expert's evidence, the role of counsel and the availability of draft reports.
- Multiple authors of expert reports.

Experience indicates that many of these questions, if considered, will depend very much on the identity and experience of counsel and the arbitral tribunal.

VI. CONCLUSIONS

6-50 This brief examination of a selection of aspects of arbitral process reveals that we are still some way from being able to say that there exists an autonomous set of international procedural rules or a consistent international arbitration practice. Undoubtedly, a number of general principles and practices have emerged, but they remain general in nature. While initiatives such as the IBA Rules and Guidelines offer the promise of developing more detailed rules and practices, we should be realistic in our expectations. In order to achieve some degree of general acceptance, any procedural rules or practices will have to be general in nature. And perhaps this is how things should be.

6-51 One of the great advantages of international commercial arbitration is the autonomy it offers the parties who are free to choose their counsel, the applicable procedural rules and the members of the arbitral tribunal. If the parties accept the responsibility of exercising their freedom of choice, they have the ability to include in their contracts detailed, predictable rules and practices to govern their arbitral process. These rules can be chosen from among those of the recognized arbitral institutions or crafted by the parties themselves. Alternatively, the parties and their counsel are free to devise, in consultation with the arbitral tribunal, a detailed set of rules at the outset of arbitral proceedings to provide a predictable and fair process. This freedom is a hallmark of arbitration and should be considered and exercised carefully by the parties and the arbitral tribunal at the outset of any arbitration. With time, more international rules and practices will develop, helping to fill the current gap and providing a useful default system. However, any such system will inevitably maintain a role for the discretion of the arbitral tribunal. The need to responsibly exercise the freedom which the autonomy of international commercial arbitration process offers will always remain.

*William W. Park**

CHAPTER 7

THE PROCEDURAL SOFT LAW OF INTERNATIONAL ARBITRATION: NON-GOVERNMENTAL INSTRUMENTS

I. THE CHALLENGE OF SOFT LAW

7-1 The conference organizers set me the daunting task of exploring arbitration's "non-national instruments," which is to say the guidelines of professional groups and non-governmental organizations related to evidence, conflicts of interest, ethics and the organization of arbitral proceedings. Frequently these procedural standards build on the lore of international dispute resolution as memorialized in articles, treatises and learned symposium papers. These guidelines represent what might be called "soft law," in distinction to the harder norms imposed by arbitration statutes and treaties, as well as the procedural framework adopted by the parties through choice of pre-established arbitration rules.

7-2 The growth of procedural soft law has accelerated during the past half-dozen years. The International Bar Association (IBA) has revised its rules on evidence[1] and issued conflicts-of-interest guidelines.[2] New American Arbitration Association ethics guidelines retreat from the longstanding AAA practice of

---

* Professor of Law, Boston University.
1 See IBA Working Party, "Commentary on the New IBA Rules of Evidence in International Commercial Arbitration", [2000] 2 *Bus Law Int'l* 14. See also Michael Bühler and Carroll Dorgan, "Witness Testimony Pursuant to the IBA Rules of Evidence in International Commercial Arbitration*", 17(1) *J Int'l Arb* 3 (2000). The rules are available at www.ibanet.org.
2 IBA Guidelines on Conflicts of Interest in International Commercial Arbitration, approved by the IBA Council on 22 May 2004, published in 9(2) *Arbitration & ADR* (IBA) 7 (October 2004); See Markham Ball, "Probity Deconstructed – How Helpful, Really are the New IBA Guidelines on Conflicts of Interest in International Arbitration", 15 *World Arb & Mediation Rep* 333 (Nov. 2004); Jan Paulsson, "Ethics and Codes of Conduct for a Multi-Disciplinary Institute", 70 *Arbitration* 193 (2004), at 198-99.

Loukas A. Mistelis and Julian D.M. Lew (eds), Pervasive Problems in International Arbitration, 141-154
© 2006 Kluwer Law International. Printed in the Netherlands

partisan party-nominated arbitrators.[3] UNCITRAL put out Notes on Organizing Arbitral Proceedings.[4] And this past autumn the American College of Commercial Arbitrators debated a compendium of "Best Practices" for business arbitration.[5]

7-3 In some cases, the compromise reached in such principles may be helpful, while less so in other instances. But in almost all cases, these guidelines will have far-reaching effects, notwithstanding that they are non-binding on their face. During heated procedural debates they will be cited *faute de mieux*, for lack of anything better. The IBA Guidelines on Conflicts of Interest – with their red, orange and green lists of illustrations indicating varying levels of arbitrator disqualification – have been contested precisely because they will in fact affect arbitrator nominations as they enter the canon of sacred writings cited when an arbitrator's independence is contested.[6]

7-4 While the increase in such guidelines is beyond cavil, it is less clear whether the trend is a healthy one. Simply put, soft law serves as a constraint on arbitral autonomy. Any regulatory instrument will limit "flexibility" and "discretion" – those hallowed words that can trigger genuflection in even the most impious of arbitrators.

---

[3] See generally Ben Sheppard Jr, "A New Era of Arbitrator Ethics in the United States", 21 *Arb Int* 91 (2005); Paul Friedland & John Townsend, "Commentary on Changes to the Commercial Arbitration Rules of the American Arbitration Association", 58 *Disp Res J* 8 (Nov 2003-Jan 2004). The new Ethics Code, adopted jointly by the AAA and the ABA, permit a party-nominated arbitrator to be non-neutral only if so provided by the parties' agreement, the arbitration rules or applicable law. See Preamble ("Note on Neutrality") and Canon X, 2004 ABA/AAA Code of Ethics for Arbitrators in Commercial Disputes. A similar change was made in the AAA domestic commercial arbitration rules, effective July 2003, which establish a presumption of neutrality for all arbitrators.

[4] "Notes on Organizing Arbitral Proceedings," finalised in New York in June 1996, published in XXVII *UNCITRAL Yearbook*, part one, paras 11-54 (1996).

[5] College of Commercial Arbitrators, *Guide to Best Practices in Commercial Arbitration* (October 2005). These build on a previous draft presented to the CCA Meeting on 30 October 2004.

[6] A "red list" describes situations that give rise to justifiable doubts about an arbitrator's impartiality. Some are non-waivable (e.g. a financial interest in the outcome of the case), while others (e.g. a relationship with counsel) may be ignored by mutual consent. An "orange list" covers scenarios (e.g. past service as counsel for a party) which the parties are deemed to have accepted if no objection is made after timely disclosure. Finally, a "green list" enumerates cases (e.g. membership in the same professional organization) that require no disclosure.

7-5 In a recent issue of *Cahiers de l'arbitrage*, the eminent Paris avocat Serge Lazareff likened procedural soft law to a loathsome skin disease, using the provocatively pejorative label *le prurit réglementaire* ("regulatory pruritus"). Serge began with a hypothetical conversation (at least I hope it was hypothetical) in which a lawyer at a hearing asks the Tribunal chairman for a pause in the testimony so he can relieve himself. "Monsieur le Président, puis-je aller aux toilettes?" Mr. Chairman, can I visit to the WC? The response is a resounding negative ("Non, mon cher Maître") bolstered by citation to provisions of the Code of Conduct for Arbitral Hearings that stipulates precise numbers of bathroom breaks in function of the length of hearings.

II. SOFT LAW AND THE ARBITRAL PROCESS

1. What Consumers Want: Balancing Fairness and Efficiency

7-6 There is certainly food for thought in our Gallic colleague's whimsical scenario attacking excessive procedural guidelines. As Talleyrand reportedly observed, anything excessive becomes insignificant: *tout ce qui est excessif devient insignifiant*.

7-7 Yet a more nuanced view might see procedural soft law as enhancing arbitration's integrity. Modern arbitration is either blessed or plagued, depending on perspective, with a lack of fixed standards related to how arbitrators conduct proceedings. Little "hard law" exists with respect to how the specifics of how an arbitral tribunal should gather evidence and hear argument in its effort to determine the facts, interpret the contract, and apply the law governing the parties' dispute.

7-8 As in other areas, the devil is in the detail. How should the case in chief be presented: written statement? Oral testimony? Both written and oral? What objections justify excluding an exhibit? What degree of relevance justifies an order to produce documents? What sanctions should be imposed for refusal to comply with a discovery order? Battlegrounds are plentiful: the process for proving applicable law; time allocation among the litigants; issue preclusion; avoiding "trial by ambush;" fixing the proper role for legal authority; and even what to do if an arbitrator is abducted.

7-9 In managing cases, arbitrators face a delicate counterpoise between efficiency and fairness. They must keep the process moving, while allowing claims to be presented and defended fully enough that the parties feel they have been treated in a just fashion. Efficiency involves making the process shorter and cheaper. Fairness, however, can implicate the additional time and cost sometimes needed to provide a meaningful right to be heard.

7-10 In arbitration, fairness requires some measure of efficiency, since justice too long delayed becomes justice denied. Likewise, without fairness an arbitral proceeding would hardly be efficient, since it would fail to deliver a key element of the desired product: a sense that justice had been respected. A chef who aimed to provide fine dining might fail either by making customers wait too long or by serving junk food instead of a gourmet meal.[7]

7-11 Discussion of these competing goals brings to mind a conversation many years ago with the secretary general of a prominent arbitral institution. He was being interviewed following his retirement after a long career during which his organisation had seen a marked increase in caseload and prestige. When asked what he considered to be his most important achievement, the eminent elder statesman replied without a moment's hesitation,

> Why, the greatest success was taking a process that had been quick and cheap and turning it into one that is now long and expensive. *Enfin!* At last we are respected.

The point, of course, was that business managers who complain about too much legal procedure also object to too little. Procedural formality is often another term for due process.

7-12 The potential benefit of procedural soft law is that it can enhance the type of fairness business managers expect in dispute resolution, helping to strike the right equilibrium between fairness and efficiency. Arbitration is neither trial by combat nor a random process such as consulting the entrails of a chicken. Rather,

---

[7] The competition between aspirations toward fairness and toward efficiency shows itself with particular starkness in connection with mass claims such as the so-called "Holocaust arbitrations" addressing insurance policies and bank accounts belonging to victims of Nazi persecution. Oral hearings can add to a sense of fairness; but with thousands of claimants, oral hearings mean considerable delay. To take another example, claims among competing heirs might normally be decided by reference to the legal system with the closest connection to the decedent account holder. In practice, however, this can mean having to decide which family member died last in a concentration camp, which might require interpreting a 1943 Hungarian simultaneous death statute. A somewhat arbitrary (*i.e.*, less legally correct) set of succession guidelines might prove a more efficient way to proceed.

arbitration implies respect for a bundle of rights often called due process, which the British sometimes label as natural justice. Once summarized as "the duty to hear before condemning,"[8] due process lies at the core of what litigants seek in both arbitration and litigation.

7-13 Like other elastic notions such as justice and equity, the term "due process" has no sacramental value in itself, but takes meaning from usage. Since one person's delay is often another's due process, notions of arbitral fairness evolve as they are incarnated into flesh and blood responses to specific problems, whose merit often depends on culturally conditioned baseline expectations. A lawyer from New York might say that fundamental fairness requires the respondent to produce certain documents even if adverse to its defence, while a lawyer from Paris or Geneva, used to a quite different legal system, would reply that the claimant should have thought about its proof before filing the claim.

7-14 Most arbitration statutes and treaties contain some notions of due process, whether or not so-labelled. Although analogous concepts exist outside Anglo-American law jurisdictions, the precise translation into Continental equivalents remains elusive.[9] French law often speaks of "the right to be heard in an adversarial process" (*droit d'être entendu en procédure contradictoire*) or "the principle of contradictory process" (*principe de la contradiction*). Germans sometimes refer to the "fair-trial principle" (*rechtsstaatliche Verfahren*)[10] or speak of a "hearing in accordance with law" (*Anspruch auf rechtliches Gehör*).[11]

7-15 The contours of arbitral due process are broad, focusing on (i) the right to be heard and (ii) an unbiased tribunal. While these rudiments of fairness often overlap, such is not always the case. Arbitrators who decide by flipping coins

---

[8] The phrase originated with the great orator and advocate Daniel Webster when he made his famous arguments to defend the charter of Dartmouth College. After asking rhetorically whether the Dartmouth trustees "lost their franchise by due course and process of law" Webster defined the concept as "law which hears before it condemns; which proceeds upon inquiry and renders judgment only after trial." See *Trustees of Dartmouth v. Woodward*, 17 US 518, 4 Wheaton's Report 518 (1818), at Wheaton 581.

[9] For a recent discussion of due process in Islamic law, see Nudrat Majeed, "Good Faith and Due Process: Lessons from the Shari'ah", 20 *Arb Int* 97 (2004).

[10] *Grundgesetz* Article 20(3) establishes a "rule of law principle" that has been interpreted by the Constitutional Court (*Bundesverfassungsgericht*) to encompass entitlement to *rechtsstaatliches Verfahren* ("procedure in accordance with the rule of law").

[11] See *Grundgesetz* Article 103(1), reading *Vor Gericht hat jedermann Anspruch auf rechtliches Gehör.* ("In the courts every person shall be entitled to a hearing in accordance with law.")

might be unbiased; but in failing to consider testimony they give no genuine opportunity for proofs to be heard. Conversely, arbitrators who go through the motions of listening attentively to witnesses might still violate due process if they enter the arbitration with minds already decided. In some instances elements of fairness exist in tension one with another. Granting a party additional time for witness examination constitutes unequal treatment, but might justify itself in exceptional circumstances if one side bears a special burden of proof.

7-16 Equality of arms among the parties constitutes yet another element of due process. An arbitrator might well decide to deny all right of oral depositions, believing the Anglo-American system to be unduly burdensome. However, the arbitrator could hardly consider requests for depositions by one side but not the other.

7-17 It is here that procedural soft law presents its potential to foster a sense of equal treatment, by promoting the perception that procedure is "regular" and according to a "rule of law" principle. Indeed, one of the essential elements of law as it has been known in the Western world is that similar cases should be treated in a similar fashion. By contrast, when arbitrators invent procedural norms as cases unfold, choosing their procedural standards after knowing who will receive the rough end of a rule, one side may perceive application of different sets of weights and measures.

2. "Judicialisation"

7-18 One oft-heard criticism of procedural soft law is that it leads to the "judicialisation" of arbitration: procedural transformation of arbitral dispute resolution to resemble court litigation more closely.[12] But is this really so bad?

7-19 At first blush, judicialised arbitration may seem a contradiction in terms. Arbitration is presumed to present an alternative to legal formalities, a phrase often stirring images of the judicial waste satirized in the Dickensian inheritance

---

[12] See generally the University of Virginia's 12th Sokol Colloquium, *International Arbitration in the 21st Century: Towards Judicialization and Uniformity?* (Richard Lillich & Charles Brower eds., 1993), with contributions by CF Amerasinghe, R Bilder, A Bucher, Th Carbonneau, A Giardina, H Holtzmann, C Larsen, R Lillich, A Rovine, D Stewart and Albert Jan van den Berg. For an exploration of the judicialisation of inter-governmental trade disputes, see JH Weiler, "The Rule of Lawyers and the Ethos of Diplomats: Reflections on the Internal and external Legitimacy of WTO Dispute Settlement", 13 *Am Rev Int'l Arb* 177 (2002). See also Gerald Phillips, "Is Creeping Legalism Infecting Arbitration?", 58 *Disp. Res. J.* 37 (Feb./April 2003).

dispute *Jarndyce v. Jarndyce*, which had become so complicated that no living soul knew what it meant, and whose legal costs consumed the entire estate.

7-20 What the Dickensian satire misses, of course, is that elements of legal process inevitably enter arbitration as soon as the litigants want a binding result. No one would much care about legal rights if either party could unilaterally elect to disregard the arbitrator's decision. But such is not normally the case. Arbitration proceeds in the shadow of judicial power, enlisted to seize assets and grant *res judicata* effect to awards.

7-21 So it is not at all surprising that litigants expect ordered arbitral proceedings. Few business managers want a lottery of inconsistent results. When cases are won or lost, rather than negotiated away, procedural rights inevitably become an object of concern. By providing sign posts to these rights, procedural soft law enhances the prospect that similar cases will be treated in similar ways.

3. Institutional Rules

7-22 At this point, the careful observer might wonder what the fuss is all about. After all, institutions can always adopt rules to define the precise nature of the practices that will satisfy the litigants' senses of arbitral due process. So why does anyone need professional guidelines?

7-23 Here we see a disjunction between rhetoric and reality. On the one hand, arbitral institutions consistently endorse flexibility and its twin sister, arbitrator discretion. On the other hand, more specific norms inhabit the less elastic world where lawyers *do* care about the "regular" way to do things.

7-24 While cynics might suggest that these two approaches cohabit so arbitrators can hedge their bets (invoking discretion as an escape hatch and customary practices as rationale), better ways exist to explain this divergent evolution. The emphasis on flexibility likely represents a Darwinian a survival mechanism, helping institutions market themselves globally by sidestepping tough questions about what fairness means when legal cultures diverge in matters such as discovery, the questioning of witnesses, use of experts and legal argument.[13] These

---

[13] See Siegfried H. Elsing & John M. Townsend, "Bridging the Common Law-Civil Law Divide in Arbitration", 18 *Arb. Int.* 59 (2002); Axel Baum, "Reconciling Anglo-Saxon and Civil Law Procedure: The Path to a Procedural Lex Arbitrationis", in: *Recht der Internationalen Wirtschaft und Streiterledigung im 21. Jahrhundert: Liber Amicorum Karl-Heinz Böckstiegel* 21 (R.

distinctions have often been noted between so-called "adversarial" and "inquisitorial" approaches, the former emphasizing the role of lawyers in controlling the proceedings (with the arbitrators simply listening to evidence and argument) and the latter granting the arbitrators a greater role in asking questions and directing the inquiry.

7-25 The prevailing orthodoxy, of course, says that flexibility strengthens arbitration, and that arbitrators should have wide discretion to do what best fits each individual case.[14] It is an exceptional arbitration conference without at least one war story about a praiseworthy arbitrator (usually the speaker himself) who exercised just the right touch of procedural *je ne sais quoi* that that made things come out right. And indeed, it would be hard to argue that proceedings should be forced into an ill-fitting straight-jacket of rules designed for some other controversy, rather than reflecting the contours of each particular case.

7-26 Major institutional rules address the conduct of proceedings simply by saying that arbitrators may establish the facts by "all appropriate means,"[15] with the "widest discretion to discharge [their] duties"[16] in "whatever manner [the tribunal] considers appropriate."[17] While this lack of direction might not matter when all arbitrators and counsel are cut from the same mould, such gaps might cause awkward confusion when one arbitrator or lawyer is doing his or her first international arbitration.

7-27 It has sometimes been suggested that the homage paid to flexibility in major arbitration rules confirms the lack of users' demand for more specific procedures. One wonders, however, whether the prevailing emphasis on flexibility indicates an absence of demand or a paucity of supply. No empirical evidence drawn from

---

Briner, L Y Fortier, K-P Berger & J Bredow, eds, Carl Heymanns Verlag 2001); Paul D Friedland, "A Standard Procedure for Presenting Evidence in International Arbitration", *Mealey's Int'l Arb Rev* 133 (1996); Markus Wirth, "Ihr Zeuge, Herr Rechtsanwalt! Weshalb Civil-Law-Schiedsrichter Common-Law-Verfahrensrecht anwenden", 1(1) *Schieds VZ* (Jan/Feb 2003); Piero Bernardini, "The Role of the International Arbitrator", 20 *Arb Int* 113 (2004); Christopher Staughton, "Common Law and Civil Law Procedures: Which is More Inquisitorial? A Common Lawyer's Response", 5 *Arb Int* 352 (1989).

[14] For a contrasting view, see John Uff, "Predictability in International Arbitration", *International Commercial Arbitration: Practical Perspectives* 151 (Construction Law Press, 2001), who provocatively suggests that "in most cases it is a matter of pure chance whether the parties to an international arbitration end up with what might objectively be called a 'good' resolution of their dispute." Ibid. at 152.

[15] ICC Arbitration Rules, Art 20.

[16] LCIA Arbitration Rules, Art 14.2.

[17] UNCITRAL Rules, Art 18; AAA International Rules, Art 16.

modern arbitration indicates that more specific rules were tried and found wanting, rather than simply not having been tried at all.

7-28 The soft law contained in the recent proliferation of professional guidelines does suggests that some of arbitration's users seek more rather than less procedural predictability. In contrast to this rhetoric of flexibility, the conduct of arbitral proceedings is often quite focused on fidelity to specific established norms. When a dispute arises over some procedural issue, such as privilege, discovery or witness sequestration, counsel frequently invoke what they believe to be the normal way to do things. These customary standards are believed to exist; they are summoned into play during procedural disagreements; and the parties' sense of having been treated fairly is linked to how well the norms have been respected.

7-29 One difficulty in evaluating the impact of procedural soft law in the chameleon-like quality of the arbitral flexibility that soft law restricts. Flexibility is a concept that changes colour depending on context – not surprising for a word defined as the ability to adapt in response to new situations.[18] On a continuum between precision and generality, a flexible approach falls toward the "generality" end. Flexibility usually involves determining the specific rule after the procedural question arises: in essence, a type of *ex post facto* rule-making.

7-30 In the real world, the flexibility implied by an absence of soft law guidelines can sometimes enhance performance of the arbitrator's tasks. But not always. And perhaps not usually. The very nature of the legal process contains an inherent tension between generality and specificity. Law would hardly be law without an aspiration to grant similar treatment to those in similar situations. An overly broad rule would fail by denying recognition to critical distinctions among different cases. No rule at all, however, will often detract from the parties' sense of fairness, which is often fostered more by fidelity to pre-established standards than by the content of the standards themselves.

7-31 Intelligent soft law can provide guidance on repeat-offender trouble spots (such as discovery and privilege) without imposing undue rigidly on all aspects of the arbitral process. The search for procedural balance (evoking the Swedish

---

[18] Usually the term is associated with words like "reasonable" and "appropriate" and used in juxtaposition or contrast to "rigid" or "strict." Of course, the difference between flexible and rigid procedures is one of degree.

word *lagom*, meaning "not too much and not too little") can be context-based without being open-ended.

4. Divergent Cultural Baselines

7-32 When arbitration takes place among lawyers who share little common legal culture, the absence of pre-established procedural standards can create special problems. This is ironic, of course, since flexibility is understandably justified as the best way to address cultural diversity.

7-33 The problem lies in the lack of common cross-cultural baselines. Parties can usually accept a ruling that follows a common pattern. Established norms articulating the "regular" way to do things reduces the risk that one side might perceive arbitrators to apply weights and measures chosen after knowing which side needs a thumb on the scale.

7-34 Without shared expectations about regular ways of doing things, however, litigants lack common assumptions about what fairness means. The absence of standards fixed in advance, while perhaps making arbitration less cumbersome in some instances, can generate feelings of inequality. The existence of two different baselines means that any *ex post* choice by the arbitrators will deviate from one side's sense of procedural integrity. Practices which constitute procedural rights in one system might elsewhere be unfamiliar, unethical or prohibited. Examples of include witness interviews[19] and oral depositions,[20] as well as the processes for appointing experts and determining admissibility of their testimony.[21]

---

[19] See, e.g., Art 13 of Geneva's *Us et coutumes de l'ordres des avocats* ("L'avocat doit s'interdire de discuter avec un témoin de sa déposition future et de l'influencer de quelque manière que ce soit"). By contrast, US lawyers would be considered lacking in diligence if they failed to rehearse their witnesses about the type of questions to be asked, in theory seen as a way to keep witnesses from being misled or surprised, and arguably making the testimony more accurate. See *Wigmore on Evidence* (4th edition, Aspen 2000) § 788; Thomas A Mauet, *Pretrial* (4th edition, Aspen, 1999) at 40.

[20] The IBA Rules of Evidence make no provision for oral depositions analogous to Federal Rules of Civil Procedure, Rule 26(b)(1).

[21] In the United States, a so-called "Daubert" motion may be made to disqualify an expert because his or her method is not sufficiently reliable. See *Daubert v. Merrell Dow Pharmaceuticals*, 509 US 579 (1993), confirmed in Federal Rules of Evidence § 702. When scientific or technical knowledge will assist in understanding evidence, an expert witness qualified may testify in the form of an opinion if "the testimony is the product of reliable principles and methods."

7-35 One example of culture clash relates to communications from in-house lawyers, which are privileged in the United States[22] but not in many European countries.[23] How should an arbitrator choose between these divergent models of privilege?

7-36 Arbitrators might give effect to the expectations relied upon at the place the relevant memo was written. Accordingly, a memo would be protected if sent by an in-house lawyer in New York. By contrast, advice given by an in-house counsel in Geneva would not be protected, since the Swiss lawyer presumably had no expectation of privilege.

7-37 Such an approach has great theoretical merit if an arbitrator single-mindedly ignores all procedural expectations other than those related to privilege. But other expectations do exist, of course. In particular, the anticipation of equal treatment is likely to be shared by both sides. Instinctively, therefore, a good arbitrator would shrink from assigning procedural benefits and burdens unequally, allowing one side but not the other an opportunity to claim privilege on the very same type of document.[24] An arbitrator who gives one side such stark procedural handicaps would be inviting award vacatur.

7-38 Procedural soft law on this much-vexed issue would have the benefit of establishing a protocols before proceedings begin – something that arbitrators and litigants often avoid, from fear of inviting unnecessary wrangling. The cost, of course, is often disruption in the serenity of the proceedings and party satisfaction. Perceptions of *ad personam* justice (what the French might call *justice à la tête du client*) increases the risk of tension between the tribunal and at least one of the parties.

---

[22] See, e.g., *NCK Organization Ltd v. Bregman*, 542 F 2d 128, 133 (2d Cir 1976).

[23] For example, in Switzerland, the notion of *avocat / Rechtsanwalt* depends on activity of an "independent" character, and the status of employee is disqualifying. See, e.g., Peter Burckhardt, "Legal Professional Secrecy and Privilege in Switzerland", *IBA International Litigation News* 33 (October 2004); Bernard Corboz, "Le secret professionnel de l'avocat selon l'article 321 CP", *Semaine Judiciaire* 77 (1993).

[24] Similarly, an American would be unlikely to have enthusiasm for a decision that allowed a Swiss company to obtain discovery from a company in New York (because that was the expectation in the United States), but did not allow discovery from the adversary in Geneva (because fishing expeditions were unknown there.)

5. Secondary Markets for Rules: Illustrating the Impact of Soft Law

7-39 Professional guidelines have evolved to mitigate some of the above-mentioned hazards of arbitral discretion. The more specific norms of "secondary market" procedures represent in essence the invention of civil procedure on several levels. The following two problems might serve as illustrations.

(a) Who Gets the Last Word?

7-40 The interaction of flexible discretion and concrete rules is illustrated by an English case decided in 2004, *Margulead v. Exide*.[25] An Israeli-American joint venture went sour, ending up in an arbitration whose official seat was London. The sole arbitrator, wanting to finish before lunch on the final day of hearings, refused a right of reply to the Claimant's lawyer. "You did [such an] admirable job of stating your case," the arbitrator said to counsel, that a reply will not be necessary. The arbitrator later denied both the claim and the counterclaim, finding that mutual mistake of fact made the parties' agreement unenforceable. The Israeli claimant challenged the award,[26] alleging serious procedural irregularity because it had not been given the last word, as apparently would have been normal in English courts for the claimant carrying the burden of proof.

7-41 An English judge upheld the award, on the basis that a rule giving final say to claimants did not apply in arbitration. The judge looked first to the procedural framework accepted by the parties, which included a well-recognized set of arbitral provisions (the UNCITRAL Rules) and the IBA Rules of Evidence. Neither authority said who gets to speak last. The judge then turned to the English Arbitration Act, which also punted the question to the arbitrator.[27]

7-42 But discretion was not enough. The reviewing court then made reference to a learned treatise that *did* set forth a rule, to the effect that in international arbitration parties normally have the right to make an *equal* number of submis-

---

[25] *Margulead Ltd v. Exide Technologies*, High Court of Justice (Q.B., Commercial Court), 16 February, [2004] EWHC 1019 (Comm.) (Colman, J.).

[26] The challenge under Section 68(2)(a) of the 1996 Arbitration Act, referring to failure to comply with section 33 of the Act, which in turn imposes a general duty for the arbitral tribunal to act fairly and impartially, giving each side a reasonable opportunity to present its case. A secondary challenge was brought under Section 68(2)(d) of the Act for failure to deal with all the issues.

[27] The act said only that the arbitrator should "decide all procedural matters [including] ... whether and to what extent there should be oral or written evidence or submission." 1996 Arbitration Act, Section 34(1) and 34(2)(h), cited in paragraphs 31 and 32 of Justice Colman's opinion.

sions.[28] Thus, the failure to give claimant the last word comported with an established practice. One can only speculate on how the case would have been decided if a treatise had indicated a different rule.

(b) Ex Parte Measures

7-43 The current debate over the arbitrator's right to grant *ex parte* interim measures of protection provides another point to ponder. Draft revisions of the UNCITRAL Model Law would permit arbitral orders on application of only one side.[29] Good arguments exist for and against the proposals.

7-44 The interesting aspect of this debate lies in what is *not* being said. Would the question arise at all if arbitrators really did have discretion on the matter? But in fact, an uncodified rule imposes a general ban on deciding matters without hearing both sides, absent the parties' specific agreement to the contrary.[30]

III. SOFT LAW AND THE IMPERIAL ARBITRATOR

7-45 Ultimately, the tension between procedural soft law and unrestrained arbitral flexibility brings us full circle to the matter of an arbitrator's fidelity to the parties' shared *ex ante* expectations. While arbitrators are not expected to wear procedural straight jackets, and procedural guidelines can certainly contain "good cause shown" exceptions, most litigants anticipate a measure of ordered procedure as a prerequisite to equal treatment and due process.

7-46 Such concerns about "*ad hoc* justice" have led some commentators to suggest that flexibility might be overrated, and to propose that arbitral institutions

---

[28] Justice Colman cited Alan Redfern and Martin Hunter, *Law and Practice of International Arbitration* (3rd ed. Sweet & Maxwell 1999), para 7-107 ("Who has the last word?") at 336, stating that the practice of giving the claimant two submission opportunities is "not widely followed, since arbitrators tend to feel, instinctively, that due process is generally served only if the parties are permitted an equal number of opportunities to make oral submissions."

[29] Draft Articles 17 and 17Bis are discussed in Hans van Houtte, "Ten Reasons Against a Proposal for Ex Parte Interim Measures of Protection in Arbitration", 20 *Arb Int* 85 (2004). See Report of the Working Group on Arbitration, 39th Session, Vienna, 10-14 November 2003, Document A/CN.9/545. See also John P. Gaffney, "Ex Parte Measures in International Arbitration", 3 *Int'l ALR* (No 4) 55 (Winter2002), providing a discussion of *ex parte* measures by courts as well as arbitrators.

[30] A similar consensus exists on the impropriety of an arbitrator's *ex parte* communications with one of the litigants, regardless of whether this leads to any ruling. Yet some major institutional rules (such as the ICC Rules) contain no explicit prohibition on *ex parte* communications between parties and arbitrators.

consider a smörgåsbord approach which would offer a menu of more specific provisions from which to choose: perhaps between procedure light and procedure heavy, or between rules with a Continental, English or an American flavor.

7-47 Such an idea was floated in the Freshfields Lecture in 2002. During the dinner following the lecture, several members of the arbitral establishment indicated that such a proposal was about as welcome as a horde of ants at a Sunday school picnic. Surprisingly, after the lecture was published[31] a large number of letters to the author expressed relief that the question had been raised openly, and shared experiences of "imperial arbitrators" whose abusive disregard of even-handedness was facilitated by the flexibility inherent in institutional rules. (And you know who you are.) But as Rudyard Kipling might have written, that is a story for another day.

---

[31] William W Park, "Arbitration's Protean Nature: The Value of Rules and the Risks of Discretion", 19 *Arb Int* 279 (2003).

*Wang Shengchang** and Cao Lijun***

CHAPTER 8

THE ROLE OF NATIONAL COURTS AND *LEX FORI* IN INTERNATIONAL COMMERCIAL ARBITRATION

8-1 Arbitration has grown into the preferred method for resolving disputes arising from international business transactions. This is mainly attributable to the emerging international climate favouring arbitration advanced by the 1958 Convention on the Recognition and Enforcement of Foreign Arbitral Awards (hereinafter referred to as "the New York Convention"), the extensive work of the United Nations Commission on International Trade Law (hereinafter referred to as "UNCITRAL") and the legislation by most jurisdictions.

8-2 An arbitration agreement is a special type of forum selection agreement and parties thereto are required to stick to it and not to litigate the dispute. However, it is not correct to say that an arbitration agreement has deprived the judicial organs of any role in the arbitral proceedings.

8-3 The court has a wide range of powers to assist and supervise international commercial arbitration proceedings. Under international conventions and national statutes, courts should decline jurisdiction and compel arbitration if the parties already agreed to have the dispute arbitrated. While the arbitration proceedings are pending, the court may step in and decide on matters regarding the appointment and removal of arbitrators. The court may also order interim measures of protection in aid of arbitration. After an award has been rendered by the arbitral tribunal, the prevailing party will have to move for recognition and enforcement of the award at the court if the losing party fails to honour the award automatically, and the losing party can oppose such a motion, or alternatively,

* Vice Chairman and Secretary General, China International Economic and Trade Arbitration Commission (CIETAC).
** Arbitrator, China International Economic and Trade Arbitration Commission (CIETAC).

Loukas A. Mistelis and Julian D.M. Lew (eds), Pervasive Problems in International Arbitration, 155-183
© 2006 Kluwer Law International. Printed in the Netherlands

move for setting aside or annulment of the award at the court. In every aspect where the court can intervene in the arbitral proceedings, the court has to rely on certain procedural rules, which are mostly from the *lex fori*, *i.e* the law of the forum state (the law of the court).

8-4 However, as party autonomy is a principle well recognized in arbitration, the role of the judicial authority has to be restricted, as has been witnessed by the 1985 UNCITRAL Model Law on International Commercial Arbitration (hereinafter referred to as "the Model Law") and legislations in many states. Under the statutes, the court cannot intervene in any arbitral proceedings except when it is statutorily permitted to do so.[1]

8-5 But has international commercial arbitration been so developed, and the public policy in its favour so advanced, that the judicial role should be reduced, if not eliminated? The answer is negative. Court assistance is fundamental to international commercial arbitration, in that it ensures the due process and fairness of arbitral proceedings and fills in the blanks in arbitration agreements, especially *ad hoc* agreements. In contrary, court assistance shall conceivably be strengthened in response to the development of arbitration.

8-6 A discussion about all aspects mentioned above is presented in this chapter. When examining the issues, reference is made to the New York Convention, the UNCITRAL Model Law and national legislations of jurisdictions where arbitration is popular.

I. *LEX FORI* AND LAWS TO BE APPLIED TO AN ARBITRATION

1. Three Laws Distinguished

8-7 For domestic arbitration, the court relies only on national laws when deciding arbitration-related matters. In the context of international commercial arbitration, however, at least three different laws come into play, which include:

---

[1] For example, Article 5 of the Model Law provides that

in matters governed by this Law, no court shall intervene except where so provided in this Law.

- The proper law of the contract, or the law applicable to the substantive issues of the dispute;
- The proper law of the arbitration agreement;
- The law applicable to the arbitral proceedings, or *lex arbitri*.

8-8 For an international business contract, the proper law is to be specified according to certain conflicts rules and is not always the substantive laws of the forum state. It is not a topic to be discussed in this chapter.[2]

8-9 When deciding the validity of the agreement to arbitrate or other procedural issues, a court may not necessarily rely on the forum law, that is to say, the *lex fori* is not necessarily the law applicable to the arbitration agreement, nor the *lex arbitri*. However the *lex fori* is still the fundamental law, as in many situations parties fail to subject the agreement or the whole arbitral procedure to a law of their choice and the *lex fori* always applies on the subsidiary basis.

2. The Applicable Laws Referred to in the New York Convention

8-10 The New York Convention provides in its Article V seven grounds for refusing recognition and enforcement of foreign arbitral awards. Under Article V(1)(a), refusal may be rendered by a competent judicial authority when a party can prove that

> the said agreement is not valid under the law to which the parties have subjected it or, failing any indication thereon, under the law of the country where the award was made.

It follows that, under the New York Convention, the parties can subject the validity of arbitration agreement to any law of their choice, and when such a choice is not available, the forum law, i.e. the law of the place of arbitration, applies.

8-11 Under Article V(1)(e), recognition and enforcement of a foreign arbitral award may be refused if the opposing party can prove that

> the award has not yet become binding on the parties, or has been set aside or suspended by a competent authority of the country in which, or under the law of which, that award was made.

---

[2] But see Chapter 3 above, by Kessedjian.

The second part of the quoted sentence is of substantial importance to the conduct of international arbitration. The court of the seat of arbitration is usually the competent authority for setting aside the award, but when the parties have agreed that the procedural law is other than that of the seat state, the court of that other country is the competent authority. The rationale behind the provision is that parties oftentimes select the seat of arbitration for its geographical convenience and do not intend to have the proceedings governed by the *lex fori*. Be that as it may, selecting a procedural law other than the *lex fori* becomes feasible only when the *lex fori* allows and recognizes such a selection.

3. Arbitration Agreement v. Lex Arbitri

8-12 Generally speaking, the arbitral procedure is subject first to the explicit agreement of the parties, followed in turn by the chosen institutional rules (only in case of institutional arbitration) – an expression of the agreement of the parties – and the *lex arbitri*, the latter being either the procedural law chosen by the parties or the law of forum state, i.e. the law of the seat of arbitration.

8-13 However it will be risky to suggest that the arbitration agreement always prevails when it differs from the *lex arbitri*, especially the mandatory rules in the *lex arbitri*.[3] Suppose that with regard to a certain procedural matter, the rules made in the parties' agreement are not in compliance with the mandatory provisions of the *lex arbitri*, arbitrators whose task is to make an internationally enforceable award may find themselves in a paradoxical situation. If they do not comply with the mandatory provisions of the *lex arbitri*, their award may be set aside and as a result lose the benefit of the New York Convention. If, on the other hand, they comply with those rules and thereby ignore the rules agreed by the parties, their award may be refused recognition or enforcement on the basis of Article V(1)(d) of the New York Convention.[4] Drafters of arbitration agreements shall be aware of this possibility and avoid making rules incompatible with mandatory provisions of the *lex arbitri*.

---

[3] See Julian D M Lew, Loukas Mistelis, Stefan M Kröll, *Comparative International Commercial Arbitration* (Kluwer Law International 2003), paras 2-42 et seq, 21-5 – 21-18.

[4] See Emmanuel Gaillard and John Savage (eds), *Fouchard Gaillard Goldman on International Commercial Arbitration* (Kluwer Law International 1999), at 990.

II. THE JUDICIAL ROLE WITH REGARD TO ARBITRATION AGREEMENT

8-14 Parties to an arbitration agreement are required to honour their undertaking to submit to arbitration any dispute covered by the agreement. But what if one party files a court action in breach of the agreement, either before or after the other party initiates the arbitration? To foster the use of international arbitration in resolving disputes, international conventions and national legislation require that national courts upheld the sanctity and honour the arbitration agreement and refer the parties to arbitration. This principle is fundamental to both domestic and international arbitration, for otherwise every arbitration agreement may be forgone by initiating court proceedings.

1. The New York Convention and National Legislations

8-15 The New York Convention sets forth in Article II(3) a guideline for judicial behaviour in dealing with disputes covered by an arbitration agreement. It provides:

> the court of a Contracting State, when seized of an action in a matter in respect of which the parties have made an agreement within the meaning of this article, shall, at the request of one of the parties, refer the parties to arbitration, unless it finds that the said agreement is null and void, inoperative or incapable of being performed.

8-16 The general rule has been incorporated into the Model Law, as well as the national arbitration statutes of the New York Convention Contracting States. The national statutes may, however, add more requirements as thresholds for the court to decline its jurisdiction.

8-17 For example, Article 8 of the Model Law provides:

> (1) A court before which an action is brought in a matter which is the subject of an arbitration agreement shall, if a party so requests not later than when submitting his first statement on the substance of the dispute, refer the parties to arbitration unless it finds that the agreement is null and void, inoperative or incapable of being performed.
>
> (2) Where an action referred to in paragraph (1) of this article has been brought, arbitral proceedings may nevertheless be commenced or continued, and an award may be made, while the issue is pending before the court.

8-18 In addition to what have been provided in Article II of the New York Convention, Article 8 of the Model Law requires that a party request for the referral before submitting his first statement on the substances of the dispute. This requirement makes legal sense, as a party who answers the substantive issues before the court of law while aware of the existence of the arbitration agreement is deemed to have submitted to the jurisdiction of the court and to have repudiated the arbitration agreement: thus it is estopped from repudiating his repudiation. The article also makes it clear that the arbitral proceedings shall be commenced or continued despite the pending court action, where the parties dispute the validity of the arbitration agreement.

8-19 A similar provision is found in Article 7 of Swiss Private International Law Statute, which provides:

> If the parties have concluded an arbitration agreement covering an arbitrable dispute, a Swiss court seized of it shall decline jurisdiction unless:
> a. the defendant has proceeded with its defense on the merits without raising any objection;
> b. the court finds that the arbitral agreement is null and void, inoperative or incapable of being performed; or
> c. the arbitral tribunal cannot be constituted for reasons manifestly attributable to the defendant.

8-20 In France, Article 1458 of the New Code of Civil Procedure, which is also applicable to international arbitration,[5] clearly states

> where a dispute submitted to an arbitral tribunal by virtue of an arbitration agreement is brought before a national court, such court shall decline jurisdiction.

8-21 In China, Article 5 of the Arbitration Law 1995, which is applicable to both domestic and international arbitration, provides that

> a people's court shall not accept an action initiated by a party to an arbitration agreement, unless the agreement is invalid.

2. Stay of the Court Action and Anti-Suit Injunctions in England and the United States

8-22 In most jurisdictions under civil law influence, a court shall decline jurisdiction (or even determine an action inadmissible) when there is a valid

---

[5] See *Fouchard Gaillard Goldman, ibid*, at 404.

arbitration agreement and the defendant relies on it. In Anglo-American legal systems, the court will grant a stay of the court proceedings until the making of the arbitral award rather than exclude the jurisdiction of the court altogether.

8-23 This approach has been traditionally adopted by the English courts and is still the case under English Arbitration Act 1996.[6] According to Article 9, Section (1) of the Act,

> [a] party to an arbitration agreement against whom legal proceedings are brought (whether by way of claim or counterclaim) in respect of a matter which under the agreement is to be referred to arbitration may (upon notice to the other parties to the proceedings) apply to the court in which the proceedings have been brought to stay the proceedings so far as they concern that matter.

8-24 It should be noted that under this provision, even if the seat of the arbitration is outside England or no seat has been designated or determined, a party seeking to rely on the arbitration agreement can apply for the stay of action before an English court.

8-25 A similar rule is found in Section 3 of the U.S. Federal Arbitration Act (hereinafter referred to as "FAA"), according to which courts confronted with an arbitration agreement must stay the proceedings until the arbitration has taken place in accordance with the terms of the arbitration agreement.

8-26 In the United States, the federal district court[7] may under Section 206 of the FAA

> direct that arbitration be held in accordance with the agreement at any place therein provided for, whether that place is within or without the United States.

Compared with the counterpart provision for domestic arbitration in Chapter 1 of the FAA[8], under which the district court is only authorized to order arbitration in

---

[6] *Ibid*, at 403-404.

[7] Under Article 205 of the FAA, where the subject matter of an action or proceeding pending in a State court relates to an arbitration agreement or award falling under the Convention, the defendant or the defendants may, at any time before the trial thereof, remove such action or proceeding to the district court of the United States for the district and division embracing the place where the action or proceeding is pending.

[8] The counterpart provision is in Section 3 of the FAA, which provides:

the district where it sits, the provision for international arbitration set forth in Section 206 is more favorable. However, Section 206 applies only if the agreement identifies a place for arbitration. The district court cannot select an arbitral forum where the agreement fails to do so, nor can a court order the parties to arbitrate in a location that they did not designate.[9] Nevertheless, under Section 208's residual application provision, if the agreement satisfies Section 202 and contains no provision for location, the court can order that the parties arbitrate in the district where the district court sits pursuant to Section 4 of the FAA.[10]

8-27 Under English law, if England is the seat of arbitration and a court action is commenced abroad, a party seeking to rely on the arbitration agreement may, instead of applying directly to the foreign court for a stay, apply for an anti-suit injunction from an English court. In issuing the injunction, which can be either a permanent one or an interim one, the English court will need to be satisfied that there has been an actual or threatened breach of the arbitration agreement.[11] Similar judicial practice also exists in many states of the US.[12]

3. Upon the Request of a Party?

8-28 Under the New York Convention and most national laws, a court hearing a dispute covered by an arbitration agreement cannot declare *ex officio* that it has no jurisdiction. If a party brings a court action in breach of the arbitration agreement and the other party does not challenge the court's jurisdiction, it is clear that the parties jointly abandon the arbitration agreement and such a joint intention shall be respected from the court. So the court will refer the parties to

---

if any suit or proceeding be brought in any of the courts of the United States upon any issue referable to arbitration under an agreement in writing for such arbitration, the court in which such suit is pending, upon being satisfied that the issue involved in such suit or proceeding is referable to arbitration under such an agreement, shall on application of one of the parties stay the trial of the action until such arbitration has been had in accordance with the terms of the agreement, providing the applicant for the stay is not in default in proceeding with such arbitration.

[9]   *Jain v. deMere*, 51 F 3d 686, 689 (7th Cir 1995), *cert denied*, 516 US 914 (1995); *Bauhinia Corp v. China Nat'l Mach & Equip Imp & Exp Corp*, 819 F 2d 247, 250 (9th Cir 1987). See also Susan Karamanian, "The Road to the Tribunal and Beyond: International Commercial Arbitration and United States Courts", 34 *Geo Wash Int'l L Rev* 17, at 39.

[10]   See Karamanian, *ibid*, at note 143.

[11]   See *Russell on Arbitration*, 22nd edition, by David St. John Sutton and Judith Gill (Sweet & Maxwell, 2003), at 297.

[12]   See Lew, Mistelis, Kröll, supra note 3, paras 15-28 – 15-33. See also Chapter 9 below by Gaillard; and Emmanuel Gaillard (ed), *Anti-Suit Injunctions in International Arbitration* (Juris and Staempfli 2005).

arbitration only when the defendant objects to its jurisdiction over the dispute. This approach has been widely accepted. For example, in France, Article 1458 of the New Code of Civil Procedure, while providing that a national court shall decline jurisdiction over any dispute submitted in breach of an arbitration agreement, whether before or after the commencement of arbitral proceedings, also arguably prohibits the court from declining jurisdiction on its own motion.

8-29 Unlike in most jurisdictions, the court in China is required under Article 5 of the Arbitration Law 1995 not to accept an action initiated by a party to an arbitration agreement, unless the arbitration agreement is invalid. That is to say, the court shall decline jurisdiction over a matter covered by an arbitration agreement which is *prima facie* valid. In contrary, when the agreement is *prima facie* invalid, the court shall accept the case and look into the validity issue only upon the subsequent objection of its jurisdiction by the defendant.

4. Null and Void, Inoperative or Incapable of Being Performed

(a) Meaning of the Terms

8-30 A null or void agreement means that it was never entered into or where it was entered into but has subsequently been found to be void *ab initio*. The agreement will be inoperative where, for example, it has been repudiated or abandoned or it contains such an inherent contradiction that it cannot be given effect. The agreement will be incapable of being performed where, even if both the parties are ready, willing and able to do so, it can not be performed by them. Poverty of the proposed claimant will not render the agreement incapable of being performed, nor will inability of the party seeking the stay to satisfy any subsequent award.[13]

(b) Which Law to Decide "Null and Void, Inoperative or Incapable of Being Performed"?

8-31 There is a controversy as to which is the applicable law for deciding whether the arbitration agreement is "null and void, inoperative or incapable of being performed." Under Article V(1)(a) New York Convention, recognition or enforcement of an arbitral award may be refused if the opposing party can prove that the arbitration agreement is invalid under the law

---

[13] Russell on Arbitration, supra note 11, at 302; Lew Mistelis & Kröll, supra note 3, paras 14-40 – 14-48.

to which the parties have subjected it or, failing any indication thereon, under the law of the country where the award was made.

However the applicable law to the arbitration agreement was omitted from Article II(3) of the New York Convention and based on the convention history, the omission was deliberate. The drafters of the New York Convention had specifically rejected a proposal to include Article V's choice-of-law rule into Article II because they were "concerned that forum might then have an obligation to enforce arbitration clauses regardless of its 'local' law."[14]

8-32 The US Court of Appeals for the Third Circuit dealt with this very issue in *Rhone Mediterranee Compagnia Francese di Assicuazioni e Riassicurazioni v. Achille Lauro.*[15] In that case, an Italian casualty insurer as a subrogee challenged the arbitration of its dispute against an Italian vessel and vessel master in Italy, alleging that the arbitration clause calling for an even number of arbitrators is null and void under Italian law. The court analysed the convention history and concluded that in deciding whether the arbitration agreement is "null and void", the forum law, which is the US law, shall apply and that under the US law, such an arbitration clause is valid. The court also opined that the "null and void" exception should apply only in limited circumstances:

> (1) when [the agreement] is subject to an internationally recognized defense such as duress, mistake, fraud or waiver or (2) when [the agreement] contravenes fundamental policies of the forum state.

The court thus affirmed the order by the lower court staying the insurer's case pending arbitration in Italy.

(c) The Judicial Review of the Existence, Validity and Scope of the Arbitration Agreement

8-33 Under Article II(3) of the New York Convention, the court shall refer the parties to arbitration if the matter before the court falls into the scope of the arbitration agreement, unless the agreement is "null and void, inoperative or incapable of being performed." This provision, which has been widely adopted by national legislations, gives the court power to review the existence, validity and scope of the arbitration agreement.

---

[14] See G Haight, Convention on the Recognition and Enforcement of Foreign Arbitral Awards: Summary Analysis of Record of United Nations Conference, May/June 1958, pp 24-28 (1958).
[15] 712 F 2d 50.

8-34 There are two types of judicial review of the existence, validity and scope of the agreement, i.e. a full review, as in England before the English Arbitration Act 1996, in Sweden[16] and the United States[17] now, and a *prima facie* review, as in French and a number of other jurisdictions. The full review of the existence, validity and scope of the agreement may somehow contradict the doctrine of Kompetenz-Kompetenz, according to which arbitrators can rule on their own jurisdiction in the arbitral procedure.

8-35 In France, the court must decline jurisdiction unless the arbitration agreement is "patently void", which amounts to a *prima facie* review of the existence and validity of the arbitration agreement.[18] Under English Arbitration Act 1996, the court may determine any question as to the substantive jurisdiction of the tribunal upon application of a party to arbitral proceedings, if the application is made with the agreement in writing of all the parties or with the permission of the tribunal.

8-36 There seems to be a trend towards *prima facie* judicial review of the issue. Without the full review at this stage, the Kompetenz-Kompetenz doctrine can be served and the arbitrators may decide on its jurisdiction in the arbitral proceedings, preferably by a preliminary arbitral award, and a party's intent of exploiting court proceedings in order to obstruct the arbitration can be frustrated. The review of arbitration agreement can be centralized in the stages of setting aside or recognizing and enforcing an award, thus reducing the cost and saving the time for the arbitral procedure.

III. THE JUDICIAL ROLE IN THE COMPOSITION OF THE TRIBUNAL

8-37 Generally parties will designate in their arbitration agreement the mechanism under which the arbitrators are to be appointed, either by designing such a mechanism in explicit terms, as in most *ad hoc* arbitration clauses, or by referring to institutional rules, which always provide in details the procedure for the composition of the arbitral tribunal. The court normally will not intervene at this stage.

---

[16] Section 2(1) of the Arbitration Act 1999.
[17] See, e.g., *Comptek Telecomm, Inc v. IVD Corp*, No. 94-CV-0827 E(H), 1995 US Dist. LEXIS 11876 (WDNY Aug. 1, 1995), see also *Fouchard Gaillard Goldman*, supra note 4, at 409.
[18] See Fouchard Gaillard Goldman, supra note 4, at 407.

1. Equal Treatment Concern

8-38 In most jurisdictions, when the fundamental principles of fairness and due process are challenged at the stage of constituting the tribunal, the court's intervention can override the agreement of the parties. What should always be considered is parties' right to equal treatment, which has been expressly provided in Article 18 of the Model Law and the national laws of many jurisdictions. Some national laws, such as the Dutch law[19] and the German law[20], has gone even further to allow the court to appoint an arbitrator in deviation of an agreement that gives one party an advantage in appointing the arbitrator or arbitrators. In jurisdictions where such a principle is not clearly set forth, a party in the unfavourable position may request the court to safeguard the principle of equal treatment in appointing arbitrator or arbitrators. This problem, if not solved during the arbitral proceedings, may ruin the enforceability of the final award, as unequal treatment of the parties may be found as being contrary to the public policy.

2. Arbitration Agreement and Lex Fori Regarding the Composition of the Tribunal

8-39 Under Article V(1)(d) of the New York Convention, recognition and enforcement of a foreign arbitral award can be refused if the opposing party can furnish proof that

> the composition of the arbitral authority or the arbitral procedure was not in accordance with the agreement of the parties, or, failing such agreement, was not in accordance with the law of the country where the arbitration took place.

That is to say, the court in the recognition or enforcement proceedings will give priority to the parties' agreement, including those that make reference to institutional rules, as to the composition of the tribunal and the law of the place of arbitration, or *lex fori*, shall apply when such an agreement is not in existence.

8-40 In line with the provisions in the New York Convention, legislations in most jurisdictions provide that, subject to the due process check mentioned in V(1)(b), the composition of the arbitral tribunal is generally a matter of the agreement by the parties, and that the *lex fori* will play a subsidiary role unless

---

[19] See Article 1028 of the Netherlands Code of Civil Procedure.
[20] See Section 1034 of the ZPO.

the parties agree otherwise.[21] This is the case in England, Switzerland, the Netherlands, and all legal systems that have adopted the Model Law.

3. The Court's Role in the Constitution and Reconstitution of the Tribunal

8-41 In practice, there might be difficulties in the composition of the tribunal, such as when one party defaults in appointing the arbitrator on his side, or when the parties disagree on the appointment of the sole or presiding arbitrator. For a well-written *ad hoc* arbitration clause, as well as for the institutional rules, which are incorporated into the agreement by mere reference, an appointing authority is always designated, which shall step in and make appointment when there are difficulties. However, for a blank arbitration clause, which mentions nothing more than that the dispute is to be settled by way of arbitration in a certain place, there is obviously no such pre-agreed appointing authority to solve the difficulties. Can a court therefore provide assistance in such a situation? Further, can a court provide assistance when the designated appointing authority declines to or is unable to fulfil such a mandate?

8-42 Under the Model Law, and all statutes enacting it, parties are free to agree on how difficulties concerning the constitution or reconstitution of the tribunal are to be solved and the court usually provides the last resort as to the difficulties unless otherwise provided by the parties. Difficulties in the initial constitution of the tribunal include (1) when the two arbitrators fail to agree on the third arbitrator; (2) when the two parties are unable to agree on the sole arbitrator; (3) when a party fails to act as per the appointment procedure agreed by the parties; (4) when the parties, or two arbitrators, are unable to reach an agreement expected of them under an appointment procedure; (5) when the appointing authority fails to perform the appointment entrusted to it.[22] After the tribunal has been constituted, a substitute arbitrator shall be appointed following the termination of the mandate of an incumbent due to his death, his withdrawal from office, a successful challenge by a party, or revocation by the parties' agreement.[23] Similar difficulties might arise during the reconstitution of the tribunal. The court not only will assist in the reconstitution of the tribunal, but may also rule on the challenge or termination of the mandate.

---

[21] It should be noted that procedural rules contained in the *lex fori* governing the constitution of the arbitral tribunal is usually not mandatory, as the parties may exclude them in the arbitration agreement.

[22] See Article 11 of the Model Law.

[23] See Articles 12 through 15 of the Model Law.

8-43 Under French law, if a difficulty arises in the composition of the tribunal in an arbitration which either has its seat or its procedural law in France, the most diligent party may, in the absence of a clause to the contrary, apply to the President of the Tribunal de Grande Instance of Paris for assistance.[24]

8-44 In England, the court is empowered to appoint arbitrators if there is failure of appointment procedure (Section 18 of the English Arbitration Act 1996), to remove arbitrators (Section 24), to grant the resigned or removed arbitrator his entitlement to fees or expenses, if any (Section 25). In making appointment, the court shall have due regard to any agreement of the parties as to the qualifications required of the arbitrators.

8-45 In China, there is no statutory provision regarding judicial assistance during the composition of an arbitral tribunal. As *ad hoc* arbitration is prohibited under the Arbitration Law 1995, all arbitration in China is institutional and whatever gap left by an arbitration agreement can only be filled by institutional rules. The institution is not only the appointing authority when there is any difficulty, but also the decision-maker when an arbitrator's impartiality and independence is challenged. The court in China only reviews the composition of the tribunal and the behaviour of arbitrators after an award has been made, either in the recognition/enforcement proceedings or when a party applies for setting aside the award.

IV. THE JUDICIAL ROLE WITH REGARD TO INTERIM MEASURES OF PROTECTION

8-46 In international arbitration, parties sometimes seek interim measures of protection in order to facilitate the subsequent enforcement of the arbitral award, to facilitate the smooth conduct of the arbitration, or to preserve the *status quo* of the dispute and prevent the prejudicial effect upon the parties. Issues relating to court-ordered interim measures are to be discussed in this section.

---

[24] See Article 1493(2) of the French New Code of Civil Procedure.

1. Which Organ to Order Interim Measures, the Court or the Tribunal?

(a) Necessity of Court-Ordered Measures

8-47 Whether a court or a tribunal is empowered to order interim measures of protection is a matter of *lex arbitri*, as well as of the agreement between parties, so long as the *lex arbitri* allows such agreement.

8-48 It is generally understood that the tribunal, as the adjudicating authority with respect to the merits of the parties' claims, is in the best position to order interim measures of protection. However, not all the tribunals are empowered to order interim measures under national legislation or the rules the parties agree upon. And there exist several situations where interim measures cannot be sought from arbitral tribunals, the fact of which justifies the grant of power of ordering interim measures upon judicial organs.

8-49 Arbitration is of contractual nature. A clear disadvantage for this nature is that the tribunal lacks the coercive power and this also explains why the outcome of arbitration needs to be enforced through the court system when the parties do not automatically follow the result rendered. With regard to interim measures, it is also due to the lack of coercive power that parties prefer to seek measures directly from a court; even if a party applies to a tribunal for the granting of a measure in the first place, he will have to turn to a court for recognition and enforcement of the measure.

8-50 For example, before the tribunal is constituted or sometimes even before the initiation of arbitration, a party to an arbitration agreement might as a matter of urgency seek attachment of the other party's assets from a national court where the assets are located or where the other party is domiciled. Even after the constitution of the tribunal, there might be such a need where a party wants to seek recourse to a court for interim measures.

8-51 Also due to the tribunal's lack of coercive power, awards or orders issued by the tribunal are generally binding only upon the immediate parties to the arbitration, or in other words, parties to the arbitration agreement. It is conceivable that an order issued by the tribunal that directs a third party to act, for example, an order that the shipper release perishable goods to the buyer in an arbitration between the buyer and the seller, is hardly binding upon that third party. In those circumstances, the party seeking the measure will opt to submit the application to the court, whose order generally binds third parties.

8-52 Even in those jurisdictions where access to both the tribunal and the court for interim measures is available, parties are more willing to choose the court for reasons of speed and immediate enforceability as they are aware of the fact that they most probably need to rely on the court for enforcement of the tribunal-ordered measures in the end.

(b) Three Approaches

8-53 Several different approaches exist as to whether the tribunal or the court is empowered to order interim measures of protection.[25] Briefly these fall into the following three categories:

- where the power is exclusively reserved to the court, as in Argentina,[26] Italy[27] and Austria[28] and China;[29]
- where it is reserved to the arbitral tribunal once it has been constituted, as in parts of the US;
- where both the arbitral tribunal and the court have such powers.[30]

8-54 In most jurisdictions, parties are allowed to apply for interim measures of protection to either the tribunal or the court, though the court will be the only body where one can apply for interim relief before the constitution of the arbitral tribunal. The tribunal and the court are said to have concurrent powers.[31] In those where the powers are divided between the court and the tribunal according to the stages at which a measure is sought (that is, the court is empowered to grant measures only prior to the constitution of the tribunal, after which the tribunal will take full charge of like matters), the tribunal and the court are said to have consecutive powers.[32]

8-55 The Model Law avails parties of access to both tribunals and courts in seeking interim relief. On the one hand, Article 9 of the Model Law provides that

---

[25] See generally Chapter 9 below, by Yesilirmak.

[26] William Wang, "International Arbitration: The Need for Uniform Interim Measures of Relief", 28 *Brooklyn J Int'l L* 1059 (2003) at 1092. See also Argentine National Code of Civil and Commercial Procedure.

[27] *Ibid.* See also Italian Code of Civil Procedure Article 818.

[28] See article 578-599 of the Austrian Code of Civil Procedure. [But note that the Austrian Law has undergone revision in late 2005].

[29] See article 28 of the Arbitration Law of the PRC.

[30] See UNCITRAL Preparation of uniform provisions on interim measures of protection: Note by Secretariat, A/CN.9/WG.II/WP.119, paragraph 20.

[31] *Ibid*, paragraph 25. See also Chapter 9 below.

[32] *Ibid*, paragraph 27.

[i]t is not incompatible with an arbitration agreement for a party to request, before or during arbitral proceedings, from a court an interim measure of protection and for a court to grant such measure.

On the other hand, Article 17 of the Model Law reads:

[u]nless otherwise agreed by the parties, the arbitral tribunal may, at the request of a party, order any party to take such interim measure of protection as the arbitral tribunal may consider necessary in respect of the subject-matter of the dispute.

8-56 In those jurisdictions that have adopted the Model Law or shaped their arbitration statute after it, parties enjoy a high level of autonomy in terms of seeking interim measures. They can choose freely to seek measures from the court or from the tribunal, whichever fits their respective needs and considerations. Under such a regime, the parties may also decide by agreement from which authority to seek interim measures and there is no risk such agreement be overridden by the statute.

8-57 In Switzerland, under the Private International Law Act of 1987, the arbitrators and the court both have power to order provisional or conservatory measures. According to Article 183 of the Act,

Unless the parties have agreed otherwise, the arbitral tribunal may, at the request of a party, order provisional or conservatory measures. If the party so ordered does not comply voluntarily, the arbitral tribunal may request the assistance of the court. Such court shall apply its own law. The arbitral tribunal or the court may make the granting of provisional or conservatory measures subject to appropriate sureties."

8-58 There are also jurisdictions, most notably England, in which the law accords to both tribunals and courts the powers to order interim measures of protection, with the court as the forum of last resort. [33] According to Section 44(1) of the English Arbitration Act 1996,

---

[33] Schaefer calls this approach "the court subsidiarity model." See Jan K Schaefer, "New Solutions for Interim Measures of Protection in International Commercial Arbitration: English, German, and Hong Kong Law Compared", at http://www.ejcl.org/22/art2-2.doc or 2.2 *Electronic J Comp L* (1998). See also William Wang, International Arbitration: The Need for Uniform Interim Measures of Relief, 28 *Brooklyn J Int'l L* 1059 (2003) at 1085.

[u]nless otherwise agreed by the parties, the court has for the purposes of and in relation to arbitral proceedings the same power of making orders about the matters listed below as it has for the purposes of and in relation to legal proceedings...

However, the court may "make orders as it thinks necessary for the purpose of preserving evidence or assets" only in case of urgency, otherwise

the court shall act only on the application of a party to the arbitral proceedings made with the permission of the tribunal or the agreement in writing of the other parties.[34]

Section 44(5) provides that

[i]n any case the court shall act only if or to the extent that the arbitral tribunal and any arbitral or other institution or person vested by the parties with power in that regard, has no power or is unable for the time being to act effectively.

8-59 In France, the arbitration part of the Code of Civil Procedure does not refer to interim measures. Nevertheless, the general power given to the courts to grant interim measures on an urgent basis, without prejudicing the subsequent decision on the merits, clearly extends to disputes which are the subject of arbitration as well as those before the courts. The court may make summary orders for interim measures in aid of arbitration even after the tribunal has been constituted. Moreover, French courts have required very explicit language to constitute waiver of the right to seek interim measures from a court in regards to a dispute subject to international arbitration.[35]

8-60 In China, the court is entrusted with the exclusive power to order interim measures of protection in the context of arbitration.[36] However, under the Arbitration Law 1995 and the Civil Procedure Law 1991, the application for the measure has to be at the first place submitted to the arbitration commission, which will then direct it to the court. It is not clearly set forth in the statutes whether the arbitration commission, in so directing the application, may exercise any power of *prima facie* scrutiny of the measure, although arbitration

---

[34] English Arbitration Act 1996, Section 44 (3) and (4).

[35] See W Laurence Craig, Willian W Park and Jan Paulsson, *International Chamber of Commerce Arbitration* (3rd edition, Oceana and ICC Publishing, 2000), at 475, 476.

[36] The two main types of interim measures are property preservation and evidence preservation. In the context of maritime arbitration, there is also maritime injunction.

institutions in China never scrutinize any measure in practice. The good point for this practice is that the arbitration commission and the tribunal are free from any doubt of procedural irregularity, or violation of due process, or any doubt as to its independence and impartiality, with regard to interim measures. The court generally orders or rejects the measure without a hearing, or even without a prior notice to the party against whom the measure is sought. Whether the *ex parte* measure so ordered is in violation of the due process doctrine is questionable. Indeed opinions as to the admission to an *ex parte* measure are highly divided. However by not hearing the parties' arguments on the measure, the court at least avoids looking into factors such as probability of the moving party's prevailing on the merits of the dispute, and thus avoids pre-judging the merits.

2. Whether Ordering Interim Measures is in Violation of the Agreement to Arbitrate?

8-61 In most jurisdictions, granting interim measures by the court is not deemed as a violation of the obligation under the New York Convention, nor is seeking a measure incompatible to the agreement to arbitrate on the part of the moving party. For example, Article 9 of the Model Law clearly provides that

> it is not incompatible with an arbitration agreement for a party to request, before or during arbitral proceedings, from a court an interim measure of protection and for a court to grant such measure.

8-62 The only major jurisdiction that holds a somehow different opinion on this issue is the United States, where courts are divided as to whether such interim measures[37] may be granted in an international commercial arbitration setting[38]. Some courts deny requests for interim measures such as pre-award attachments on the ground that such remedies are contrary to the parties' agreement to arbitrate, and thus to the New York Convention. Other courts avail the parties of pre-award attachments as a type of preliminary remedy.

---

[37] US law permits American courts to bar the removal of assets from a jurisdiction through the use of temporary injunctions and orders for pre-judgment attachment. See Fed R Civ P 64, 65. Many states have similar provisions. See, e.g. NY Civ. Prac. L. & R. 6201 (McKinney 1980)

[38] Unlike the courts' division concerning interim measures for international arbitration, there is uniform practice for domestic arbitrations. See Section 8 FAA and *Murray Oil Products Co v. Mitsui & Co Ltd* 146 F 2d 381 (2d Cir 1944).

8-63 Neither Federal Rule of Civil Procedure 64 (which deals with seizure of person or property, including attachment)[39] nor Rule 65 (which governs injunctions), contain explicit reference to attachment in international commercial settings. It was precisely the lack of explicit provisions as to the interim measures in support of international commercial arbitration in the rules, statutes, as well as the conventions that the United States has been acceded, that brought up uncertainty and division among the U.S. judiciary.

8-64 The leading case that shows the unfavourable judicial attitude towards granting interim measures supporting international commercial arbitration is *McCreary Tire & Rubber Co. v. CEAT S.p.A.*[40] The leading case on the opposite side is *Carolina Power & Light Co. v. Uranex.*[41]

3. Judicial Enforcement of Interim Measures in Support of International Commercial Arbitration

(a) Enforcement of Tribunal-Ordered Measures

i. Form of the measures (interim award or procedural order?)

8-65 An interim measure ordered by the tribunal may take the form of either an interim award or a procedural order. Whether a measure is established in the form of an interim award or anything else is a matter of discretion on the part of the tribunal. However the tribunal's choice about the form of the measure, or the word the tribunal chooses to title its order, has significant implications on the enforcement of the measure by the court.

8-66 When an interim measure ordered by a tribunal is to be enforced in a court of the seat of arbitration, it is the *lex arbitri* that governs the recognition and enforcement, regardless whether the measure is in the form of an interim award or most often, an order. In such enforcement proceedings, an interim award might receive more reverence than a procedural order.

---

[39] The remedies available under Rule 64 include "arrest, attachment, garnishment, replevin, sequestration, and other corresponding or equivalent remedies."
[40] 501 F 2d 1032 (3d Cir 1974).
[41] 451 F Supp 1044 (ND Cal 1977).

8-67 Whether an interim award containing an interim measure that has been rendered outside a jurisdiction can be enforced by a national judicial authority of that jurisdiction under the New York Convention is a matter of interpretation of the New York Convention. The New York Convention defines the term "arbitral award" as

> not only awards in the State made by arbitrators appointed for each case but also those made by permanent arbitral bodies to which the parties have submitted.[42]

It says nothing about whether the "award" therein refers only to final awards (or at least partial awards) on the merits of disputes, or it may also include both final awards and procedural orders which tribunals employ so frequently during the arbitral process.

8-68 Legal systems take abruptly different attitudes as to the interpretation. Some jurisdictions interpret the "arbitral award" as only those that deal with all or part of the substances of a dispute. An interim measure even in the form of an interim award will not fall into that category and thus a national court is not obligated to enforce it under the New York Convention.[43] Some jurisdictions treat an interim award that addresses an interim measure as an award enforceable under the New York Convention. Some go even further to regard a procedural order that contains an interim measure as an award enforceable under the said convention.[44]

---

[42] Article I(2) of the New York Convention.

[43] For an illustration of this attitude, see *Resort Condominiums International Inc v. Ray Bolwell and Resort Condominiums Pty Ltd*, 9(4) Mealey's IAR A1 (1994) XX YBCA 628 (1995) (Supreme Court Queensland, 29 October 1993);, see also Craig, Park and Paulsson, supra note 37. In that case, the Supreme Court of Queensland, Australia denied the enforcement of an arbitral award rendered in the US in order to preserve the *status quo* between a US licensor and an Australian licensee during the pendency of the arbitration. The award ordered the licensee not to enter into any competing arrangements and to require the deposit into an escrow account of all revenues received as a consequence of the license agreement. Justice Lee concluded in that case that the award was clearly of an interlocutory and procedural nature and did not finally put an end to any arbitral dispute or to establish the legal rights of the parties. According to the decision, the award was not enforceable under the New York Convention.

[44] This is illustrated in *Sperry International Trade v. Government of Israel*, 532 F Supp 901 (SDNY 1982). In an arbitration between a US company as the claimant and the Government of Israel as the respondent, the tribunal issued an interim award requiring Israel to pay the proceeds of a letter of credit into an escrow account in the joint names of the two parties, and the following language are contained in the text of the award,

> This order shall constitute an Award of the arbitrators and either party is at liberty to apply forthwith to the United States District Court for the Southern District of New York for confirmation and/or enforcement thereof.

8-69 In an era where arbitration has grown into the major mechanism for resolving private international disputes and where most jurisdictions consider as a strong public policy the use of arbitration for settling disputes, a more flexible interpretation in favour of promoting arbitration is bound to provide the commercial community with more benefits. Given the difficulty of putting into force a new convention replacing the New York Convention or even of modifying the New York Convention, it is advisable to explore ways to grant wider meaning to the terms used in the New York Convention.[45] It is also helpful to harmonize, as being done by the UNCITRAL Working Group, the legal provisions of different jurisdictions to achieve a similar result by adjusting the existing statutes.

ii. Enforcement of tribunal-ordered interim measures by national courts

8-70 In most jurisdictions, there exists no statutory provision with regard to the enforcement by courts of tribunal-ordered measures. Even the Model Law provides nothing as to whether a national court shall enforce an interim measure rendered by a tribunal within or without its jurisdiction, except that Article 27[46] stipulates a court's power in assisting the tribunal in taking evidence. Given that courts are empowered for intervention and assistance in arbitral proceedings only in those circumstances as expressly provided in the Model Law, there are clouds over the justification of court enforcement of tribunal-ordered measures in those nations that have adopted the Model Law.

8-71 After the Model Law has been put into force for almost 20 years, experts are now trying to strengthen the use of interim measures through making amendments to the Model Law. Part of the efforts are targeted at granting tribunals extensive power in ordering a variety of measures and correspondingly, another part of the efforts are to secure courts' enforcement of tribunal-ordered measures, without which measures ordered by tribunals could be abortive.

The award was found to be a final, albeit partial, award and was enforced under the New York Convention.

[45] There were new interpretations as to the meaning of "agreement in writing", for example.

[46] Article 27 of Model Law provides that

The arbitral tribunal or a party with the approval of the arbitral tribunal may request from a competent court of this State assistance in taking evidence. The court may execute the request within its competence and according to its rules on taking evidence.

(b) Enforcement Of Court-Ordered Measures by the Court of Another Jurisdiction

8-72 As the significance and necessity of court-ordered interim measures are widely recognized, enforcement of these measures is also part of the picture about enforcement of interim measures of protection in the context of international commercial arbitration. The court that grants a measure in aid of arbitration is not necessarily the appropriate forum for the enforcement of the measure. And if the enforcement of the measure is sought in another jurisdiction, it should be statutorily justified.

8-73 A judicial order in favour of arbitration cannot be as easily enforced as an arbitral award due to the lack of a universal convention like New York Convention. However it is still enforceable under some other mechanisms, such as the EC (Brussels) Regulation 44/2001 that existed within the European Union. A foreign judicial order granting an interim measure can however be enforced under the principle of reciprocity or international comity even without any convention or treaty. Under all the regimes stated above, the enforcement court will have to examine the measure and will refuse enforcement when there is violation of due process or violation of public policy of the enforcement forum. Although the standard for enforcement varies, it is correct to say that a standard that is stricter than that of enforcement of arbitral awards is imposed.

V. COURT REVIEW OF ARBITRAL AWARDS

1. Two Types of Review and Applicable Laws

8-74 After an international arbitral award is made, it is widely enforceable under international conventions. However the universal enforceability will not be conceivable if the court cannot exert any review upon the content of the award and the procedural context in which the award had been made.

8-75 The court review takes place either at the seat of the arbitration (or the country under the law of which the award was made) where the losing party requests the court to set aside the award, or in certain places where the recognition or enforcement of the award is sought.

8-76 The law to be applied in the setting aside proceedings is the *lex arbitri*, which is either the law of the seat of the arbitration, or the law under which the award was made. The law applicable to the recognition or enforcement proceedings is that of the country where the recognition or enforcement is sought, including international conventions of which that country is a member, as those conventions has been incorporated into the national legal system of the member country. As has been mentioned in the preceding parts of this Chapter, when deciding certain issues during these proceedings, the applicable law will lead the court to adopt a different law. For example, the court may apply the law of the parties' choice as to the validity of the arbitration agreement.

2. Grounds for Refusing Recognition and Enforcement and Grounds for Setting Aside

8-77 For international arbitral awards, the judicial authorities in the member states of the New York Convention may only refuse the recognition or enforcement upon grounds expressly provided in Article V of the New York Convention. The list of grounds is exhaustive and excludes any revision of the merits of the award. Though the court may take a more liberal stance so as to decline the request for refusal even when certain grounds exist, it cannot deny recognition or enforcement on a ground other than those listed in Article V.

8-78 The New York Convention makes a distinction between two types of grounds on which recognition and enforcement may be refused: those that must be raised by the opposing party and those that can be raised by the court.

8-79 The grounds that must be raised by the party opposing recognition or enforcement are set forth in Article V(1) and include: (a) the existence of an invalid arbitration agreement; (b) breach of due process; (c) the award fails to comply with the terms of the arbitration agreement; (d) irregularities affecting the composition of the tribunal or the arbitral proceedings and (e) the award has not become binding, or has been suspended or set aside.

8-80 The grounds that may be raised by the court on its own motion are set forth in Article V(2) and include: (a) the non-arbitrability of the subject-matter and (b) the recognition and enforcement will be contrary to the public policy.

8-81 The grounds on which an international arbitral awards may be set aside or annulled are generally the same as the grounds for refusing recognition or enforcement contained in the New York Convention. This is true under the Model Law, as well as national legislations adopting it. Article 36 of the Model Law, which provides the grounds for setting aside arbitral awards, mirrors the grounds for refusing recognition or enforcement listed in Article V of the New York Convention.

3. Delocalized Awards

8-82 In the past twenty years, there is a new trend in national legislations towards "delocalisation" or "denationalisation" of international commercial arbitration. In Belgium, a law dated March 27, 1985 introduced a new Article 1717 into the Judicial Code, providing that:

> The Belgian courts can only hear an action to set an award aside if at least one of the parties to the dispute decided by the arbitral award is either an individual having Belgian nationality or residence, or a legal entity constituted in Belgium or having a subsidiary or other establishment in Belgium.

8-83 In 1987, the Swiss legislature introduced a similar, but less radical, provision in Article 192 of the Swiss Private International Law Statute, according to which

> where none of the parties has its domicile, its habitual residence, or a business establishment in Switzerland, they may, by an express statement in the setting aside proceedings, or they may also limit such proceedings to one or several of the grounds [on which an award can be set aside] listed in Article 190, paragraph 2.

8-84 Unlike the above-mentioned Belgian law, the Swiss law gives the parties option to exclude one or all grounds for setting aside only when they expressly agreed to do so. This principle was followed in the Tunisian Arbitration Code 1993 (Article 78(6)) and the Swedish Arbitration Act 1999[47]. The Belgian law of May 19, 1998[48] also stepped backwards and adopted the less radical approach.[49]

---

[47] Section 51 of the Swedish Arbitration Act 1999 provides, *inter alia*, that

> where none of the parties is domiciled or has its place of business in Sweden, such parties may in commercial relationship through an express written agreement exclude or limit the application of the grounds for setting aside an award…An award which is subject to such an agreement shall be recognized and enforced in Sweden in accordance with the rules applicable to a foreign award.

[48] The new provision indicates that

> the parties may, by an explicit declaration in the arbitration agreement or by a later agreement, exclude any application for the setting aside of an arbitral award, in case none

8-85 The "delocalisation" trend reflects that the courts in those states are willing to lax the standard of review of arbitral awards and give the parties more autonomy in designing the arbitral procedure. Sometimes the parties choose the arbitration seat for geographical convenience, not because they want the arbitral procedure to be subject to the law of the place of arbitration and this is especially true if the parties have no physical or legal connection with the seat. In those cases, it would be out of the parties' intention if the local court exerts any judicial intervention to the arbitral procedure. Hopefully the example set up by the above legislations will be followed elsewhere in the world.

8-86 There is argument that a delocalised arbitral award can be enforced under the New York Convention. Most scholars agree that the New York Convention does not in its text exclude delocalised awards from its scope. The Convention awards are those binding foreign awards, subject to reciprocity. It would unquestionably be adding to the text of the New York Convention to consider that it applies only to foreign awards that may be the object of an action to set them aside in the sear of arbitration. At least in Sweden, a delocalised award can be "recognized and enforced in accordance with the rules applicable to a foreign award."[50]

4. Enforcement Despite the Existence of a Ground for Refusal

8-87 In recent years, another new trend has been developed by judiciaries in several countries, whereby a foreign arbitral award is enforceable even if the opposing party successfully establishes a ground contained in Article V of the New York Convention, usually the existence of procedural irregularity or the setting aside of the award at the seat of arbitration. A court order enforcing an award despite the existence of such a ground is not contradictory to the international obligation under the New York Convention, as Article V of the New York Convention only laid down the grounds upon which recognition and enforcement of a foreign award "*may*" be refused. That is to say, the court can in its own discretion decide whether to grant enforcement or not. The new trend reflects the pro- enforcement judicial attitude, which in turn is helpful for the development of international commercial arbitration.

---

of them is a physical person of Belgian nationality or a physical person having his normal residence in Belgium or a legal person having its main seat or a branch office in Belgium.

[49] See Fouchard Gaillard Goldman, supra note 4, at 910-912.

[50] See supra note 47.

(a) Enforcement of an Award in Spite of its Being Set Aside

8-88 After an award has been set aside in the state where the arbitration took place, can it nevertheless be recognized and enforced in another state? It has been argued the setting aside of an award eliminates only its enforceability in the same state, not its existence and further, its enforceability elsewhere. This argument has been recognised in some jurisdictions.

8-89 The French court in *Pabalk v. Norsolor*[51] held that the New York Convention merely represent the minimum recognition of awards that the contracting States undertake to provide, and that they do not prevent the recognition and enforcement in France of an award which has been set aside at the seat of the arbitration. The approach was unequivocally confirmed by the Cour de cassation in its 1994 *Hilmarton* decision, whereby it was held that the award, which has been set aside in Switzerland

> was an international award which [was] not integrated in the legal system of that State, so that it remains in existence even if set aside and its recognition in France [was] not contrary to international public policy.[52]

Also the recognition in the French legal order of an award set aside outside France obviously prevents the recognition or enforcement in France of a second award made after the setting aside of the first award at the seat of arbitration, The French Cour de cassation clarified this point in its June 10, 1997 decision in the *Hilmarton* matter.[53]

(b) Enforcement Despite Procedural Irregularities

8-90 The arbitral procedure is conducted in accordance with the parties' agreement and the procedural law of the arbitration. Generally if the procedure is not in compliance with the agreement or the procedural law, the award subsequently rendered may be set aside or its recognition or enforcement be refused. But will the award be doomed upon any, even minor, alleged non-compliance?

---

[51] *Société Norsolor v. Société Pabalk Ticaret Sirketi*, 108 Clunet 836 (1981).

[52] Cour de cassation, 23 March 1994, *Société Hilmarton Ltd v. Société Omnium de traitement et de valorisation (OTV)*, XX YBCA 663 (1995), 121 Clunet 701 (1994), Rev Arb 327 (1994), see also *Fouchard Gaillard Goldman*, supra note 4, at 914, 915

[53] *Ibid*; see also Lew, Mistelis, Kröll, supra note 3, paras 26-106 – 26-110.

8-91 In some jurisdictions, it has been observed that if the arbitral award could not have been difficult had the procedural irregularity not occurred, the court is willing to enforce the award.

8-92 The Hong Kong Court of Appeal upheld this principle in *Apex Tech Investment Limited v. Chuang's Development (China) Limited*[54], the subsequent enforcement proceedings of a CIETAC arbitral award on a dispute between the purchaser and the vendor of a block of flats in China. In that case, the defendant contended that there was a procedural irregularity, as the tribunal had made inquiries to a land use authority in China and relied on the result of the inquiries in reaching its conclusion, but unfortunately, the tribunal did not give the defendant any notice of inquiries and any opportunity to make further submissions. On that the judge of the court of first instance agreed. But after having examined the materials put forward by the defendant which it submitted would have been available to put before the tribunal, he came to the conclusion that the result of the arbitration could not have been different even if the opportunity to be heard had been granted. The judge then exercised his discretion to order enforcement in spite of his finding of a procedural irregularity under section 44(2) of Hong Kong Arbitration Ordinance, which is identical to Article V of the New York Convention. The judges of the Court of Appeal agreed on the principle articulated in the lower court's ruling, although they reversed the ruling based on a conclusion that the outcome of the arbitration could have been different had the defendant been given opportunity to make further submissions.

VI. CONCLUSION

8-93 Although party autonomy has been widely recognised as the underlying principle for international commercial arbitration, procedural rules contained in the *lex arbitri* (which is *lex fori* in most circumstances) and court assistance and intervention are still indispensable in the success of an international arbitration procedure. The roles of the *lex fori* and the court have been examined in this Chapter.

8-94 This Chapter only focuses its discussion of the roles of the court and *lex fori* in the four most noticeable areas, namely the arbitration agreement, the constitution of arbitral tribunal, the interim measures of protection and the award. However the court may also have power in other aspects, such as in extending

---

[54] Court of Appeal, Civil Appeal No. 231 of 1995.

time limits for commencing the arbitral proceedings and for making the award, in determining points of law and in determining the recoverable costs of the arbitration in some given jurisdictions. These powers vary according to national laws.[55]

8-95 So far, there is no sign of diminishing judicial role in assisting international commercial arbitration, although in some jurisdictions, the court tends to lax its intervention upon the arbitral process. The recent arbitration legislations and court decisions in most jurisdictions all indicate a trend in growing favour of international commercial arbitration.

---

[55] See generally Lew, Mistelis, Kröll, supra note 3, Chapter 15.

Ali Yesilirmak[*]

CHAPTER 9

PROVISIONAL MEASURES

I. INTRODUCTION

9-1 In the beginning of the 20th century, businesspersons in international trade started to frequently use arbitration as a dispute resolution mechanism for protection of their rights. The reasons for the use of arbitration in those days were essentially the same as the reasons why businesspersons choose to arbitrate today: neutrality, expertise, flexibility, speed, cost.[1] The main aim for the use of arbitration, however, is the final protection of rights. This aim originated with the Arbitration Plan agreed upon between the *Bolsa de Commercio* of Buenos Aires and the United States Chamber of Commerce in 1915 ("1915 Plan").[2] This Arbitration Plan was the origin of many arbitration rules adopted by several local chambers within the US.[3] The 1915 Plan also affected arbitration plans entered into between the US Chamber of Commerce and trade institutions in Brazil, Ecuador, Panama, Paraguay, Uruguay, Venezuela, and Columbia.[4] Further, this Plan, to a great extent, adopted by the International Chamber of Commerce

---

[*] LLB, LLM, PhD, Visiting Professor, Yeditepe University Faculty of Law, and Attorney-at-Law, Istanbul.
[1] Obviously, there are some other reasons that prompt contracting parties to arbitrate. On these reasons, see Martin Domke, *Commercial Arbitration* (Prentice-Hall 1965); Pieter Sanders, *Quo Vadis Arbitration? – Sixty Years of Arbitration Practice* (Kluwer Law International 1999), 2-9.
[2] For the text of the 1915 Plan, see American Arbitration Association ("AAA"), *Year Book on Commercial Arbitration in the United States* (Oxford University Press 1927), 823. On the Plan, see also Horacio Grigera Naón, "Latin American Arbitration Culture and the ICC Arbitration System" in Stefan Frommel / Barry Rider (eds), *Conflicting Legal Cultures in Commercial Arbitration – Old Issues and New Trends* (Kluwer Law International 1999), 117.
[3] AAA, *ibid*, at 824.
[4] *Ibid.*

Loukas A. Mistelis and Julian D.M. Lew (eds), Pervasive Problems in International Arbitration, 185-200
© *2006 Kluwer Law International. Printed in the Netherlands*

Arbitration Rules 1923 ("1923 Rules").[5] These Rules in turn influenced directly or indirectly many national and international legislative bodies.

9-2 The 1915 Plan and 1923 Rules dealt with many aspects of arbitration procedure. One of these aspects was related to provisional measures[6] aimed at interim protection of arbitrating parties' rights pending final resolution of their dispute. Such protection was thought to be as important as the final protection sought in arbitration. This was probably for the simple reason that final protection of a right would be meaningless without the availability of interim protection of that right in appropriate circumstances. Despite the growth in importance of provisional measures in the last 90 years,[7] the problems relating to such measures have not been completely resolved. Indeed, a Working Group attached to the United Nations Commission on International Trade Law ("UNCITRAL") is currently undertaking a study of most of such problems.[8] The main problem is related to the selection of forum to obtain provisional measures: an arbitral tribunal or a court? In today's world, court assistance to arbitration is still necessary for enhancing effectiveness of arbitration and better distribution of justice.[9] Nonetheless, the arbitral tribunal should be the "natural forum" for

---

[5] Ali Yesilirmak, *Provisional Measures in International Commercial Arbitration* (Kluwer Law International 2005), paras 2-10 – 2-14.

[6] This term is used to refer to all relieves, measures, or remedies aimed to protect arbitrating parties' rights on an interim basis. For the types of provisional measures commonly seen in arbitration, see note 30 below and accompanying text.

[7] On the growth of the importance, see Yesilirmak, supra note 5, paras 1-17 – 1-21.

[8] See, e.g., UN Doc A/53/17, and A/CN.9/WG.II/WP.108. UNCITRAL's work deals with arbitral provisional measures, enforcement of such measures, and judicial provisional measures.

[9] See, generally, Yesilirmak, supra note 5, paras 3-20 – 3-24. However, some laws provide for exclusive judicial powers for interim protection of rights. See, e.g., Argentina, Article 753 of the National Code of Civil and Commercial Procedure 1982; Brazil, see Matthew Heaphy, "The Intricacies of Commercial Arbitration in the United States and Brazil: A Comparison of Two National Arbitration Statute", 37 *USFL Rev* 441, 455 (2003); China, Articles 28 and 46 of the Arbitration Law; Czech Republic, Section 22 of the Law on Arbitral Proceedings and Enforcement of Arbitral Awards 1994; El Salvador, Hans Smit/Vratislav Pechota, *The World Arbitration Reporter* (Juris Publishing 2003), 1558; Finland, Section 5(2) of the AA 1992; Italy, Article 818 of the CCP 1990; Libya, Article 758 of the CCP; Liechtenstein, Article 605 of the CCP; Malaysia, J. Stewart McClendon (ed), *Survey of International Arbitration Sites,* (3rd ed., AAA 1993), 73); Oman, Smit/Pechota, 2205; Panama, Article 1444 of the Judicial Code 1988; and Quebec, Article 940(4) of the Arbitration Law. In contrast, for instance, in accordance with Article 26 of the International Convention for Settlement of Investment Disputes ("ICSID"), and Article 39(5) of the ICSID Arbitration Rules, unless parties agree otherwise, the rule of exclusive remedy is adopted. As the issue of court's role for interim protection of rights is dealt with in Chapter 8 by Shengchang/Lijun above, this chapter refrains from examining this issue.

acquiring final as well as provisional remedies.[10] This view supported by most national laws, arbitration rules, and scholarly opinions essentially arises from contracting parties' choice of arbitration as a dispute resolution mechanism.[11]

9-3   However, there are three salient problems concerning the arbitral power to grant provisional measures.[12]

- *First*, the arbitral tribunal's power extends, in principle, only to parties. Since such power essentially derives from the arbitration agreement, the extension of this power to third parties would be out of question.[13]
- *Second*, prior to the formation of the tribunal, no interim protection is available from the tribunal as it has yet to come into power. This problem is resolved by the availability of such emergency measure rules as pre-arbitral referee rules, which complement arbitration concerning interim protection of rights ("complementary mechanisms").[14]
- *Third*, the tribunal does not have coercive powers to enforce measures it grants on an interim basis.[15] This problem is resolved by lending the authority of state courts to arbitration for enforcement.[16]

9-4   Further, the predictability as to the standards of procedure and principles for arbitrators' power to grant provisional measures is fairly low.

9-5   The aim of this Chapter is to briefly examine: (1) the essential issues and problems concerning the sources and standards of principles and procedure for the grant of arbitral provisional measures, (2) the complementary mechanisms, and (3) the enforcement of such measures.

II. Arbitral Provisional Measures

9-6   This section deals with: (1) power of arbitrators, and (2) standards of principles and procedures for granting provisional measures.

Further, for the draft article 17 ter (to the UNCITRAL Model Law) prepared by the UNCITRAL Working Group, see UNCITRAL Doc A/CN.9/WG.II/WP.125, para. 42.

[10]   See, e.g., Catherine Kessedjian, "Court Decisions on Enforcement of Arbitration Agreements and Awards", 18(1) *J Int'l Arb* 1, 7 (2001); and Yesilirmak, supra note 5, para 3-3.

[11]   See, generally, Yesilirmak, supra note 5, paras 3-5 et seq.

[12]   For full account of the problems, see, e.g., *ibid*, para. 3-24.

[13]   But see, e.g., *ibid*, Chapter 3, notes 90-93 and accompanying text.

[14]   On which, see section III below.

[15]   On which see, para 9-35 below.

[16]   On which see, para. 9-39 below.

1. Jurisdiction of Arbitrators

9-7   One of the main problems concerning provisional measures relates to the power of an arbitral tribunal to grant provisional measures. This problem has, to a great extent, been resolved in the last twenty years in favour of the arbitral tribunal having the power to grant interim protection of rights.[17] There are several reasons that have assisted in resolution of the above problem, such as[18]

- Utmost respect for contracting parties' choice of arbitration;
- Non-interference with risk allocation concerning the avoidance of foreign laws and/or court practices;
- Avoidance of the use of the process for interim protection as dilatory tactic or offensive weapon by arbitrators;
- Less disruptive effect of arbitral provisional measures on arbitrating parties' commercial relationship than litigation;
- Confidentiality in arbitration;
- Arbitrators' flexibility in crafting the most appropriate provisional measure in arbitration; and
- Often involvement of less costs in arbitration than litigation for interim protection of rights.

9-8   The most common source of an arbitral tribunal's power to grant interim protection is found in the arbitration agreement,[19] generally through incorporation of arbitration institutional rules.[20] In cases where such rules are silent, however, national laws generally provide for default powers in that respect.[21] Further, if needed, implied, inherent or other powers of arbitrators may be used for the interim protection.[22]

2. Standards, Principles and Procedure

9-9   In general, standards and principles for the granting of provisional measures are not indicated in arbitration rules and laws. I suggest that there are three

---

[17]   Indeed, in more recent arbitration statutes, their approaches to such power change from negative or neutral to positive. See Yesilirmak, *supra* note 5, Chapters 3, 5, and Annex.

[18]   See, *e.g.*, *ibid.*, para. 3-5.

[19]   *Ibid.*, para. 3-8.

[20]   See, *e.g.*, Article 23 ICC Rules, Article 26 UNCITRAL Rules. See also Yesilirmak, *ibid*, Annex.

[21]   See, *e.g.*, Article 17 Model Law. However, laws of some states do not provide for default powers. See English Arbitration Act 1996. On the issue of judicial powers to grant provisional measures in assistance to arbitration, see also Yesilirmak, *supra* note 5, at paras 3-8 – 3-9.

[22]   See, e.g., Yesilirmak, *supra* note 5, at paras 3-10 – 3-12.

reasons behind the lack of elaborate regulation. The *first* reason is to enable the arbitrators to craft the most appropriate measure for the case, the subject matter in dispute, and the parties before them. The *second* reason is that this area of arbitration law has been in the process of great flux and development. The *final* reason is related to individuality of arbitration. Each arbitration is and should be considered distinct from another.[23] This arises from one of the benefits of arbitration: it can be tailor-made to dispute and parties. Thus, it had been left to the discretion of arbitral tribunals to be flexible in order to craft the most appropriate standards for the dispute and parties before them.

9-10 The standards and principles for the granting of provisional measures are important to determine as they assist in the effectiveness of the arbitration process by making it consistent and predictable.[24] The consistency and predictability along with flexibility make arbitration a more effective dispute resolution mechanism.

9-11 As to such standards and principles, arbitration laws and rules generally give broad discretion to arbitrators.[25] In using this discretion, the arbitrators rarely apply or adopt the principles set out under the applicable law(s) (*e.g.* the law of place of arbitration).[26] The arbitrators generally take guidance from such sources as arbitration laws and rules, arbitral case law, and scholarly opinions in establishing the standards and principles.[27] The comparative analysis of these sources demonstrates that there are emerging principles and standards regarding transnational procedural rules on arbitral provisional measures[28], which rules are coincidentally in great harmony with the ALI/UNIDROIT Principles of Transnational Civil Procedure[29]. In light of such analysis, I suggest that the following principles and standards should be put in place for the arbitral tribunal to grant provisional measures.[30]

9-12 *First*, it is for a party to generally make a request for an interim measure of protection because such a request would honour the principle of party autonomy.

---

[23] See, e.g., Julian Lew / Loukas Mistelis / Stefan Kröll, *Comparative International Commercial Arbitration* (Kluwer Law International 2003), page v, and para 1-16.

[24] Yesilirmak, supra note 5, para 5-1.

[25] *Ibid*, para 5-2.

[26] *Ibid*, para 5-3.

[27] This is demonstrated by most cases cited in *ibid*, Chapter 5. See also *ibid*, paras 5-4 – 5-5.

[28] *Ibid*, para 5-5.

[29] See, particularly, Principles 5 and 8.

[30] Yesilirmak, supra note 5, paras 5-9 – 5-106.

In rare cases, an arbitral tribunal may, in the absence of a request, grant such measure in order to avoid aggravation of a dispute.

9-13 *Second*, the request should at least include the relevant right whose protection is sought, type of the measure applied for, and the circumstances that necessitate such measure. The request may be made orally or in writing.

9-14 *Third*, the request, as it is generally the case in practice, should be given priority and handled within as a short period of time as possible.

9-15 *Fourth*, the requirements for the granting of a measure are not clearly defined under arbitration rules or laws, although many of them leave the determination of the requirements to the discretion of the tribunal. Experience demonstrates that there are positive and negative requirements for the grant of arbitral provisional measures. The positive requirements are
1. *prima facie* establishment of jurisdiction,
2. *prima facie* establishment of case,
3. urgency,
4. imminent danger, serious or substantial prejudice to the moving party if the request for the measure is denied, and
5. proportionality.

The request for interim protection may be denied where
1. it necessitates examination of merits of the case in question,
2. it seeks to acquire final relief in the form of a provisional measure,
3. the moving party does not have "clean hands",
4. the measure sought is not capable of being carried out;
5. the measure requested is not capable of preventing the alleged harm; or
6. the request is moot.

9-16 The tribunal may seek the satisfaction of some or all of the above requirements. The tribunal may further require the applicant to provide a security for damages and costs. Alternatively, the tribunal may deny the request upon receipt of an undertaking by the respondent that it will not infringe the right whose protection was sought with the request. Even if the tribunal refrains from granting the measure requested, it should nevertheless consider the necessity of an expedited proceeding to avoid any potential or actual prejudice to the applicant.

9-17 *Fifth*, an arbitral provisional measure traditionally takes the form of either an order or an award. This measure may also be granted in the form of a decision, direction, request, proposal, recommendation, or temporary restraining order. In fact, the parties are free to agree on the form of the measure. In the absence of such agreement, however, an arbitral tribunal generally has the discretion to determine the most appropriate form. In making such a determination, the tribunal should take into account the parties' will, the potential savings of time and costs, and the overall effectiveness and efficiency of the arbitration. In any case, the tribunal ought to take into consideration mandatory provisions of *lex arbitri* (law applicable to arbitration). The form of "award" is chosen where, among others, enforcement of the decision is necessary. In cases of urgency, the tribunal may initially issue an *ex parte* order (preliminary order or order without notice) and then, if necessary, incorporate it into an award or a (further) order following *inter partes* proceedings. The *ex parte* order may take the form of a temporary restraining order.

9-18 *Sixth*, due to the temporal nature of arbitral jurisdiction, the arbitral tribunal could issue a provisional measure from its formation until it becomes *functus officio*.

9-19 *Seventh*, because provisional measures have an interim effect, they may be amended or revoked under changed circumstances or in light of new facts or evidence. Alternatively, the measure may be confirmed in the final award.

9-20 *Eighth*, arbitration laws and, particularly, arbitration rules generally, in the absence of party agreement, leave the discretion to determine the types of measures[31] to the arbitral tribunal. The laws and rules generally empower the tribunal to grant any and all types of provisional measures. In this respect, the tribunal is given wide discretion which invites flexibility. The tribunal may generally grant any measure available under *lex arbitri*, *lex causae*, and *lex*

---

[31] Provisional measures may be divided into three broad categories: (1) measures related to preservation of evidence, (2) measures related to conduct of arbitration and relations between the parties during arbitral proceedings, and (3) measures aimed to facilitate later enforcement of award. In this respect, it is noteworthy that anti-suit injunctions should not considered as one of the traditional types of provisional measures since the main aim of such injunctions are not the protection of parties' rights but that of arbitrators' jurisdiction. This is despite the fact that some times the arbitral power to grant interim protection is, in practice, relied upon wrongly to render a decision on anti-suit injunctions. See id., Chapter 1, note 44, and paras 5-78 – 5-79. But see Konstantinos D. Kerameus, "Anti-Suit Injunctions in ICSID Arbitration" in: Emmanuel Gaillard (ed.), *Anti-Suit Injunctions in International Arbitration* (Juris / Staempfli 2005), 131 et seq.

executionis. The tribunal may also grant the types of measures that are generally granted in arbitration practice. To this end, experience demonstrates that arbitral tribunals generally grant on an interim basis

- measures for preservation of evidence,
- injunctions or remedies,
- security for payment,
- security for costs, and
- provisional payment.

9-21 *Ninth*, arbitral provisional measures are usually granted in *inter partes* proceedings. However, where there is utmost urgency or where the element of surprise is required, there is a need to have measures in *ex parte* arbitration proceedings. *Ex parte* provisional measures should be available in arbitration provided that certain safeguards are taken.

9-22 *Tenth*, costs regarding provisional measure proceedings should generally be borne by the losing party in order to deter or punish any vexatious applications.

9-23 *Finally*, in cases where provisional measures granted prove to be unjustified or disobeyed, damages caused by such measures or disobedience may, in principle, be recoverable.

9-24 The text, which is being prepared by the UNCITRAL Working Group, deals with almost all issues discussed above.[32] The text intends to bring predictability and consistency to the granting of arbitral provisional measures but should not underestimate the flexibility that is one of the attractions of international commercial arbitration. Thus, the balance set out in the text between predictability and flexibility should be improved in favour of the latter.

III. COMPLEMENTARY MECHANISMS

9-25 The period between the spark of a dispute and the formation of the tribunal ("pre-formation stage") constitutes an important stage of arbitration.[33] A survey conducted in the US indicates that a majority of disputes settle prior to a trial.[34]

---

[32] This text is set out in "draft Article 17" of the Model Law. For the current text, see UNCITRAL Doc A/CN.9/WG.II/ WP.131, para 4 and UNCITRAL Doc A/CN.9/573, paras 11-69.

[33] Yesilirmak, *supra* note 5, at para. 4-1.

[34] See Herbert M Kritzer, "Adjudication to Settlement: Shading in the Gray", 70(3) *Judicature* 161, 163 (1986). Before the U.S. District Courts, more than 75% of the cases settle prior to trial

Further, 47% and 48% of the ICC and AAA cases respectively are settled between the request for arbitration and first hearing.[35] Indeed, in many occasions, parties use or at least consider using interim measures as a tool for settlement.[36] A successful party in a provisional measure request from a court would generally be in a commending position to force its opponent to settle the case at hand.

9-26 At the pre-formation stage, a provisional measure is normally available from a court. However, channelling contracting parties directly to a court is mainly against their desire to resolve the disputes before an independent and impartial third person, an arbitrator and is often an open invitation for abuse.[37] Mainly, because of these reasons, it is thought that parties would be served better and abuses of court-ordered interim measures may, to a great extent, be avoided if provisional measures are available from an arbitrator-like independent and impartial third person.

9-27 The above idea is not new. The 1915 Plan contained a mechanism under which interim protection of rights was available from a party-determined authority at the pre-formation stage.[38] Today, interim protection in that stage is

---

during the twelve-month period ended 30 September 1997. Heather Russell Koenig, "The Eastern District of Virginia: A Working Solution For Civil Justice Reform", 32 *U Rich LR* 799, 829 (1998). See also *Hubbard v. Vosper* [1972] 2 QB 84, 96. In addition, once a judicial provisional measure is granted, such order becomes final in 95% in the Netherlands and 70% in France of the cases in dispute. See V V Veeder, "The Need for Cross-Border Enforcement of Interim Measures Ordered by a State Court in Support of the International Arbitral Process" in: Albert J van den Berg (ed), *New Horizon in International Commercial Arbitration and Beyond* ICCA Congress Series No 12 (Kluwer Law International 2005), 242, 247. Further, many international disputes settle right after exchanges of statement of claim and defence. See, in this respect, Eric Schwartz, "The Powers of the Arbitrator and The Experience of the Arbitral Institutions – The Practices and Experience of the ICC Court" in: ICC (ed), *Conservatory and Provisional Measures in International Arbitration*, ICC Publication No 519 (ICC Publishing 1993), 45, 55. Recognising the importance of this period, a change has been suggested to Article 39 of the ICSID Arbitration Rules extending the power of the ICSID Secretary General to fix time limits for filing observations of the parties on the provisional measure application. ICSID Secretariat, *Suggested Changes to the ICSID Rules and Regulations* (A Working Paper, 12 May 2005) available at <http://www.worldbank.org/ icsid/052405-sgmanual.pdf> last visited on 30 May 2005. Although it is certainly a positive move, such amendment would not be sufficient to provide necessary speed for interim measures of protection at the pre-formation stage. It is also necessary to speed up the process for appointment of arbitrators if there is a request for interim protection along with request for arbitration.

[35] According to William Slate, President, American Arbitration Association.

[36] Yesilirmak, supra note 5, at para 4-1.

[37] *Ibid*, para 4-2.

[38] *Ibid*, paras 2-10 – 2-11. See also, note 1 above and accompanying text.

available for either (1) a head or an organ of or (2) under emergency arbitral provisional measures procedures adopted by some arbitration institutions.

1. Emergency Measures from a Head or Organ of an Arbitral Institution

9-28 Like the 1915 Plan, certain arbitration rules empower an organ of the relevant institution to grant certain emergency provisional measures. For instance, Article 12(1) of the Arbitration Rules 2002 of the Arbitration Court Attached to the Economic Chamber of Commerce of the Czech Republic empowers the president of the court to preserve evidence in urgent cases. Similarly, further to Article R37 of the Procedural Rules 1994 of the Court of Arbitration for Sport, the president of the relevant sports division is empowered to grant provisional measures prior to transfer of case file to the arbitral panel.[39]

2. Emergency Arbitral Provisional Measure Procedures

9-29 There are four sets of arbitration rules where emergency arbitral provisional measures are available. These are the ICC Pre Arbitral Referee Procedures, the European Court of Arbitration Pre-Arbitral Referee Rules, the Summary Arbitral Proceedings of the Netherlands Arbitration Institution, and the Optional Rules for Emergency Measures of Protection of the American Arbitration Association.

9-30 The main characteristics of the emergency measure procedures are[40]

1. They envisage resolution of a dispute, on an interim basis, by an independent and impartial third person in a judicial manner.[41] This person may thus be called an emergency arbitrator or an arbitrator.

---

[39] See also Section 1(6) of the Arbitration Rules 1995 of the International Commercial Arbitration Court at the Chamber of Commerce and Industry of the Russian Federation, Articles 2 and 8 of the Rules for International Arbitration 1994 of the Italian Association for Arbitration, and Article 13 of the Arbitration Rules of the French Arbitration Association.

[40] Yesilirmak, supra note 5, paras 4-25 – 4-101.

[41] But see mainly Klaus Peter Berger, "Pre-Arbitral Referees: Arbitrators, Quasi-Arbitrators, Hybrids or Creatures of Contract Law?" in Gerald Aksen / Karl-Heinz Böckstiegel / Michael J Mustill / Paolo Michele Patocchi / Anne Marie Whitesell (eds), *Global Reflections on International Law, Commerce and Dispute Resolution - Liber Amicorum in honour of Robert Briner* (ICC Publishing 2005), text accompanying footnote 28 (arguing that pre-arbitral referee procedures "should be considered as instruments of a truly contractual, not a procedural nature." As the task of the emergency arbitrator is not merely fact finding and the decision concerning a request for a provisional measure necessitates the emergency arbitrator's juridical assessment like a judge or an arbitrator of the facts, this author disagrees with Berger's opinion.

2. Under these procedures, a provisional measure request may be handled in a speedy manner.

3. The parties are generally able to appoint their own arbitrators.

4. Under these procedures, an emergency arbitrator is generally given broad powers to conduct proceedings.

5. The determination of the requirements to grant emergency provisional measures are generally left to the discretion of the emergency arbitrator: urgency and immediate damage or irreparable loss may be required.

6. The emergency arbitrator is generally empowered to issue any measure such arbitrator deems appropriate.

7. The form of the decision would be an order or an award. Whichever form the decision on emergency measure takes, the arbitrator should be able to subsequently modify or revoke it.

8. The decision of the emergency arbitrator should not in any way pre-judge the substance of the case in dispute.

9-31 Where parties make a reference to an emergency provisional measure procedure, they are expected to voluntarily comply with the decision of their emergency arbitrator. For non-compliance, there are several remedies:[42] the emergency measure may be backed with liquidated damages where permitted or damages caused by the failure or costs of the emergency measure procedures may be compensated from the recalcitrant party in arbitration. Would an emergency measure granted in the form of an award[43] be enforceable under the United Nations Convention on the Recognition and Enforcement of Foreign Arbitral Awards?[44] There is no clear-cut answer. It is arguable that where the award is binding at the place where it was rendered then such award should be enforceable under the New York Convention.[45]

---

[42] For detailed information on these remedies, see Yesilirmak, supra note 5, paras 4-73 – 4-79.

[43] *Société Nationale des Petroles du Congo v. Republique du Congo*, extracts of the English translation from the French original published in Emmanuel Gaillard / Philippe Pinsolle, "The ICC Pre-Arbitral Referee: First Practical Experiences", 20(1) *Arb Int* 13, 16, 33-37 (2004) (Court of Appeal, Paris, 29 April 2003) (holding, among others, that the pre-arbitral referee is not an arbitrator and that the pre-arbitral referee's decision only had a contractual value). On this decision see, e.g., Gaillard/Pinsolle, 16 *et seq;* Yesilirmak, supra note 5, at paras 4-74 – 4-75.

[44] Done at New York, 10 June 1958, 330 UNTS 38, No. 4739 (the "New York Convention").

[45] See Francis Gurry, "The Need for Speed" in: Biennial IFCAI Conference (24 October 1997, Geneva, Switzerland), 3 4 (unpublished); Sigvard Jarvin, "Alternative Solutions to the Intervention of the Engineer" in: Albert Jan van den Berg (ed.), *I. Preventing Delay and Disruption of*

9-32 The complementary procedures do not provide for total exclusion of court assistance to arbitration.[46] Where parties make a reference to these procedures, the role of court remains to be complementary. That is to say court assistance should be available where there is a need to have a measure against third parties to arbitration or where the enforcement of measures inherently necessitates the use of coercive powers (*e.g.*, attachments).[47]

9-33 The complementary mechanisms are very useful.[48] That is because, first, they diminish, to a great extent, the court intervention at the pre-formation stage.[49] In this way, party autonomy is foremost upheld. Second, the very existence of the complementary mechanisms may deter a party to act in bad faith.[50] Indeed, the use of such mechanisms is on the increase.[51] These mechanisms will soon become very trendy.

9-34 Complementary mechanisms have not received the attention they deserve from the UNCITRAL Working Group, other international legislative bodies or from most arbitration institutions.

IV. ENFORCEMENT OF ARBITRAL PROVISIONAL MEASURES

9-35 Arbitral provisional measures are, unlike judicial provisional measures, not self-executing. However, these measures traditionally have a certain weight because the arbitral tribunal has some persuasive powers over the arbitrating parties.[52] Thus, the losing party often complies with the tribunal's decision on interim protection of rights.[53] There may, however, be occasions where that

---

Arbitration – II. Effective Proceedings in Construction Cases, ICCA Congress Series No. 5 (Kluwer 1991), 385, 403; and Yeşilırmak, supra note 5, para 4-76.

[46] Yesilirmak, supra note 5, para 4-31.

[47] This is indeed what seems to be envisaged by Section 44(5) of the English Arbitration Act 1996.

[48] Yesilirmak, supra note 5, paras 4-92 – 4-97.

[49] *Ibid*, para 4-34.

[50] See, e.g., Humphrey Lloyd, "What is Pre-Arbitral Expertise and How Does it Differ from the Pre-Arbitral Referee Procedure?" in: Institute of Business Law and Practice, Conference on Arbitration and Expertise (Paris, 12 April 1991), 18-19 (unpublished);

[51] Yesilirmak, supra note 5, para 4-97. For instance, six references were made under the ICC Pre-Arbitral Referee Rules from their inception. (E-mail of Emmanuel Jolivet, General Counsel of the ICC International Court of Arbitration, to the author).

[52] Yesilirmak, *ibid*, para 6-2.

[53] For instance, according to Aboul-Enein, all four of the measures granted in 2000 were complied with in arbitrations administered by the Cairo Regional Centre for International Commercial Arbitration. M I M Aboul-Enein, "Issuing Interim Relief Measures in International Arbitration in the Arab States", 3(1) *J World Inv* 77, 81 (2002). Further, a survey done by the AAA reflects that, in 90 % of the international and national cases (45 out of 50 cases surveyed), arbitrating

decision is not followed. For such occasions, the arbitral tribunal has two main sanctions for disobedience.[54] The tribunal may draw adverse inference from the disobedience; however, such inference is generally only drawn in cases involving the interim protection of evidentiary matters. In addition, the recalcitrant party may be held liable for costs and/or damages related to its non-compliance. Further, the tribunal may impose time limits for compliance, which has the effect of a form of psychological coercion. Moreover, the tribunal may, if permitted, impose a penalty for failure to comply with its decision.

9-36 The weight and effectiveness of the above sanctions differ.[55] Thus, the need for enforceability of an arbitral provisional measure varies. The need is absolute for measures aimed to facilitate later enforcement of awards. Further, there may also be a need for enforcement of measures related to conduct of arbitration and to relations between arbitrating parties after a dispute arisen. However, the need for enforcement of measures relating to the preservation of evidence is minimal because drawing an adverse inference[56] against a recalcitrant party could provide for full protection.

9-37 Due to the above need, it is generally felt that the tribunal's lack of power to enforce its decision causes a problem because it may result in the infringement of a parties' right and may hamper the effectiveness of the arbitration.[57]

9-38 In order to make arbitration more effective, a number of legislatures offer various solutions to the problem of an arbitral provisional measure's enforceability by lending the coercive powers of the judiciary to the arbitral tribunal.[58] Laws of some states provide for enforcement of arbitral provisional measures where the tribunal has its seat in that state whereas laws of a small

---

parties comply with their tribunal's decision on interim relief. Richard W Naimark / Stephanie E Keer, "Analysis of UNCITRAL Questionnaires on Interim Relief", 16(3) *Mealey's IAR* 23, 26 (2001). It is further interesting to note that in all five cases, the decisions of the pre-arbitral referees in ICC arbitration were directly or indirectly (through settlement) observed. Gaillard / Pinsolle, 19-20. See also Alan Redfern, "Interim Measures" in: Lawrence W. Newman / Richard D. Hill, *The Leading Arbitrators' Guide to International Arbitration* (Juris Publishing 2004), 217, 239; and W Michael Reisman / W Laurence Craig / William W Park / Jan Paulsson, *International Commercial Arbitration: Cases, Materials and Notes on the Resolution of International Business Disputes* (Foundation Press 1997), 755, note 143.

[54] Yesilirmak, supra note 5, paras 6-4 – 6-11.
[55] *Ibid*, paras 6-16 – 6-18.
[56] This is to say drawing adverse inferences from the failure and making the award on the basis of information and evidence before the tribunal.
[57] Yesilirmak, supra note 5, para 6-12.
[58] See *ibid*, paras 6-16 – 6-41.

number of states envisage enforcement of such measures regardless of the seat of arbitration.

9-39 On the enforcement of arbitral provisional measures at the seat of arbitration, the approach of national laws varies

1. Under the *first* approach, an arbitral provisional measure is directly enforceable as if it is a decision of the court.[59]
2. According to the *second* approach, a national court lends its executory assistance for the enforcement of an arbitral provisional measure.[60] Under this approach, a court enforces, upon request of either an arbitral tribunal or a party, an arbitral provisional measure without any further (or at least limited) examination. Further, court assistance may take the form of enforcing a decision on an arbitral provisional measure by equating and then enforcing such measure as if it were an arbitral award.
3. In accordance with the *third* approach, an arbitral decision, in certain cases, is transposed into a court order where the original decision cannot be enforced as it stands.[61]
4. Under the *fourth* approach, a court issues, basing its decision on an arbitral provisional measure, a separate order for interim protection of rights.[62]

9-40 The combined reading of the second and third approaches should be preferable because there is a pro-enforcement bias. Moreover, the approaches allow for court assistance but still provide safeguards for protecting the interests of the state and arbitrating parties. The first approach has no such safeguards whereas the fourth approach requires a second court proceeding to give executory assistance to an arbitral provisional measure.

---

[59] See Article 9(3) of the Ecuadorian Law on Arbitration and Mediation 1997.

[60] See, *e.g.*, Article 36 of the Bolivian Law on Arbitration & Conciliation 1997, Section 1297(92) of the Californian Code of Civil Procedure, Sections 41(1), (5) and 42 of the English Arbitration Act 1996, Section 2GG of the Hong Kong Arbitration Ordinance.

[61] Section 1041(2) of the German Code of Civil Procedure.

[62] See, e.g., Article 7(2) of the Kenyan Arbitration Act 1995, Article 9(3) of the New Zealand Arbitration Act, and Section 1-567(39) of the North Carolina International Commercial Arbitration Act.

9-41 The jurisdictions adopting any of the above approaches generally deal with enforcement at the seat of arbitration. However, the seat often has nothing to do with the parties or the dispute in question as it is often chosen for merely its geographical convenience. Accordingly, cross-border enforcement of an arbitral provisional measure is of paramount importance. The cross-border enforcement may be permitted under a national law or an international treaty. Laws of a few states[63] allow enforcement of a provisional measure rendered by an arbitral tribunal whose seat is in a foreign state. Further, there are a few bilateral treaties, but no multilateral treaty, that enable cross-border enforcement of an arbitral provisional measure.[64]

9-42 Whether or not the New York Convention allows enforcement of an arbitral provisional measure is not clear. The text and preparatory materials on the Convention are silent on that issue. In addition, both courts and commentators have divergent views.[65] The Convention requires that, *inter alia*, an award is to be binding for its enforcement in accordance with Article V(1)(e) under the law of the state where the award was rendered. That should be sufficient for the enforcement of an award on provisional measure. However, an arbitral decision may, under one interpretation, be required to be final under the New York Convention.[66] Further, the finality of an award may be required under the law where it was rendered. In such cases, for its enforcement under the Convention, an award is required to be binding and final. Arbitrating parties either explicitly accepted binding nature of the award or the binding nature arises from the fact that the authority to grant provisional measures is vested with the tribunal.[67] As to the finality, it should be accepted that an interim award on provisional measures is final in regard of the issues it deals with so long as the issues separable from the other issues in dispute.[68] This interpretation is in line with the purpose and

---

[63] Australia, Articles 22 and 23 of the International Arbitration Act 1974, as amended; Hong Kong, Section 2GG of the Arbitration Ordinance; and Switzerland, Pierre A Karrer, "Interim Measures Issued by Arbitral Tribunals and the Courts: Less Theory Please" in: Albert J van den Berg (ed), *International Arbitration and National Courts: The Never Ending Story*, ICCA Congress Series No. 10 (Kluwer Law International 2001), 98, 108.

[64] Yesilirmak, supra note 5, para 6-35.

[65] For those arguments see, e.g., *ibid*, para 6-39.

[66] See, e.g., *Resort Condominiums International Inc v. Ray Bolwell and Resort Condominiums (Australasia) Pty Ltd,* excerpts published in XX YCA 628-650 (1995) (Supreme Court of Queensland, 29 October 1993).

[67] Yesilirmak, supra note 5, para 6-40.

[68] *Ibid*. para. 6-41. See also, e.g., *Sperry International Trade, Inc v. Government of Israel*, 532 F Supp 901 (SDNY), aff'd., 689 F 2d 301 (2 Cir 1982).

objective of the Convention: enhancing arbitration's effectiveness. It, however, has no wide acceptance.

9-43 The need for regulation of the issue of and for harmonisation of laws on enforcement of arbitral provisional measures is clear from what has been discussed above. The UNCITRAL Working Group, in drafting the text on enforcement of arbitral provisional measures as tentatively numbered Article 17 bis of the Model Law[69] rightly took into account three principles, which have paramount importance: (1) taking the system created for the enforcement of arbitral awards in the Model Law, which was based on the New York Convention as model; (2) adopting that system to the specific features of arbitral provisional measures; and (3) providing for discretion to enforcing court. This author believes that the amendment to the Model Law in respect of the enforcement of arbitral provisional measures is not sufficient to reach harmonisation as there has already been and is likely to be disharmony in existing/future laws. Thus, an addition to the New York Convention is essential.[70]

V. Conclusion

9-44 For effectiveness of arbitration, the interim protection of arbitrating parties' rights is essential. In this respect, both international and national legislative bodies as well as arbitration institutions should resolve the problems concerning such protection. In resolving these problems, their nature should be taken into account in order to tackle each individual problem.

---

[69] For the current text, see UNCITRAL Doc A/CN.9/WG.II/WP.125, para 4.

[70] See, e.g., Lew/Mistelis/Kröll, para 23-95 (who do not argue an amendment to the New York Convention, but the need of a specific international convention); V. V. Veeder, "Provisional and Conservatory Measures" in: *Enforcing Arbitration Awards under the New York Convention – Experience and Prospects* (United Nations 1999), 21-23, Hakan Pekcanıtez, "Milletlerarası Tahkimde Geçici Hukuki Himaye Tedbirleri" in: TOBB, *Milletlerarası Tahkim Semineri* (Ankara 2003), 152; William Wang, "International Arbitration: The Need for Uniform Interim Measures of Relief", 28 *Brooklyn J Int'l L* 1059 (2003); and Yesilirmak, supra note 5, para 6-44. But see, e.g., Pieter Sanders, "The Making of the Convention" in: *Enforcing Arbitration Awards, ibid*, 3, 4; and Albert Jan van den Berg, "Striving for Uniform Interpretation" in: *Enforcing Arbitration Awards, ibid*, 41, 43.

*Emmanuel Gaillard**

CHAPTER 10

REFLECTIONS ON THE USE OF ANTI-SUIT INJUNCTIONS IN INTERNATIONAL ARBITRATION

I. INTRODUCTION

10-1 Traditionally, anti-suit injunctions, a well-known device in common law systems, are issued upon the request of a party that the other party be enjoined from initiating or from proceeding with a legal action in a different jurisdiction.[1] Courts in civil law countries are increasingly willing, in certain circumstances, to enjoin a party to suspend or terminate an action brought in another country.[2]

---

*   Professor of Law, University of Paris XII; Head of the International Arbitration Group, Shearman & Sterling LLP.
[1] In English law, the seminal case was *Cohen v. Rothfield* [1919] 1 KB 410, in which the Court of Appeal ordered a party to withdraw an action commenced in Scotland. Originally designed to prevent foreign litigation that was "oppressive or vexatious," this practice has become a method for enforcing the English view of the most convenient forum. The criteria for the granting of such an injunction were laid out by the Privy Council in the *Société Nationale Industrielle Aerospatiale v. Lee Kui Jak* [1987] 1 AC 871. In the United States, the practice was intended to avoid "an irreparable miscarriage of justice." See, e.g., *Laker Airways Ltd v. Sabena Belgian World Airlines*, 731 F. 2d 909, 927 (D.C. Cir. 1984). On the evolution of the criteria applied in common law systems, see, e.g., Jonathan Arkins, "Borderline Legal: Anti-Suit Injunctions in Common Law Jurisdictions", 18(6) *J Int'l Arb* 603 (2001); Horatia Muir-Watt, note under House of Lords, 13 December 2001, 2003 *Rev Crit DIP* 116.
[2] Examples of anti-suit injunctions can be found in the following civil law jurisdictions: for Quebec, see Superior Court of Quebec, Civil Chamber, July 9, 1999 and Court of Appeal of Quebec, November 29, 1999 in the matter of *Lac d'Amiante du Canada Ltée et 2858-0702 Quebec Inc v. Lac d'amiante du Québec Ltée*, discussed by Stewart Shackleton in 3 *Int ALR* N-6 (Jan. 2000). For Germany, see Markus Lenenbach, "Antisuit Injunctions in England, Germany and the United States: Their Treatment Under European Civil Procedure and The Hague Convention", 20 *Loy LA Int'l & Comp LJ* 257 (1998). For France, see Cass. 1e civ., November 19, 2002, *Banque Worms v. Epoux Brachot et autres*, which upheld, in the context of an international bankruptcy, the decision of a French judge to order a creditor to stop a real property seizure proceeding brought in Spain against the debtor's building, 2003 Dalloz 797,

Loukas A. Mistelis and Julian D.M. Lew (eds), Pervasive Problems in International Arbitration, 201-213
© *2006 Kluwer Law International. Printed in the Netherlands*

These measures are commonly requested to preclude parasite litigation of a dispute before a different court, whether because the first court seized has issued a ruling or because its decision is pending. Violations of such injunctions may result in heavy penalties connected to the notion of contempt of court. The court that retains its jurisdiction or anticipates that it will do so thus seeks to protect its jurisdiction or, more generally, the jurisdiction of the forum it deems to be the most appropriate.[3]

10-2 The introduction of anti-suit injunctions into international arbitration is a recent trend. Directed at arbitral proceedings or at court proceedings surrounding an international arbitration, they vary in their form and are requested either in an attempt to disrupt the arbitral process or, to the contrary, to try to protect it.[4] It is however anti-suit injunctions aimed at preventing an arbitral tribunal from hearing a claim or obstructing the enforcement of an arbitral award that have seen the most spectacular development in recent years, prompting a debate on the adequacy of anti-suit injunctions in international arbitration.

II. THE VARIED USE OF ANTI-SUIT INJUNCTIONS IN INTERNATIONAL ARBITRATION

10-3 In the context of international arbitration, anti-suit injunctions are generally issued either during the arbitral process in order to prevent an arbitral tribunal from hearing the claim or, at the end of the arbitral process, to obstruct the enforcement of the arbitral award.

10-4 When they are requested during the course of arbitral proceedings, anti-suit injunctions are usually directed against the parties in the form of an order to

---

note by G. Kairallah; *Gaz Pal*, June 25-26, 2003, at 29, note by M-L Niboyet. For Brazil, see Curitiba Court of First Instance, June 3, 2003, *Companhia Paranaense de Energia (COPEL) v. UEG Arancaria Ltda*, 21 *Revista de Direito Bancário e de Mercado de Arbitragem* 421 (2003). More generally, for Latin American countries see Horacio Grigera Naón, "Competing Orders Between Courts of Law and Arbitral Tribunals: Latin American Experiences", in *Global Reflections on International Law, Commerce and Dispute Resolution. Liber Amicorum in honour of Robert Briner*, ICC Publication 335 (2005).

3   See Emmanuel Gaillard, "Introduction", in *IAI Series on International Arbitration No 2, Anti-Suit Injunctions in International Arbitration* 1 (Emmanuel Gaillard ed., Juris Publishing, 2005); see also Emmanuel Gaillard, "Il est interdit d'interdire: Réflexions sur l'utilisation des anti-suit injunctions dans l'arbitrage commercial international", 2004 *Rev Arb* 47.

4   For anti-suit injunctions in favour of international arbitration, see Axel Baum, "Anti-Suit Injunctions Issued by National Courts To Permit Arbitration Proceedings", in *Anti-Suit Injunctions in International Arbitration*, supra note 3, at 19. See also the discussion below on *KBC v. Pertamina*.

suspend or terminate the arbitral proceedings.[5] They may, however, be also directed against the arbitral tribunal itself, with the consequence that the tribunal is, either explicitly or implicitly, denied the power to rule on its own jurisdiction. The following cases illustrate the diversity of the situations where the injunction requested by one party and ordered by the courts attempts to reach the other party as well as the members of the tribunal.[6]

10-5 In *Hubco v. WAPDA*, a dispute arose between the Hubco Corporation and the Water and Power Development Authority of Pakistan (WAPDA) regarding a US\$ 1.8 billion project to construct a power station in Pakistan. The disputed contracts contained an arbitration clause under which disputes had to be resolved by ICC arbitration in London. After an arbitral proceeding was commenced in July 1998 concerning the method of calculating the price of the electricity produced, WAPDA, deeming certain contracts to be illegal and claiming that they had been obtained by fraud and corruption, presented these questions to the Pakistani courts and asked them to order the claimant to suspend the arbitration. The courts granted this request and, in a judgment dated 14 June 2000, the Supreme Court of Pakistan upheld their decision, finding that the allegation of corruption rendered the matter non-arbitrable.[7]

10-6 Similar mistrust towards arbitration and conversely favourable approach towards anti-suit injunctions were displayed in *SGS v. Pakistan*, an investment arbitration case involving the Swiss corporation SGS and the Government of Pakistan. SGS filed a claim under the auspices of the International Centre for Settlement of Investment Disputes (ICSID) on the basis of the bilateral investment protection treaty between Switzerland and Pakistan, requesting a finding that Pakistan had violated its obligations under the treaty. The Government of Pakistan requested an order from its own courts enjoining SGS to

---

[5] See Julian Lew, "Anti-Suit Injunctions Issued by National Courts To Prevent Arbitration Proceedings", in *Anti-Suit Injunctions in International Arbitration*, supra note 3, at 25; Mathieu de Boisséson, "Anti-Suit Injunctions Issued by National Courts at the Seat of the Arbitration or Elsewhere", *ibid*, at 65; José Carlos Fernández Rozas, "Anti-Suit Injunctions Issued by National Courts. Measures Addressed to the Parties or the Arbitrators", *ibid*, at 73.

[6] For other examples, see the Interim Award of May 14, 2001 in ICC Case No 8307, reported in *Anti-Suit Injunctions in International Arbitration*, supra note 3, at 307; see also the cases discussed in the articles cited at footnote 5; the report of the *Four Seasons/Consorcio Barr* case in Grigera Naón, supra note 2, at 337 et seq.

[7] See the transcript of the judgment of the Supreme Court of Pakistan published in 16 *Arb Int* 439 (2000). The dispute is reported to have subsequently settled, see Louise Barrington, "*Hubco v. WAPDA*: Pakistan Top Court Rejects Modern Arbitration", 11 *Am Rev Int'l Arb* 385 (2000).

suspend the arbitral proceeding, on the basis of the arbitration agreement contained in the underlying contract and providing for local arbitration in Pakistan. By order of July 3, 2002, the Supreme Court of Pakistan granted this request, essentially finding that the bilateral treaty did not bind Pakistan.[8]

10-7 The Arbitral Tribunal, however, disregarded the effect of this order and ordered for its part that Pakistan, as the respondent State in the arbitration, not take any step to initiate a complaint for contempt; in the alternative, it ordered that Pakistan

> take all steps to inform the [Pakistani] Court of the current standing of this proceeding and of the fact that this Tribunal must discharge its duty to determine whether it has the jurisdiction to consider the international claim on the merits.[9]

It further recommended that the local arbitration initiated in Pakistan be stayed until such time as the Tribunal could determine in a final manner whether or not it had jurisdiction.

10-8 A similar chain of decisions was issued in the ICC arbitration between *Salini Costruttori S.p.A. and the Federal Democratic Republic of Ethiopia, Addis Ababa Water and Sewerage Authority*.[10] By contrast to the *SGS v. Pakistan* case, the orders issued by the local courts in *Salini* were directed to the Claimant as well as to the Arbitral Tribunal.[11] At the early stages of the arbitral proceeding,

---

[8] "SGS [...] is hereby restrained from taking any step, action or measure to pursue or participate or to continue to pursue or participate in the ICSID arbitration." (para 77). The decision was published in 19 *Arb Int* 179 (2003) with a commentary by Lau, "Note on *Société Générale de Surveillance SA v. Pakistan, through Secretary, Ministry of Finance*".

[9] *SGS Société Générale de Surveillance SA v. Islamic Republic of Pakistan* (ICSID Case No ARB/01/13), Procedural Order No 2 dated October 16, 2002, published in *Anti-Suit Injunctions in International Arbitration*, supra note 3, at 213.

[10] *Salini Costruttori SpA v. The Federal Democratic Republic of Ethiopia, Addis Ababa Water and Sewerage Authority* (hereinafter "*Salini*"), Award regarding the Suspension of the Proceedings and Jurisdiction dated December 7, 2001, excerpts in 21 *ASA Bulletin* 59 (2003) and full text in 20(3) *Mealey's IAR* A1 (2005) with a commentary by Frédéric Bachand, "Must An ICC Tribunal Comply With An Anti-Suit Injunction Issued By The Courts Of The Seat Of Arbitration?", at 47; see also Reza Mohtashami, "In Defense of Injunctions Issued By The Courts of the Place of Arbitration: A Brief Reply to Professor Bachand's Commentary on *Salini Costruttori SpA v. Ethiopia*", 20(5) *Mealey's IAR* 44 (2005); see also the full text of the *Salini* award in *Anti-Suit Injunctions in International Arbitration*, supra note 3, at 227.

[11] For another example of an injunction against the members of the tribunal by the courts of Venezuela, resulting in the resignation of the Venezuelan member of the tribunal so as to avoid being

the Respondent, a State entity in Ethiopia, obtained a series of decisions by the Ethiopian courts, amongst which the Supreme Court's "temporary injunction against the Arbitral Tribunal ordering the suspension of the arbitration proceedings with immediate effect."[12] The Respondent had taken steps to serve the order on the arbitrators.[13] The Respondent had also commenced a separate action before the Federal First Instance Court of the Federal Democratic Republic of Ethiopia for the purposes of obtaining a judgment that the Tribunal lacked jurisdiction over the arbitration. That Court issued an order "enjoining the Claimant from proceeding with the arbitration pending its decision on the Tribunal's jurisdiction."[14]

10-9 In the Award it rendered on the Suspension of the Proceedings and Jurisdiction on 7 December 2001, the Tribunal decided not to give effect to the decisions issued by the Ethiopian courts and to pursue the arbitral proceedings. Unlike the Tribunal's decision in *SGS v. Pakistan*, which was in essence an anti-anti-suit injunction to the Respondent State, the Award in *Salini* addressed the *effect* of an anti-suit injunction on the Tribunal's power to proceed with the arbitration and on its jurisdiction over the dispute:

> The Arbitral Tribunal accords the greatest respect to the Ethiopian courts. Nevertheless, [...] the Tribunal considers that it is not bound to suspend the proceedings as a result of the particular injunctions issued by the Federal Supreme Court and the Federal First Instance Court and that, in the particular circumstances of the case, it is under a duty to proceed with the arbitration.[15]

The grounds for the Tribunal's decision were (a) its primary duty to the parties to ensure that their arbitration agreement is not frustrated; (b) its duty to make every effort to render an enforceable award; and (c) that a State or State entity cannot

---

held in contempt of court, see the report of the *Four Seasons/Consorcio Barr* case in Grigera Naón, supra note 2, at 339.

[12] *Salini*, supra note 10, at para 76.

[13] *Ibid*, at para 83. In its submissions, the Respondent threatened that, under the provisions of the Ethiopian Code of Civil Procedure, a court could attach the property of, or sentence for contempt of court, any person breaching a temporary injunction, *ibid*, at para 78. It also submitted that the Arbitral Tribunal was under the obligation to comply with the injunction and that, if it did not,

> "the arbitrators would be in contempt of court and would then be unwilling to travel to Ethiopia [the seat of the arbitration], preventing them from fulfilling their functions under the ICC Rules and necessitating their replacement.",

Ibid, at para 81.

[14] *Ibid*, at para 88.

[15] *Ibid*, at para 124.

resort to the State's courts to frustrate an arbitration agreement. The Tribunal held in particular that,

> [i]n the event that the arbitral tribunal considers that to follow a decision of a court would conflict fundamentally with the tribunal's understanding of its duty to the parties, derived from the parties' arbitration agreement, the tribunal must follow its own judgment, even if that requires non-compliance with a court order. To conclude otherwise would entail a denial of justice and fairness to the parties and conflict with the legitimate expectations they created by entering into an arbitration agreement. It would allow the courts of the seat to convert an international arbitration agreement into a dead letter, with intolerable consequence for the practice of international arbitration more generally.[16]

10-10 In the context of post-arbitral proceedings, anti-suit injunctions are sought by the losing party as a means to obstruct the enforcement of the arbitral award. One of the most spectacular illustrations is found in *KBC v. Pertamina*, in which both an anti-suit injunction and an anti-anti-suit injunction were ordered by Indonesian and American courts respectively. The dispute in that case arose between the Indonesian national company Pertamina and KBC as the contractor over the construction and development of a geothermal plant in Indonesia. After the project was suspended by the Indonesian Government, KBC commenced an arbitral proceeding in Switzerland pursuant to the UNCITRAL rules, on the basis of arbitration clauses in the disputed contracts. In December 2000, the Arbitral Tribunal ordered Pertamina to pay KBC US$ 260 million in damages.[17] After an action before the Swiss courts to set aside the award was rejected in April 2001 for untimely payment of court costs, Pertamina filed a request to annul the award in the Central District Court of Jakarta in March 2002, along with a request for an injunction prohibiting KBC from enforcing the award abroad. KBC had in fact obtained, in December 2001, the recognition of the award in the United States by the United States District Court for the Southern District of Texas, which granted summary judgment in favour of KBC.[18] On April 1, 2002, the Indonesian court

---

[16] *Ibid*, at paras 142-143. For a critical view of this decision, see Eric Schwartz, "Do International Arbitrators Have a Duty to Obey the Orders of Courts at the Place of the Arbitration? Reflections on the Role of the *Lex Loci Arbitri* in the Light of a Recent ICC Award", in *Liber Amicorum in honour of Robert Briner*, supra note 2, at 795.

[17] *Karaha Bodas Co LLC (KBC) v. Perusahaan Pertambangan Minyak Dan Gas Bumi Negara (Pertamina) and PT, PLN (Persero)*, Decision of 18 December 2000, 16(3) *Mealey's IAR* C-2 (2001).

[18] In the matter of an arbitration between *Karaha Bodas Co LLC (KBC) v. Perusahaan Pertambangan Minyak Dan Gas Bumi Negara (Pertamina)*, 190 F Supp 2d 936 (SD Texas 2001).

provisionally granted Pertamina's motion for an injunction and prohibited KBC from attempting to enforce the award in any country. On August 27, 2002, the Central Jakarta District Court annulled the award, finding that it was contrary to the 1958 Convention on the Recognition and Enforcement of Foreign Arbitral Awards (the "New York Convention") and Indonesian arbitration law. The court also issued a permanent injunction forbidding KBC from enforcing the award abroad, under penalty of having to pay a fine of US$ 500,000 per day.[19]

10-11   After Pertamina asked the Indonesian Courts to annul the award and enjoin its enforcement, KBC hastened to move the US Courts to force Pertamina to suspend its request for an injunction in Indonesia. On March 29, 2002, the United States District Court in Texas granted a temporary restraining order requiring Pertamina to withdraw its request for an injunction made to the Court in Jakarta. After the Indonesian Court granted the provisional injunction forbidding KBC from enforcing the arbitral award, KBC asked the District Court to find Pertamina in contempt. On April 2, 2002, the Texas Court again ordered Pertamina to withdraw its request in the Indonesian Court and found Pertamina in contempt. Although Pertamina then asked (over the objection of a sister company) to suspend proceedings before the Indonesian Court, the Indonesian Court rejected the request and decided to annul the arbitral award and prohibit its enforcement in the United States. Thereafter, on 26 April 2002, the Texas District Court once again reaffirmed its decision to grant summary judgment to KBC.[20]

10-12   This case illustrates the counterproductive nature of anti-suit injunctions rendered by both the Indonesian Courts and the US District Court on the basis of an overbroad understanding of their judicial power and on the presumption that their respective decisions had an absolute extraterritorial effect. However, the effectiveness of the Indonesian and the US orders outside Indonesia and the United States was far from clear. Each party was faced with a different anti-suit injunction (in the United States for Pertamina and in Indonesia for KBC) and

---

[19]   The Jakarta court's decision of 27 August 2002 is available on http://www.mealeysonline.com (document #05-021125-013Z). In a positive development, the Indonesian Supreme Court overturned the Jakarta court's decision on 23 November 2004, finding that the lower court had no "authority to examine and adjudicate" on the dispute between the companies. Unfortunately, it appears that the text of the Court's decision is not available, although it was reported in the media.

[20]   See *Karaha Bodas Co. LLC (KBC) v. Perusahaan Pertambangan Minyak Dan Gas Bumi Negara (Pertamina)*, 335 F 3d 357, 360-63 (5th Cir 2003). For the decision on appeal, see below, III.

with substantial financial penalties in different countries (Pertamina being held in contempt of the Texas District Court, while KBC appeared to be confronted with "draconian enforcement penalties" in Indonesia as a result of the Indonesian injunction[21]). The decision by the Texas Court had little effect in Indonesia where it is probable that it would not have been recognized or enforced, in the same way as the Indonesian injunction had little effect in the US.[22]

10-13 In light of these examples and the variety and complexity of the circumstances in which anti-suit injunctions are requested and issued by national courts, the recurrently debated question is whether and to what extent anti-suit injunctions should be permitted in international arbitration, even if they are ordered in support of international arbitration. In this respect, the *Pertamina* case is of particular interest as it reflects both the doctrine of judicial intervention (as viewed by both the Indonesian Courts whose decisions were hostile to international arbitration and to the resulting award, and by the US District Court whose decisions were aimed at preserving the enforceability of the award) and that of judicial self-restraint (as viewed, on appeal, by the US Fifth Circuit Court of Appeals). The latter doctrine, as will now be discussed, could persuasively be set as the applicable standard in relation to the parties' increasing temptation to have recourse to anti-suit injunctions in international arbitration.

III. THE INADEQUACY OF ANTI-SUIT INJUNCTIONS IN INTERNATIONAL ARBITRATION

10-14 The approach adopted by the courts in the above examples show that anti-suit injunctions are inefficient – and possibly harmful – in the context of international arbitration. They show that, faced with such measures, courts in other countries may be tempted to retaliate by forbidding the party targeted by the injunction from complying with the first court's decision enjoining it from going forward in the form of anti-anti-suit injunctions.[23]

---

[21] See Order, supra note 18, at 4.

[22] On this decision in general, see Emmanuel Gaillard, "The Misuse of Anti-Suit Injunctions", *NYLJ*, August 1, 2002.

[23] See Philippe Fouchard, "Anti-Suit Injunctions in International Arbitration – What Remedies?", in *Anti-Suit Injunctions in International Arbitration*, supra note 3, at 153. For another example of conflicting injunctions, see the report of the *Four Seasons/Consorcio Barr* case in Grigera Naón, supra note 2, at 337.

10-15 By contrast to the position taken by the US District Court in *KBC v. Pertamina* enjoining Pertamina from relying on the Indonesian decision and finding the company in contempt, the US Fifth Circuit Court of Appeals, faced with an appeal from the District Court decision, reversed the preliminary injunction and the contempt order against Pertamina by adopting a measured approach and underscoring the fundamental notion that the courts of any enforcement jurisdiction have discretion to enforce a foreign arbitral award regardless of any surrounding decisions rendered by the courts of other countries.[24]

10-16 In accordance with the general approach used by American Courts in such situations, the Court of Appeals' reasoning focused on the balance of domestic judicial interests regarding the prevention of vexatious or oppressive litigation and the protection of the court's jurisdiction against concerns of international comity.[25] As regards the first principle, the Court analysed the effects that the Indonesian decision annulling the award would be likely to have in the United States in order to determine whether the litigation in Indonesia was "vexatious or oppressive" and determined that none of the factors that usually contribute to vexatiousness and oppressiveness were at play in the case at hand. The Court concluded, in remarkable fashion given the controversy on the issue,[26] and citing the *Chromalloy* case,[27] that

---

[24] *Karaha Bodas Co LLC (KBC) v. Perusahaan Pertambangan Minyak Dan Gas Bumi Negara (Pertamina)*, 335 F 3d 357 (5th Cir 2003).

[25] On these aspects of the decision, see Emmanuel Gaillard, "'*KBC v. Pertamina*': Landmark Decision on Anti-Suit Injunctions", *NYLJ*, October 2, 2003. See also Emmanuel Gaillard, "Anti-suit injunctions et reconnaissance des sentences annulées au siège: une évolution remarquable de la jurisprudence américaine", 130 *JDI (Clunet)* 1105 (2003).

[26] See, e.g., in favour of the enforcement of awards annulled in their country of origin, David Rivkin, "The Enforcement of Awards Nullified in the Country of Origin: The American Experience", in *ICCA Congress Series no 9, Improving the Efficiency of Arbitration Agreements and Awards: 40 Years of Application of the New York Convention* 528 (1999). For a critical view, see Eric Schwartz, "A Comment on Chromalloy: Hilmarton à l'américaine", 14(2) *J Int'l Arb* 125 (1997); Dana Freyer, Hamid Gharavi, "Finality and Enforceability of Foreign Arbitral Awards: From 'Double Exequatur' to the Enforcement of Annulled Awards: A Suggested Path to Uniformity Amidst Diversity", 13 *ICSID Rev-FILJ 101* (1998). On the position taken by the courts of other countries, see, e.g. Emmanuel Gaillard, "The Enforcement of Awards Set Aside in the Country of Origin", 14 *ICSID Rev-FILJ.* 16 (1999).

[27] *Chromalloy Aeroservices v. Arab Republic of Egypt*, 939 F Supp 907 (DDC 1996) (enforcing in the United States an award annulled in Egypt). The French courts took the same action in a related case: Paris Court of Appeals, 14 January 1997, *République arabe d'Egypte v. Société Chromalloy Aero Services*, 1997 *Rev Arb* 385.

an American court and courts of other countries have enforced awards, or permitted their enforcement, despite prior annulment in courts of primary jurisdiction.[28]

In other words,

> other enforcement courts can and sometimes do conduct their own independent analyses of substantive challenges to the enforcement of the foreign award.[29]

10-17 As regards the interests of international comity, the Court observed that

> [t]he doctrine of [international] comity contains a rule of 'local restraint' which guides courts reasonably to restrict the extraterritorial application of sovereign power[30].

The Court further held that,

> even if the Indonesian court acted wrongly in its decision to annul the Award as a purported court of primary jurisdiction under the New York Convention, we need not directly address the propriety of that court's injunction and annulment. Contrary to the district court's conclusions, legal action in Indonesia, regardless of its legitimacy, does not interfere with the ability of US courts, or courts of any other enforcement jurisdictions for that matter, to enforce a foreign arbitral award.[31]

Thus, the Fifth Circuit recognized that its response to a possibly illegitimate anti-suit injunction by a foreign court did not need to entail issuing a similar injunction itself.

10-18 This reasoning begs the question, more generally, of whether anti-suit injunctions (including anti-anti-suit injunctions) are justified when they are issued in order to protect international arbitration or whether judicial self-restraint is a virtue in all circumstances. The Fifth Circuit's response to this

---

[28] *Pertamina*, 335 F 3d at 367. This is also what the Hong Kong Courts did in the *Pertamina* case (see *Karaha Bodas Co LLC v. Perusahaan Pertambangan Minyak Dan Gas Bumi Negara*, High Court of the Hong Kong Special Administrative Region, 27 March 2003, 2003 HKCU Lexis 378. The decision is based on the debatable ground that the Indonesian Courts did not have jurisdiction to annul the award, although the outcome is justified). More recently, on 9 December 2004, the Court of Queen's Bench of Alberta also recognized the December 2000 award (see 20(1) *Mealey's IAR* 6 (2005)).

[29] *Pertamina*, 335 F 3d at 367-68.

[30] *Ibid*, at 371.

[31] *Ibid*, at 372.

question is that no justification should be found, while issuing an anti-suit injunction, in the fact that it is rendered in favour of arbitration: although it "empathiz[ed] with the district court and shar[ed] its frustrations at the acts of Pertamina and its counsel" who requested and obtained the Indonesian anti-suit injunction and annulment judgment, the Court justifiably concluded that

> [t]he [1958 New York] Convention already appears to allow for some degree of forum shopping, and, as with many treaties, the efficacy of the Convention depends in large part on the good faith of its sovereign signatories. Upholding the district court's injunction could only further exacerbate the problem, diplomatically if not legally as well.[32]

In other words, although anti-anti-suit injunctions may appear to be the appropriate response to counter a court order aimed at obstructing arbitral proceedings or the enforcement of an arbitral award, they may exacerbate, rather than solve, the problems created by anti-suit injunctions by triggering an escalation of injunctions that lead to the frustration of the arbitral process as a whole.

10-19 Principles of international arbitration law further suggest that, as far as national courts are concerned, self-restraint is the proper response in all circumstances to the parties' attempt to bypass the arbitration agreement through an abusive recourse to the local courts. Indeed, anti-suit injunctions negate the very basis of arbitration, that is, the parties' consent to submit their disputes to arbitration.[33] When a party consents to an arbitration agreement, it undertakes to refer disputes that may arise with the other party to arbitration, to take part in the proceedings in good faith and to carry out the award that will be rendered.[34] As a

---

[32] *Ibid*, at 375-76.
[33] On this issue, see, e.g., Grigera Naón, supra note 2, at 339-340; see also the Award in *Salini*, supra note 10 and accompanying text.
[34] See, e.g., the Interim Award of May 14, 2001 in ICC Case No 8307, supra note 6, at 313:

> [...] the agreement to arbitrate implies that the parties have renounced to submit to judicial courts the disputes envisaged by the arbitral clause. If a party despite this commences a judicial action when an arbitration is pending, it not only violates the rule according to which a dispute between the same parties over the same subject can be decided by one judge only, but also the binding arbitration clause. In such a case, according to Art. II § 3 of the New York Convention which has been ratified by [country X], the judicial court has the obligation to refer the matter to the arbitral tribunal. It is not contested that an arbitrator has the power to order the parties to comply with their contractual commitments. The agreement to arbitrate being one of them, its violation must be dealt with in the same manner when it is patent that the action initiated in a state court is outside the jurisdiction of such court and is therefore abusive. This is also a guarantee of the efficiency and credibility of international arbitration.

result, when a party requests that a court issues an anti-suit injunction to prevent an arbitral tribunal from hearing a claim or to obstruct the enforcement of an arbitral award, it too may be said to fail to honour its commitment to be bound by the arbitration agreement.

10-20 At the stage of the enforcement of an arbitral award, each legal system is equally entitled to sovereign rights and to the discretion to recognize and enforce foreign arbitral awards on the basis of its own standards of review. The temptation to use anti-suit injunctions cannot be justified by the fact that it is issued in favour of the arbitral process. By definition, each measure is restricted in the scope of its effects to the legal system in which it is issued. As a result, the only viable alternative ensuring the efficiency of international arbitration is that each legal system should decide for itself and on the basis of its own standards of public policy whether or not to recognize and enforce foreign arbitral awards.

10-21 By the same token, at the stage of the arbitral proceeding, judicial self-restraint is the most appropriate standard in light of the arbitral tribunal's jurisdiction to rule on its own jurisdiction, *i.e.* the bedrock principle of competence-competence. It is indeed critical that the jurisdiction of the arbitral tribunal to determine its own jurisdiction be safeguarded and that the courts of any given legal system do not encroach on the jurisdiction of an arbitral tribunal. In other words, until such time as the award is rendered, the courts of different countries should limit their intervention on the basis that the arbitral tribunal has *prima facie* jurisdiction. Conversely, arbitral tribunals should be given the opportunity to fully exercise their power to rule on their own jurisdiction, either by way of a positive order to the parties to comply with their contractual commitments until such time as the tribunal has been in a position to determine its own jurisdiction (as in the *SGS v. Pakistan* case) or by way of a final decision on the issue of whether an anti-suit injunction should be given effect as regards the tribunal's jurisdiction to rule on its own jurisdiction (as in the *Salini v. Ethiopia* case).[35] In that context, the arbitral tribunal itself may issue an order to the parties that could be characterized as an 'anti-suit injunction': the arbitral tribunal would then be acting within the confines of its power, derived from the parties' arbitration agreement, to direct the parties not to act in any way that would jeopardize its *prima facie* jurisdiction until such time as the tribunal has formed its own judgment on its jurisdiction and established in a final manner whether it

---

[35] See also Laurent Lévy, "Anti-Suit Injunctions Issued by Arbitrators", in *Anti-Suit Injunctions in International Arbitration*, supra note 3, at 115.

has been established on the basis of an existing and valid arbitration agreement and whether the scope of that agreement includes the dispute that has been brought before it. After that determination is made, the issuance by the arbitral tribunal of an anti-suit injunction is even less problematic. Yet, after the arbitral tribunal issues an award, the courts of each legal system recover their discretion to determine whether that award meets the enforcement conditions of the law and standards applicable in that country. This is the necessary counterpart for the arbitrators' license to decide first on their own jurisdiction.[36]

10-22 Against this background, national courts should ensure the lowest level of interference in the arbitration by limiting the possibility for the parties to resort to such devices as anti-suit injunctions, which may or may not be legitimate in the context of ordinary judicial matters, but which, when transposed automatically into the realm of international arbitration, are inappropriate.

---

[36] On the arbitral tribunal's power of first determination of its jurisdiction, see Emmanuel Gaillard, "Prima Facie Review of Existence, Validity of Arbitration Agreement", *NYLJ*, December 1, 2005; Emmanuel Gaillard, "La reconnaissance, en droit suisse, de la seconde moitié du principe d'effet négatif de la compétence-compétence", in *Liber Amicorum in honour of Robert Briner*, supra note 2, at 311.

PART III

INTERNATIONAL ARBITRATION AND STATE PARTIES

*Nigel Blackaby**

CHAPTER 11

INVESTMENT ARBITRATION
AND COMMERCIAL ARBITRATION
(OR THE TALE OF THE DOLPHIN AND THE SHARK)

I. INTRODUCTION

11-1 The last five years have seen the dramatic emergence of a hitherto little-known species in the otherwise well-charted waters of international arbitration: the international investment arbitration. True, the species was known to exist and there had been sporadic catches by individual investors since the early 1990s. Prior to that time, it had been listed in textbooks but the only regular observations had been limited to those made by an international coastguard ship, "HMS Diplomatic Protection".

11-2 No doubt the increased catches by individual investors were due to their recent rights to sail in treaty claim waters formerly reserved for states alone. No longer did the claimant investor have to convince its home state to set sail from the safe harbour of international relations on its behalf. State claims were suddenly democratised and a small trickle of brave adventurers has eventually led to a small armada of private investors leaving port.

11-3 Many claims were brought under the rules of the International Centre for the Settlement of Investment Disputes (ICSID), the institution specifically established by the 1965 Convention on the Settlement of Investment Disputes between States and Nationals of Other States.[1] Others were brought under the rules more familiar to commercial practitioners, UNCITRAL, the Arbitration

* Partner, International Arbitration Group, Freshfields Bruckhaus Deringer, Paris. He may be contacted at nigel.blackaby@freshfields.com.

[1] Otherwise known as the ICSID Convention or the Washington Convention.

Loukas A. Mistelis and Julian D.M. Lew (eds), Pervasive Problems in International Arbitration, 217-233
© 2006 Kluwer Law International. Printed in the Netherlands

Institute of the Stockholm Chamber of Commerce or the ICC. These rules were the domain of a group of lawyers who had anchored their careers on the vagaries of international commerce and whose battles were principally private in nature. Yet the underlying substance of these new disputes was to be addressed under a governing law, public international law, which was often unfamiliar territory to these lawyers.

11-4 The issue that I have to consider is whether these new investment arbitrations are in fact the same animal as the commercial arbitrations which have preceded them or whether they are a different species? Like the dolphin and the shark, is their superficial similarity deceptive? Is one fish and the other mammal? As the United States Government argued in the context of an investment arbitration under the NAFTA:[2]

> [investor-state disputes are] to be distinguished from a typical commercial arbitration on the basis that a State [is] the Respondent, the issues [have] to be decided in accordance with a treaty and the principles of public international law and a decision on the dispute could have a significant effect extending beyond the two Disputing Parties.

11-5 That is a good summary – but the list is not exhaustive. I will attempt to identify the key differences before focusing on the similarities and then reach some tentative conclusions as to whether the shark and the dolphin should be swimming together in the same pool at the zoo.

II. THE DIFFERENCES

11-6 So what are these differences?

1. Source of the Consent to Arbitrate

11-7 In a commercial arbitration, the source of the consent to arbitration is usually the arbitration clause of the contract whose breach is under debate (the "*clause compromissoire*"). Occasionally it may be found in an agreement to refer the specific dispute to arbitration through a submission agreement (the "*compromis*"). The parties to the arbitration will be one or more of the parties to the contract or the submission agreement. In all cases, the agreement is limited to

---

[2] *Methanex Corporation v. United States of America*, NAFTA case, under UNCITRAL Rules, Decision on Amici Curiae, 15 January 2001, 9, para 17. Text available on the ITA website: http://ita.law.uvic.ca/chronological_list.htm._

disputes which arise out of (or sometimes in connection with, depending on the wording of the clause) the specific contract.

11-8 In an investment arbitration, the consent of the state is exhibited through an open offer to arbitrate disputes with investors having the nationality of another sovereign state in relation to defined classes of investment. This offer is contained in a treaty concluded with one or more sovereign states to which the class of protected investor is not a party – it therefore cannot in itself constitute a consent to arbitrate. It requires the consent or acceptance of a member of the class, usually exhibited through the submission of a dispute by a covered investor to arbitration through the presentation of a Request for Arbitration under the applicable rules.

11-9 The state's offer is often broad and provides a protected investor with a range of dispute resolution options some of which may foreclose others (in the presence of a so-called "fork in the road" provision). A state is therefore unaware of the specific identity of potential disputants until they are notified of the existence of a dispute under the relevant Treaty. This type of arbitration has been christened "arbitration without privity" since there is no need for a direct contractual link between the state and the investor.[3]

11-10 This was of course a remarkable development: – the granting of directly enforceable rights against a sovereign state to investors of the other Contracting State. Its function was clear: to depoliticise foreign investment disputes which depended until then upon the exercise by the investor's home state of diplomatic protection. Such protection had grave limitations as Professor Brierley observed 40 years ago:[4]

> [The investor] has no remedy of his own, and the state to which he belongs may be unwilling to take up his case for reasons which have nothing to do with its merits; and even if it is willing to do so, there may be interminable delays before, if ever, the defendant state can be induced to let the matter go to arbitration ... It has been suggested that a solution might be found by allowing individuals access in their own right to some form of international tribunal for the purpose, and if proper safeguards against merely frivolous or vexatious claims could be devised, that is a possible reform which deserves

---

[3] Jan Paulsson, "Arbitration Without Privity", 10 *ICSID Review – FILJ* 232 (1995).
[4] J L Brierley, *The Law of Nations*, (6th edition, Oxford University Press), p 277.

to be considered. For the time being, however, the prospect of states accepting such a change is not very great.

11-11 However, states were eventually convinced of the need for this change. The solution was ingenious: in the absence of a permanent tribunal, an individual right of action would be created through an open offer to arbitrate by the state. The elegance of the solution was unquestionable and could be served by the recently created ICSID, an institution established under the auspices of the World Bank dedicated to disputes between states and investors of other states. Principally conceived to provide a better adapted regime for state contracts with foreign investors, the proposed solution of ICSID arbitration for investment disputes fell neatly within ICSID's purpose.

2. The Amicable Negotiation Period

11-12 Often before consent can be perfected through a Request for Arbitration, investment treaties include other preconditions usually absent from commercial arbitrations. To seek to minimise the number of cases which advance to arbitration, the offer of most states to arbitrate investment disputes is conditioned on the conclusion of an amicable negotiation period of between three to six months. This is perhaps the reverse of the coin of an open offer to arbitrate. Prior to being drawn into a long and expensive international procedure with potentially adverse political consequences, states have insisted on a prior notification and a "cooling off" period within which they could seek to resolve the dispute amicably. Such a condition was aimed at providing respondent states with an opportunity to enter into a dialogue with the disgruntled investor before being exposed to the risk of a claim whose existence would almost certainly enter the public domain with a negative impact on the state's investment profile.

11-13 It is a pity that few states have seriously used this period to explore potential settlements and its original purpose appears to have been largely ignored by most states which refuse to engage in a dialogue during this period.[5] Indeed, some tribunals have categorised this requirement as procedural rather

---

[5] It has been suggested to me that one reason for this failure to engage (at least in relation to most Latin American jurisdictions) is the personal liability that civil servants may incur if they are considered not to have fulfilled their public duty. As a consequence, few functionaries are prepared to authorise a settlement (however reasonable) – an adverse award represents less personal risk than a positive settlement. I have heard of a case where a US$1 million settlement with a South American state was approved by five separate ministries in order to avoid the risk of any allegation of corruption or breach of the duties of public office.

than jurisdictional in order to break free from an excessive formalism that it might otherwise impose at a time when action needed to be taken. On the basis of this theory, if and when it is clear that the state does not intend to engage in discussions with the disgruntled investor, the failure to observe the waiting period does not operate as a jurisdictional bar.

11-14   In *Ronald S Lauder v. The Czech Republic,*[6] the tribunal waived the six-month waiting period in the US – Czech Republic Treaty in the following terms:

> However, the Arbitral Tribunal considers that this requirement of a six-month waiting period of Article VI(3)(a) of the Treaty is not a jurisdictional provision, i.e. a limit set to the authority of the Arbitral Tribunal to decide on the merits of the dispute, but a procedural rule that must be satisfied by the Claimant (*Ethyl Corp. v. Canada*, UNCITRAL June 24, 1998, 38 I.L.M. 708 (1999), paragraphs 74-88). As stated above, the purpose of this rule is to allow the parties to engage in good-faith negotiations before initiating arbitration.[7]

Moreover, in the tribunal's view,

> [t]o insist that the arbitration proceedings cannot be commenced until 6 months after the 19 August 1999 Notice of Arbitration would, in the circumstances of this case, amount to an unnecessary, overly formalistic approach which would not serve to protect any legitimate interests of the Parties.[8]

11-15   How does this step differ from purely commercial arbitrations? It is true that such clauses may be introduced into private contracts in the context of staged dispute resolution provisions. Indeed, the provisions are often more complex with the integration of mediation and non-binding expertise as required steps prior to initiating arbitration. However, such staged clauses remain generally limited to complex infrastructure contracts where the ongoing nature of the works mandates a dispute resolution procedure which maximises the possibility of settlement at an early stage. Otherwise, the increasing length of traditional arbitration procedures provides ample opportunity to engage in parallel settlement discussions during the life of the arbitration.

---

[6]   *Ronald S Lauder v. The Czech Republic*, Final Award, 3 September 2001. Text available on the CME website at: http://www.cetv-net.com/arbitration.asp. The text is also available on the ITA website.
[7]   *Ibid*, para 187.
[8]   *Ibid*, para 190.

3. Nature of the Issues

11-16 Turning to the nature of the issues, most commercial arbitrations concern whether there has been a breach of an international commercial contract. Most investment arbitrations, on the other hand, concern whether a state, through the actions of its various branches of government, has breached its international law commitments towards foreign investments under the investment protection provisions of a treaty.[9] The task of the tribunal in such a case is therefore to assess compatibility of municipal state conduct through the optic of international law.

11-17 It will be readily observed that the two exercises are radically different. In particular, the commercial arbitration will usually come equipped with a detailed guide to the respective rights and obligations of the parties, the contract. An investment treaty dispute comes equipped with a parallel source of rights, the treaty, which will include on its face a number of broadly worded concepts such as "fair and equitable treatment" which are of little assistance to the uninitiated.

11-18 It is true that in any international commercial arbitration there will often be a governing law in the contract with which one or more arbitrators may be unfamiliar. However, its role is often peripherally limited to rules of interpretation and the definition of the outer limits of public policy. In investment arbitrations, international law is always at the very heart of the substantive debate. This brings us to the fourth difference, applicable law.

4. Applicable Law

11-19 In commercial cases, the choice of law is usually made by the parties in their contract (governing law clause) and is nearly always a system of municipal law. In investment arbitrations, the interpretation of a treaty is subject to the Vienna Convention on the Law of Treaties and thus principally to international law. The principles of international law in question form the common guiding rules of decision in all investment arbitrations.

---

[9] Investment protection provisions are most commonly found in bilateral investment treaties (of which there are over 2300) but may also be found in multilateral investment treaties such as the Energy Charter Treaty or in the investment chapters or protocols of bilateral or multilateral free trade agreements (e.g. the North American Free Trade Agreement (NAFTA); the US-Chile Free Trade Agreement; or the as yet unratified Colonia Protocol to the Mercosur Agreement).

11-20 The exercise of the international tribunal is to establish whether the state has breached substantive treaty obligations such as "expropriation without prompt, adequate and effective compensation"; "fair and equitable treatment" or "full protection and security" rather than contractual obligations. As the annulment panel in *Vivendi* stated:

> Whether there has been a breach of the treaty and whether there has been a breach of contract are different questions. Each of these claims will be determined by reference to its own proper or applicable law – in the case of the [Treaty], by international law, in the case of the Concession Contract, by the proper law of the contract ... A treaty cause of action is not the same as a contractual cause of action; it requires a clear showing of conduct which is in the circumstances contrary to the relevant treaty standard.[10]

11-21 Consequently, the violation or not of an investment treaty requires an international law analysis drawing on international law precedents on the protection of foreign investment or alien property, whether originating from the International Court of Justice, the Mixed Claims Comissions, the Iran-US Claims Tribunal or more recent cases decided under investment treaties.

11-22 Some confusion has been thrown on this issue by Article 42 of the ICSID Convention which refers the parties back to the municipal law of the state of the investment where there is no contrary agreement. When interpreting this article, it should not be forgotten that ICSID's original purpose was to provide a contractual dispute resolution mechanism in state contracts. Where a state contract did not contain a governing law clause in a contract referring to ICSID arbitration, it is not surprising that preference was to be given to the municipal law of the host state of the investment. However, municipal laws simply do not provide rules for decision of an international instrument. In the case of *MTD v. Chile*, the tribunal was unequivocal:

> the parties have agreed to this arbitration under the BIT. This instrument being a treaty, the agreement to arbitrate under the BIT requires the tribunal to apply international law.[11]

---

[10] *Compañia de Aguas del Aconquija SA & Vivendi Universal v. Argentine Republic*, ICSID Case No ARB/97/3, Decision on Annulment, 3 July 2002, paras 96 and 113. Text available on the ICSID website at: http://www.worldbank.org/icsid/cases/awards.htm

[11] *MTD Equity Sdn Bhd & MTD Chile SA v. Chile*, ICSID Case No ARB/01/7, Award, 25 May 2004, at para 87. Text available at: http://ita.law.uvic.ca/chronological_list.htm

11-23 This is eminently logical. The interpretation of the Treaty cannot change depending upon the location of the investment and the nationality of the claimant – it must have a single meaning which the two parties intended when signing. As the tribunal in *LESI DIPENTA v. Algeria* observed:

> Dealing with an international treaty, the meaning to be applied must be that which the two parties could give it and not that which one of the parties would like to emphasise in light of its national legislation.[12]

11-24 This is not to say that municipal law has no relevance. In the vast majority of cases it is precisely the legality under the Treaty of measures of municipal law which is under consideration.

11-25 Unfortunately, the complexities of applicable law do not end there. In many investment treaties, there is a clause commonly known as the "respect for undertakings" clause or "umbrella clause". There is a lively jurisprudential dispute as to whether these clauses elevate ordinary contractual breaches in state contracts to treaty breaches.[13]

11-26 Insofar as the thesis is upheld that such clauses do elevate ordinary contractual breaches to the level of an international wrong, the tribunal in *SGS v. Philippines* rightfully noted that the international wrong was dependent upon a prior conclusion that there was a breach of the contract under the municipal law applicable to that contract. International law would not inform the debate of whether such a breach had occurred in the first place.[14]

---

[12] *Consortium Groupement LESI-DIPENTA v. Algeria*, ICSID Case No ARB/03/08, Decision on Jurisdiction, 10 January 2005, at para 24. Text available on the ITA website: http://ita.law.uvic.ca/chronological_list.htm

[13] See, e.g., *SGS Société Générale de Surveillance SA v. Islamic Republic of Pakistan*, ICSID Case No ARB/01/13, Decision of the Tribunal on Objections to Jurisdiction, 6 August 2003; *SGS Société Générale de Surveillance SA v. Republic of the Philippines*, ICSID Case No. ARB/02/6, Decision of the Tribunal on Objections to Jurisdiction, 29 January 2004; *CMS Gas Transmission Company v. Argentina*, ICSID Case No ARB/01/8, Award on Jurisdiction, 17 July 2003; *Eureko BV v. Republic of Poland*, UNCITRAL, Partial Award and Dissenting Opinion, 19 August 2005. Text of decisions at: http://ita.law.uvic.ca/chronological_list.htm.
The history of these clauses is developed in Anthony Sinclair, "The Origins of the Umbrella Clause in the International Law of Investment Protection", 20(4) *Arb Int* 411– 434 (2004).

[14] *SGS Société Générale de Surveillance SA v. Republic of the Philippines*, ICSID Case No ARB/02/6, Decision on Jurisdiction, 29 April 2004, at paras 126-128. Text available on the ITA website: http://ita.law.uvic.ca/chronological_list.htm

11-27 The effect of a common set of decision-making rules also creates a precedential value for investment arbitration decisions usually absent from an ordinary commercial case based upon a particular municipal law that will likely be of interest only to the parties themselves as I will consider further below.

5. *State Participation*

11-28 The fifth point of comparison is the participation of a nation state in the proceedings. Whilst the participation of states or state entities in commercial arbitrations is not uncommon, it is a *sine qua non* of an investment arbitration. Even where a state does participate in a commercial arbitration it is usually doing so in a commercial capacity, *jure gestionis*.

11-29 Investment arbitrations, on the other hand, have at their heart measures of the state which go beyond mere contractual breaches and may raise broader political issues. So whilst public interest groups and other third parties rarely show interest in international commercial arbitration, they have sought to participate in investment arbitrations on the basis that the interests in question go beyond those of the parties in dispute. This has happened with cases brought under NAFTA concerning environmental measures where the possibility of an *amicus curiae* brief was not considered incompatible with an arbitration brought under the UNCITRAL Rules.[15] Whilst a similarly liberal approach was rejected in the context of a claim concerning the termination of a water concession in Bolivia[16], it was accepted by the tribunal in the case of *Aguas Argentinas et al v. Argentina*[17] where the tribunal found no inherent prohibition on such briefs in the ICSID Rules but subjected them to a strict test requiring the author to demonstrate its legitimacy and the relevance of its submission based loosely on criteria applied to the acceptance of similar briefs before the US Supreme Court.[18]

---

[15] See supra note 2; Chapter 16 by Friedland, below; and Loukas Mistelis, "Confidentiality and Third Party Participation in Investment Arbitration", in 21(2) *Arb Int* 211-231 (2005) = Todd Weiler (ed), *International Investment Law and Arbitration: Leading Cases from the ICSID, NAFTA, Bilateral Treaties and Customary International Law* (Cameron May, 2005) 169-199.

[16] See Letter by the President of the Tribunal David D Caron, dated 29 January 2003, refusing to admit *Amicus Curiae* briefs. Text available on http://www.earthjustice.org/news/documents/2-03/ICSIDResponse.pdf.

[17] *Aguas Argentinas SA, Suez, Sociedad General de Aguas de Barcelona, SA and Vivendi Universal, SA v. Argentine Republic*, ICSID Case No ARB/03/19, Order in Response to a Petition for Transparency and Participation as Amicus Curiae, 19 May 2005. Text available on the ITA website: http://ita.law.uvic.ca/chronological_list.htm.

[18] The Tribunal ruled that the acceptance of *Amicus Curiae* briefs should depend on three basic criteria: (i) the appropriateness of the subject matter of the case, characterised by the existence

6. Transparency

11-30 Linked to this recognition of the possible impact of investment arbitration decisions outside of the parties in conflict, there have been calls by states for greater transparency in the process to allow possibly affected third parties to participate.

11-31 The degree of transparency will depend upon whether the investment case is under the ICSID rules or other commercial arbitration rules. ICSID imposes a degree of transparency by requiring publication on its website of the existence of a case and the parties, together with major procedural steps. There are no such requirements in investment cases conducted under other rules. However, in practice many non ICSID investor-state arbitrations come to light in the event of a challenge to the award or revelation by the parties. Indeed, governments who voluntarily pay an adverse award will have to account publicly for the disbursement.

11-32 Specific rules have been applied by the signatory states to NAFTA where the United States and Canada make pleadings publicly available pursuant to freedom of information legislation. Other states such as Argentina have made public the names of counsel and have indicated they will publish pleadings.[19] This is all very different from the traditions of commercial arbitration where confidentiality is still presumed to reign. However, the presumption has little basis in concrete rules and the fortress of confidentiality has often turned out to be a castle of cards, even in commercial cases.[20]

11-33 Another aspect of transparency has been the call for public hearings in investment cases. Whilst the latest model US Bilateral Investment Treaty includes such a provision[21], most investment cases are conducted under the ICSID

---

of issues of public interest – illustrated *in casu* by the analysis of the legal framework of a public utility service system affecting millions of people; (ii) the suitability of a given non party to act as amicus curiae, hinging on sufficient expertise, experience and independence (iii) the particular procedure determined by the Tribunal. In applying these criteria the Tribunal added that consideration had to be given to the views of the parties, the extra burden placed on the proceedings as well as the degree to which the proposed brief was likely to assist the Tribunal in arriving at its decision.

[19] See the website of the Procuración Nacional del Tesoro: www.ptn.gov.ar. See also Mistelis, supra note 15.

[20] See discussion on confidentiality in Redfern & Hunter with Nigel Blackaby, Constantine Partasides, *Law & Practice of International Commercial Arbitration* (4th edition Sweet & Maxwell 2004), at pp 27 –34. See also Chapter 4 by Veeder, above and Mistelis, supra note 15.

[21] 2004 US Model BIT, Article 29(2). Text available at www.stategov/e/eb/rls/othr/38602.htm.

rules or UNCITRAL rules which do not. In these cases, public hearings require the consent of both parties which is rarely forthcoming. Ironically, in those cases where such consent has occurred, the clamour surrounding the secrecy of the usually "secret courts" (as the newspapers have baptised them) quickly gives way to lethargy – in one recent case, after just a few days of hearings, the journalistic interest had all but disappeared.

11-34 The question of a public hearing has rarely arisen in commercial arbitrations where, by their very nature, questions of private interest are debated. Any further move towards a generalised public hearing in investment cases would consequently represent a fundamental difference between the two systems.

7. Publicity of Decisions

11-35 The decisions of the average commercial arbitration tribunal are not public. Unless the decision is subject to a challenge procedure, the awards will often never be known outside of the parties and the institutional secretariat. Moreover, even if they were public, their substantive aspects would cause little excitement. To take an example, what eminent Swiss, French and German arbitrators conclude about a particular question of Brazilian law is unlikely to attract the attention of Brazilian lawyers or be called in aid of a case before the Brazilian courts. Insofar as the decisions are published in redacted form, they are interesting more for their interpretations of the arbitrators' powers, the procedural issues that may have arisen or the occasional reference to international public policy or *lex mercatoria* rather than substantive issues of the applicable law.

11-36 The decisions of investment arbitration tribunals, on the other hand, are nearly always public. In the case of ICSID, either party may release the award even though there is some debate about whether the other party's consent is required.[22] Indeed, the Secretariat encourages the publicity of awards. In the case of investment arbitrations under commercial rules, publicity is not universal but the stakes are usually such that the losing party will often seek to set aside the award before the courts of the forum at which moment the award is revealed.

---

[22] The ICSID rules require the consent of both parties for the Centre to publish the award (Rule 48 (4)). However, this does not necessarily imply that the parties need each other's consent for such publication. In reality, it is common for one or other party to publish the award on its website or release a decision unilaterally to publications such as the *International Law Reports* or *Mealey's Arbitration Report*.

11-37 This lack of publicity gives international arbitrators in commercial arbitrations an advantage over international arbitrators in investment arbitrations: they can focus on the case at hand and ignore wider implications on the development of jurisprudence. As a result, the tension between the need for justice in the specific case and the danger of creating an unfortunate precedent does not usually arise.

11-38 In the light of the increased publicity of investment arbitration awards, the investment arbitrator has a new responsibility for establishing a corpus of law. Unlike commercial arbitration where applicable law varies, the arbitrators in these cases are consistently applying a limited number of concepts under public international law. They have thus become *ad hoc* judges whose decisions are scrutinised and commented as if they were decisions of a domestic Supreme Court. The arbitration community has rarely basked in such publicity as lawyers attempt to define the frontiers of abstract concepts such as "fair and equitable treatment" or "full protection and security". Quite naturally, recognising this broader role, arbitrators have begun to act like judges – often commenting on issues not strictly necessary for the resolution of the dispute in *obiter dicta*. The award also becomes a showcase for legal erudition since the reputation of the arbitrator will depend on the perceived quality of the decision by the peer group. The interests of the consumers (the investor and the state) to have the specific dispute resolved promptly in the most cost effective manner may have been lost in the crescendo of academic debate that has left them all too often as helpless bystanders. The process takes on a life of its own which grinds forward at a pace so slow that the passage of generations of in-house counsel soon forget the origin of the dispute.[23] In between the constitution of the tribunal, the hearing of bifurcated jurisdictional objections and frequent arbitrator challenges, there is much that a respondent state can do to wear down the resolve of the most persistent

---

[23] In the worst cases, a comparison with the progress of the case of *Jarndyce v. Jarndyce* in Dickens's *Bleak House* would not be out of place.

> *Jarndyce and Jarndyce* drones on. This scarecrow of a suit has, in course of time, become so complicated that no man alive knows what it means. The parties to it understand it least, but it has been observed that no two Chancery lawyers can talk about it for five minutes without coming to a total disagreement as to all the premises. Innumerable children have been born into the cause; innumerable young people have married into it; innumerable old people have died out of it. ... The little plaintiff or defendant who was promised a new rocking-horse when Jarndyce and Jarndyce should be settled has grown up, possessed himself of a real horse, and trotted away into the other world.

(Charles Dickens, *Bleak House*, Chapter One)

claimant on the slimmest of arguments. Commercial organisations are shocked to be told that an investment dispute will take four years to resolve (without counting an eventual annulment application to add a further 18 months to two years). An award on jurisdiction frequently takes six months or more; an award on the merits up to a year. We are a long way from the alleged benefit of arbitration as a time and cost efficient dispute resolution mechanism.

11-39 It is true that the length of the average commercial arbitration has increased over the years. Yet, in the absence of any publicity for the awards or the sense of a higher jurisprudential purpose, the focus tends to remain firmly fixed on resolving the commercial dispute between the parties.

11-40 Another fundamental difference that arises from the publicity of awards and that consequently raises little concern in the world of commercial arbitration is the impact of the dual role of counsel and arbitrator. Counsel in commercial cases can move seamlessly to a role as arbitrator in another commercial case. The factual and legal issues in each case will be radically different and the decisions will usually remain in the private domain. However, arbitrators and counsel in treaty cases will be working repeatedly with a small number of legal concepts. As a consequence, in a much discussed case, the independence and impartiality of an arbitrator who was allegedly adopting a particular position on a pertinent issue in a case as counsel was successfully challenged.[24]

8. Importance of Lex Arbitri

11-41 The eighth point of comparison is the importance of the *lex arbitri*. Once again, there is no clear dividing line since the difference will depend entirely on whether the investment arbitration is under the ICSID regime or commercial rules. Under the ICSID regime, the critical role of the *lex arbitri* has been abandoned in favour of a self-contained hermetic system of international justice. Under arbitrations conducted under the ICSID Convention, the national courts of

---

[24] See District Court of The Hague, 18 October 2004, Challenge No. 13/2004 *Telekom Malaysia v. Ghana*; Petition No HA/RK 2004.667; an unofficial English translation of the judgment can be found at: www.transnational-dispute-management.com.
This decision, concerned the challenge of the arbitrator nominated by Ghana on the basis that Ghana relied on a decision, *RFCC v. Morocco,* where the arbitrator had been advising RFCC on a potential challenge to the award. The Dutch court gave the arbitrator the option of ceasing such representation or resigning as arbitrator.

the place of arbitration have no traditional supervisory role. Article 26 expressly provides that

> consent of the parties to arbitration under this Convention shall, unless otherwise stated, be deemed consent to such arbitration to the exclusion of any other remedy.

Likewise pursuant to article 52 applications to annul the award must take place within the system itself. However, under investment arbitrations conducted under the scope of commercial institutions or rules such as those of UNCITRAL, the ICC or the Stockholm Chamber of Commerce, the courts of the place of arbitration continue to play an important role in challenge proceedings in the same way as in any commercial case. Here, however, the situation is more delicate than in a purely commercial matter. The courts of a third state sit in judgment over an international law decision which exonerates or condemns the state party to the arbitration. Although the scope of such review is limited, there is an inherent tension in the idea that the courts of British Columbia, Sweden or the United Kingdom have had in their hands questions concerning the liability of Mexico, the Czech Republic or Ecuador.[25] Indeed, in the recent discussion concerning potential modifications to the ICSID rules, the possibility of an "option" to the ICSID system of review was discussed for those arbitrations held under the Additional Facility of ICSID[26] where normally the courts of the seat would have jurisdiction for such an exercise.

9. International Legal Effect

11-42 The last difference I want to highlight is the different international legal effect of most investment cases compared with commercial cases. But once

---

[25] In the case of *Metalclad v. Mexico*, the Supreme Court of British Columbia in a decision dated 2 May 2001, Supreme Court of British Columbia, 2001 *BCSC* 664, partially set aside the award in favour of the claimant; in the case of *CME v. Czech Republic*, the Svea Court of Appeals in Sweden in a decision dated 15 May 2003, Svea Court of Appeal Case no T 8735-01, available at http://ita.law.uvic.ca/documents/CME2003-SveaCourtofAppeal_001.pdf, also 42 *ILM* 919, considered a challenge to the US$300 million decision in favour of the claimant; in the case of *Occidental Exploration and Production Company v. Republic of Ecuador*, the English Court of Appeal confirmed in a decision dated 9 September 2005, [2005] EWCA Civ 1116, its jurisdiction to review the US$60 million award of an arbitral tribunal which had sat in London to determine the liability of Ecuador for an alleged breach of the United States-Ecuador BIT.

[26] The Additional Facility of ICSID may be available in the event that either the state of the investor or the host state of the investment is not a party to the ICSID Convention.

again, this is a function of whether the arbitration is under the auspices of ICSID or other commercial rules.

11-43 A winning party in a commercial arbitration may seek enforcement in the courts of any state party to the 1958 New York Convention on the Recognition and Enforcement of Foreign Arbitral Awards (the NY Convention). The courts of that state are obliged to apply the provisions of the NY Convention to the case in point by executing the award and in the event of objection to enforcement, will hear arguments by the losing party under Article V NY Convention. Failure to execute the award or provide such a possibility to raise objections will be a breach of that state's international obligations under the NY Convention.

11-44 A state in compliance with its obligations under the NY Convention will interpret its obligations to enforce and provide a forum for challenge. In the event of enforcement, the apparatus of the state to enforce final judgments must be available. Provided the court has purported to apply the tests of the NY Convention then there is no further review or international objection to be made.

11-45 In the case of an investment arbitration under commercial rules, the NY Convention will also apply. However, in the event that the court fails to provide a proper means of enforcement of the award or adds extra obstacles to enforcement not included in Article V of the NY Convention, the state will be in breach of its obligations under the NY Convention *and* the relevant treaty pursuant to which the arbitration took place. The risk of such a breach is far more acute in investment arbitrations since the natural place to execute an award adverse to a state is in the territory of the state itself. The temptation is for the state to introduce additional hurdles such as constitutional compatibility which provide an ample opportunity for local courts to intervene. However, the introduction of such hurdles is not only a breach of the NY Convention but also the relevant investment treaty. International law is not interested in municipal law compatibility: once a state has ratified the international treaty its international liability is engaged, and domestic law cannot limit its international obligations. It is therefore no defence for a state on the international stage to say that the treaty obligations are unconstitutional as has been suggested by Argentina or that they have not been properly incorporated into domestic law (as was once suggested by Pakistan). In such circumstances, failure to limit the domestic review to NY Convention conditions will be a breach of two international treaties.

11-46 In the case of an arbitration under the ICSID rules, there is less "wriggle room". The ICSID Convention is clear that the award must be executed without further analysis by the domestic judiciary[27]- the control of Article V of the NY Convention having been replaced by the self-contained annulment proceedings. There is therefore no scope for arguing that a domestic court can review the award under grounds similar to Article V NY Convention. Put simply, failure to execute an ICSID award is immediately the violation of two international treaties: the ICSID Convention and the specific treaty pursuant to which the award was rendered.

11-47 International breach is important here. The breach is towards the other states signatory to the treaties and may be the subject of a subsequent inter-state arbitration. It may also give rise to a diplomatic complaint. The United States has gone a stage further through the so-called "Hickenlooper Amendment" which mandates a US veto in international financing institutions for those states who have expropriated the property of US citizens without compensation[28].

11-48 Our biological analysis has demonstrated that the two creatures have some fundamental differences. But are there sufficient similarities to put them in the same tank at the zoo?

III. SIMILARITIES

11-49 Subject to the important differences which surround the source of the consent, the increased transparency, the relationship with national courts and the international legal effect, the actual arbitration procedure is remarkably similar. This is perhaps not surprising: the arbitrators called upon to decide investment arbitrations are largely trained in the sphere of commercial arbitration and the forensic middle ground between the common law and civil law traditions applicable in commercial cases is reflected in investment cases.

11-50 As a consequence, there is usually an exchange of written memorials of claim, defence, reply and rejoinder which annex pertinent documents and signed statememts of experts and fact witnesses. It is not uncommon for the IBA Rules of Evidence and (more recently) the IBA Guidelines on Conflicts of Interest in International Arbitration to be relied upon.

---

[27] Articles 53 and 54 ICSID Convention.

[28] Amendment to the Foreign Assistance Act 1961, approved on December 16, 1963, 77 Stat 386 (22 USC 2370).

11-51 The oral presentation of the case does not have any distinguishing features from commercial arbitration with each party presenting its witnesses who are subject to limited examination-in-chief, cross examination and re-examination with ample opportunity for the arbitrators to ask questions. A person witnessing an investment arbitration through sound-proof glass would not be able to distinguish it from a purely commercial arbitration.

IV. Conclusion

11-52 Having played the role of the vivisectionist and dissected the two animals on the laboratory table, can we legitimately conclude that investment arbitration and commercial arbitration belong to the same family? Or are their superficial similarities deceptive? Is one a mammal and the other a fish?

11-53 The investment arbitration, by its very nature, analyses under the optic of international law measures of a state which are usually public in nature and may have an impact beyond the parties in dispute. The commercial arbitration, on the other hand, analyses under the optic of domestic law the conduct of a party in the context of a private relationship enshrined in a document that is aptly called by the civil law systems "the law of the parties". Whilst the boundaries are not always clear, the essentially public nature of investment arbitration will inevitably require ever greater transparency and accountability. Commercial arbitration should, however, remain essentially a private affair of the parties subject only to a control of due process. If it is dragged into the public arena by its relationship to investment arbitration, many of its essential attributes will be lost.

11-54 The physiological differences must therefore be recognised and appropriate precautions taken. Although the same actors participate in both types of arbitration, they should be wary of all too readily transferring concepts from one to the other as this may pollute some of the essential qualities and flexibility of commercial arbitration. In this context, a salutary exercise is to read the arbitration provisions of the latest model United States BIT and imagine those concepts transferred to a commercial case. It would cause more than one corporation to think twice before inserting an arbitration clause in its contract! So beware, there is a danger in putting the sharks and the dolphins together in the same aquarium at the zoo. The dolphin may be sacrificed!

*Matthew Weiniger**

CHAPTER 12

JURISDICTION CHALLENGES IN BIT ARBITRATIONS –
DO YOU READ A BIT BY READING A BIT
OR BY READING INTO A BIT?

I. OVERVIEW

12-1 Jurisdiction challenges have been featuring in ICSID arbitrations since the very first ICSID arbitration, *Holiday Inns*.[1] The Respondent State challenged the tribunal's jurisdiction to hear the claim in three of the first four ICSID arbitrations. In the last three years, out of approximately 56 awards or decisions arising out of arbitrations registered by ICSID,[2] the Respondent State has or is in the process of challenging the tribunal's jurisdiction in approximately 47 arbitrations. To this figure of 47, one should add that in a further eight cases (where the tribunal has already been constituted) the Respondent State is Argentina and it is likely to challenge jurisdiction in accordance with its current practice.

12-2 In recent years Claimants in bilateral investment treaty (BIT) arbitrations have become more aggressive in formulating the jurisdictional basis of their claims. This is manifested in a willingness to bring claims based upon legal theories that stretch the very limits of acceptable BIT interpretation. In deciding whether to admit claims, tribunals have had difficulties in interpreting BITs. Some tribunal members have insisted on following the literal wording of the treaty. Others have wanted to take a more rounded view, addressing issues of

---

* Partner, International Arbitration Group, Herbert Smith, London
[1] *Holiday Inns SA and others v. Morocco*, Decision on Jurisdiction, 12 May 1974. Unpublished. For a detailed description see Pierre Lalive, "The First 'World Bank' Arbitration (*Holiday Inns v. Morocco*) – Some Legal Problems", 51 *BYbIL* 123 (1980) and 1 *ICSID Reports* 645.
[2] This is assuming that where a hearing on jurisdiction or a filing of rejoinder/memorial on jurisdiction has taken place according to ICSID, an award has been given.

Loukas A. Mistelis and Julian D.M. Lew (eds), Pervasive Problems in International Arbitration, 235-256
© 2006 Kluwer Law International. Printed in the Netherlands

substance and policy as part of the interpretive exercise. The result is that tribunals' findings are becoming more controversial, both among tribunals themselves and amongst those commenting on published awards. This chapter will examine in detail four jurisdiction decisions which illustrate this point, as well as look in passing at other decisions raising similar issues. The four decisions are (1) *CMS v. Argentina*,[3] (2) *SGS v. Pakistan*,[4] (3) *SGS v. Philippines*[5] and (4) *Tokios Tokelés v. Ukraine*.[6]

12-3 These four decisions well reflect the nature of the problem. They show tribunals trying to address the issue of whether a BIT should be read as a stand-alone text, or whether a tribunal should reach a decision having departed from a literal reading by taking account of the treaty's proper political, legal and economic context. They also show a range of views being expressed both between tribunals, and within tribunals. Of these four decisions, one distinguished another on a crucial legal finding (*SGS v. Philippines* distinguishing *SGS v. Pakistan*), two feature strong dissents (*SGS v. Philippines, Tokios Tokelés*), one follows the letter of the treaty to create a situation which arguably makes little economic or legal sense (*CMS v. Argentina*) and one goes to the heart of what the ICSID system is supposed to be about (*Tokios Tokelés v. Ukraine*). Yet every decision (and every dissent!) is defensible. The reason these decisions should be considered together is that they raise the same central problem – how should a tribunal read a BIT? Should the tribunal consider the plain wording of the BIT, without regard to the wider consequences of its decision? Or should the tribunal read the wording of BITs with circumspection, always mindful of the fact that such treaties are supposed to be balanced and *bilateral*,[7] and thus should not be interpreted in a manner which places all the benefits on one side and the burdens on the other? In these four cases the literal wording of the BIT points one way while a "broader" view, moving from the literal words, points in the opposite direction.

---

[3] *CMS Gas Transmission Company v. The Republic of Argentina*, Decision on Jurisdiction, 17 July 2003, 42 ILM 788 (2003).

[4] *SGS Société Générale de Surveillance SA v. Islamic Republic of Pakistan*, Decision on Jurisdiction, 6 August 2003, 18 ICSID Rev-FILJ 301 (2003), 42 ILM 1290 (2003).

[5] *SGS Société Générale de Surveillance SA v. Republic of the Philippines*, Decision on Jurisdiction, 29 January 2004, available at www.worldbank.org/icsid/cases/SGSvPhil-final.pdf.

[6] *Tokios Tokelés v. Ukraine*, Decision on Jurisdiction, 29 April 2004, available on the ICSID website at www.worldbank.org/icsid/cases/tokios-decision.pdf.

[7] Hans van Houtte, *The Law of International Trade* (Sweet & Maxwell, 1995) at para 7.15.

12-4 The purpose of this chapter is not to take sides. Instead I will outline the contours of the problem as it arose in each case. The eminence of the voices on each side of the debates shows that there is no right answer. It is not a question of showing a pro-State or a pro-investor bias. Indeed, the State or investor interest in the interpretive question will depend upon the issue being raised. The only moral, if there is one, is *caveat litigators* – choose your arbitrators with care because if your jurisdiction case could be interpreted in a similar fashion it is important to make sure that your party-appointed arbitrator will see the case your way.

12-5 The rest of this chapter will develop in 6 sections. I will begin by introducing the question of how ICSID tribunals approach situations where a literal reading and wider policy considerations divide (Section II). I will then address each of the four illustrative awards in chronological order (Sections III to VI) followed by a conclusion (Section VII).

II. SUBSTANCE V. APPEARANCE IN ICSID ARBITRATIONS

12-6 The years before the explosion of BIT based claims[8] represented what was perhaps a simpler age for ICSID arbitration.[9] In those days the jurisdictional basis of an ICSID arbitration would be a concession agreement between investor and State. In 1991 Carolyn B. Lamm in an article entitled "Jurisdiction of the International Centre for Settlement of Investment Disputes"[10] was able to consider jurisdiction challenges made to date and conclude "ICSID tribunals have not taken a formalistic approach to the issue of consent".[11] In the light of the recent difficulties faced by ICSID tribunals in interpreting BITs[12] one could no longer conclusively state that ICSID tribunals have not taken a formalistic approach.

---

[8] The first was *Asian Agricultural Products Limited v. Democratic Socialist Republic of Sri Lanka* in 1987 (Award, 27 June 1990, 6 ICSID Rev-FILJ 526 (1991); 30 ILM 577 (1991); 6(5) Mealey's IAR, at Section A (May 1991); 17 YBCA 106 (1992) (excerpts); 4 ICSID Rep. 246 (1997)). Before this case there had been 23 ICSID arbitrations in 14 years. Since then there have been 65 concluded cases in only 18 years and there are 85 pending cases.

[9] Of course, not all treaty arbitrations are ICSID arbitrations, but a majority of the most important published treaty decisions have been rendered under ICSID or ICSID Additional Facility auspices

[10] Carolyn B Lamm, "Jurisdiction of the International Centre for Settlement of Investment Disputes", 6 *ICSID Rev - FILJ* 462 (1991).

[11] *Ibid*, p 464.

[12] For example *CMS v. Argentina*, supra note 3, and *Tokios Tokelés v. Ukraine*, supra note 6.

12-7 In reviewing the approach taken to what had been at that time the most frequently arising jurisdictional difficulty, the scope of the ICSID Convention Article 25 (2)(b) nationality exception, Ms Lamm stated that:

> These more recent cases may be viewed as indicative of a trend amongst ICSID tribunals to expand the definition of foreign juridical persons aggressively to provide the protection of the Convention to all parties involved. Thus, ICSID tribunals have moved from a somewhat rigid, narrow approach regarding issues of jurisdiction and national sovereignty to a less stringent one enabling the Centre to resolve a greater number of investment disputes.[13]

12-8 Again, one could not make a similar statement today. Firstly, one cannot say that, as a general rule, ICSID tribunals are approaching questions of jurisdiction in a manner that enables ICSID to resolve more claims. (Perhaps even then it was dangerous to try and identify trends. For example, in *Amco Asia v. Indonesia*[14] the tribunal stated that an arbitration agreement

> is not to be construed *restrictively*, nor as a matter of fact, *broadly* or *liberally*. It is to be construed in a way which leads to find out and respect the common will of the parties.[15]

There are many modern instances of tribunals denying jurisdiction where it would have been reasonable to find otherwise, even when the wording of BITs would have *prima facie* allowed jurisdiction.[16] Secondly, a review of jurisdiction awards shows that a "rigid, narrow" approach is not always the one advocated by the Respondent State and a "less stringent one" is not always advocated by the Claimant investor.

---

[13] Lamm, supra note 10, p 473

[14] *Amco Asia Corporation and others v. Republic of Indonesia*, Decision on Jurisdiction, 25 September 1983, 89 ILR 379 (1992); 1 ICSID Rep. 389 (1993)

[15] *Ibid*, para 14. [Emphasis in original]

[16] For example *SGS v. Pakistan* (supra note 4), *SGS v. Philippines* (supra note 5), the original decision in *CAA and Vivendi Universal (CGE) v. Argentina*, Decision on Jurisdiction, 21 November 2000, 40 ILM 426 (2001), and *Salini Costruttori SPA and Italstrade SPA v. The Hashemite Kingdom of Jordan*, Decision on Jurisdiction, 29 November 2004, available at http://www.worldbank.org/icsid/cases/salini-decision.pdf, where the tribunal gave a narrow reading to a most favoured nation clause.

12-9 Perhaps the most aggressive attempt by a claimant to establish jurisdiction in a concession agreement case was in *Banro v. Congo.*[17] Two Banro companies were involved in this arbitration. The first, Banro Resource Corporation, was the parent company which had signed the concession agreement (here a Mining Concession with an ICSID arbitration clause) with the Congolese State. However, Banro Resource Corporation was a Canadian company and thus ineligible to bring a claim under the ICSID Convention. The second Banro was the claimant, Banro American Resource, an American company which was wholly owned by the Canadian Banro Resource Corporation. Banro Resource Corporation had transferred its rights under the concession agreement to Banro American Resource. Notwithstanding this transfer, if the tribunal was to read the concession agreement literally it would have to recognise that it did not have jurisdiction to hear disputes brought by the claimant. Congo had not consented to arbitrate disputes with the American subsidiary and the company with which it had consented to arbitrate was not eligible to bring claims under the ICSID system.

12-10 The tribunal found that it did not have jurisdiction. It favoured a literal, rather than an expansive, reading of the concession agreement's arbitration provision. It rejected the American claimant's arguments asking it to construe the consent to arbitrate widely so as to give legal effect to the parties' ICSID arbitration agreement and refused to pierce the corporate veil to look at the financial rather than the legal reality. The tribunal showed little flexibility in its approach. It was decidedly not taking a non-formalistic approach as described by Ms Lamm; it justified its lack of flexibility by stating that:

> What the Claimants are asking the tribunal in the present case, is not to uncover the reality behind the matter or to find a true investor behind the formalities and procedural appearances, but rather; on the contrary, to base its inquiry on the formal and procedural appearance and to turn a blind eye to the reality behind the relationships deriving from the investment.[18]

12-11 In *Banro* the tribunal felt it was appropriate to stick to the literal wording of the concession agreement rather than let itself be persuaded to consider wider issues. In the next sections we shall see how the tribunal reacted to a similar

---

[17] *Banro American Resources, Inc. and Société Aurifère du Kivu et du Maniema SARL v. Democratic Republic of the Congo*, Award, 1 September 2000, 17 ICSID Rev-FILJ 382 (2003) (excerpts).

[18] Pierre Lalive, "Some objections to Jurisdiction in Investor-State Arbitration" (Procès-verbaux de l'ICCA, May 2002), p 18.

interpretive question in four separate cases. As these interpretive questions arise under BITs, rather than under concession agreements, the potential effect of the tribunals' decisions is far wider. There are now more than 2,300 BITs[19] in force worldwide, as well as a number of multilateral investment treaties such as the Energy Charter Treaty and the ASEAN Agreement for the Promotion and Protection of Investments. The provisions of these treaties can be similar. A decision under one may increase the confidence of investors in wholly different States to seek to assert jurisdiction under different treaties containing similar provisions. A BIT may be *lex specialis* but that law is not so special when the identical special regime may be generally in force. Thus the effect of tribunals construing BITs will be felt much more widely than decisions on concession agreements.

12-12 The four awards considered in the next sections all arise under BITs. They demonstrate the difficulties tribunals have faced in deciding whether to base their inquiry "on the formalities and procedural appearances" or whether to consider more widely "the relationships deriving from the investment".

III. CMS GAS TRANSMISSION COMPANY V. THE REPUBLIC OF ARGENTINA[20]

12-13 This is the first one of the many ICSID arbitrations brought against Argentina arising out of that country's economic crisis in 1999. The Claimant CMS is a US company which brought its claim under the 1991 US –Argentina BIT.

12-14 The jurisdictional basis of the CMS claim was unusual. CMS was a minority shareholder in an Argentinian company Transportadora de Gas del Norte (TGN). In 1992, TGN had obtained a licence for the transportation of gas. Under the arrangements made for privatisation of the Argentine gas sector, tariffs were to be calculated in US dollars and expressed in Argentine pesos at the exchange rate at the time of billing. They were also to be adjusted semi-annually in accordance with the United States Producer Price Index. Following the economic and financial crisis, Argentina enacted various measures including the devaluation of the currency and the adoption of additional financial and administrative measures. These measures also included the restructuring and renegotiation of public and private contracts made in foreign currency, extinguishing the right of licensees in the regulated public sector to link tariffs to US price indexes and re-

---

[19] See Chapter 9 of the World Development Report 2005, *International Rules and Standards*, available at http://siteresources.worldbank.org/INTWDR2005/Resources/11_WDR_Ch09.pdf.
[20] *CMS Gas Transmission Company v. The Republic of Argentina*, supra note 3.

denominating rates and tariffs into pesos at the exchange rate of one peso per dollar.

12-15   These measures affected the value of TGN's asset, the gas transportation licence. As a result CMS claimed that it was entitled to bring an arbitration under the provisions of the US-Argentina BIT to protect the rights associated with its investment as a minority shareholder in TGN. In asserting jurisdiction CMS relied upon "the plain language of the [BIT's] provisions and their legal context."[21]   It is indeed difficult to see how a literal reading of these provisions could do anything but support the CMS case.   CMS is claiming that it had made a protected investment in Argentina.   Article I(1) of the BIT defined "investment" in the following broad terms[22]:

> (a) 'investment' means every kind of investment in the territory of one Party owned or controlled directly or indirectly by nationals or companies of the other Party, such as equity, debt and service and investment contracts; and includes without limitation:
> (…)
> (ii)   a company or shares of stock or other interests in a company or interests in the assets thereof …

12-16   CMS emphasised that it was not claiming for rights pertaining to TGN. It was not claiming as TGN, which would have been impossible under the ICSID system given that TGN was an Argentinian company. It was also not claiming for impairment of the licence which it did not own and thus could not have been covered under the US-Argentina treaty. Its claim was for compensation for loss connected with its minority shareholding in TGN. It argued that its minority shareholding in TGN qualified as an investment covered under the treaty giving it the right to claim for compensation in the case of a dispute that arises directly out of its investment in the shares. Such a dispute would not relate to TGN's rights but to those CMS possessed arising from the treaty.[23]

12-17   The tribunal supported CMS' view. It found:

> … no bar in current international law to the concept of allowing claims by shareholders independently from those of the corporation concerned, not even if those shareholders are minority or non-controlling shareholders … as

---

[21]   *Ibid*, para 60.
[22]   *Ibid*, para 57
[23]   *Ibid*, para 67.

noted above, the rights of the Claimant can be asserted independently from the rights of TGN and those relating to the License, and because the Claimant has a separate cause of action under the Treaty in connection with the protected investment, the Tribunal concludes that the present dispute arises directly from the investment made and that therefore there is no bar to the exercise of jurisdiction on this count.[24]

12-18 Argentina had tried to draw the tribunal's attention to "the reality behind relationships deriving from the investment"[25]. These were characterised by the tribunal as "assumed consequences"[26] Argentina had mentioned three such consequences:

(i) TGN could come to a successful finalization of the negotiation process under way and, separately, an ICSID tribunal could reach a different conclusion;

(ii) the eventual discrimination which could take place between domestic and foreign investors in TGN as only the latter have access to arbitration; and

(iii) the eventual multiplication of international claims by investors of different nationalities and under separate treaties.[27]

12-19 Argentina also pointed out that as a minority shareholder in TGN, CMS had no guarantee that it would receive any compensation if any were ultimately to be awarded to TGN by Argentina.

12-20 Taken together these "objections on assumed consequences"[28] show a marked imbalance between the position of the two parties under the BIT. CMS, as an investor, had little to lose in framing the novel basis of its claim. If it won it would be able to place itself in a better position than the company which actually owned the asset and had been directly affected by Argentina's actions. It would also find itself in a better position than any of its fellow shareholders who happened to be either Argentinean nationals or nationals of companies which did not have a BIT with Argentina. If it lost it would still be able to take advantage, albeit as a minority shareholder, of any negotiated settlement TGN could ultimately obtain.

---

[24] *Ibid*, paras 48 and 68.
[25] Lalive, supra note 17, p 18.
[26] Part of the heading to para 83 of *CMS v. Argentina*, supra note 3.
[27] *CMS v. Argentina*, supra note 3, Decision on Jurisdiction at para 83.
[28] Full heading of para 83 of *CMS v. Argentina*, supra note 3.

12-21   In contrast, Argentina had everything to lose from an expansive approach to the jurisdictional rights of minority shareholders. It could face itself open to a multitude of claims from an unknowable number of previously unidentified foreign shareholders of Argentine companies. Each shareholder would have the right to bring its own arbitration. There could be a number of different arbitrations arising out of the same set of facts with a real risk that different tribunals could reach different conclusions.

12-22   In arriving at its decision dismissing Argentina's jurisdiction objection the tribunal chose to ignore the wider issues, including the potential for chaos, and took a rigid formalistic approach to interpreting the investment provisions of the BIT. It stated that:

> The Tribunal notes in respect that the Centre [ICSID] has made every effort possible to avoid a multiplicity of tribunals and jurisdictions, but that it is not possible to foreclose rights that different investors might have under different arrangements. The Tribunal also notes that, while it might be desirable to recognize similar rights to domestic and foreign investors, this is seldom possible in the present state of international law in this field.[29]

12-23   The shortcomings in this award may be explained on the grounds that the tribunal appeared in some way to confine itself only to questions of jurisdiction, not of admissibility:

> The distinction between admissibility and jurisdiction does not appear quite appropriate in the context of ICSID as the Convention deals only with jurisdiction and competence.[30]

12-24   If this is the case, the tribunal would be reserving the wider issues as discussed in this article for the merits stage. Nonetheless, as can be seen from the other awards discussed in this article, other tribunals have not felt that the ICSID Convention's lack of admissibility, as opposed to jurisdiction, criteria prevents them from considering matters within their proper political, legal and economic context.

---

[29]   *Ibid*, para 86.
[30]   *Ibid*, para 41.

IV. SGS SOCIETE GENERALE DE SURVEILLANCE SA V. ISLAMIC REPUBLIC OF PAKISTAN[31]

12-25   Much attention has been paid to this award and to the award of the next case to be considered, *SGS v. Philippines*. Much of the interest generated by these awards arises from the two tribunals' different approaches to the umbrella clauses contained in the respective BITs upon which the arbitrations were based. In this chapter the awards will be considered on the basis that the two tribunals' differing approaches to the construction of the umbrella clauses reflect the tension between interpreting the wording of the clauses literally and having a regard to the wider circumstances of the matter.

12-26   In *SGS v. Pakistan*, SGS had entered into a pre-shipment inspection agreement dated 29 September 1994 with Pakistan whereby SGS was to provide certain pre-shipment inspection services with respect to goods to be exported to Pakistan (PSI Agreement). The PSI Agreement contained a dispute settlement provision pursuant to which all claims were to be resolved by arbitration in Pakistan.

12-27   The PSI Agreement entered into force on 1 January 1995. It was subsequently performed by both parties in the sense that services were rendered by SGS and invoices issued by it were paid by Pakistan. Both parties disputed the adequacy of the other's performance. In 1998 SGS, a Swiss company, commenced proceedings in the courts of Switzerland seeking relief against what it alleged was Pakistan's unlawful termination of the PSI Agreement. These claims were dismissed by the Swiss Federal Tribunal after a process lasting 22 months. Pakistan commenced an arbitration against SGS under the PSI Agreement arbitration clause in September 2000. Related proceedings were also brought in the Pakistani courts. On 12 October 2001 SGS filed a Request for Arbitration at ICSID under the provisions of the Switzerland – Pakistan BIT.

12-28   Pakistan objected to the ICSID tribunal's jurisdiction on a number of grounds, including that the dispute between the parties arose out of a contract rather than under the BIT. SGS however contended that, as a result of BIT Article 11, contractual disputes between the parties could be elevated to treaty disputes. BIT Article 11, the "umbrella clause", provides:

---

[31] *SGS Société Générale de Surveillance SA v. Islamic Republic of Pakistan*, supra note 4.

Either Contracting Party shall constantly guarantee the observance of the commitments it has entered into with respect to the investments of the investors of the other Contracting Party.[32]

12-29 The tribunal refused to allow SGS to use the clause to assert that any breaches of contract by Pakistan would amount to breaches of Pakistan's commitments under the BIT. The tribunal accepted that a literal reading of Article 11 would support SGS:

As a matter of textuality therefore, the scope of Article 11 of the BIT, while consisting in its entirety of only one sentence, appears susceptible of almost indefinite expansion.[33]

12-30 However, the tribunal refused to adopt a literal meaning which would have given rise to such a broad effect. In doing so its approach differed completely from that adopted by the *CMS v. Argentina* tribunal which refused to consider any issues beyond the literal meaning of the treaty provisions themselves. The tribunal refused to attribute consequences to Article 11 of the BIT that are

so far–reaching in scope, and so automatic and unqualified and sweeping in their operation, so burdensome in their potential impact upon a Contracting Party

without

clear and convincing evidence that such was indeed the shared intent of the Contracting Parties to the Swiss - Pakistan Investment Protection Treaty in incorporating Article 11 in the BIT.[34]

The tribunal thus avoided being confined to a literal reading by stating that any literal reading that would provide far-reaching consequences would have to be supported by evidence of the treaty's drafting history. Such evidence would need to indicate clearly that such wide-reaching consequences were intended.

12-31 Having freed itself from having to follow a literal reading of the treaty, the tribunal was able to spell out "in some detail"[35] the consequences of accepting

---

[32] *Ibid*, para 163.
[33] *Ibid*, para 166.
[34] *Ibid*, para 167.
[35] *Ibid*, para 168.

SGS' reading of Article 11 of the BIT. These are set out in paragraph 168 of the award where the tribunal reflects three extra-textual policy reasons why the Claimant's arguments should not be followed. This paragraph of the award is thus an unconscious echoing of paragraph 83 of the *CMS v. Argentina* award where the tribunal set out the three extra-textual policy reasons put forward by Argentina as to why the literal reading of the investment provisions of that treaty should not be followed.

12-32   The three extra-textual reasons noted by the tribunal in *SGS v. Pakistan* were:

- the extreme consequences of reading Article 11 as amounting to an incorporation by reference of an unlimited number of State contracts and other municipal law instruments with the effect that any alleged violation of those contracts and other instruments could be treated as a breach of BIT;
- SGS' reading of Article 11 would make Articles 3 to 7 of the BIT superfluous. "There would be no real need to demonstrate a violation of those substantive treaty standards if a simple breach of contract, or of municipal statute or regulation, by itself, would suffice to constitute a treaty violation on the part of a Contracting Party and engage the international responsibility of the Party."[36]
- If an investor were able to use an umbrella clause to elevate contract claims into BIT claims, the investor would be able to choose at will to nullify any freely negotiated dispute resolution provisions in State contracts. The tribunal emphasised the importance of neutrality in pointing out how allowing the investor to choose at will to nullify domestic dispute resolution provisions would create a situation where the benefit "would flow only to the investor." The tribunal refused to countenance such a situation because: "Article 11 of the BIT should be read in such a way as to enhance mutuality and balance of benefits in the inter-relation of different agreements located in differing legal orders."[37]

12-33   However, by moving away from a literal interpretation the *SGS v. Pakistan* tribunal created an interpretive difficulty for itself. If Article 11 of the Swiss – Pakistan BIT did not mean what it said, then what did it mean? The tribunal was only able to say that it amounted to non-binding "confirmation" that

---

[36]   *Ibid*, para 168.
[37]   *Ibid*, para 168.

a contracting party's obligations entered into elsewhere were binding but would only have binding legal effect "under exceptional circumstances".[38]

12-34 In reaching its decision about the meaning of Article 11 of the Swiss – Pakistan BIT the tribunal was following policy considerations rather than canons of interpretation. The problem with interpretation by reference to policy is that policy issues usually cut both ways. This is illustrated by the next award to be considered, *SGS v. Philippines*.

V. SGS SOCIÉTÉ GÉNÉRALE DE SURVEILLANCE SA V. REPUBLIC OF THE PHILIPPINES[39]

12-35 The tribunal in *SGS v. Philippines* reached the opposite conclusion on the meaning of the umbrella clause from that reached by the *SGS v. Pakistan* tribunal. The *SGS v. Pakistan* tribunal favoured a literal reading of the BIT. This is not to say that it did not use policy considerations in arriving at its decision. Rather, the policy considerations it took into account led it to its literal reading. Taken together the two SGS awards are an illustration of the limitations inherent in relying upon policy considerations in interpreting treaties as the policy considerations taken into account by the *SGS v. Philippines* tribunal were directly opposite to the policy considerations relied upon in *SGS v. Pakistan* and led to the opposite result.

12-36 The dispute in *SGS v. Philippines* arose out of an agreement for the provision of comprehensive import supervision services (the CISS Agreement) dated 23 August 1991. Pursuant to the CISS Agreement SGS was to provide specialised services to assist in improving the customs clearance and control processes of the Philippines. The dispute in *SGS v. Philippines* was less wide-ranging than in *SGS v. Pakistan*. In *SGS v. Philippines* it was limited to a claim for contractual amounts due. SGS contended that it should be able to avoid the contractually agreed dispute resolution provisions, which would have led to the courts in the Philippines, because of a clause in the Switzerland-Philippines BIT elevating contract claims into treaty claims. This provision, Article X(2) provided that:

---

[38] *Ibid*, para 172.
[39] *SGS Société Générale de Surveillance SA v. Republic of the Philippines*, supra note 5.

Each Contracting Party shall observe any obligation it has assumed with regard to specific investments in its territory by investors of the other Contracting Party.[40]

12-37 In contrast, the Philippines contended, as Pakistan had done before it, that the tribunal did not have jurisdiction over contractual claims.

12-38 The tribunal signalled its intent to keep to a literal interpretation by stating that:

One must begin with the actual text of Article X.[41]

12-39 Before examining the decision in *SGS v. Pakistan* the tribunal stated its "provisional conclusion" as being that the umbrella clause "Article X(2) means what it says".[42] Rather than following the *SGS v. Pakistan* tribunal and using policy considerations to take away from the literal meaning of the clause, the *SGS v. Philippines* tribunal used policy considerations to support the award:

The object and purpose of the BIT supports an effective interpretation of Article X(2). The BIT is a treaty for the promotion and reciprocal protection of investments. According to the preamble it is intended "to create and maintain favourable conditions for investments by investors of one Contracting Party in the territory of the other". It is legitimate to resolve uncertainties in its interpretation so as to favour the protection of covered investments.[43]

12-40 In the light of this policy:

Interpreting the actual text of Article X(2), it would appear to say, and to say clearly, that each Contracting Party shall observe any legal obligation it has assumed, or will in the future assume, with regard to specific investments covered by the BIT. Article X(2) was adopted within the framework

---

[40] *Ibid*, para 34.

[41] *Ibid*, para 114. The text of the clause in *SGS v. Pakistan,* (supra note 4) ("Either Contracting Party shall constantly guarantee the observance of the commitments ...") was slightly weaker than that in *SGS v. Philippines* ("Each Contracting Party shall observe any obligation ..."). However, while this point was noted by the *SGS v. Philippines* tribunal (para 119), the difference between the two awards cannot be explained by reference to this alone

[42] *Ibid*, para. 119. And compare this with the *SGS v. Pakistan* (supra note 4) tribunal's belief that the clause was "susceptible of almost indefinite expansion" at paragraph 166 of the decision

[43] *Ibid*, para 116.

248

of the BIT, and has to be construed as intended to be effective within that framework.[44]

12-41 The tribunal then went on to criticise the broader reasons given by the *SGS v. Pakistan* tribunal for rejecting a literal interpretation, and provided some broader reasons of its own. For example, it stated that:

> It is a conceivable function of a provision such as Article X(2) of the Swiss-Philippines BIT to provide assurances to foreign investors with regard to the performance of obligations assumed by the host State under its own law with regard to specific investments ... this is the proper interpretation of Article X(2).[45]

12-42 However, despite their statements of intent to keep to the "actual text"[46] in their conclusion the majority of the tribunal decided not to follow the literal meaning of the clause to its full extent. They stated that:

> Article X(2) makes it a breach of the BIT for the host State to fail to observe binding commitments, including contractual commitments, which it has assumed with regard to specific investments. But it does not convert the issue of the *extent* or *content* of such obligations into an issue of international law.[47]

12-43 Accordingly, the tribunal's conclusion was that jurisdiction existed under the BIT to enforce contractual obligations but that the international law tribunal would not be permitted to determine the extent or content of those obligations. These issues were to be determined pursuant to the CISS Agreement's dispute resolution provisions and the majority of the tribunal granted a stay to allow the designated tribunal (certain courts in the Philippines) to do so. The merits or otherwise of the majority's decision are beyond the scope of this article. For present purposes we need note only the unusual nature of a decision determining that a tribunal granted the power to enforce an obligation should not be granted the power to determine the extent or content of such obligation. The unusual nature of the majority's decision is an indication that an element of policy has crept into the literal reading that it previously stated it was going to follow.

---

[44] *Ibid*, para 115.
[45] *Ibid*, para 126.
[46] *Ibid*, para 114.
[47] *Ibid*, para 128.

12-44   The award was subject to a dissent on this point from the Claimant's party-appointed arbitrator, Professor Antonio Crivellaro. The manner in which policy considerations can both support or derogate from a literal interpretation is further highlighted in Professor Crivellaro's Dissenting Declaration. Professor Crivellaro did not examine the wording of the umbrella clause. Indeed, he did not have to do this given that the majority had accepted "it means what it says"[48]. However, his Declaration contains many statements of policy. In a manner which further highlights the subjective nature of any treaty interpretation exercise depending on policy, Professor Crivellaro's Declaration sets out his view on the policy which should influence the interpretive process. Professor Crivellaro's favoured policy is not one stated either by the tribunal in the *SGS v. Pakistan* award nor by the majority in *SGS v. Philippines*.

12-45   Accordingly, any reader trying to find a consistent policy yardstick by which a BIT may be interpreted will not be assisted by these two high-profile awards made by eminent tribunals. The policy considerations which would have motivated Professor Crivellaro to find that the tribunal had jurisdiction over all aspects of the contractual claim were that:

> It is my understanding that the most significant advantage which, in practice, is granted by a BIT to foreign investors is, precisely, the right to select, amongst the alternative forums made available by the BIT, the forum that the investor deems the most suitable <u>to him</u> ... the really innovating contribution of a BIT is given by the investor's privilege to choose a preferential forum amongst those offered by the host State after that the dispute has arisen (together with, when stipulated, the s.c. "umbrella clause") ... Here SGS claims that the Respondent has violated Article X(2) of the BIT ... Consequently SGS's claim seemed to me fully admissible before our Tribunal...[49]

VI. TOKIOS TOKELÉS V. UKRAINE[50]

12-46   This award features a powerful dissent. Most unusually, the dissent in this case came from the President of the tribunal who was outvoted by his co-arbitrators. Having publicly stated that he did not consider the tribunal to have jurisdiction to consider the substantive issues he has subsequently resigned.

---

[48]   *Ibid*, para 119.
[49]   *Ibid*, Dissenting Declaration at paras 5, 6 and 11.
[50]   *Tokios Tokelés v. Ukraine*, supra note 6.

12-47 This award perhaps illustrates the issue addressed in this Article in the starkest manner. The literal reading of the treaty unambiguously points in one direction while the wider considerations of substance emphasised by the dissenting President are of the most fundamental importance to the ICSID framework.

12-48 The claimant, Tokios Tokelés, was a business enterprise established under the laws of Lithuania. It was engaged primarily in the business of advertising, publishing and printing in Lithuania and outside its borders. In 1994, Tokios Tokelés created Taki spravy, a wholly owned subsidiary established under the laws of Ukraine. Taki spravy was in the business of advertising, publishing and printing in Ukraine and outside its borders. The claimant alleged that governmental authorities in Ukraine had engaged in a series of actions with respect to its local subsidiary, Taki spravy. These actions had breached the obligations contained in the BIT between Ukraine and Lithuania.

12-49 The complication in this claim arose from the fact that the claimant, while being a legally established entity under the laws of Lithuania, was 99% owned by Ukraine nationals. Accordingly, following formal and procedural appearances, the dispute was properly characterised as being between a Lithunian legal person and the Ukraine. However, when one takes into account financial and economic realities as well as the relationships deriving from the investment the dispute was between Ukrainian nationals and Ukraine. It would thus not be suitable for ICSID arbitration.

12-50 The decision of the majority of the tribunal members was based squarely on a literal reading of the relevant provisions of the Ukraine-Lithuania BIT. Article 1(2)(b) of the Ukraine-Lithuania BIT defines the term "investor" with respect to Lithuania as:

> any entity established in the territory of the Republic of Lithuania in conformity with its laws and regulations.[51]

12-51 The majority noted that:

> The Treaty contains no additional requirements for an entity to qualify as an "investor" of Lithuania.[52]

---

[51] *Ibid*, para 28.
[52] *Ibid*, para 28.

12-52 The majority refused to imply any additional requirements themselves. They noted that many BITs contain a so-called "denial of benefits" provision whereby the contracting parties reserve the right to deny the advantages of the treaty to any company controlled by nationals of a third state or nationals of the denying party with no real economic activity on the territory of the denying party. However, no such denial of benefits clause appeared in the Ukraine-Lithuania BIT. Thus, according to the majority:

> In our view, it is not for tribunals to impose limits on the scope of BITs not found in the text, much less limits nowhere evident from the negotiating history. An international tribunal of defined jurisdiction should not reach out to exercise a jurisdiction beyond the borders of the definition. But equally an international tribunal should exercise, and indeed is bound to exercise, the measure of jurisdiction with which it is endowed ... under the terms of the Ukraine-Lithuania BIT, interpreted according to their ordinary meaning, in their context, and in light of the object and purpose of the Treaty, the only relevant consideration is whether the Claimant is established under the laws of Lithuania. We find that it is. Thus, the Claimant is an investor of Lithuania under Article 1(2)(b) of the BIT.[53]

12-53 This conclusion provides resounding support for the idea that tribunals, in interpreting BITs, should have regard only to the literal provisions and not take account of policy considerations that may lead them to consider wider issues that are not expressed in the treaty itself. Referring specifically to *SGS v. Pakistan*, the majority stated that:

> While some tribunals have taken a distinctive approach, we do not believe that arbitrators should read into BITs limitations not found in the text nor evident from negotiating history sources.[54]

12-54 In a footnote[55] the tribunal specifically criticised the *SGS v. Pakistan* tribunal's construction of the umbrella clause in the Switzerland-Pakistan BIT stating that the tribunal had "decided – without support from the text or evidence of the parties' intent" that the umbrella clause did not mean what it said.

---

[53] *Ibid*, paras 36 and 38.
[54] *Ibid*, para 52.
[55] *Ibid*, footnote 42.

12-55   In formulating its decision, the majority was clear in spelling out the manner in which it was interpreting the Ukraine-Lithuania BIT and its policy for so doing:

> This tribunal, by respecting the definition of corporate nationality in the Ukraine-Lithuania BIT, fulfils the parties' expectations, increases the predictability of dispute settlement procedures, and enables investors to structure their investments to enjoy the legal protections afforded under the Treaty. We decline to look beyond (or through) the Claimant to its shareholders or other juridical entities that may have an interest in the claim.[56]

12-56   Yet, the President was just as clear in setting out the reasons motivating him to take the opposite approach. He rejected the literal wording of the BIT in favour of considering its "object and purpose":

> If I have decided to dissent, it is because the approach taken by the Tribunal on the issue of principle raised in this case for the first time in ICSID's history is in my view at odds with the object and purpose of the ICSID Convention and might jeopardize the future of the institution.[57]

12-57   The President refused to ignore "the reality behind the relationships deriving from the investment".[58] He emphasised that:

> … the ICSID arbitration mechanism is meant for *international* investment disputes, that is to say, for disputes between States and *foreign* investors … The Decision rests on the assumption that the origin of the capital is not relevant and even less decisive. This assumption is flying in the face of the object and purpose of the ICSID Convention and system …[59] (Emphasis in original).

12-58   The President was not prepared to consider the literal meaning of the Ukraine-Lithuania BIT and the ICSID Convention as decisive. Instead:

> What *is* decisive in our case is a simple, straightforward, objective fact that the dispute before this ICSID tribunal is not between the Ukrainian State and a foreign investor but between the Ukrainian State and an Ukrainian investor – and to such a relationship and to such a dispute the ICSID Convention was not meant to apply and does not apply … It is this very

---

[56] *Ibid*, para 40.
[57] *Ibid*, Dissenting Opinion at para 1.
[58] Lalive, supra note 17, p 18.
[59] *Tokios Tokelés v. Ukraine,* supra note 6, Dissenting Opinion at paras 5 and 6.

same rationale of giving effect to the economic reality over and above the legal structure that should have led the tribunal to decide that an investment made in Ukraine by Ukrainian citizens with Ukrainian capital – albeit through the channel of Lithuanian corporation – cannot benefit from the protection of the ICSID mechanism … Since the object and purpose of this provision – and, for that matter, of the whole ICSID Convention and mechanism – is to protect *foreign* investment, it should not be interpreted so as to allow domestic, national corporations to evade the application of their domestic, national law and the jurisdiction of their domestic, national tribunals.[60] (Emphasis in original).

VII. CONCLUSION

12-59   As treaties, BITs are to be interpreted in accordance with principles of public international law. Treaties are generally interpreted in accordance with the principles contained at Articles 31 to 33 of the 1969 Vienna Convention on the Law of Treaties. These principles would apply in interpreting a BIT even if the State contracting parties were not parties to the Vienna Convention as they reflect customary international law.[61] In practice the principles contained in the Vienna Convention are not wholly useful in resolving difficult questions of BIT interpretation as the guidance they provide is insufficiently concrete.

12-60   The cases analysed above demonstrate how the provisions of BITs are capable of being melded in any direction the tribunal wishes.   Consider the following interpretive principles announced by the various tribunal members in just these four cases:

- Far-reaching effects arising out of the text of BITs must be confirmed by clear and convincing evidence of the State parties' intent;[62]
- BIT terms should be read in such a way as to enhance mutuality and balance of benefits;[63]
- It is legitimate to resolve uncertainties in the interpretation of a BIT so as to favour the protection of covered investments;[64]

---

[60]   *Ibid*, Dissenting Opinion at paras 21 and 23.
[61]   Robert Jennings and Arthur Watts *Oppenheim's International Law* (Longman, 9th edition, 1992), vol 1 pt 2-4, p. 602 to 607; *Salini v. Jordan,* supra note 2, para 75.
[62]   *SGS v. Pakistan*, supra note 4 paras 166-167.
[63]   *Ibid*, para 168.
[64]   *SGS v. Philippines,* supra note 5, para 116.

- A tribunal cannot read into a BIT words of limitation that are not found in the text;[65]
- Provisions granting rights to investors should be read in the way that is most favourable to the investor;[66]
- Tribunals should not read into BITs limitations not found in the text nor evident from negotiating history sources;[67]
- BITs must be applied and interpreted having regard to the object and purpose of the ICSID system.[68]

12-61   This array of often contradictory "principles" of interpretation shows the level of controversy engendered by modern BIT practice. The days when Dr Francis Mann could declare of BITs that they "do not seem to have given rise to much difficulty or contention in practice"[69] have long gone. It is tempting to try to categorise these decisions by reference to whether they are pro-State or pro-investor, and indeed given that these decisions could have gone either way it is not possible to discount the effect of the arbitrators' inherent biases.[70] In their book *Bilateral Investment Treaties* Professor Rudolf Dolzer and Ms Margrete Stevens offer guidance as to the interpretation of BITs depending on whether such treaties should be viewed as either evidence of the parties' intentions to enhance the protection of the foreign investor or as providing a fair and balanced protective regime.[71]

12-62   The purpose of this chapter was to highlight the very different approaches to construing BITs adopted by tribunals in some recent awards. The exercise of standing back and reviewing the practice of tribunals should bring benefits – it may enable tribunals to produce awards which are more consistent with one another, or more explicit as to why they are differing. It also provides

---

[65]   *Ibid*, para 118.
[66]   *Ibid*, Dissenting Declaration of Professor Crivellaro, para 10.
[67]   *Tokios Tokelés v. Ukraine,* supra note 6, para 52.
[68]   *Ibid*, Dissenting Opinion of Professor Weil, paras 19, 23 and 29.
[69]   F A Mann, "British Treaties for the Promotion and Protection of Investments", 52 *BYbIL* 242 (1981). This is a fascinating article, both for the trends that Dr Mann predicted and those that he did not, as well as for his clear understanding of the wide effect of umbrella clauses (at p 246).
[70]   For another award, on the issue of quantum rather than jurisdiction, where the tribunal split along these lines see the Final Award in *CME Czech Republic BV v. The Czech Republic*, Final Award, 14 March 2003, available at http://ita.law.uvic.ca/documents/CME-2003-Final_001.pdf and Professor Brownlie's Separate Opinion on Final Award, 14 March 2003, available at http://ita.law.uvic.ca/documents/CME2003-SeparateOpinion_001.pdf.
[71]   Dolzer & Stevens, *Bilateral Investment Treaties* (Kluwer Law International, 1995), p 15 and 16.

counsel with more advocacy ammunition in urging certain interpretations upon tribunals. One thing that cannot be done is to increase certainty by enabling parties and lawyers to predict better the results of particular cases. There are too many treaties in force around the world with well known *lacunae* which can be filled in so many different directions. The only solution for those who seek consistency is the long-term one currently being pursued by the United States. The various provisions in the new United States model BIT[72] are drafted to take account of all known awards and to provide a text which fills in the holes existing elsewhere. In the absence of any wholesale unifying effort, the difficulties and contentions will continue.

---

[72] United States Model Bilateral Investment Treaty, 15 September 2004, available at http://www.state.gov/documents/organization/38710.pdf

Gabrielle Kaufmann-Kohler[*]

CHAPTER 13

INTERPRETATION OF TREATIES: HOW DO ARBITRAL TRIBUNALS INTERPRET DISPUTE SETTLEMENT PROVISIONS EMBODIED IN INVESTMENT TREATIES?

I. THE QUESTION: HOW TO APPROACH IT AND WHY IT IS RELEVANT

13-1 How do arbitral tribunals interpret dispute resolution provisions in investment treaties? This is the question this chapter seeks to review. The review will have coherence and consistency as the two guiding principles.

13-2 Do arbitral tribunals reach consistent interpretations on identical or similar treaty provisions? Or do they adopt inconsistent interpretations? If the interpretations are inconsistent, is it because the treaty provisions are different, or because the tribunals adopt divergent interpretations of identical provisions? Bearing this focus in mind, this contribution will examine interpretation in three steps:
- First, it will set out a reminder of the basics of treaty interpretation and attempt a comparison with contract interpretation (section II);
- Second, it will examine the application of the rules of treaty interpretation identified in section II to dispute settlement provisions in investment treaties (section III);
- Third and last, it will attempt to formulate an answer to the question posed at the outset and open some perspectives (section IV).

13-3 Before addressing the first of these three topics, it may be worthwhile to pause and ask why the question is relevant at all. The question of the interpreta-

---

[*] Professor, University of Geneva; Partner, Schellenberg Wittmer, Geneva; Honorary President of the Swiss Arbitration Association.

Loukas A. Mistelis and Julian D.M. Lew (eds), Pervasive Problems in International Arbitration, 257-276
© *2006 Kluwer Law International. Printed in the Netherlands*

tion of investment treaties is relevant for a combination of two reasons. First because all investment treaties protect investments by granting investors certain rights which are materially identical or comparable, and second because there is no doctrine of precedent. Or, in the words of the arbitral tribunal in *SGS v. Philippines*:

> ... there is no doctrine of precedent in international law, if by precedent is meant a rule of the binding effect of a single decision. There is no hierarchy of international tribunals, and even if there were, there is no good reason for allowing the first tribunal to resolve issues for all later tribunals.[1]

13-4 In international commercial arbitration, there is no doctrine of precedent and no hierarchy of tribunals either. Yet the absence of a doctrine of precedent raises no difficulty because each decision involves a single or a series of contracts particularly negotiated between business partners. The position is different in treaty arbitration where a multiplicity of treaties often grants materially identical rights. Even where their wording differs, the purpose of protecting and promoting investment is common to all treaties.

13-5 With the present boom of investment arbitration,[2] there will be more and more awards dealing with the same protections, the same issues, and the same or similar provisions of bilateral or multilateral investment treaties.

II. A REMINDER: BASICS OF TREATY INTERPRETATION

1. The Vienna Convention

13-6 Although they are familiar, a brief reminder of the main rules of treaty interpretation may be useful to set the stage.[3] Article 31 of the Vienna Convention on the Law of Treaties, which codifies customary international law, provides for the primary means of interpretation in the following terms:

---

[1] *SGS Société Générale de Surveillance SA v. Republic of the Philippines* (referred to as *SGS v. Philippines*), Decision on jurisdiction, 29 January 2004, para 97, available on the ICSID website at www.worldbank.org/icsid/cases/SGSvPhil-final.pdf.

[2] For figures, see Stanimir Alexandrov, "The "Baby Boom" of Treaty-Based Arbitrations and the Jurisdiction of ICSID Tribunals: Shareholders as "Investors" and Jurisdiction *ratione temporis*", *The Law and Practice of International Courts and Tribunals*, Leiden 2005, vol 4, 19-59.

[3] For a historic commentary of these rules see the International Law Commission (ILC), *Yearbook of the International Law Commission*, vol II, 218 et seq (1966).

A treaty shall be interpreted in good faith in accordance with the ordinary meaning to be given to the terms of the treaty in their context and in the light of its object and purpose.

13-7 Accordingly, the general rule requires focusing
- first on the ordinary meaning of the terms;[4]
- second, on the context; and,
- third, on the object and purpose of the treaty.

13-8 The second paragraph of Article 31 specifies that the context comprises:

[…] in addition to the text, including its preamble and annexes:
(a) any agreement relating to the treaty which was made between all the parties in connection with the conclusion of the treaty;
(b) any instrument which was made by one or more parties in connection with the conclusion of the treaty and accepted by the other parties as an instrument related to the treaty.

13-9 If these primary means lead to an obscure or manifestly absurd result or to one that needs confirmation, the interpreter may rely on supplementary means under Article 32, *i.e.*, on the preparatory work and the circumstances of the conclusion of the treaty:

Recourse may be had to supplementary means of interpretation, including the preparatory work of the treaty and the circumstances of its conclusion, in order to confirm the meaning resulting from the application of article 31, or to determine the meaning when the interpretation according to article 31:
(a) leaves the meaning ambiguous or obscure; or
(b) leads to a result which is manifestly absurd or unreasonable.[5]

---

[4] In its commentary on treaty interpretation, the ILC adopted the textual approach noting that the text must be presumed to be the authentic expression of the intentions of the parties; and that, in consequence, the starting point of interpretation is the elucidation of the meaning of the text, not an investigation *ab initio* into the intentions of the parties (ILC Commentary, *ibid*, 220).

[5] The rules for treaty interpretation were discussed in detail in the very first arbitral award based on a BIT, which was rendered in 1990 in *Asian Agricultural Products Limited v. Democratic Socialist Republic of Sri Lanka* (referred to as *AAPL v. Sri Lanka*), 30 ILM 577 (1991).

2. A Comparison with Contract Interpretation

13-10 Does treaty interpretation differ from contract interpretation? The question arises because counsel and arbitrators who have a commercial or private law background increasingly act in investment arbitrations. They are used to construing arbitration agreements by application of the rules of contract interpretation. Is contract and treaty interpretation the same exercise? If it is different, then how does it differ?

13-11 These are questions which could give rise to a long debate. In the present context, it suffices to make two points. First, the interpretation tools are comparable and so are the approaches. Indeed, there are different approaches to interpretation in private law as well as in public international law. National contract laws adopt either a subjective theory, where investigation into the intentions of the parties prevails, or an objective theory, which relies primarily on the meaning of the text, or sometimes a mixed approach, where the meaning of the text is only taken into consideration if and to the extent that the intentions of the parties cannot be established.[6] Similarly, there are different schools of thought for interpretation in public international law: according to the subjective school, the goal of the interpretation is to ascertain the intent; pursuant to the objective school, the goal of interpretation must be to ascertain the meaning of the text, there being a presumption that the parties' intent is reflected in this text; and in the teleological school, the focus is primarily placed on the object and purpose of the treaty.[7]

13-12 Second, in spite of these resemblances, there is one basic difference which impacts the interpretation. An arbitration agreement in a contract is specific by its very nature. It is shaped to meet the needs of a given transaction. Moreover, both drafters are present in the arbitration and may thus explain their intentions. Whatever the contents of the applicable contract law, the arbitration will take ample account of these intentions.[8] When contracts are interpreted in international commercial arbitration, one may indeed venture to say that the search for the real intentions dominates. By contrast, dispute resolution provisions in treaties define jurisdiction in the abstract for an unlimited number of

---

[6] Marcel Fontaine / Filip De Ly, *Droit des contrats internationaux* (Bruylant 2003) 120.

[7] Ian Sinclair, *The Vienna Convention on the Law of Treaties* (2nd ed., Manchester University Press 1984) 114-5; Ian Brownlie, *Principles of Public International Law*, (6th ed., Oxford University Press, 2003) 602 et seq.

[8] Gabrielle Kaufmann-Kohler, "Annulment of ICSID Awards in Contract and Treaty Arbitrations: Are there Differences?", in Emmanuel Gaillard and Yas Bonifatemi (eds.), *Annulment of ICSID Awards* (Juris and Staempfli, 2004) 206.

future investments. In arbitration proceedings, only one of the drafters is present, the respondent State[9]. For the claimant, the dispute resolution provision is *res inter alios acta*. As a result, in treaty arbitration more objective criteria will by essence prevail and the subjective element will play a lesser role.

13-13 It remains to be seen whether the increasing presence on international tribunals of arbitrators trained in commercial arbitration will influence interpretation methods[10]. It may be too early to make an assessment, but there are signs pointing in this direction. For instance, is a reference to the UNCITRAL Model Law on Commercial Arbitration in the context of the interpretation of the most favoured nation clause in an investment treaty in *Plama v. Bulgaria*, an award rendered by three "commercial" arbitrators, an indication of an emerging trend? Or is it another indication that, in applying the nationality requirement under Article 25 of the ICSID Convention, a tribunal also composed of arbitrators with a commercial background determined that, in the silence of the treaty, the parties to the investment agreement were free to define nationality as long as the definition was reasonable[11] and that a renowned specialist of public international law disagreed with this determination[12]? Even if it is premature to venture any statement, this is certainly an evolution to be watched carefully.

---

[9] Subject to the reservation that in NAFTA Chapter 11 arbitrations, the NAFTA states not party to the arbitration may make submissions to the Tribunal on questions of interpretation of the NAFTA (Art. 1128 NAFTA). As noted by Mark W. Friedman, "Non-Party States' Efforts to Influence Ongoing Proceedings, in Appeals and Challenges to Investment Treaty Awards: Is it Time for an International Appellate System?", 2(2) *Transnational Dispute Management* 45 (2005), in at least nine NAFTA cases, states have put in Article 1128 submissions.

[10] In *Loewen*, the Tribunal held that

> it is true that some aspects of the resolution of disputes arising in relation to private international commerce are imported into the NAFTA system via Article 1120.1(c), and that the handling of disputes within that system by professionals experienced in the handling of major international arbitrations has tended in practice to make a NAFTA arbitration look like the more familiar kind of process.

(*The Loewen Group, Inc and Raymond L Loewen v. United States of America*, Award, 26 June 2003, available on www.naftalaw.org).

[11] *Autopista Concesionada de Venezuela, CA v. Bolivarian Republic of Venezuela*, Decision on jurisdiction, 27 September 2001, 16(2) *ICSID Rev - FILJ* para 64 (2001).

[12] See Prosper Weil in his dissenting opinion in *Tokios Tokelés v. Ukraine,* dissenting opinion dated 29 April 2004, is available at www.worldbank.org/icsid/cases.

III. THE APPLICATION OF TREATY INTERPRETATION RULES TO DISPUTE
SETTLEMENT PROVISIONS IN INVESTMENT TREATIES

13-14 How are the rules of treaty interpretation referred and applied to dispute
settlement provisions in investment treaties? In order to review this question, this
chapter will elaborate on the following four topics:

- The distinction between treaty and contract claims and some of its effects,
  specifically the significance of contractual choice of court or arbitration
  clauses and of "fork in the road" provisions;
- The definition of "disputes with respect to investments";
- The meaning of umbrella clauses;
- The application of the most favoured nation clause (MFN) to dispute
  resolution.

1. Treaty v. Contract Claims

13-15 Most treaty arbitrations involve an investment that gave rise to a
contract. The jurisdictional issues in treaty arbitration are particularly complex
because of the difficult co-existence of treaty and contract dispute resolution
mechanisms. In addition to reviewing notions such as investor, investment, and
consent, the assessment of jurisdiction over a treaty claim will often involve
drawing the line between treaty and contract claims and between treaty and
contract dispute settlement methods. The distinction between treaty and contract
claims in itself appears well accepted. The following quote from the *Vivendi*
annulment decision could be replicated by many others:

> A state may breach a treaty without breaching a contract, and *vice versa,*
> and this is certainly true of these provisions of the BIT ... Whether there has
> been a breach of the BIT and whether there has been a breach of contract
> are different questions. Each of these claims will be determined by reference
> to its own proper or applicable law – in the case of the BIT, by international
> law; in the case of the Concession Contract, by the proper law of the
> contract ...[13].

---

[13] *Compañia de Aguas del Aconquija SA and Vivendi Universal v. Argentina* (referred to as
Vivendi v. Argentina), Decision on annulment, 3 July 2002, 19(1) *ICSID Rev – FILJ* paras 95-96
(2004). A distinction between treaty claims and contract claims was also made by other ICSID
tribunals, e.g., *SGS Société Générale de Surveillance SA v. Islamic Republic of Pakistan*
(referred to as *SGS v. Pakistan*), Decision on jurisdiction, 6 August 2003, 18(1) *ICSID Rev –
FILJ* paras 146 et seq (2003); *Azurix Corp v. Argentina* (referred to as *Azurix v. Argentina*),
Decision on jurisdiction, 8 December 2003, paras 75 et seq. and 88 et seq, available on

13-16   The distinction between treaty and contract claims is especially useful when the investment contract contains an exclusive choice of court or an arbitration clause. In the presence of such a clause, can the investor nevertheless resort to investment arbitration? The distinction between treaty and contract claims yields the answer: yes, the investor can resort to investment arbitration for treaty claims, but not for contract claims. This answer is found in *CMS v. Argentina*, among other cases:

> As contractual claims are different from treaty claims, even if there had been or there currently was a recourse to the local courts for breach of contract, this would not have prevented submission of the treaty claims to arbitration.[14]

13-17   Or in the words of the Vivendi *ad hoc* Committee:

> In a case where the essential basis of a claim brought before an international tribunal is a breach of contract, the tribunal will give effect to any valid choice of forum clause in the contract. [15]

13-18   And further:

> Where "the fundamental basis of the claim" is a treaty laying down an independent standard by which the conduct of the parties is to be judged, the existence of an exclusive jurisdiction clause in a contract between the claimant and the respondent state or one of its subdivisions cannot operate as a bar to the application of the treaty standard.[16]

13-19   The question of the effect of a choice of court clause in a contract is sometimes linked to a so-called "fork in the road" provision contained in the investment treaty. The fork in the road provides that the investor has the right to start arbitration under specified rules, most often under the ICSID Convention or the UNCITRAL Rules, provided that it has not submitted the dispute to the local courts or to a previously agreed dispute settlement procedure.[17]

---

www.asil.org; CMS *Gas Transmission Company v. Argentina* (referred to as *CMS v. Argentina*), Decision on jurisdiction, 17 July 2003, 42 ILM 788 (2003), para 80.

[14]   *CMS v. Argentina* (supra note 13), para. 80*; Azurix v. Argentina* (supra note 13), para 89*;* see also Christoph Schreuer, "Investment Treaty Arbitration and Jurisdiction over Contract Claims – The *Vivendi I* Case Considered", in Todd Weiler (Ed.), *International Investment Law and Arbitration: Leading Cases from ICSID, NAFTA, Bilateral Treaties and Customary International Law* (Cameron May 2005) 289 et seq.

[15]   *Vivendi v. Argentina*, Decision on annulment (supra note 13), para 98.

[16]   *Vivendi v. Argentina*, Decision on annulment (supra note 13), para 101.

[17]   See, e.g., Art. VII(2) and (3) of the US-Argentina BIT:

13-20   Here again, the distinction between treaty claim and contract claim is useful. If no treaty claim was brought before the local courts or in a previously agreed procedure, the treaty arbitration option remains available. A difficulty arises, however, because treaty and contract claims often overlap in terms of the actual losses they seek to recover. Is the overlap an obstacle to the distinction? What requirements must a treaty claim meet to be distinct from a contract claim? It is doubtful that the consistency observed so far also prevails on this fact issue. Recent awards in Argentinean cases hold that the claims are distinct whenever they do not involve the same parties, "cause of action", and "instrument". This is the view expressed for instance in *CMS v. Argentina*:

> [...] even if TGN had done so [i.e., applied to local courts], – which is not the case –, this would not result in triggering the "fork in the road" provision against CMS. Both the parties and the causes of action under separate instruments are different.[18]

---

(2) In the event of an investment dispute, the parties to the dispute should initially seek a resolution through consultation and negotiation. If the dispute cannot be settled amicably, the national or company concerned may choose to submit the dispute for resolution:
(a) to the courts or administrative tribunals of the Party that is a party to the dispute; or
(b) in accordance with any applicable, previously agreed dispute-settlement procedures; or
(c) in accordance with the terms of paragraph 3.
(3) (a) Provided that the national or company concerned has not submitted the dispute for resolution under paragraph 2 (a) or (b) and that six months have elapsed from the date on which the dispute arose, the national or company concerned may choose to consent in writing to the submission of the dispute for settlement by binding arbitration:
(i) to the International Centre for the Settlement of Investment Disputes ("Centre") established by the Convention on the Settlement of Investment Disputes between States and Nationals of other States, done at Washington, March 18, 1965 ("ICSID Convention"), provided that the Party is a party to such convention: or
(ii) to the Additional Facility of the Centre, if the Centre is not available; or
(iii) in accordance with the Arbitration Rules of the United Nations Commission on International Trade Law (UNICTRAL); or
(iv) to any other arbitration institution, or in accordance with any other arbitration rules, as may be mutually agreed between the parties to the dispute.
(b) Once the national or company concerned has so consented, either party to the dispute may initiate arbitration in accordance with the choice so specified in the consent.

[18]   *CMS v. Argentina* (supra note 13), para 80; see also *Azurix v. Argentina* (supra note 13), para 89; *Enron Corporation and Ponderosa Assets, L P v. Argentina* (referred to as *Enron v. Argentina*), Decision on jurisdiction, 14 January 2004, para 97, available on www.asil.org.

13-21 This approach appears to restate the traditional requirements set to the application of the principles of *res judicata* or *lis alibi pendens*, i.e. identity of parties, object or *petitum*, and ground or *causa petendi*.[19]

13-22 As opposed to this line of cases, an *obiter dictum* in the *Vivendi* annulment decision seems to imply that treaty and contract claims are not distinct as soon as they involve the same facts:

> In the Committee's view, a claim by CAA against the Province of Tucumán for breach of the Concession Contract, brought before the contentious administrative courts of Tucumán would *prima facie* ... constitute a "final" choice of forum and jurisdiction, if that claim was coextensive with a dispute relating to investments made under the BIT.[20]

13-23 This is a different test than the one applied in CMS. In other words, if the principle is well-established, its implementation varies.[21]

2. *"Disputes with Respect to Investments"*

13-24 Another related issue deals with the scope of the dispute settlement option offered in investment treaties or similar formulas. Certain treaties are quite specific and give the investor the right to initiate a treaty arbitration over "disputes under this Agreement"[22] or similar language. Other treaties use broader language such as "disputes with respect to investments". Does this language

---

[19] For a discussion of these principles with further references, see August Reinisch, "The Use and Limits of *Res Judicata* and *Lis Pendens* as Procedural Tools To Avoid Conflicting Dispute Settlement Outcomes", *The Law and Practice of International Courts and Tribunals*, Leiden 2004, vol 3, 37-77, 61 et seq.

[20] *Vivendi v. Argentina*, Decision on annulment (supra note 13), para. 55; applying equally the sole requirement of identity of facts in connection with the waiver under Art. 1121 NAFTA, *Waste Management, Inc v. United Mexican States* (referred to as *Waste Management v. Mexico*), Award, 2 June 2000, 15(1) *ICSID Rev FILJ* (2000).

[21] For a discussion of various cases on fork in the road provisions, see in particular Christoph Schreuer, "Travelling the BIT Route – Of Waiting Periods, Umbrella Clauses and Forks in the Road", 5(2) *J World Inv & Trade*, 239 et seq (2004).

[22] See, e.g., the alternative version of Art. 8(1) of the United Kingdom Model BIT:

> Disputes between a national or company of one Contracting Party and the other Contracting Party concerning an obligation of the latter under this Agreement in relation to an investment of the former which have not been amicably settled shall, after a period of three months from written notification of a claim, be submitted to international arbitration if the national or company concerned so wishes.

include contract disputes? At first sight at least, disputes on an investment contract certainly qualify as "disputes with respect to investment".

13-25 On this issue one may distinguish three lines of cases[23]. First, *Salini v. Morocco*[24] considers that the phrase includes contract disputes. More precisely, the *Salini* tribunal held that the terms of Article 8 of the applicable Morocco/Italy BIT[25] were "very general" and that the

> reference to expropriation and nationalisation measures, which are matters coming under the unilateral will of a State, cannot be interpreted to exclude a claim based in contract from the scope of application of this Article.[26]

To reach this conclusion, the *Salini* tribunal ruled out the effect of a contractual choice of the local administrative courts on the ground that the jurisdiction of such courts cannot be prorogated or chosen by the parties but exists by operation of law.[27] This appears to be an insufficient reason for denying effect to the contract clause providing for the jurisdiction of these disputes. Indeed, even if such jurisdiction cannot be prorogated, the very fact that the parties expressly stated their common intent to have contract disputes resolved in such courts should be sufficient to grant effect to this clause.

13-26 The second line is found in *SGS v. Philippines*. The *SGS v. Philippines* tribunal held that such language in the Swiss-Philippines treaty included contract claims, but that the treaty tribunal should not exercise its jurisdiction as long as the contract judge had not ruled on the scope of the contract obligation. In other words, jurisdiction of a contract dispute under the treaty was limited to performance of the contract obligations and did not extend to their scope or amount.[28]

---

[23] For a discussion of the relevant ICSID jurisprudence, see Emmanuel Gaillard, "Investment Treaty Arbitration and Jurisdiction over Contract Claims – the SGS Cases Considered", in Weiler (ed), *International Investment Law and Arbitration*, supra note 14, 331 et seq.

[24] *Salini Construttori SpA and Itaestrade SpA v. Kingdom of Morocco* (referred to as *Salini v. Morocco*), Decision on jurisdiction, 23 July 2001, *Journal du droit international* (2002), no 1, 196 et seq. (an English translation of the French original is published in 42 *ILM* 609 (2003)).

[25] Art. 8 of the applicable Italy-Morocco BIT used the terms "tutte le controversie o divergenze ... in relazione ad un investimento" in order to define ICSID jurisdiction.

[26] *Salini v. Morocco* (supra note 24), para 59.

[27] *Salini v. Morocco* (supra note 24), para 27.

[28] *SGS v. Philippines*, Decision on jurisdiction (supra note 1), paras 130 et seq and para 155.

13-27   The third line is represented by *SGS v. Pakistan*, where the tribunal held that similar language under the Swiss-Pakistani treaty covered only treaty claims.[29]

3. Umbrella Clause

13-28   The fifth and penultimate topic addressed here deals with umbrella clauses. A quotation from the Swiss-Pakistani BIT serves to illustrate the topic:

> Either Contracting Party shall constantly guarantee the observance of the commitments it has entered into with respect to the investments of the investors of the other Contracting Party.[30]

13-29   Another example is excerpted from the Philippines BIT between the Philippines and Switzerland. It reads as follows:

> Each party shall observe any obligation it has assumed with regard to specific investments in its territory by investors of the other Contracting Party.[31]

13-30   The question which arises is whether the words "any obligation" or "commitments" include contractual obligations and, if so, whether contract rights are transformed into or elevated to treaty rights by the operation of this provision. In other words, are contractual obligations "put under the treaty's protective umbrella"?[32]

13-31   Are the clauses just quoted different? They differ somewhat in the words used: "consistently guarantee the observance of" *versus* "observe"; "commitments" *versus* "any obligation"; "it has entered into with respect to the investment of the investors of the other Contracting Party" versus "it has assumed with respect to specific investments ... by investors of the other Contracting Party". Do these variations imply a different meaning of the clause? *SGS v. Pakistan* and *SGS v. Philippines* answered in the affirmative.

---

[29] *SGS v. Pakistan*, Decision on jurisdiction (supra note 13), paras 161 and 162.
[30] Art 11 Swiss-Pakistan BIT.
[31] Art X(2) Swiss-Philippines BIT.
[32] Schreuer, supra note 14, 299. On the history of the umbrella clause, see Anthony C. Sinclair, "The Origins of the Umbrella Clause in the International Law of Investment Protection", 20(4) *Arb Int* 411-434 (2004); see further Thomas W Wälde, "The "Umbrella" Clause in Investment Arbitration, A Comment on Original Intentions and Recent Cases", 6(2) *J World Inv & Trade* 183 et seq. (2005).

13-32   The *SGS v. Pakistan* tribunal held that the text fell considerably short of the alleged "elevator effect", that the legal consequences of the elevator effect were so far reaching that it could only be accepted on the basis of clear and convincing evidence of the shared intent of the contracting States, which evidence was not adduced. It also relied on the fact that the clause was placed at the end of the treaty, separate from the substantive protections. Specifically, it held the following:

> A treaty interpreter must of course seek to give effect to the object and purpose projected by that Article and by the BIT as a whole. That object and purpose must be ascertained, in the first instance, from the text itself of Article 11 and the rest of the BIT. Applying these familiar norms of customary international law on treaty interpretation, we do not find a convincing basis for accepting [...] that Article 11 of the BIT has had the effect of entitling [...] SGS, in the face of a valid forum selection contract clause, to "elevate" its claims grounded solely in a contract [...] to claims grounded on the BIT [...].[33]

13-33   The *SGS v. Philippines* tribunal reached the contrary view. In its opinion, the text was clear and the object and purpose of the BIT pleaded in favour of a broad interpretation:

> The object and purpose of the BIT supports an effective interpretation of Article X(2). The BIT is a treaty for the promotion and reciprocal protection of investments ... It is legitimate to resolve uncertainties in its interpretation so as to favour the protection of covered investments.[34]

13-34   It is interesting to contrast this interpretation in favour of the investment and the investor with the one given by *SGS v. Pakistan*, which is reflected in the following passage:

> On the reading of Article 11 urged by the Claimant, the benefits of the dispute settlement provisions of a contract with a State also a party to a BIT, would flow only to the investor. ... Article 11 of the BIT should be read in such a way as to enhance mutuality and balance of benefits in the inter-relation of different agreements located in differing legal orders.[35]

---

[33]   *SGS v. Pakistan*, Decision on jurisdiction (supra note 13), para 165.
[34]   *SGS v. Philippines*, Decision on jurisdiction (supra note 1), para 116.
[35]   *SGS v. Pakistan*, Decision on jurisdiction (supra note 13), para 168.

13-35 Accordingly, *SGS v. Pakistan* seeks to balance the interests of the State and the investor, while *SGS v. Philippines* privileges the interests of the investor over those of the State.[36]

13-36 On their face, these holdings would appear to reach radically opposed results; the reality is different. The *Philippines* tribunal accepted that contract claims fell within the umbrella clause and that it thus had jurisdiction over the contract claims. Its jurisdiction was, however, limited to the *performance* of contract obligations and did not extend to the scope of the obligation. The scope, here the amount of the debt due, remained within the jurisdiction of the local courts chosen in the contract. This reservation substantially mitigates the difference in outcome of the two cases. Depending on the circumstances, however, the mitigation may not always work. Moreover, the approach in the two cases to the umbrella clause remains fundamentally different.

4. Most Favoured Nation Clause

13-37 Many investment treaties provide that neither contracting State shall submit the investors of the other State to treatment less favourable than that which it accords to investors of any third country.[37] The obvious question in our

---

[36] For a discussion of theses cases, see in particular Gaillard, *supra* note 23, 251 et seq. See also Schreuer, *supra* note 21, 249 et seq; Stanimir Alexandrov, "Introductory Note to International Centre for the Settlement of Investment Disputes (ICSID): SGS Société Générale de Surveillance S.A. v. Pakistan", 42 *ILM* 1285 (2003); Judith Gill / Matthew Gearing / Gemma Birt, "Contractual Claims and Bilateral Investment Treaties – A Comparative Review of the SGS Cases", 21(5) *J Int'l Arb* 397-412. (2004).

[37] See, e.g., Art. 3 of the United Kingdom Model BIT:

(1) Neither Contracting Party shall in its territory subject investments or returns of nationals or companies of the other Contracting Party to treatment less favourable than that which it accords to investments or returns of its own nationals or companies or to investments or returns of nationals or companies of any third State.

(2) Neither Contracting Party shall in its territory subject nationals or companies of the other Contracting Party, as regards their management, maintenance, use, enjoyment or disposal of their investments, to treatment less favourable than that which it accords to its own nationals or companies or to nationals or companies of any third State.

(3) For the avoidance of doubt, it is confirmed that the treatment provided for in paragraphs (1) and (2) above shall apply to the provisions of Articles 1 to 11 of this Agreement.

On most favoured nation treatment, see generally Georg Schwarzenberger, "The Most-Favoured-Nation Standard in British State Practice", 22 *BYbIL* 96 et seq. (1948). According to Schwarzenberger (at 99 seq.),

context is whether such "no less favourable treatment" also applies to the dispute settlement options. Can one incorporate into a treaty a dispute resolution provision of another treaty in whole or in part? Here again, one faces divergent solutions.

13-38   In *Maffezini v. Spain*, the tribunal had to decide whether a time limit in one treaty could be applied in another one on the basis of the MFN clause in the basic treaty, *i.e.,* the treaty containing the most favoured nation clause.[38] More precisely, if the provisions on dispute settlement contained in the basic treaty are more favourable than those in another treaty, can the former provisions be extended to the beneficiary of the latter treaty by operation of the MFN clause?

13-39   The *Maffezini* tribunal decided in the affirmative on the ground that procedural and substantive rights were intimately connected:

> The tribunal considers that there are good reasons to conclude that today dispute settlement arrangements are inextricably related to the protection of foreign investors.[39]

> [the MFN standard's] main function consists in forming an agency of equality. It prevents discrimination and establishes equality of opportunity on the highest possible plane: the minimum discrimination and the maximum of favours conceded to any third State .... It is clear that m.f.n. clauses serve as an insurance against incompetent draftsmanship and lack of imagination on the part of those who are responsible for the conclusion of international treaties .... Unforeseen problems necessarily arise and changes occur which make desirable the adaptation of treaties to changed circumstances. As long as a country is content to enjoy treatment equal to that of the most-favoured third country, and the subject-matter of the treaty lends itself to such treatment, the use of the m.f.n. standard leads to the constant self-adaptation of such treaties and greatly contributes to the rationalization of international affairs.

[38]   *Emilio Agustín Maffezini v. Kingdom of Spain* (referred to as *Maffezini v. Spain*), Decision on jurisdiction, 25 January 2000, 16(1) *ICSID Rev – FILJ* (2001), para 44. For a commentary of this decision see, e.g., Jürgen Kurtz, "The Delicate Extension of Most-Favoured-Nation Treatment to Foreign Investors: Maffezini v. Kingdom of Spain", in Weiler (ed), *International Investment Law and Arbitration*, supra note 14, 523 et seq; Francisco Orrego Vicuña, "Bilateral Investment Treaties and the Most-Favoured-Nation Clause: Implications for Arbitration in the Light of a Recent ICSID Case", in *Investment Treaties and Arbitration, ASA Special Series* No. 19 (2002) 133 et seq..

[39]   *Maffezini v. Spain,* Decision on jurisdiction (supra note 38), para 54. In *Siemens AG v. Argentina* the Tribunal followed the *Maffezini* Tribunal, stating that

> access to [dispute settlement] mechanisms is part of the protection offered under the Treaty. It is part of the treatment of foreign investors and investments and of the advantages accessible through a MFN clause. ... This conclusion concurs with the findings of the arbitral tribunal in *Maffezini*

and

> If a third party treaty contains provisions for the settlement of disputes that
> are more favorable to the protection of the investor's rights and interests
> than those in the basic treaty, such provisions may be extended to the bene-
> ficiary of the most favored nation clause as they are fully compatible with
> the *ejusdem generis* principle.[40]

13-40 By contrast, *Plama v. Bulgaria* did not extend the most favoured nation
clause to arbitration. The claimant argued that it was entitled to select the ICSID
dispute resolution mechanism provided in another treaty instead of the *ad hoc*
arbitration offered in the "basic" treaty. The tribunal did not accept this substitution of dispute resolution systems because it was not clear from doubt that such
an extension or incorporation of language from a third treaty reflected the intent
of the contracting States:

> An MFN provision in a basic treaty does not incorporate by reference
> dispute settlement provisions in whole or in part set forth in another treaty,
> unless the MFN provisions in the basic treaty leaves no doubt that the
> Contracting Party intended to incorporate them.[41]

13-41 Among more recent cases, *Salini v. Jordan* shares this view expressing
fears over treaty shopping.[42]

IV. THE ANSWER: CONSISTENT AND OTHER SOLUTIONS, AND POSSIBLE REMEDIES

13-42 Where does this all lead? What is the answer to our question? The
answer can be divided in three parts: the first deals with consistent solutions; the

---

(*Siemens AG v. Argentina*, Decision on jurisdiction, 3 August 2004, paras. 102-103, available on www.asil.org).

[40] The *ejusdem generis* principle implies that the extension is only admissible to matters of the same category. See Endre Ustor "Most-Favoured-Nation Clause", in *Encyclopedia of Public International Law*, vol 8 (North-Holland 1985) 414-5) according to who

> the beneficiary State can only claim rights which belong to the subject-matter of the clause, which are within the time-limits and other conditions and restrictions set by the agreement, and which are in respect of persons or things specified in the clause or implied from its subject-matter.

See also *Maffezini v. Spain,* Decision on jurisdiction (supra note 38), para 56.

[41] *Plama Consortium Limited v. Republic of Bulgaria* (referred to as *Plama v. Bulgaria*), Decision on jurisdiction, 8 February 2005, para 223, available on www.worldbank.org/icsid.

[42] *Salini Construttori SpA and Italtrade SpA v. the Hashemite Kingdom of Jordan*, Decision on jurisdiction, 29 November 2004, para 115, available on www.worldbank.org/icsid.

second with divergent solutions due to different treaty provisions; and the third with remaining inconsistencies and possible remedies.

1. Consistent Solutions

13-43   First, there are indeed a number of consistent solutions which emerge from the review of treaty interpretations above. The main one consists in the distinction between contract and treaty claims and its implementation in terms of the effect of contractual choice of court clauses or arbitration agreements, or of the impact of fork in the road provisions. The consistent interpretation is not so much a result of the application of treaty interpretation methods, but rather arises from the recognition of the distinct nature of different instruments and of the rights flowing from such instruments.

13-44   Whether the distinction and its consequences, which involve a plurality of *fora*, with the inherent waste of resources, the risk of conflicting decisions and double recovery, is a good distinction or not is a different question. In the present state of the law, it appears to be an unavoidable feature of investment arbitration. Consistency and coherence of results as well as legal certainty will undoubtedly benefit if the distinction is rigorously applied.

2. Divergent Solutions due to Different Treaty Provisions

13-45   Second, certain divergent solutions are justified by the different meanings of treaty provisions or different underlying intentions. Modern investment treaties have many common features and their texts mostly derive from previous treaties. Nevertheless, there are sometimes substantial differences from one treaty to the other.[43]

13-46   Among the illustrations discussed above, the *Plama* award on MFN probably falls within this category. Indeed, the elements on record, especially evidence of later negotiations, showed that the parties' intent was not to incorporate the dispute resolution mechanisms from other treaties.[44]

---

[43]   Thomas Wälde/Todd Weiler, "Investment Arbitration Under the Energy Charter Treaty in the Light of New NAFTA Precedents: Towards a Global Code of Conduct for Economic Regulations", in Weiler (ed,) *Investment Treaties and Arbitration*, supra note 38, 166, note 19; Jeswald W Salacuse / Nicholas P Sullivan, "Do BITs Really Work?: An Evaluation of Bilateral Investment Treaties and Their Grand Bargain", 46(1) *Harvard Int'l L J* 85-6 (2005).

[44]   *Plama v. Bulgaria*, Decision on jurisdiction (supra note 41), para 195.

3. Remaining Inconsistencies and Remedies

13-47   Third, certain inconsistencies in interpretation leading to irreconcilable outcomes remain. The interpretation of the umbrella clause, and of the words "disputes with respect to investment" are examples of such remaining inconsistencies. There are and there will be others. Are there possible remedies? One may think of the following:

- Improving the manner in which arbitral tribunals interpret treaties. However, the application of treaty interpretation rules by arbitral tribunals does not appear to be the problem. An extensive review of arbitral awards[45]

---

[45] *Metalclad Corp v. United Mexican States*, Award, 30 August 2000, 16(1) *ICSID Rev – FILJ* (2001); *Marvin Feldman v. United Mexican States*, Award, 16 December 2002, 18(2) *ICSID Rev – FILJ* (2003); *Tokios Tokelés v. Ukraine*, Decision on jurisdiction, 29 April 2004 (available on www.worldbank.org/icsid); *Salini v. Jordan*, Decision on jurisdiction (supra note 42); *Mihaly International Corp v. Democratic Socialist Republic of Sri Lanka*, Award, 15 March 2002, 17(1) *ICSID Rev – FILJ* (2002); *Consortium RFCC v. Kingdom of Morocco*, Decision on jurisdiction, 22 December 2003 (available on www.worldbank.org/icsid); *Ethyl Corp v. Canada*, Decision on jurisdiction, 24 June 1998 (available on www.naftalaw.org); *United Parcel Service of America Inc. v. Canada*, Decision on jurisdiction, 22 November 2002 (available on www.naftalaw.org); *Cross-Border Trucking Services*, Final Report of the Panel, 6 February 2001 (available on www.naftalaw.org); *Fireman's Fund Insurance Company v. United Mexican States*, Decision on jurisdiction, 17 July 2003 (available on www.naftalaw.org); *Pope & Talbot Inc v. Canada*, Award, 10 April 2001 (available on www.naftalaw.org); *SGS v. Philippines*, Decision on jurisdiction (supra note 1); *SGS v. Pakistan*, Decision on jurisdiction (supra note 13); *Loewen Group, Inc. and Raymond L. Loewen v. United States of America*, Decision on jurisdiction (9 January 2001) and Award (26 June 2003), supra note 10; *S.D. Myers, Inc. v. Canada*, Award, 13 November 2000 (available on www.naftalaw.org); *Técnicas Medioambientales Tecmed S.A. v. United Mexican States*, 29 May 2003, 19(1) *ICSID Rev - FILJ* (2004); *Maffezini v. Spain*, Decision on jurisdiction (supra note 38); *Champion Trading Co and Ameritrade International, Inc. v. Arab Republic of Egypt*, Decision on jurisdiction, 21 October 2003, 19(1) *ICSID Rev – FILJ* (2004); *Banro American Resources, Inc. and Société Aurifère du Kivu et du Maniema S.A.R.L. v. Democratic Republic of the Congo*, Award, 1 September 2000, 17(2) *ICSID Rev – FILJ* (2002); *Waste Management v. Mexico*, Award, 2 June 2000 (supra note 20); *Plama v. Bulgaria*, Decision on jurisdiction (supra note 41); *ADF Group Inc. v. United States of America*, Award, 9 January 2003, 18(1) *ICSID Rev – FILJ* (2003); *AAPL v. Sri Lanka*, Award (supra note 5); *Consorzio Groupement LESI – DIPENTA v. Algeria*, 10 January 2005 (available on www.worldbank.org/icsid); *Fedax NV v. Republic of Venezuela*, Award, 9 March 1998, 5 *ICSID Reports*, 200 et seq, *Lanco International, Inc v. Argentina*, Decision on jurisdiction, 8 December 1998, 5 *ICSID Reports*, 367 et seq.; *Siemens AG v. Argentina*, Decision on jurisdiction (supra note 39); *Victoir Pey Casado and Fondation Président Allende v. Republic of Chile*, Decision on provisional measures, 25 September 2001, 16(2) *ICSID Rev – FILJ* (2001); *Alex Genin, Eastern Credit Limited, Inc and AS Baltoil v. Republic of Estonia*, Award, 25 June 2001, 17(2) *ICSID Rev – FILJ* (2002); *Azurix v. Argentina*, Decision on jurisdiction (supra note 13); *CMS v. Argentina*, Decision on jurisdiction (supra note 13); *Enron v. Argentina*, Decision on jurisdiction (supra note 18); *Compañía de Aguas del Aconquija SA & Vivendi Universal v. Argentine*

shows that arbitrators do apply treaty interpretation rules rather conscientiously, with variations of course, some being more text-bound and others more intent-bound. The differences in solutions are not due to a misapplication of treaty interpretation rules, but rather to varying assessments of the meaning and respective weight of the different elements playing a part in the interpretation. The differences in the role assigned to the object and purpose of the treaty in the *SGS* cases are a good illustration.

- Introducing a doctrine of precedent or *stare decisis*. In addition to being unrealistic, this solution would not serve much of a purpose.[46] It is striking how ICSID tribunals pay deference to precedents, in particular to ICSID awards and ICJ cases. Subject to exceptions such as the *SGS v. Philippines* case, past cases have considerable influence on future arbitral tribunals. Is it because "arbitrators tend to go with the flow" and because "placing oneself within the collegial continuity is a condition for continuing practice of guild membership"?[47] These factors may play a role, but one would doubt that they are decisive. In any event, for our purposes what matters is that arbitrators are indeed rather deferential.

- What else then may be done? Would the introduction of an appeal facility promote consistency[48]? The existence of an appeal would bring certain advantages, including increased consistency if the appellate procedure is well designed. It would, however, also bring along substantial drawbacks. Justice would take longer and be more expensive. No party dissatisfied with an award could afford *not* to file an appeal, be it only for internal

---

Republic, Award, 21 November 2000, 16(?) *ICSID Rev – FILJ*; *Autopista Concesionada de Venezuela, CA v. Bolivarian Republic of Venezuela*, Decision on jurisdiction (supra note 11).

[46] On this point, see, *e.g.*, Barton Legum, "Visualizing an Appellate System", *in Appeals and Challenges to Investment Treaty Awards: Is it Time for an International Appellate System?*, supra note 9, 68-9), who points out that

> it is doubtful that a formal system of *stare decisis*, such as that applicable in common-law courts, is either necessary or desirable. It is of doubtful necessity because international tribunals seem to accord considerable weight to earlier decisions whether or not a formal *stare decisis* system is in place … A rigid system of binding precedents may not be suited for an environment in which many different treaties, with many different histories, contexts and provisions, are in play.

On this aspect and other reform proposals see also Susan D Franck, "The Legitimacy Crisis in Investment Treaty Arbitration: Privatizing Public International Law Through Inconsistent Decisions", 73 *Fordham L Rev* 1611 et seq (2003).

[47] Wälde/ Weiler, supra note 43, 166.

[48] On this issue, see, e.g., the contributions of Doak Bishop, Judith Gill and Nigel Blackaby in *Appeals and Challenges to Investment Treaty Awards: Is it Time for an International Appellate System?*, supra note 9, 8 et seq.

reasons. Whether the additional cost and time involved would produce a superior quality of justice is questionable at best.[49]

- Rather than an appellate mechanism, would it be preferable to introduce a permanent investment court, an ICJ of investment disputes? Investment arbitration is shaped on the model of commercial arbitration which may not always be adapted to investment disputes.[50] Hence, investment arbitration may be in a state of transition and evolve towards a permanent court. Ruling as a sole instance, a permanent body would not have the drawbacks of an appellate mechanism, but it would certainly have other disadvantages, such as feasibility and the risk of politicisation.

- Further, for jurisdictional purposes (the same would not be true for the merits), the annulment mechanism under Article 52 of the ICSID Convention could very well offer some remedy against inconsistency. Article 52 provides for annulment in the event of "manifest excess of power", which applies to the merits as well as to decisions on jurisdiction. It is submitted that any exercise of jurisdiction when jurisdiction is not given and any failure to exercise jurisdiction when jurisdiction is given, is a manifest excess of power in and of itself.[51] There are no degrees in terms of jurisdiction: either a tribunal has jurisdiction or it does not. Hence, there can be no degrees in the review of a decision on jurisdiction at the annulment stage. This understanding of the ground for annulment would allow for an unrestricted review of decisions on jurisdiction and would thereby greatly foster coherence and consistency in treaty interpretation. This being said, it is not entirely satisfactory. Indeed, like the arbitral tribunals, the annulment committees change from one proceedings to the other. Thus, even with a full review of jurisdictional objections, complete uniformity cannot be taken for granted.

---

[49] On the pros and cons of an international appellate system, see in particular the contributions of Bette Shifman, Barton Legum, Guido Tawil and Thomas Wälde in *Appeals and Challenges to Investment Treaty Awards: Is it Time for an International Appellate System?*, supra note 9, pp. 60 et seq.

[50] Brigitte Stern, "International Economic Relations and the MAI Dispute Settlement System", 16(2) *J Int'l Arb* 127-8 (1999).

[51] Although not expressed in so many words, this appears to be the meaning of an *obiter* in *Vivendi v. Argentina*, Decision on annulment (supra note 13), para 86. On "manifest excess of power" and jurisdictional review of ICSID awards, Philippe Pinsolle's contribution "Appeals and Challenges to Investment Treaty Awards: Is it Time for an International Appellate System?", supra note 9, 28 et seq; Kaufmann-Kohler, supra note 8, 197-198.

- Finally, another possible solution may be to introduce a consultation mechanism at the level of the arbitration proceedings. Any ICSID tribunal could request guidance about legal issues from a permanent consultative body.[52] A possible model may be provided by the procedure of Article 234 (formerly 177) of the EC Treaty, pursuant to which national courts of Member States request interpretative rulings from the European law. If properly designed, such a mechanism would ensure consistency, without the drawbacks of a full-fledged appellate procedure. Which of these possible remedies will develop in practice remains to be seen in the years to come.

---

[52] Such a function of an independent body with interpretative jurisdiction is very different from the one provided in Art. 1131(2) of the NAFTA, pursuant to which the States party to the Treaty, may issue joint interpretations of the treaty. It is submitted that the proposed consultation mechanism would meet the definition of a "similar mechanism" in Section 2102(b)(3)(G)(iv) of the US Federal Trade Act.

PART IV

INTERNATIONAL ARBITRATION AND THIRD PARTIES

*Bernard Hanotiau**

CHAPTER 14

GROUPS OF COMPANIES
IN INTERNATIONAL ARBITRATION

I. INTRODUCTION

14-1 In international arbitration, groups of companies raise a number of different issues. Some of them concern mainly the substance of the dispute, others seem to be more of a procedural nature, although I would hesitate to refer to a distinction between procedural and substantive issues, which might be to some extent incorrect or even confusing. Issues mainly concerning the substance of the dispute are themselves quite various: may a mother company, claimant in an arbitration procedure, request the payment by a respondent of not only the damage it has suffered as a consequence of respondent's wrongful conduct or breach of contract but also of the damage suffered by its subsidiaries (pass-through claims)? Is it possible that a mother company be declared jointly and severally liable for the breaches of contract committed only by one of its subsidiaries, both being parties to the arbitration? These, and others issues, which mainly concern the substance of the claim, are not really specific to arbitration. I will therefore only briefly address at the end of this presentation the issue of pass-trough claims since it has given rise to a recent important English Commercial Court decision of 4 February 2004.[1]

14-2 If one considers on the other hand the questions which are more of a procedural nature – at first impression at least – various issues may also arise. The most classical one is the issue whether a member of a group of companies may be added as additional claimant or as additional respondent, while the

---

*   Member of the Brussels and Paris Bar, Professor at the University of Louvain; Partner, Hanotiau and van den Berg.
[1]   *Peterson Farms Inc v. C & M Farming Ltd* [2004] All ER (D) 50; (2004) EWHC 121 (Comm).

Loukas A. Mistelis and Julian D.M. Lew (eds), Pervasive Problems in International Arbitration, 279-290
© 2006 Kluwer Law International. Printed in the Netherlands

contract containing the arbitration clause was entered into by another member of the group? This is the so-called issue of extension of the arbitration clause to non signatories. Or may other companies of a group request to be joined to the arbitration procedure beside the original claimant, another company of the same group? Or may a respondent request the joinder to the arbitration procedure of one or several other members of the group of companies to which claimant belongs? This last issue is a classical issue of joinder which is not really specific to groups of companies and which I will therefore not address here. In the same context, an issue of appointment of the members of the Arbitral Tribunal may also arise when several claimants, members of a group of a company, start an arbitration procedure against several respondents, members of another group. But again, this is not peculiar to groups of companies. It may arise in relation to any multiparty arbitration. I will therefore focus this presentation on the issue of extension of the arbitration clause to other members of a same group of companies, non signatories, as additional claimants or respondents: other companies of the group, directors or shareholders.[2]

14-3 In this respect, a few preliminary remarks should be made. In the first place, one must make a distinction between the issues arising from the circumstances in which the project at the center of the dispute has been negotiated and performed by one or more companies that belong to a group, some of which are not signatories of the arbitration clause, and the issues arising from the fact that the dispute involves or concerns a variety of problems originating from, or in connection with, two or more agreements entered into by the same and/or different parties and which do not all contain the same – or at least compatible – arbitration clauses. In this second scenario, the fact that the parties to the contracts may belong to a group is *a priori* irrelevant, although it may in some cases help clarify or resolve the issues that arise from the existence of a group of contracts. This was the case in the decision of the Paris Court of Appeal of 31 October 1989 in *Re Société Kis France v. Société Générale*,[3] where the existence of a group of companies was decisive in reaching the conclusion of the existence of a group of contracts. But this situation is rather unusual.

14-4 In other words, the question of extension of the arbitration clause to non signatory members of a group of companies, and the question whether and to

---

[2] For a thorough analysis of the case law, see in particular Bernard Hanotiau, "Problems raised by complex arbitrations involving multiple contracts-parties-issues – An Analysis", 18(3) *J Int'l Arb* 251-360 (2001).

[3] 1992 *Rev Arb* 90; XVI *YBCA*. 145 (1991).

what extent it is possible to bring into one arbitral proceeding all the parties that have participated in a single economic transaction through various agreements and to decide in the same proceeding all the issues arising from the latter, should be clearly distinguished and are indeed in the main the subject of distinct case law.

14-5 On the other hand, the widely used concept of extension of the arbitration clause to non signatories is a misleading concept, and moreover, is probably wrong to a large extent since, in most cases, courts and arbitral tribunals still base their determination of the issue on the existence of a common intent of the parties and, therefore, on consent. The basic issue therefore remains: who is party to the clause, or has adhered to it, or eventually is estopped from contending that it has not adhered to it. This is in other words a classic problem of contract law. The real issue therefore becomes whether in international arbitration, given its specific character and taking into consideration the usages of international trade, one should follow the same rules as are applicable to ordinary civil and commercial cases or adopt a more liberal approach; and in the latter case, what approach should be adopted.

14-6 The existence of a group of companies gives a special dimension to the issue of conduct or consent. Several authors have pointed out that when there is a group of companies, one may presume that the parent company binds its subsidiaries; but on the other hand, only the companies that have been substantially involved in the negotiation and performance of the agreement containing the arbitration clause will be considered parties to the latter. The case law is not always entirely clear in this respect. In most cases, it seems that only a substantial involvement is considered sufficient to constitute consent or ratification. Some cases however suggest that a party's conduct should not necessarily be regarded as an expression of a party's implied consent; rather a party's substantial involvement in the negotiation and performance of the contract and the knowledge of the existence of the arbitration clause have a standing of their own, as a substitute for consent, just as reliance is a substitute for consideration. In any case, it is the author's opinion that, whatever the factual scheme, the issue of extension of the arbitration clause to other companies of the group should indeed be analyzed in terms of consent, rather than by determining whether the so called group of companies doctrine is known or unknown in the relevant legal system.[4]

---

[4] See on this issue, Bernard Hanotiau, *Complex Arbitrations, Multiparty, Multicontract, Multi-issue and Class Actions* (Kluwer Law International 2006), paras 104 et seq.

II. Leading Cases

14-7 One will note in this respect the difference between the wording of two leading decisions, the first one, the *Dow Chemical* award in ICC case no 4131 of 1982[5] and the decision of the Paris Court of Appeal of 22 March 1995[6] in the *SMABTP* case.

14-8 In the first decision, the Arbitral Tribunal formulated its reasoning as follows:

> considering, in particular, that the arbitration clause expressly accepted by certain of the companies of the group should bind the other companies which by virtue of their role in the conclusion, performance or termination of the contract containing said clauses, and in accordance with the mutual intention of all parties to the proceedings, appear to have been veritable parties to these contracts or to have been principally concerned by them and the disputes to which they may give rise.[7]

14-9 In the Paris Court of Appeal's decision, the reasoning was much more liberally formulated:

> the arbitration clause inserted in an international contract has self-standing validity and effectiveness which requires that its application be extended to parties which are directly implicated in the performance of the contract and in the dispute that may arise therefrom as long as it is established that their situation and their activities give rise to the presumption that they were aware of the existence and the scope of the arbitration clause, eventhough they were not signatories of the contract which provides for it.[8]

14-10 Before turning to the scenarios which present themselves in the case law (arbitral awards and court decisions), one should wonder why one does want to join non signatory companies as additional claimants or as additional respondents? The reasons are various and pertain to strategy: for example, the real party in interest is not the company which signed the relevant agreement but rather a

---

[5] ICC case no. 4131, 1982, Interim Award, *Dow Chemical France et al v. Isover Saint Gobain*, IX *YBCA* 131 (1984); *Collection of ICC Arbitral Awards* (Kluwer Law and Taxation 1994) 146.

[6] (1st Ch D), 1997 *Rev Arb* 550.

[7] ICC case no. 4131, 1982, Interim Award, *Dow Chemical France et al v. Isover Saint Gobain*, IX *YBCA* 131 (1984); Jarvin, Derains, Arnaldez (eds), *Collection of ICC Arbitral Awards* (Kluwer Law and Taxation 1994) 146 at 151.

[8] (1st Ch D), 1997 *Rev Arb* 550.

subsidiary or the mother company of the group; or the company which has signed the arbitration clause is insolvent while the other subsidiaries of the group of the mother company are not; or the damage resulting from a breach of contract or from a tort committed by respondent, is not the company which signed with respondent the contract containing the arbitration clause but other companies of the group. Other parties invoke the fact that justice would not be well administered if a specific additional non signatory respondent could not be a party to the arbitration. I will immediately point out that this is not a good argument. Whatever the stretch that one is ready to give to the concept of consent (and it goes as far as considering a certain specific conduct as a substitute for consent), one should not forget that consent is the fundamental pillar of international arbitration.

14-11   What are the various factual schemes which are encountered in the disputes submitted to arbitral tribunals and national courts in relation to the extension of the arbitration clause to one or more additional, non signatory, member(s) of a group of companies? In reality, arbitral awards and court decisions may be subdivided into some twelve different factual patterns which may themselves be put into two groups: the extension of the clause is requested to one or several other defendants and the extension is claimed by one or several other claimants.

14-12   In the first case, Claimant (or Claimants) request(s) the extension of the clause:
- to the parent company of the group;
- to a State;
- to one or more subsidiaries or one or more companies of the group that are not subsidiaries;
- to a sister corporation and an employee;
- to another company, unrelated to the signatory;
- to a director or general manager or CEO or the owner of the group;
- to an individual, possibly a majority shareholder of the group, and another company within the group.

14-13   On the other hand, the signatory Claimant may want to join as additional Claimant (or Claimants):
- the parent company of the group;
- to a State;
- an individual (possibly a majority shareholder of the group) and other companies within the group;
- one or more subsidiaries or one or more companies within the group that are not subsidiaries;

- a director and principal shareholder.

14-14 I do not have enough space in this chapter to review the hundreds of arbitral awards and national court decisions in relation to which the arbitrators or courts have been confronted with these different schemes. I will just try to draw from the analysis that I have personally performed[9] a number of tentative conclusions, being made clear that depending on who decides, the conclusions are not always the same.

14-15 But before drawing these conclusions, I would like to briefly analyze a very important recent decision of the Swiss Federal Supreme Court of 16 October 2003[10] which had the opportunity to address a fundamental issue in relation to the extension of the arbitration clause to non signatory members of a group of companies, which I will name the "formal" issue. One will not dispute that an arbitration clause in writing is necessary to give jurisdiction to an arbitral tribunal. But by definition, if you want to join a non signatory, it means that this particular company has not signed the arbitration clause. Can one say that there is therefore no arbitration clause in writing in relation to this particular company and that therefore it may not be joined to the arbitration? The Swiss Federal Court answered in the negative. From the moment there is an arbitration clause, the issue of extension to a non signatory may be considered. The fact that the clause or the contract containing the clause was not signed by the "non signatory" is not a formal bar to the extension. In the own words of the Swiss Federal Court:

> this formal requirement (contained in article 178 al. 1 of the Swiss Law on Private International Law) only applies to the arbitration agreement itself, that is to the agreement ... by which the initial parties have reciprocally expressed their common will to submit the dispute to arbitration. As to the question of the subjective scope of an arbitration agreement formally valid under article 178 al. 1 – the issue is to determine which are the parties which are bound by the agreement and eventually determine if one or several third parties which are not mentioned therein nevertheless enter into its scope ratione personae –, it belongs to the merits and should consequently be decided in the light of article 178 al. 2 LDIP.[11]

---

[9] Hanotiau, supra note 4, Chapter II.

[10] *X S.A.L., Y S.A.L. et A v Z, SARL et Tribunal Arbitral CCI*, BGE 129 III 727.

[11] *Ibid*, at page 736.

(which provides that the arbitration agreement is valid, as to its substance, if it meets the conditions either of the law chosen by the parties, either of the law governing the subject matter of the dispute and in particular the law applicable to the main agreement, either of Swiss law).

III. TENTATIVE CONCLUSIONS

14-16 Let us now turn to the tentative conclusions which may be drawn from the existing case law. In reality, it is really difficult to draw general conclusions. The "extension" of the arbitration clause to other companies of the group – non signatories – started in France, and still today, its courts and arbitrators are among the most innovative in the development of this jurisprudence. Swiss courts on the other hand appeared in the first place extremely reluctant to accept the extension of an arbitration clause to non signatories but the Swiss Federal Court has recently relaxed its jurisprudence. On the other hand, the German approach seems still to be more restrictive and so seems to be also the position in England, where the doctrine of group of companies is said to be inconsistent with the principle of privity of contract, the principle of the corporate veil and the treatment of derivative actions. Moreover, the principles of *lex mercatoria* are not part of English law. The issue of who is a party to the arbitration clause is therefore mainly viewed as an issue of consent, but "extension" may nevertheless be achieved by recourse to such other theories as agency, trust or piercing the corporate veil. The same theories are also applied in the United States, which to some extent appears to be one of the most liberal jurisdiction with respect to the extension of the arbitration clause to non signatories.

14-17 Subject to these reservations, a first conclusion may be drawn from the awards and court decisions to the effect that the determination whether an arbitral clause should be extended to other companies of the group or its directors or shareholders, is "fact specific" and may differ depending upon the circumstances of the case. As was expressed by the Arbitral Tribunal in its first interim award in ICC case no 9517:[12]

> the question whether persons not named in an agreement can take advantage of an arbitration clause incorporated therein is a matter which must be decided on a case-to-case basis, requiring a close analysis of the circumstances in which the agreement was made, the corporate and practical relationship existing on one side and known to those on the other side of the

---

[12] 30 November 1998, unpublished.

bargain, the actual or presumed intention of the parties as regards rights of non signatories to participate in the arbitration agreement, and the circumstances under which non signatories subsequently became involved in the performance of the agreement and in the dispute arising from it.

14-18 A second conclusion is that arbitral tribunals do not often base their decision to extend the clause or not on a prior determination of the applicable law. Starting from the principle of autonomy of the arbitration clause, they generally feel free to determine their competence according to what they consider to be – on the basis of the facts of the case – the common intention of the parties, also taking into consideration the usages of international trade.

14-19 There seems to be an agreement that the existence of a group of companies is not *per se* a sufficient element to allow the extension to a non signatory of an arbitration agreement concluded by another member of the group. In most cases, courts and tribunals require proof of the existence of an intention at least implicit of all the parties that the non signatories be parties to the underlying contract and its arbitration clause. Some courts however limit themselves to an awareness of the clause and the requirement that the additional Claimant or Defendant be concerned by the dispute. But the company concerned must always have played a role in the conclusion and the performance of the agreement and this has to be proved by the party requesting the extension of the clause.

14-20 The analysis of the arbitral awards also leads to the emergence of a rebutable presumption that a parent company binds its subsidiaries[13] but that, on the other hand, only companies that have participated in the conclusion and performance of the agreement will be bound by the contract and the arbitration clause.

14-21 Various other elements equally play a role in the decision to extend the clause to a non-signatory:
- the fact that the other party has obviously entered into the agreement with a group as a whole and did not really care which companies would be involved in its performance; it is assumed that the determination of the

---

[13] See also Klaus Peter Berger, *The Creeping Codification of the Lex Mercatoria*, (Kluwer Law International 1999) principle 50 at 300; Michael Mustill, "The New Lex Mercatoria – the First Twenty-five Years" in Bos & Brownlie (eds), *Liber Amicorum for Lord Wilberforce* (Clarendon Press, 1987), 149-183, principle no. 8 at 176.

signatory companies only concerns the details of performance of the contract;

- or the fact that all the companies concerned have participated in the rights and obligations of the contractual relationship (in what has sometimes been called "a total confusion").

14-22 On the other hand, the application of the theory of lifting the corporate veil is generally considered to be limited to cases of fraud, abuse of rights and violation of mandatory rules. It is also admitted that the extension of the clause can never be considered a sanction of the conduct of the non-signatory. I would also like to point out in relation to lifting the corporate veil that this theory is very often wrongly presented and applied by advocates. They invoke the theory to extend the arbitration clause, beyond the company whose corporate veil has allegedly to be lifted, to the owners of the company. In most legal systems, this is not correct. Lifting the corporate veil means that the legal personality of the company is disputed and has to be lifted and that therefore the action should be directed only to its owners, those who stand "behind the corporate veil". In other words, it is "the shareholders instead of the company" and not "the company plus the shareholders". Before raising such a theory one should therefore have in the first place a good understanding of basic principles of corporate law, which is not always the case.

14-23 One other conclusion is that arbitral tribunals and courts have emphasized the right to use a group structure as appropriate, but once such choice has been made, it must be fully assumed. In this respect, the use of a company vehicle for tax or other reasons is not per se an argument to justify extending the arbitration clause to the underlying shareholder(s).

14-24 It seems also that at least in a great number of cases, a good test to decide whether an extension of the clause is appropriate is to determine whether the same conclusion would be justified if the situation was reversed. In other words, it is tentatively suggested that the principles used to determine the eventual extension of the clause to additional defendants should also be applied when the case concerns additional claimants and vice versa.

14-25 Finally, it appears that in relation to the issue of extension of the clause to non-signatories, American law is much more liberal than any in Europe, at least in some Circuits, the paramount concern of the courts being the "federal policy favouring arbitration".

IV. PETERSON FARMS

14-26   I will conclude this paper by a brief presentation of the recent English Commercial Court decision of February 4, 2004,[14] in which the Court had to decide on a challenge under section 67 of the 1996 Arbitration Act of an award in which the Tribunal had decided that it did have jurisdiction to consider and determine the damage claims of other entities within the Claimant's group, which were not parties to the arbitration.

14-27   The facts of the case were as follows. In September 1996, the parties entered into a contract for the sale of live poultry. The Claimant Indian company was the purchaser and the Defendant, a company incorporated under the laws of State of Arkansas, was the seller. The contract provided for ICC arbitration and for the application of the law of Arkansas. Under the agreement, the Claimant was sold male "grandparent" birds. It mated the birds to produce "parent" males which it would sell on as hatching eggs or day-old chicks to other "group entities" and to other purchasers. The other group entities used the parent males to breed with parent females to produce broiler chicks. It transpired that the poultry was infected with an avian virus.

14-28   The Claimant initiated arbitration. One of the issues for the Tribunal was whether it had jurisdiction to consider and determine the damage claims of other entities within the Claimant's group which were not named as parties to the agreement. The Tribunal held that it did have jurisdiction on the ground of the "group of companies doctrine" and further on the ground that the Claimant had entered into the agreement as agent for the other entities. It awarded the Claimant damages, a large portion of which comprised losses suffered by the other group entities. The Tribunal rejected the Defendant's submission that the dispute was governed by Arkansas law. It held that the right of the Indian company to make claims for its group was a question of interpretation of the arbitration agreement; in the absence of any choice of law made by the parties with regard to the arbitration agreement itself, the Tribunal had to determine this question in accordance with the common intent of the parties. In this respect, the Tribunal considered that Peterson, the seller, was aware throughout the negotiating period and at the time of contracting that it was dealing with the C&M group and would have obligations to all C&M companies. It was logical to have the name of one member of the group as the contracting partner with Peterson. C&M group, as

---

[14]   See supra note 1.

such, was not a legal entity and therefore could not contract in its own name. The purchaser contracted on behalf of and as the agent for the whole group. This was clearly understood by Peterson. According to the Arbitral Tribunal,

> the group of companies doctrine provides that an arbitration agreement signed by one company in a group of companies entitles (or obligates) affiliate non signatory companies, if the circumstances surrounding negotiation, execution, and termination of the agreement show that the mutual intention of all the parties was to bind the non signatories.[15]

This was the case here.

14-29 Following the challenge procedure, the Commercial Court decided that in this particular case, the identification of the parties to the agreement was a question of substantive and not procedural law; that "the autonomy" of the arbitration agreement was not in point; that the question was whether it was governed by Arkansas law. The judge decided that it was and added that in the context of the group of companies doctrine, the parties agreed that Arkansas law was the same as English law and that excluded the doctrine of group of companies. The judge also reached the conclusion that the award could not be sustained on the basis of agency by application of the same law of Arkansas. The Court therefore concluded that Peterson was entitled to have that part of the Award which awarded payment of losses by a group entities set aside for lack of jurisdiction.

14-30 Was the issue submitted to the Commercial Court a real issue of jurisdiction in relation to a group of companies? Was it not rather an issue of the extent of the damages which could be recovered by the purchasers? In other words, could the latter, beyond the damages they had suffered, also recover the damages suffered by companies closely connected to them and to the contractual scheme? From a discussion of this issue the author of these lines had recently with a number of lawyers from England and the continent, it appears that all of them would agree that, although the reasoning of the Court is correct from the strict point of view of English law in relation to the group of companies doctrine, the approach to the problem in the award and in the Commercial Court decision is quite unusual. A more usual approach would have been to consider that the Tribunal had jurisdiction *ratione personae* and then to address with the merits the issue whether Claimant could also recover the damages suffered by members of

---

[15] See supra note 1.

its group. In this respect, I would like to emphasize that the issue of "pass-through claims" is not specific to groups of companies and does not necessarily have to be decided on the basis of this doctrine. For example, it is not unusual for a main contractor to claim from the owner not only its own damages but also the damages suffered by its sub-contractors, which the main contractor has already indemnified. Whether this pass-through claim should be granted as such is function of the applicable law, which will most probably be the law applicable to the main agreement.

14-31 Does the Peterson Farm case mean the end of any possibility of extension of the arbitration clause to a non-signatory company when the underlying contract is governed by English law? We do not think that the Commercial Court decision inevitably commands such a conclusion. In the first place, we consider that it is probably better to avoid restricting oneself to the formula "group of companies doctrine" as a tool for legal reasoning in relation to the "extension" of an arbitration clause. As we already pointed out above, the existence of a group of company is not the ground on the basis of which courts and arbitral tribunals usually extend arbitral clauses to non signatories. They generally base their decision on consent or on conduct as an expression of implied consent or as a substitute for consent. It is mainly in this context that the fact that the signatory and the non-signatories are part of a group plays a role in their determination. Moreover, the extension of an arbitration clause to a non-signatory may still be considered on the basis of other theories, such as agency, trust or piercing the corporate veil.

*Stephen Jagusch and Anthony Sinclair**

CHAPTER 15

THE IMPACT OF THIRD PARTIES ON INTERNATIONAL ARBITRATION – ISSUES OF ASSIGNMENT

I. Introductory Remarks

15-1 International commerce and trade require that contractual rights and *choses in action* be capable of assignment.[1] Indeed, the assignment of *choses in action* is routine practice. However, where assigned rights are to be enforced by arbitration a number of complex issues arise out of the introduction of a stranger to the arbitration clause.[2] For some time it was not clear in English law, or in other legal systems, that an arbitration agreement could be assigned, or, if it could be assigned, what steps were required in law for the assignment to be perfected. In particular, given the doctrine of separability (or autonomy) of the arbitration clause,[3] the question was asked whether, in order to assign an arbitration agreement, it was necessary to effect a distinct transfer of those rights and

---

[*] Allen & Overy LLP, London.

[1] See VV Veeder, "Towards a Possible Solution: Limitation, Interest and Assignment in London and Paris", Albert Jan van den Berg (ed), *Planning Efficient Arbitration Proceedings: The Law Applicable to Arbitration* (ICCA Congress Series No. 7, Kluwer Law International, 1996) 268, 283 (hereinafter "Veeder").

[2] Of the published studies on the topic see: Daniel Girsberger and Christian Hausmaninger, "Assignment of Rights and Agreement to Arbitrate", 8 *Arb Int* 121 (1992) (hereinafter "Girsberger and Hausmaninger"); Veeder, *ibid*; Emmanuel Gaillard and John Savage (eds) *Fouchard Gaillard Goldman on International Commercial Arbitration* (Kluwer Law International, 1999) 417 et seq. (hereinafter "*Fouchard Gaillard Goldman*"); Mauro Rubino-Sammartano, *International Arbitration Law and Practice* (2nd edition, Kluwer Law International, 2001) 291 et seq. Noting some of the complexities that have arisen in ICC arbitration, see JA Cremades, "Problems that arise from Changes affecting one of the Signatories to the Arbitration Clause", 7(2) *ICC Bulletin* 28 (1996), 29.

[3] UNCITRAL Model Law, Article 16(1); English Arbitration Act 1996, section 7; UNCITRAL Arbitration Rules, Article 21(2); ICC Arbitration Rules, Article 6(4); LCIA Arbitration Rules, Article 23(1); AAA International Arbitration Rules, Article 15(2).

Loukas A. Mistelis and Julian D.M. Lew (eds), Pervasive Problems in International Arbitration, 291-319
© 2006 Kluwer Law International. Printed in the Netherlands

obligations in addition to the assignment of the contract as a whole. In practice, what is frequently at issue is whether signatories may compel arbitration against non-signatory assignees, and vice versa.

15-2 In either case, on closer analysis a host of subsidiary issues arise including whether an assignee may join an arbitration which is already underway and the effect that will have on the standing, obligations and interests of the assignor and the signatory counterparty, as well as the composition and jurisdiction of the tribunal. As shall be seen from a review of English arbitration law, interspersed by examples drawn from other jurisdictions, a robust and sound substantive solution is emerging to these contemporary problems, which, it is submitted, is consistent with the expectations of the parties in international commercial arbitration and conducive to the needs of business.

1. Kompetenz-Kompetenz

15-3 Hand in hand with these questions is the important matter of whether it is for the tribunal or the local courts to rule on the existence or validity of an assignment, *i.e.* the transfer of an arbitration clause. Different legal systems have different approaches to the competence of tribunals to determine their own jurisdiction, but since this is not an issue unique to assignment it suffices to note that the prevailing view seems to favour application of the principle of Kompetenz-Kompetenz (*compétence-compétence*) with the result that, in the first instance, it is for tribunals to decide upon their own jurisdiction.[4] This will necessarily include findings on the existence or validity of the assignment.[5]

2. The Importance (and Problem) of Consent

15-4 At the heart of the problems which can arise is that arbitration is a consensual process. Tribunals cannot accommodate non-signatories to the arbitration clause in the same way that a court may join third parties. Arbitration is not litigation: whilst parties may, even absent their consent, be compelled by force of law to submit to the jurisdiction of local courts, this is not so in international arbitration. This is a concept taught to and quickly grasped by all new students of arbitration. It is also a principle enshrined in the New York Conven-

---

[4] UNCITRAL Model Law, Article 16(1); English Arbitration Act 1996, section 30; UNCITRAL Arbitration Rules, Article 21(1), (2); ICC Arbitration Rules, Article 6(2); LCIA Arbitration Rules, Article 23(1); AAA International Rules, Article 15(1).

[5] This was the conclusion in the *Bulbank* arbitration, discussed infra.

tion,[6] which provides that the courts of a Contracting State shall respect agreements to arbitrate.[7] The New York Convention requires an arbitration agreement to be "in writing" and "signed by the parties or contained in an exchange of letters or telegrams",[8] but it does not expressly answer the question whether an assignment of an agreement automatically includes assignment of the arbitration clause.[9] Likewise, the 1961 European Convention on International Commercial Arbitration does not contain an express provision addressing the assignment of the arbitration clause.[10]

15-5 In 1985, UNCITRAL adopted a model law (the "Model Law"[11]) designed to "assist States in reforming and modernising their laws on arbitral procedure so as to take into account the particular features and needs of international arbitration". The Model Law has since been enacted wholly or substantially in many jurisdictions around the world. To similar effect as the New York Convention, the Model Law provides that courts shall respect agreements to arbitrate,[12] and that an agreement to arbitrate is

> an agreement by the parties to submit to arbitration all or certain types of dispute … An arbitration agreement may be in the form of an arbitration clause in a contract or in the form of a separate agreement.[13]

---

[6] Convention on the Recognition and Enforcement of Foreign Arbitral Awards, signed 10 June 1958 at New York, N.Y in force 7 June 1959, (1958) 330 *UNTS* 3 (hereinafter the "New York Convention") available online at www.uncitral.org/en-index.htm. The New York Convention is more commonly known for its obligations to enforce foreign arbitral awards, but of at least equal significance is the power it confers on parties to compel arbitration. This compulsion is, however, subject to the stated requirement that there be *an agreement in writing*.

[7] New York Convention, Article II(1) provides that:

> Each Contracting State shall recognise an agreement in writing unless which the parties undertake to submit to arbitration all and any differences which have arisen or which may arise between them in respect of a defined legal relationship, whether contractual or not, concerning a subject matter capable of settlement by arbitration.

[8] New York Convention, Article II.

[9] Girsberger and Hausmaninger, supra note 2, 131-132.

[10] European Convention on International Commercial Arbitration, (1963-4) 484 *UNTS* 364.

[11] UNCITRAL Model Law on International Commercial Arbitration, as adopted by UNCITRAL on 21 June 1985, available online at www.uncitral.org/en-index.htm.

[12] Model Law, Article 8, entitled "Arbitration Agreement and Substantive Claim before Court" provides:

> (1) A court before which an action is brought in a matter which is the subject of an arbitration agreement shall, if a party so requests … refer the parties to arbitration ….

[13] Model Law, Article 7(1); also English Arbitration Act 1996, Section 6(2).

Article 7(2) of the Model Law requires that an arbitration agreement be "in writing" which may be "in a document signed by the parties or in an exchange of letters, telex, telegrams or other means of telecommunication which provide a record of the agreement", and a party is a party to an arbitration agreement.[14]

15-6 Of course the need for an arbitration agreement in order for one party to compel another to arbitrate is neither new nor controversial. The importance of the consent does not, however, begin and end with compulsion to participate in arbitration proceedings. Under both the New York Convention and the Model Law, awards – ultimately the product of arbitration proceedings – may not be recognised and enforced in the absence of a binding agreement to arbitrate.[15] The New York Convention requires the party seeking recognition or enforcement of the award to supply the original agreement to arbitrate.[16] This is mirrored in the Model Law.[17] Further, in 1976 UNCITRAL approved arbitration rules which have since become a standard for *ad hoc* arbitrations. The UNCITRAL Arbitration Rules, at Article 1, beneath the heading "Scope of Application", begin by stating that they apply "where the parties have agreed in writing" to arbitrate their disputes.[18] Other major sets of international commercial arbitration rules

---

[14] Model Law, Articles 7(2) and 2(1)(h); Arbitration Act 1996, Section 5.

[15] New York Convention, Article V(1)(a):

> Recognition and enforcement of the award may be refused ... where ... the parties to the agreement ... were, under the law applicable to them, under some incapacity, or the said agreement is not valid under the law to which the parties have subjected it or, failing any induction thereon, under the law of the country where the award was made;

Model Law, Article 36(1)(a).

[16] New York Convention, Article IV(1)(b).

[17] Model Law, Article 35(2).

[18] For a comprehensive analysis of the writing requirement, see Toby Landau, "The Requirement of a Written Form for an Arbitration Agreement: When 'Written' Means 'Oral'", Albert Jan van den Berg (ed), *International Commercial Arbitration: Important Contemporary Questions* (ICCA Congress Series No. 11, Kluwer Law International, 2003) 19. See also Lucy F Reed, "Experience of Practical Problems of Enforcement", Albert Jan van den Berg, *Improving the Efficiency of Arbitration Agreements and Awards: 40 Years of Application of the New York Convention* (ICCA Congress Series No. 9, Kluwer Law International, 1999) 557 noting the risk of enforcement difficulties. See, e.g., A S Komorov, "Enforcement Experience in the Russian Federation", van den Berg, *Improving the Efficiency of Arbitration Agreements and Awards: 40 Years of Application of the New York Convention* (ICCA Congress Series No. 9, *ibid*) 583 referring to the case *Re Application of IMP Group (Cyprus) Ltd for Enforcement of the Arbitral Award*, Ruling of the Judicial Collegium for Civil Cases of the Moscow District Court, 21 April 1997, reported in XXIII *YBCA* 745-749 (1998), in which the Moscow District Court found that an arbitration clause had not been effectively assigned, and hence an ICC tribunal was wrong to

also contain a writing requirement.[19]   None of these sets of rules contain any express guidance on the matter of assignment and arbitration, which ultimately is a matter for the applicable substantive laws.

15-7 It is worth recalling that the formal writing requirement that applies to the arbitration agreement itself is distinct from any other requirements for an effective assignment of that agreement as prescribed by the law applicable to the assignment.[20] These requirements of form apply merely to the initial conclusion of an agreement to arbitrate and do not apply thereafter to any assignment of it. This is principally because to comply would be cumbersome for the efficient transfer of rights and obligations,[21] and, as a matter of policy, the form requirement does not purport to protect later assignees.[22] An assignee is thought to be sufficiently warned in the case of an assignment of an existing arbitration agreement and has the opportunity to scrutinise it in advance of accepting the assignment.[23]

3. Particular ICSID and Other Investor-State Issues

15-8 It is worth digressing on the specific requirements of jurisdiction in some investor-state arbitrations. For those arbitrations conducted under the auspices of the ICSID Convention, there is, in addition to becoming a party to the ICSID Convention, an added requirement of an expression of consent on the part of the host state to submit the particular investment dispute to ICSID arbitration. It is

---

find jurisdiction because of the autonomy of the arbitration agreement from the main contract and because the assignee had not specifically consented to the arbitration clause.

[19] UNCITRAL Arbitration Rules, Article 3(3)(c); AAA International Arbitration Rules, Article 1; LCIA Arbitration Rules, Article 1.1(b). While there is no express requirement as such in the ICC Arbitration Rules, (cf. Article 6(2)) signing the Terms of Reference is likely to be sufficient: W Laurence Craig, William W Park and Jan Paulsson, *International Chamber of Commerce Arbitration* (3rd edition, Oceana, 2000) 59 (hereinafter "Craig, Park and Paulsson").

[20] The conclusion that it is not a prerequisite for the assignment of an arbitration agreement that the assignee sign it or the main contract was confirmed, e.g., in a Decision of the Swiss Courts, of 7 August 2001, summarised in (2002) 1 *ASA Bulletin* and noted M Scherer, 5(2) *Int ALR* N-15 (2002). See also Alan Redfern and Martin Hunter, *Law and Practice of International Commercial Arbitration* (4th edition, with Nigel Blackaby and Constantine Partasides, Sweet & Maxwell, 2004) 151 (hereinafter "Redfern and Hunter"); CB Lamm and JA Aqua, "Defining the Party – Who is a Proper Party in an International Arbitration before the American Arbitration Association and other International Institutions", 34 *Geo Wash Int'l L Rev* 711 (2003) 721 (hereinafter "Lamm and Aqua").

[21] Veeder, supra note 1, 283.

[22] Girsberger and Hausmaninger, supra note 2, 142 et seq.

[23] Philip Habegger, "Extension of Arbitration Agreements to Non-Signatories and Requirements of Form", 22 *ASA Bulletin* 398 (2004).

not clear that the benefit of the latter consent may be assigned to a third person, at least not without the host state's consent.[24] In *Amco Asia Corporation, Pan American Development Ltd and PT Amco Indonesia v. The Republic of Indonesia*, shares were assigned from the original investor to the eventual claimant. Indonesia objected to jurisdiction of ICSID on the basis that it had not consented to arbitration in respect of the assignee. In that case, however, Indonesia had consented to the assignment of the shares, and on that basis the Tribunal dismissed the objection:

> the right acquired by Amco Asia to invoke the arbitration clause is attached to its investment, represented by its share in P.T. Amco, and may be transferred with those shares. To be sure, for such a transfer to be effective, the government of the host-country must approve it, which approval has as its consequence that said government agrees to the transferee acquiring all rights attached to the shares, including the right to arbitrate, unless this latter right would be expressly excluded in the approval decision. Such approval having been given in the instant case, it constitutes, together with Amco Asia's Request to transfer the shares, the agreement in writing to submit to ICSID arbitration the disputes with the transferee, requested by the Convention (article 25).[25]

15-9 In the event of an assignment from an investor having the nationality of an ICSID Contracting State to a third person who does not have the nationality of a Contracting State, an ICSID tribunal would lack jurisdiction, although the arbitration may proceed under the ICSID Additional Facility Rules. Again, however, the claimant will have to demonstrate the state's consent to the assignment. The problem (albeit involving an assignment from a national of a non ICISD Contracting State to a national of a Contracting State) arose in *Mihaly International Corp v. Democratic Socialist Republic of Sri Lanka*,[26] which, as the respondent put it, concerned:

---

[24] See also Georges R Delaume, "ICSID Arbitration: Practical Considerations", 1 *J Int'l Arb* 101 (1984); Pierre Lalive, "Some Objections to Jurisdiction in Investor-State Arbitration", Albert Jan van den Berg (ed), *International Commercial Arbitration: Important Contemporary Questions* (ICCA Congress Series No. 11, Kluwer Law International, 2003) 376, 385-387.

[25] In *Amco Asia Corporation, Pan American Development Ltd and PT Amco Indonesia v. The Republic of Indonesia*, Decision on Jurisdiction of 25 September 1983, 1 *ICSID Rep* 377 (1993) para. 31; also *Amco: Resubmitted Case*, Decision on Jurisdiction of 10 May 1988, 1 *ICSID Rep* 543 (1993) 569.

[26] *Mihaly International Corp v. Democratic Socialist Republic of Sri Lanka*, Award and Individual Concurring Opinion of 15 March 2002, 6 *ICSID Rep* 310 (2004).

a claim by a Canadian Company, allegedly assigned to this US Claimant but without Sri Lanka's consent, for reimbursement of expenditures made pursuing a possible investment in a proposed power project in Sri Lanka that never happened.[27]

15-10   As Canada was/is not a party to the ICSID Convention, the Tribunal held that the Canadian assignor could not, by way of an assignment to a company that was a national of a Contracting State, put that assignee in any better position to have the claim arbitrated under the auspices of ICSID with or without, and especially without, the express consent of Sri Lanka. The Tribunal insisted that

[a] claim under the ICSID Convention with its carefully structured system is not a readily assignable *chose in action* as shares in the stock-exchange market or other types of negotiable instruments, such as promissory notes or letters of credit.[28]

To allow such an assignment to operate in favour of ICSID jurisdiction would defeat the object and purpose of the ICSID Convention, the Tribunal said, as well as the sanctity of the privity of international agreements not intended to create rights and obligations for non-Convention parties or other nationals.

15-11   The nationality requirements of bilateral investment treaties (BITs) may also give rise to specific obstacles. The *ad hoc* Committee in *Compañía de Aguas del Aconquija SA and Vivendi Universal (formerly Compagnie Générale des Eaux) v. Argentine Republic* expressed grave doubts that, as a matter of law, a ripe claim arising under one BIT could be effectively assigned to another investor having a different nationality, with the effect that the latter could bring a claim against the host state under a separate BIT in respect of the assigned investment.[29] In *Vivendi* the *ad hoc* Committee was not called upon to make this ruling, but the Committee did warn that:

if Dycasa [the assignor] had a Spanish treaty claim prior to March 1996 questions might arise as to how the claim could be later transferred to a French company [the assignee] or as to how CGE [the assignee] could have acquired a French treaty claim in respect of conduct concerning an

---

[27]   *Ibid*, para 11.

[28]   *Ibid*, para 24.

[29]   *Compañía de Aguas del Aconquija SA and Vivendi Universal (formerly Compagnie Générale des Eaux) v. Argentine Republic*, Decision of *ad hoc* Committee on Annulment of 3 July 2002, 6 *ICSID Rep* 340 (2004).

investment which it did not hold at the time the conduct occurred and which at that time did not have French nationality. At least such questions might affect the quantum of recovery, but they might have further and even more basic legal consequences.[30]

15-12   In the case of *Loewen v. the United States*[31] the assignment by Loewen Group, Inc (a Canadian company) of its NAFTA claims to a US company was considered a ground for refusing jurisdiction for failing to meet the NAFTA requirement of diversity of nationality. This reasoning, applying a rule requiring continuous nationality, has been the subject of some debate.[32] It does, however, present further evidence of the complications of assignment in the context of ICSID and other investor-state disputes.

II. CONTRACTUAL PERMISSIONS AND RESTRICTIONS

15-13   Given that the principal arbitration rules and laws provide little or no express guidance on the validity and effect of an assignment of an agreement to arbitrate, the question to be asked is whether parties can take matters into their own hands. In other words, with appropriate drafting, can parties definitively provide for, or exclude, the assignability of an agreement to arbitrate?

15-14   On the one hand, it is clear that parties are free expressly to exclude any assignment of an arbitration agreement. Moreover, clauses prohibiting assignment of the main contract as a whole are often taken to exclude assignment of the arbitration agreement.[33] If, on a proper construction of the arbitration clause it was the parties" intention not to allow an assignment, this should be respected –

---

[30]   *Ibid*, para 50. No difficulties arose in the case of an assignment prior to the cause of action aris-ing in *Fedax NV v. Republic of Venezuela*, Decision on Objections to Jurisdiction of 11 July 1997, 5 *ICSID Rep* 186 (2002) paras. 18-19 (involving endorsement of a promissory note from a Venezuelan national to the claimant).

[31]   *Loewen Group, Inc and Raymond L Loewen v. United States of America*, NAFTA / ICSID Addi-tional Facility, Case No. ARB(AF)/98/3.

[32]   The reasoning of the Tribunal in *Loewen* has been widely criticised. See, e.g., Jan Paulsson, "*Continuous Nationality in Loewen*, a Note", 20(2) *Arb Int* 213 (2004).

[33]   *Linden Gardens v. Linesta Sludge* [1994] 1 AC 85, 108 *per* Lord Browne-Wilkinson; *Yeandle v. Wynn Realisations Ltd* (1995) 47 Con LR 1; *R v. Chester and North Wales Legal Aid Area Office (No 12), ex parte Floods of Queensferry Ltd* [1998] 1 W.L.R. 1496; *Bawejem Ltd v. MC Fabrications* [1999] 1 All ER (Comm) 377. For examples from other jurisdictions see Decision of Swiss Courts of 9 April 1991, reprinted in 8(2) *J Int'l Arb* 21 (1991); *United States v. Panhandle Eastern Corp*, 672 F Supp 149 (D Del 1987).

arbitration is, after all, a consensual process.[34] Such an intention may be evident where the agreement to arbitrate has a personal element. (That is, where the identity of the particular parties to the agreement was integral to including the right to arbitrate.) Thus, in 2001, the Swiss Courts set aside an award because the tribunal in question had taken jurisdiction (albeit on an interim basis) in respect of a claimant assignee without noting that the contract contained a clause which prohibited assignment and a declaration that the contract was concluded with strict regard to the assignor.[35] A purported assignment of the arbitration clause in this type of situation might be effective but only if the counterparty subsequently agrees to the substitution of the assignee.[36] In practice, it is seldom the case that an arbitration agreement is entered into *intuitu personae*. The contemporary assumption is that the mere presence of an arbitration clause in a contract does not in itself prevent the contract being assigned,[37] and an arbitration agreement is not presumed to be a personal covenant incapable of being assigned.[38] To the contrary, there is now a presumption that an arbitration agreement may be assigned, and that assignees may validly take the benefit of it.[39]

15-15 One other situation in which a purported assignment of an arbitration clause may be denied effect is where it would lead to a deterioration of the signatory counterparty's position. Lew, Mistelis and Kröll agree with this suggestion and provide the example of the assignee who may not be in a financial position to meet the signatories'' costs should the signatory be successful in the arbitration.[40]

15-16 On the other hand, while business people are again free to negotiate and include in their agreements arbitration clauses that purport to bind them and their

---

[34] E.g., *Clearstar Ltd v. Centromor*, Swiss Courts, 9 April 1991, note Werner, "Jurisdiction of Arbitrators in Case of Assignment of an Arbitration Clause: On a Recent Decision by the Swiss Supreme Court", 2 *J Int'l Arb* 13 (1991).

[35] *O v. P*, Swiss Federal Court, 16 October 2001, summarised in (2002) 1 *ASA Bulletin* and note Matthias Scherer, 5(2) *Int ALR* N-15 (2002).

[36] *Fouchard, Gaillard and Goldman*, supra note 2, paras 721-722.

[37] Hugh Beale (gen ed) *Chitty on Contracts: Vol 1: General Principles* (29th edition, Sweet & Maxwell, 2004) (hereinafter "*Chitty on Contracts*"), 1187 para 19-054; Michael Mustill & Stewart Boyd, *Commercial Arbitration* (2nd edition, Butterworths, 1989) 137 (hereinafter "Mustill & Boyd"); *Fouchard, Gaillard and Goldman*, supra note 2, para 718.

[38] See *Cottage Club Estates Ltd v. Woodsite Estates Co (Amersham) Ltd* [1928] 2 KB 463; and *Russell on Arbitration* (13th edition.) 45 with D Sutton and J Gill, *Russell on Arbitration* (22nd edition, Sweet & Maxwell, 2003) 85 (hereinafter "*Russell on Arbitration*").

[39] *Fouchard, Gaillard and Goldman*, supra note 2, paras 716-717.

[40] Julian DM Lew, Loukas A Mistelis and Stefan M Kröll, *Comparative International Commercial Arbitration* (Kluwer Law International, 2003) 147-148 (hereinafter "Lew, Mistelis and Kröll").

assigns,[41] ultimately the enforceability of the arbitration agreements by or against assignees will depend on the applicable substantive law.

III. RELEVANT LAWS

15-17   The assignment of the arbitration clause can and frequently does give rise to complex choice of law questions depending on the approach adopted in the relevant legal system to characterisation of the issue (as one of substance, procedure, or both). Even within a single legal system decisions frequently exhibit inconsistency in their approach to applicable law issues, with the effect that an assignment of an arbitration clause may fall to be construed according to the proper law of the contract assigned, the arbitration agreement (if different) the law applicable to the assignment agreement itself, or the law of the forum. Without delving into complex choice of law issues beyond the scope of this chapter,[42] in principle two laws are most relevant to determine the effect of an assignment of a contract containing an arbitration clause: the law governing the assignment itself, and the law governing the arbitration agreement (which will typically be the proper law of the main contract).[43] As Fouchard Gaillard Goldman succinctly states:

> [t]he law governing the arbitration agreement determines the assignability of the agreement, the conditions to which the assignment is subject, and the consequences of the assignment, at least as far as relations between the assignor and its initial co-contractor are concerned… By contrast, relations between assignor and assignee are governed by the law chosen by those parties for that purpose.[44]

15-18   In practice therefore, the relationship between the original counterparty and the assignee will necessarily be governed by the law which originally governed the contract, and unless the assignor and assignee have specified a different law to govern the assignment, it may be presumed that they intended the law governing the assigned contract to apply.[45]

---

[41] Gary Born, *International Arbitration and Forum Selection Agreements: Planning, Drafting and Enforcing* (Kluwer Law International, 1999) 80-81; see also MF Rosenberg, "Chronicles of the *Bulbank* Case – The Rest of the Story", 19 *J Int'l Arb* 1 (2002) suggesting that better drafting might avoid legal arguments in the courts later.

[42] See further, Horacio Grigera Naón, *Choice of Law Problems in International Commercial Arbitration* (Mohr, 1992) 106 et seq.; and Girsberger and Hausmaninger, supra note 2, Part III.

[43] Redfern and Hunter, supra note 20, 151.

[44] *Fouchard Gaillard Goldman*, supra note 2, para 698.

[45] *Ibid*, para 697.

15-19   The Model Law, as with the Arbitration Act 1996 (England and Wales) (the "Act") does not expressly deal with the question whether assignment or transfer of rights under an agreement has any effect on the right or obligation to submit a dispute to arbitration based on an arbitration clause contained in the agreement. As the Departmental Advisory Committee[46] explained, this subject was omitted from the Act for two reasons. The first is that complex conflicts of law issues could arise given that assignment of a contract is governed by the law applicable to the contract, whereas the effectiveness of the assignment is governed by the assignment itself – and the Act does not deal with conflicts issues as such. The second is that the distinction between legal and equitable assignments, a distinction seemingly peculiar to English law,[47] would require complex drafting that would not sit well with the rest of the Act.[48]

15-20   However, the Act is not entirely silent on the matter. Unlike the Model Law, section 82(2) of the Act defines a party to an arbitration agreement as including "any person claiming *under or through* a party to the agreement". English courts have held that this provision recognises a rule in English law that an assignee of a contract may become a party to the arbitration agreement contained in that contract, whether the assignment is legal or equitable in nature.[49] In *Through Transport Mutual Insurance Association (Eurasia) Ltd v. New India Assurance Co Ltd*, Moore-Bick J confirmed that an assignee seeking to rely on an arbitration clause in an assigned contract to enforce its rights clearly came within section 82(2) because the assignee claimed *under or through* the assignor which had signed the arbitration clause.[50] On this basis it may be said that the Act contemplates arbitration proceedings brought by or against assignees. English law, however, contemplates three different forms of assignment, and the particular

---

[46] The Committee established by the UK Department of Trade and Industry responsible for drafting the Arbitration Act 1996.

[47] Including many Commonwealth laws derived from English law.

[48] Departmental Advisory Committee on Arbitration Law, *Report on the Arbitration Bill* (1996) para 46. See also Robert Merkin, *Arbitration Act 1996* (LLP, 2000) 33 (hereinafter "Merkin").

[49] *Montedipe SpA v. JTP-RO Jugotanker, The "Jordan Nicolov"* [1990] 2 Lloyd's Rep 11; *Phoenix Finance Ltd v. Féderation Internationale de l'"Automobile, Formula One Management Ltd and Formula One Administration Ltd* (unreported, High Court, 22 May 2002), available online at http://www.austlii.edu.au/~andrew/bailii/Joe/Data/EW_EWHC_Ch_2002_1028.html; *Through Transport Mutual Insurance Association (Eurasia) Ltd v. New India Assurance Co Ltd* [2005] EWHC 455, para 25. See also Veeder, supra note 1, 285-286; Mustill & Boyd, supra note 37, 137; *Russell on Arbitration*, supra note 38, 85.

[50] *Through Transport v. New India Assurance, ibid*, para 25.

form an assignment takes may have an impact on the enforceability of an arbitration agreement.[51]

15-21 As stated earlier, a common question arising when contracts containing arbitration agreements are assigned is whether assignees (*i.e.* non-signatories to arbitration agreements) may compel signatory counterparties to arbitrate disputes arising under such assigned contracts. The English Law of Property Act 1925, section 136, upholds the rights of legal assignees provided the assignment is absolute (not merely by charge), is in writing, and provided that express notice has been given to the other party. Such an assignment transfers "all legal and other remedies" including the right to invoke the arbitration clause.[52] There is no difficulty in an assignee of rights to claim under a contract which contains an arbitration agreement submitting those claims to arbitration in its own name.[53] A legal assignee may enjoy the full benefit of the arbitration clauses, as Hobhouse J held in *Montedipe SpA v. JTP-RO Jugotanker, The "Jordan Nicolov"*:[54]

> The assignee of causes of action under a contract which is covered by an arbitration clause has the right to invoke the arbitration clause, take arbitration proceedings, and if successful on the merits, obtain an award.[55]

15-22 English law also contains the concept of an equitable assignment. An equitable assignment is either an assignment of a legal interest which fails to meet the criteria described above, or an assignment of an equitable interest. An equitable assignment is not always effective to transfer the remedies in respect of a *chose in action*, including the right to submit disputes to arbitration.[56] However, if an equitable assignment is to transfer the benefit of an arbitration clause certain requirements must be met. The first requirement is that both the assignee and assignor must be parties to arbitration proceedings to enforce a debt.[57] This creates obvious problems when assignors refuse to co-operate. In this situation there is little that a tribunal can do as its jurisdiction does not extend to the legal relations between an assignor and an assignee. An application by an assignee to the courts to obtain an order either compelling the assignor to execute a legal

---

[51] See *Russell on Arbitration*, supra note 38, 85-86.
[52] Mustill & Boyd, supra note 37, 137 fn. 7.
[53] *Rumput (Panama) SA and Belzetta Shipping Co SA v. Islamic Republic of Iran Shipping Lines, The "Leage"*, [1984] 2 Lloyd's Rep. 259.
[54] *The "Jordan Nicolov"* supra note 49, 11.
[55] *Ibid.*, 17 *per* Hobhouse J.
[56] *Herkules Piling Ltd v. Tilbury Construction Ltd* (1992) 61 BLR 107.
[57] *Chitty on Contracts*, supra note 37, 1180 para 19-038; and *Russell on Arbitration*, supra note 38, 86.

assignment or allowing the assignee to proceed under the assignor's name, may resolve this stumbling block, though note that the assignee might be expected to provide an indemnity as to costs.[58] By way of contrast, long-standing English legal principles dictate that a *legal* assignment has the effect of extinguishing the cause of action of the assignor against its original counterparty so that the assignor will thereafter not be able to invoke an arbitration clause in the underlying contract and seek an award.[59] It may be that an assignor disputes the assignee's standing to bring (or defend) a claim. In the case of a legal assignment, it is plausible that the assignor may remain involved in pending proceedings but if it does it will recover nothing.[60] If there is a genuine dispute as to the existence and effect of an assignment and neither the assignor nor the assignee is able to establish which of them has title to sue, a tribunal should render an award in favour of the respondent signatory counterparty because the tribunal cannot make a joint award "since on any view there is no joint right in the plaintiffs – only one or the other can be entitled to an award".[61] In the case of doubt, the assignor and assignee may resolve any uncertainty with a further instrument of assignment.

15-23 The second requirement before an equitable assignee may compel arbitration is that it must notify the signatory counterparty of the assignment. If the assignment occurs prior to any arbitration commencing this requirement is unlikely to present many difficulties since if the assignee later commences an arbitration, the request for (or notice of) arbitration itself should be sufficient notice to the signatory counterparty. Similarly, if the signatory counterparty commences arbitration against the assignee it must necessarily have had notice of the assignment.

15-24 English law has yet another category of assignments: statutory assignments. These are assignments that take effect by operation of law, as opposed to party agreement. A statutory assignee can generally bring an action without joining the assignor as party to the action. The most common form of statutory assignment is the case of succession to the estate of a deceased, followed closely by trustees in bankruptcy.[62] Contracts of insurance also occasionally lead to a

---

[58] Mustill & Boyd, supra note 37, 138, at note 13.
[59] *Read v. Brown* (1889) LR 22 QBD 128, 132 *per* Lord Esher MR, affirmed in *The Jordan Nicolov* [1990] 2 Lloyd's Rep 11, 15.
[60] *Cottage Club Estates Ltd v. Woodsite Estates Co (Amersham) Ltd* [1928] 2 KB 463.
[61] *The Jordan Nicolov* [1990] 2 Lloyd's Rep 11, 20.
[62] Insolvency Act, section 108.

statutory assignment. In *The Padre Island (No 1)* and *The Padre Island (No 2)* an issue raised was whether the transferee of an insolvent insured's rights against his insurer pursuant to the Third Parties (Rights against Insurers) Act 1930 was bound by the arbitration clause contained in the relevant policy. In the former decision, Leggat J held that:

> [t]he 1930 Act transfers to the plaintiffs not the claim but the contractual rights of the insured. Those contractual rights are subject to the arbitration clause…

15-25 In the latter case, Lord Goff held that:

> [t]he agreement to arbitrate is one which regulates the means by which the transferred right is to be enforced against [the insurer]. As such, it is inevitable that such an agreement must be treated as transferred to the statutory transferee as part of, or as inseparably connected with, the member's right against [the insurer] under the rules in respect of the relevant liability.[63]

15-26 A recent decision on the Contract (Rights of Third Parties) Act 1999 (the "CRTP Act") has opened up new possibilities for arbitration by third parties. In *Nisshin Shipping Co Ltd v. Cleaves & Co Ltd & Others*,[64] the respondent ship-brokers negotiated charters on behalf of the applicant, each of which contained an arbitration clause, and for which they were promised a commission. When their commissions went unpaid, the shipbrokers commenced arbitration proceedings against Nisshin under those arbitration agreements notwithstanding that it was not a party to them. The Tribunal upheld its jurisdiction referring to the CRTP Act. Section 8(1) of the CRTP Act provides that where a third person is given the right to enforce a substantive term of an agreement which is also subject to a term of a contract that provides for disputes to be submitted to arbitration, the third person is required to submit to arbitration if he wishes to enforce his rights and he shall be treated as a party to the arbitration agreement for the purposes of the Arbitration Act 1996. Section 8(2) of the CRTP Act provides that where a third person is the beneficiary of the right to arbitrate and seeks to exercise that right, the third party shall be treated as a party to the arbitration agreement for the purposes of the Arbitration Act 1996. In *Nisshin Shipping*, on an application to have the award set aside, Colman J. upheld the Tribunal's decision. The promise to pay the shipbrokers a commission was a promise made to and enforceable by the relevant charterers, but by virtue of section 1 of the

---

[63] *The Padre Island (No 2)* [1990] 2 Lloyd's Rep 191, 200.

[64] *Nisshin Shipping Co Ltd v. Cleaves & Co Ltd & Others* [2003] EWHC 2602; see also Philip Capper, *International Arbitration: A Handbook* (3rd edition, LLP, 2004) 45-46.

CRTP Act, the shipbrokers were entitled to bring claims for it in their own right. Their entitlement was subject, however, to the obligation contained in the charterparties that disputes shall be submitted to arbitration. The striking result of this case is that if the CRTP Act is not expressly excluded from contracts then third parties may have recourse to the arbitration clauses contained therein.[65]

15-27   In other countries it is sometimes still debated whether, in order to assign an arbitration agreement, it is necessary to effect a distinct transfer of those rights and obligations in addition to the assignment of the contract as a whole. Unlike under English law, where separate evidence of intention to transfer a right to arbitrate is not a requirement, in France the historical approach has been that the assignee must indeed consent to the assignment of an arbitration agreement. As explained below, the French courts seem to get around this with a fairly robust presumption of such an agreement. This general requirement is sometimes explained by reference to cases involving chains of contracts.[66] For instance, in 1991 the Cour de cassation ruled in the case of *Fraser v. Compagnie Européenne des Pétroles* that

> an arbitration clause remains subject to the principles of privity of contracts and cannot therefore circulate in a chain of contracts, unless the parties have expressly provided otherwise.[67]

In *SMABTP v. Statinor*, the Paris Cour d'appel explained this result as the product of the rule that the assumption of obligations requires knowledge of such obligations on the part of the assignee.[68]   Redfern and Hunter explain this particular requirement of French law as the product of a certain view that arbitration agreements create mostly duties and not rights.[69] Girsberger and Hausmaninger seem to agree when they explain the approach as evidence of a readiness in civil law systems "to analogise arbitration agreements to security interests or accessory rights which attach to the claim they relate to".[70] Where the assignee's consent is established, however, the assignee will become a party to the arbitration agreement and will be bound by it in the event of a dispute.

---

[65]   Note however that the CRTP Act applies only to contracts entered into after 11 May 2000 and some earlier contracts which expressly provide for the CRTP Act's application.

[66]   See *Fouchard Gaillard Goldman*, supra note 2, 417 et seq.

[67]   *Fraser v. Compagnie Européenne des Pétroles*, Cour de cassation, 6 November 1990 reprinted in (1991) *Rev. Arb.* 73, 74, translation supplied in Redfern and Hunter, supra note 20, 151.

[68]   *SMABTP v. Statinor*, Paris Cour d'appel, 22 March 1995 reprinted (1997) *Rev Arb* 550, 552.

[69]   Redfern and Hunter, supra note 20, 151, citing ICC Case 6962 of 1991, XVIIII YBCA 184 (1994) where it is observed that in French law one can assign rights, not duties.

[70]   Girsberger and Hausmaninger, supra note 2, 138.

15-28   As indicated, the difficulties which may be created by the need in French law for the assignee's separate or express consent are to some extent alleviated by a presumption that if the assignee has accepted the assignment of the underlying contract as a whole, it will be considered to have accepted the assignment of the arbitration agreement as well. With this presumption, French courts have rejected the far-too-theoretical dilemma that the principle of autonomy of the arbitration agreement requires a separate and written acceptance on the part of the assignee in order to be binding:[71]

> the assignee of a contract who enjoys the benefit of the rights assigned cannot avoid the application of the arbitration clause contained in that contract. … The principle of the autonomy of the arbitration agreement does not require proof that the parties had two distinct intentions – one regarding the main contract, one regarding the arbitration agreement – in the case of assignment any more than for the initial arbitration agreement.[72]

15-29   In *CCC Filmkunst GmbH v. EDIF* the Paris Cour d'appel suggested that there was a presumption that the right to arbitration was automatically transferred along with the assignment of the main contract because assignment

> necessarily implies that the assignor transfers the benefit of the arbitration clause – which forms part of the economics [of the] contract – to the assignee.[73]

This presumption stemmed from the fact that the contract contained a typically broad arbitration clause but also in light of the widespread acceptance of arbitration as a means to resolve disputes in modern trade and commerce.[74] By the same token, any suggestion that the nature of the arbitration agreement also requires the agreement of the signatory counterparty for it to be effectively assigned was also rejected. The basis for the court's decision was recognition of the fact that arbitration has now become a normal method of resolving disputes in international trade such that it was "legitimate to assume that the initial co-contractor had accepted the possibility of an assignment of the arbitration agreement".[75] It

---

[71]   See Veeder, supra note 1, 284-285; *Fouchard Gaillard Goldman*, supra note 2, para 712.

[72]   *Fouchard Gaillard Goldman*, supra note 2, para 712.

[73]   *CCC Filmkunst v. EDIF*, Paris Cour d'appel, 28 January 1988 reprinted in (1988) *Rev Arb* 568, 569 translation supplied in *Fouchard Gaillard Goldman*, supra note 2, para 718.

[74]   *Ibid.*

[75]   *Ibid.*

is surely right that business people today must be presumed to anticipate the possibility of assignment of arbitration agreements.

15-30 This approach has found favour with commentators,[76] and it has been endorsed in France by both the Paris Cour d'appel and the Cour de cassation. In *Société Clark International Finances v. Société Sud Matériels Service*, the Cour d'appel ruled that an arbitration clause in an international contract had its own validity and effectiveness which required that it be extended to an assignee along with the contract or contractual rights assigned, provided that the dispute came within the scope of the clause.[77] In *Banque Worms v. Bellot*, the Cour de cassation held that

> the international arbitration agreement, the validity of which is based exclusively on the will of the parties, is assigned together with the rights [to which it relates], in the same shape and form as those rights existed between the assignor and the original co-contractor.[78]

That principle was echoed by the Cour de cassation also in 1999 in the case *Société Taurus Films v. Les Film du Jeudi*, where the court confirmed also that a signatory counterparty may rely on an arbitration clause in an assigned contract against the assignee just as it might have done against the assignor.[79] In *SA Burkinabe des ciments et matériaux v. Société des Ciments d"Abidjan* the Paris Cour d"appel went so far as to suggest that this might be a general principle of international commercial arbitration law.[80]

15-31 An illustrative example of contemporary practice comes from Sweden. Prior to the *Bulbank*[81] arbitration triggering a re-evaluation of the implied duty of

---

[76] *Fouchard Gaillard Goldman*, supra note 2, para 718; Lew, Mistelis and Kröll, supra note 40, 148.

[77] *Société Clark International Finances v. Société Sud Matériels Service*, Paris *Cour d"appel*, 20 April 1988 reprinted in (1988) *Rev Arb* 570.

[78] *Banque Worms v. Bellot*, *Cour de cassation*, 5 January 1999 reprinted in (2000) *Rev Arb* 85, 86 translation supplied in *Fouchard Gaillard Goldman*, supra note 2, para 718. See also *Société Taurus Films v. Les Film du Jeudi*, Cour de cassation, 8 February 2000 reprinted in (2000) *Rev Arb* 280.

[79] *Société Taurus Films v. Les Film du Jeudi*, Cour de cassation, 8 February 2000 reprinted in (2000) *Rev Arb* 280.

[80] *SA Burkinabe des ciments et matériaux v. Société des Ciments d' Abidjan*, Paris Cour d"appel, 25 November 1999 reprinted in (2001) *Rev Arb* 165; noted Lew, Mistelis and Kröll, supra note 40, 148.

[81] Supreme Court, 27 October 2000, *Bulgarian Foreign Trade Bank Ltd v. AI Trade Finance Inc*, 15(11) Mealey's IAR B 1 (2000), 13(1) WTAM 147 (2001).

confidentiality, the case in fact involved a question of assignment. Bulgarian Foreign Trade Bank (Bulbank) entered into a Credit Facility Agreement (which contained an arbitration clause) with an Austrian bank, GiroCredit, Bank Aktiengesellschaft der Sparkassen (GiroCredit) by which GiroCredit would provide credit to Bulbank to facilitate transactions between Bulgarian importers and Austrian creditors. GiroCredit entered into a "Silent Risk Participation Agreement" with AI Trade Finance, Inc (AIT) which, as its name suggests was a confidential arrangement by which AIT guaranteed payments from time to time owed by Bulbank under the Credit Facility Agreement. In 1990 Bulgaria faced financial difficulties which required its government to declare a moratorium on the repayment of Bulbank's foreign debts while it entered into negotiations with the London Club. AIT fulfilled its obligations to GiroCredit and then turned to Bulgaria to recover the sums paid out. GiroCredit formally assigned to AIT all of GiroCredit's rights against Bulbank with respect to the obligations guaranteed and paid by AIT and notified Bulbank of the assignment. AIT proceeded to commence arbitration proceedings against Bulbank under the terms of the Credit Facility Agreement. Bulbank contested the Tribunal's jurisdiction in respect of AIT arguing that the arbitration clause was a separate and independent contract that had not been validly assigned to AIT. In a decision on jurisdiction, which AIT controversially but famously released for publication, the Tribunal rejected Bulbank's arguments.[82] Relying on Girsberger and Hausmaninger's article the Tribunal held that policy arguments required that the doctrine of separability of the arbitration clause did not mean that the clause should be treated separately in a situation of transfer of rights.[83] Nor should the fact of an assignment allow one or the other of the signatory counterparties to avoid an obligation to arbitrate.[84] Like the French approach in *Filmkunst*, on the one hand the assignee could not be placed in a better position than the assignor by being able to avoid the obligation to arbitrate; on the other, the counterparty was deemed to accept the transferability of the arbitration clause unless there were special circumstances, such as clear evidence that the arbitration agreement was entered into out of personal considerations dependent on the identity of the other contracting party, or the assignment was calculated to hurt the signatory counterparty's interests.[85] It was also notable that Bulbank had notice of the assignment. (The risk that the assignee

---

[82] *Ibid.* The Tribunal was constituted under the ECE Arbitration Rules. See also Rosenberg, "Chronicles of the *Bulbank* Case – The Rest of the Story", 19(1) *J Int'l Arb* 1 (2002) (hereinafter "Rosenberg").

[83] Supra note 8, at B-14.

[84] *Ibid.*

[85] *Ibid*, B-15.

may be less able than the assignor to pay the costs of a fruitless claim was not in this case a sufficient hardship to defeat the assignment.)

15-32   Under the US Federal Arbitration Act, courts will apply "ordinary principles of contract and agency" to determine whether an obligation to arbitrate attaches to a person other than the signatory.[86] It is frequently held in US decisions that the assignee of a contract is able to invoke the arbitration clause contained within it.[87]   However, unlike contemporary French law, there is no presumption that assignment will automatically have this effect, as the courts are careful to scrutinise the particular arbitration clause to ensure that any ruling on jurisdiction *ratione personae* is consistent with the parties" intentions.   In some cases US courts have denied effect to a purported assignment of an arbitration agreement through the assignment of the main contract.[88]

15-33   In Italy, the presumption of transferability of the arbitration agreement is accepted,[89] and although no means free from doubt, a recent decision in China reached the same conclusion.[90] German law similarly contains a presumption that an arbitration clause will be assigned along with the assignment of the main contract.[91] Over a period of some years, decisions of the Swiss Courts have con-

---

[86] *Thomson-CSF SA v. American Arbitration Association and Evans & Sutherland Computer Corp,* 64 F.3d 773, 776 (2d Cir 1995).

[87] See *Banque de Paris et des Pays-Bas v. Amoco Oil Company* 573 F Supp 1464, 1469 (SDNY 1983); *Instituto Cubano v. The MV Driller*, 148 F Supp 739 (SDNY 1957); *Application of Reconstruction Finance Corp*, 106 F Supp 358 (SDNY 1952). cf. *Lachmar v. Trunkline LNG Co*, 753 F 2d 8 (2d Cir 1988); *United States v. Panhandle Eastern Corp*, 672 F Supp 149 (D Del 1987).   See also Girsberger and Hausmaninger, supra note 2 and authorities cited at notes 2 et seq.; Gary Born, *International Commercial Arbitration* (2nd edition, Transnational Publishers and Kluwer, 2001) 668-671.

[88] E.g., *Britton v. Co-op Banking Group*, 4 F 3d. 742, 746 (9th Cir 1993).

[89] *SA Assicuriazioni e Riassicurazioni "Lloyd Continental" SpA v. Navigazione Alga (Italy)*, Corte di cassazione, 11 September 1979 summarised in VI *YBCA* 230 (1981) 232:

> The endorsement of the bill of lading entitled the endorsee to the exercise of all the rights deriving from the contract of transportation, including the right to act against the transporter for damages incurred to the cargo.

[90] Although the law is reportedly unsettled (on which see Z Jianlin and L Yuwu, "China's New Contract Law: Implications for Arbitration", 3(5) *Int ALR* 157 (2000) 161) in a recent decision the PRC People's Supreme Court held that an arbitration clause in an assigned contract was, with the assignee's consent, binding and enforceable by the assignee against the original counterparty: *CNIEC Henan Corporation v. Liaoning Bohai Nonferrous Metals I/E Ltd*, Decision of 16 August 2000 noted L Yuwu, "Assignment of Arbitration Clause", 4(2) *Int ALR* N-11 (2001).

[91] See authorities cited in Lew, Mistelis and Kröll, supra note 40, 147, at note. 73; Redfern and Hunter, supra note 20, 151 at note. 17.

firmed that under Swiss law an assignment of rights under a contract, or of the contract as a whole, entails the transfer of the right to arbitrate contained in the contract save where the assignment is restricted or forbidden in the contract or by law.[92]   In two 2001 decisions the Federal Court upheld the rule that a valid assignment automatically transfers the arbitration agreement,[93] and that it is not a prerequisite for the assignment of an arbitration agreement that the assignee sign it or the main contract.[94]

15-34   In some cases an assignor may assign not the whole contract but only certain rights, while excluding others. This may be the case, for instance, with certain security interests. A careful analysis of the agreement to assign will be required in order to determine whether the arbitration clause has been transferred.[95] In one LCIA arbitration,[96] involving a commodities purchase agreement between an African State Agency (the purchaser) and a North American supplier, the State Agency had entered into financing arrangements with an African Bank. The Bank had taken a floating security over the State Agency's assets including its rights under the commodities contract. When a dispute arose the Bank sought to commence arbitration proceedings against the defaulting supplier. The supplier refused to appear, vigorously opposing the jurisdiction of the LCIA and the Arbitrator on a number of grounds including that the Bank lacked standing to sue.   The Arbitrator found that the rights under the commodities agreement, including the right to arbitrate, had been validly assigned to the Bank which was entitled to bring its claim. The objection to jurisdiction was accordingly rejected.

15-35   If the assignor did not intend to assign the arbitration clause along with certain contractual rights, common sense would suggest that an exclusion ought to be expressed, otherwise the assignor, not the assignee, is the party able to

---

[92]   E.g., *Muller v. Bossard,* 25 January 1977; *Clearstar Ltd v. Centromor*, 9 April 1991, noted Werner, "Jurisdiction of Arbitrators in Case of Assignment of an Arbitration Clause: On a Recent Decision by the Swiss Supreme Court", 2 *J Int'l Arb* 13 (1991); *Transkei v. FJ Berger and Steyr-Daimler-Puch AG*, 13 October 1992 summarised in (1992) *ASA Bulletin* 68.

[93]   *Nextrom Holding SA and Nextrom SA v. Watkins International*, 9 May 2001 summarised in (2002) 1 *ASA Bulletin* and noted Scherer, 5(2) *Int ALR* N-15 (2002).

[94]   Decision of 7 August 2001, summarised in (2002) 1 *ASA Bulletin* and noted in Scherer, *ibid.*

[95]   E.g., J Tackaberry, "Assignment of the Right to Arbitration", 17 *Const LJ* 287 (2001).

[96]   Noted by Baum in Comments on the topic "Non-Party Participation – The Extent to which Non-Contracting Parties may be encouraged or compelled to Join Proceedings", LCIA/AMINZ Arbitration Seminar, 20 February 2003, Auckland, New Zealand.

compel arbitration against the signatory counterparty, but it may have assigned its relevant substantive interests and therefore lack standing to pursue them.[97]

IV. PENDING ARBITRATIONS

15-36   When an assignment occurs whilst arbitration proceedings are pending, interesting questions arise concerning its effect on the standing, obligations and interests of the parties to the arbitration as well as the composition and jurisdiction of the tribunal.

15-37   Such an assignment does not make the assignee *automatically* a party to the arbitration, nor must the assignee start proceedings afresh to bring its claims (in which case any number of difficulties may arise, such as, *inter alia*, time bar issues[98]). English law will permit the assignee to join the proceedings provided it gives notification to the other party and submits to the jurisdiction of the tribunal.[99]   Provided the assignee serves notice (which must be given within a reasonable time[100]) it will succeed to the assignor's rights in the arbitration and will have legal standing to then continue with the prosecution (or defence) of the proceedings in its own name:

---

[97]   *Fouchard Gaillard Goldman*, supra note 2, para 712.

[98]   *Compania Colombiana de Seguros v. Pacific Steam Navigation Co* [1963] 2 Lloyd's Rep 479; and see Mustill & Boyd, *Commercial Arbitration – 2001 Companion to the Second Edition* (Butterworths, 2001) 146.

[99]   *The Jordan Nicolov* [1990] 2 Lloyd's Rep 11, 18; followed in *Baytur SA v. Finagro Holdings SA* [1992] QB 610; and see *Charles M Willie & Co (Shipping) Ltd v. Ocean Laser Shipping Ltd, The "Smaro"* [1999] 1 Lloyd's Rep 225, 241-43 *per* Rix J approving these authorities in a case concerning novation.

[100]   In the *Jordan Nicolov* case, notice of the assignment given prior to the conclusion of the arbitration hearing was adequate notice to the Tribunal. In *NBP Developments Ltd and Others v. Buildko and Sons Ltd (formerly William Thomson and Sons Ltd) (in liquidation)* (1992) 8 Const LJ 377 the delay of 12 months on the part of the legal assignee to inform the arbitrator in writing of the assignment justified the court exercising its discretion to terminate the arbitration agreement. It is obviously desirable for the assignee to give notice as, for example, in a claim for debt, the absence of notice may allow the original party to discharge its debt to the assignor, or indeed the lack of notice may affect priorities in recovering debt. However, an equitable assignment of an equitable chose in action must be in writing, as stated in the Law of Property Act 1925, section 53(1)(c).

the assignee is entitled to enforce the assignor's rights in the pending arbitration... [and] is entitled to an award from the [respondent] if he can prove his case on the merits, including his title to sue.[101]

15-38 In an institutional arbitration, common sense would suggest that the assignee should also serve notice on the supervising institution, although the authors are not aware of any case in which this was said to be a legal requirement.[102]

15-39 In circumstances where an assignee joins pending proceedings in this manner, an interesting question arises concerning the assignee's acceptance of the choice of arbitrators[103] and the assignee's relationship with them. It is of course fundamental to arbitration that the parties have a right to choose the persons who will determine their dispute, or the process by which they will be chosen, but in these circumstances the assignee will have played no part in their selection. In *The Jordan Nicolov* Hobhouse J. held that a legal assignment post-commencement of arbitral proceedings did not lead to any right on the part of the assignee to appoint a new tribunal. Rather, by accepting the assignment, the assignee was taken, sensibly, to have adopted the performance already given by the assignor, including its appointment of an arbitrator. Moreover, he held that notice to the Tribunal of the assignment perfects the assignee's legal relationship vis-à-vis the Tribunal.[104] Fouchard Gaillard Goldman come to the same conclusion. Those authors consider that "too much emphasis" is placed on the idea that each party has a right to participate in the constitution of a tribunal. They point out that an assignment of a contract containing an arbitration clause does not create a new arbitration agreement; rather, it "transfers an existing agreement which must continue to operate as it did before the assignment".[105] Thus, if an assignment gives the assignee the option unilaterally to maintain or replace an existing tribunal it would confer advantages on the assignee not available to the assignor and allow the proceedings to be frustrated and delayed.

---

[101] *The Jordan Nicolov* [1990] 2 Lloyd's Rep 11, 19. Also *Aspell v. Seymour* [1929] WN 152; *Shayler v. Woolf* [1946] 1 Ch. 320 *per* Lord Greene MR (although strictly not a decision on the right of an assignee to sue, since the claimant was enforcing its rights in court rather than arbitration: Mustill & Boyd, supra note 37, 138 at note 8). See further Merkin, supra note 48, 33; *Russell on Arbitration*, supra note 38, 85.

[102] Also Veeder, supra note 1, 287.

[103] See *Fouchard Gaillard Goldman*, supra note 2, paras 723, 725 and *The Jordan Nicolov* [1990] 2 Lloyd's Rep. 11, 20.

[104] *Montedipe SpA v. JTP-RO Jugotanker, The Jordan Nicolov* [1990] 2 Lloyd's Rep 11, 16.

[105] *Fouchard Gaillard Goldman*, supra note 2, para 725.

15-40 For an equitable assignee (under English law) to join a pending arbitration it must provide adequate and timely notice of the assignment to the counterparty and the tribunal. In *Baytur SA v. Finagro Holdings SA*[106] the English Court of Appeal considered the legal effect on claims submitted to arbitration of an equitable assignment in the absence of notice to the other party and the Tribunal of the assignment. In this case, unbeknown to the Tribunal, the Claimant was dissolved while the claims it had submitted to arbitration were pending. The Claimant's assets and liabilities were transferred to other companies. The Tribunal rendered an award in the putative Claimant's favour, which the Respondent then challenged. The Court of Appeal held that award was void because the Tribunal's jurisdiction had lapsed with the demise of the Claimant. It considered that there could not be a valid arbitration where one of the two parties had ceased to exist and that the equitable assignment did not *ipso facto* render the assignees parties to the arbitration. The assignees could become parties to the arbitration and hence claim the benefit of the award only if they had given notice of the assignment to the Respondent and submitted to the jurisdiction of the Tribunal before the assignor ceased to exist,[107] although Lloyd LJ left open the possibility that in the event of some equitable assignments it may be that the consent of a tribunal and the other party would also be required.[108]

15-41 It is worth noting that the assignee who joins pending arbitration proceedings may be liable for an order of costs.[109] It will not ordinarily be forced to bear the burden of earlier phases of the arbitration as the assignor will be responsible for costs already incurred.[110] This is subject to the warning of Lloyd LJ in *Baytur v. Finagro* that if an insolvent assignor is subsequently liquidated, the assignee must bear the risk that it will be held liable for the full costs of the arbitration in the event that it is unsuccessful.[111]

V. ASSIGNMENT AND THE BURDEN OF AN ARBITRATION AGREEMENT

15-42 The other main question which arises in this area is the flipside of the first, namely, whether a signatory to the arbitration agreement may rely on it to

---

[106] *Baytur SA v. Finagro Holdings SA* [1992] QB 610.
[107] *Ibid.*
[108] *Ibid.*, 619.
[109] *Montedipe SpA v. JTP-RO Jugotanker, The Jordan Nicolov* [1990] 2 Lloyd's Rep 11.
[110] *Ibid.*, 19; also *Baytur SA v. Finagro Holdings SA* [1992] QB 610.
[111] *Baytur, ibid.*

compel arbitration against the assignee, notwithstanding that the assignee is a non-signatory to the arbitration agreement. Under English law, a legal assignment transfers not only the benefit, but also the burden of the arbitration clause. That is, an assignee may invoke the arbitration agreement to pursue a claim but it will also be bound by the arbitration agreement in the event of a claim by signatories to the arbitration agreement, as Hobhouse J. also noted in *The Jordan Nicolov*:

> [the assignee] is bound by the arbitration clause in the sense that he cannot assert the assigned right without also accepting the obligation to arbitrate.[112]

15-43   In *Schiffahrtsgesellschaft Detlev Von Appen GmbH v. Voest Alpine Intertrading GmbH, The Jay Bola*,[113] the question to be answered was whether the insurers of a cargo for carriage from Brazil to Thailand under a voyage charter were entitled to present claims against a time charterer in the English courts, notwithstanding an arbitration clause binding on its insured. Hobhouse LJ, with whom Sir Richard-Scott V-C agreed, held that it was not. The arbitration clause bound the assignee (the insurer) just as it would have bound the assignor relying on section 136 of the Law of Property Act 1925 by which the assignee obtains the benefit of all remedies for enforcing the *chose in action* assigned to it but subject to the equities, including both the right and the obligation to arbitrate. Indeed, the English courts will ordinarily uphold the arbitration agreement by way of anti-suit injunction.[114] As Sir Richard Scott V-C concluded:

> [the insurer] is bound by the arbitration agreement not because there is any privity of contract between [the insurers] and [the time charterers] but because [the voyage charterer's] contractual rights under the sub-charterparty to the benefit of which [the insurer] has become entitled by subrogation are, subject to the arbitration agreement which, too, is part of the sub-charterparty. [The insurer] cannot enforce those contractual rights without accepting the contractual burden, in the form of the arbitration agreement to which those rights are subject…[115]

---

[112] *The Jordan Nicolov* [1990] 2 Lloyd's Rep 11, 15; also *The Leage* [1984] 2 Lloyd's Rep 259.

[113] *Ibid.*

[114] E.g., *The Leage* [1984] 2 Lloyd's Rep 259; *The Jay Bola* [1997] 2 Lloyd's Rep 279, 285; and also the discussion from paragraphs 14 et seq. of the decision dated 21 March 2005 in *Through Transport Mutual Insurance Association (Eurasia) Ltd v. New India Assurance Co Ltd* [2005] EWHC 455 (Comm) (Moore-Bick J).

[115] *The Jay Bola* [1997] 2 Lloyd's Rep 279, 291.

15-44   The principle was recently confirmed in a 2002 decision of the High Court in the interesting case of *Phoenix Finance Ltd v. Féderation Internationale de l'Automobile, Formula One Management Ltd & Formula One Administration Ltd.*[116]   The dispute concerned Phoenix's unsuccessful bid to secure the right to participate in the 2002 Formula One motor racing season as a result of an assignment of assets from racing great Alain Prost's insolvent racing team, Prost Grand Prix (PGP).   Sir Richard Scott V-C held that PGP's rights to participate in the 2002 season had been automatically extinguished by its insolvency and its failure to participate in the first event of the racing calendar, the Australian Grand Prix.   Naturally Phoenix, as assignee, could not be put in any better position than PGP as assignor, so its hopes of competing were dashed.   At the same time, Phoenix was also bound by the assignment to present its grievances with the Formula One authorities to ICC arbitration in accordance with the overarching Formula One "Concorde" agreement, and the High Court proceedings were accordingly stayed:

> [t]he rights, if any, of Phoenix are derived from those of PGP under the Concorde and their sale by PGP and its liquidator to Phoenix.   Phoenix is the assignee of PGP.   It must take those rights subject to the obligation imposed by clause 17.3 to refer to arbitration any dispute in connection with their existence or extent.[117]

15-45   Under English law the legal assignee of contractual rights takes them subject to the equities, which includes the obligation to pursue claims by arbitration, as a recent case illustrates.   In early April 2005, judgment was delivered in the case of *Through Transport Mutual Insurance Association (Eurasia) Ltd v. New India Assurance Co Ltd*, where Moore-Bick J concluded that according to English authorities, the foremost being *The Jay Bola*:

> a person who obtains by an assignment or transfer of some other kind the right to pursue a claim under a contract can only enforce that right in accordance with the terms of the contract and subject to any restrictions or limitations which those terms may impose.   In other words, what he obtains is a *chose in action* whose precise scope is determined by the contract under

---

[116] *Phoenix Finance Ltd v. Féderation Internationale de l'Automobile, Formula One Management Ltd and Formula One Administration Ltd* (unreported, High Court, 22 May 2002) available online at http://www.austlii.edu.au/~andrew/bailii/Joe/Data/EW_EWHC_Ch_2002_1028.html.
[117] *Ibid.*, para 82.

which it arises and which is inherently subject to certain incidents, in this case a requirement that it be enforced by arbitration.[118]

15-46 In this case the result was that, whether or not New India Assurance Co Ltd was the statutory transferee of certain rights in respect of its insured, or merely the beneficiary of independent statutory rights arising under a foreign law, it was effectively seeking to enforce the obligations of Through Transport Mutual Insurance Association under a contract of insurance. As such, Moore-Bick J held that

> the right it enjoys is a right to enforce a *chose in action* which is itself subject to certain inherent limitations. One of those is … the obligation to enforce any claim by arbitration in London.[119]

15-47 Relying in part on the *Bulbank* Tribunal's jurisdictional award,[120] the Swedish Supreme Court in *MS Emja Braack Schiffahrts KG v. Wärtsila Diesel Aktiebolag* held that an arbitration clause is binding on both assignee and assignor, unless special circumstances apply, such as the inability to pay the arbitration costs.[121] At stake was a contract for the supply of components from a Finnish engineering company to a Dutch shipbuilder. The contract contained an ICC arbitration clause. Upon purchase of the ship, the purchaser acquired "all the rights" of the shipbuilder as against the engineering company, so when the machinery proved to be faulty, the purchaser brought claims against the engineering company, but it preferred to litigate these claims in the Swedish courts. The Finnish respondent applied to the courts for a stay, arguing that the arbitration clause in the contract was binding on the claimant as assignee. The Supreme Court of Sweden upheld that argument, ruling that the assignee was indeed bound by the arbitration agreement. The Court reasoned that an original counter-party would be disadvantaged if an assignee of a contract were not bound by an

---

[118] *Through Transport Mutual Insurance Association (Eurasia) Ltd v. New India Assurance Co Ltd* [2005] EWHC 455, para 22.

[119] *Ibid.*, para 24. The outcome of this particular decision was that it granted the claimant's application under section 18 of the Arbitration Act and exercised its discretion to appoint an arbitrator to determine the dispute between the parties.

[120] On which see Rosenberg. The Decision on Jurisdiction was also upheld on the assignment issues in subsequent Swedish court proceedings but this issue was quickly overwhelmed by the ensuing confidentiality debate.

[121] *MS Emja Braack Schiffahrts KG v. Wärtsila Diesel Aktiebolag*, Swedish Supreme Court, 15 October 1997, summarised in XXIVa *YBCA* 317-320 (1999) and noted Sallnas and Dyer, "Sweden: Arbitration and Assignment of Contract, Case Comment" 2(1) *Int ALR* N2-3 (1999).

arbitration clause contained within it, because otherwise an assignor could not avoid its obligation to arbitration by way of a simple assignment.[122]

15-48 In France, the position for signatories seeking to compel arbitration against assignees is consistent with the reverse position, described earlier, when an assignee seeks to compel arbitration against signatories. Here, the signatory must prove the assignee's consent to be bound by the assigned arbitration clause.[123] The burden of this requirement is lifted, somewhat, by the presumption that the assignee, by accepting an assignment of the contract, has consented to assignment of the agreement to arbitrate.[124] In respect of US jurisdictions, Hosking notes that, in most states,

> where the rights and obligations under a contract are validly assigned and the assigned contract contains an arbitration provision, that arbitration provision is binding on all parties including the original contracting parties (both promisor and promisee) and the assignee.[125]

15-49 In the early but oft-cited case of *Hosiery Mfg Corp v. Goldston*, the New York Court of Appeal observed that arbitration agreements would be worthless if either party could escape them by assigning claims subject to arbitration between the original parties to third parties.[126] In 1983 in the case of *Banque de Paris et des Pays-Bas v. Amoco Oil Company* this was said to be a basic principle in the case law.[127] For a modern illustration, in the 1997 case of *Cedrela Transport Ltd v. Banque Cantonale Vaudoise*, Cedrela entered into a charterparty with Knotts whereby Cedrela chartered a vessel in return for which it undertook to make

---

[122] See also Redfern and Hunter, supra note 20, 151.

[123] See *Fouchard Gaillard Goldman*, supra note 2, 417 et seq.

[124] E.g., *CCC Filmkunst v. EDIF*, Paris Cour d'appel, 28 January 1988 reprinted in (1988) *Rev Arb* 568, 569 translation supplied in *Fouchard Gaillard Goldman*, supra note 2, para 718.

[125] James Hosking, "Non-Signatories and International Arbitration in the United States: the Quest for Consent", 20(3) *Arb Int* 289 (2004). See e.g., *Cedrela Transport Ltd v. Banque Cantonale Vaudoise*, 67 F Supp 353 (SDNY, 1999) and Bernard Hanotiau, "Problems Raised by Complex Arbitrations Involving Multiple Contracts-Parties-Issues", 18(3) *J Int'l Arb* 251 (2001) 263; JJ Sentner, "Who is Bound by Arbitration Agreements? Enforcement by and Against Non-Signatories" 6 *Business Law International* 55 (2005), 70; Lamm and Aqua, supra note 20, 727-728.

[126] *Hosiery Mfg Corp v. Goldston* (1924) 143 NE 779, 780; 238 NY 2d 22.

[127] *Banque de Paris et des Pays-Bas v. Amoco Oil Company* 573 F Supp 1464, 1469 (SDNY 1983). See also *Instituto Cubano v. The MV Driller*, 148 F Supp 739 (S.D.N.Y. 1957); *Application of Reconstruction Finance Corp*, 106 F Supp 358 (S.D.N.Y. 1952). cf. *Lachmar v. Trunkline LNG Co*, 753 F 2d 8 (2d Cir 1988); *United States v. Panhandle Eastern Corp*, 672 F Supp 149 (D Del 1987). See also Girsberger and Hausmaninger, supra note 2 and authorities cited at notes 2 et seq.; Gary Born, *International Commercial Arbitration* (2nd edition, Transnational Publishers and Kluwer, 2001) 668-671.

certain payments. The charterparty contained an arbitration clause. When Knotts refinanced the vessel with Banque Cantonale by way of security, it assigned to the bank all its rights, title and interest in and to all moneys under the Charter as well as all other rights and benefits. Cedrela was notified of, and duly acknowledged, the assignment. When Cedrela fell behind on its payments, Banque Cantonale demanded arbitration of the dispute pursuant to the arbitration clause in the charterparty. Cedrela applied to the court arguing that the Banque Cantonale was not a party to the arbitration agreement. The US District Court for the Southern District of New York rejected that argument, upholding a line of authority that assignees may be entitled to compel signatories to an agreement containing an arbitration clause to submit to arbitration.[128]

VI. CONCLUSIONS

15-50 One should not presume from the foregoing that the complex issues regarding arbitration and assignment are all entirely settled. There have been many cases where automatic assignment of an arbitration agreement with assignment of the main contract has been denied, at least in the absence of an express approval of the assignee, the counterparty or both. For instance, in *All-Union Foreign Trade Association ("Sojuzneftexport") v. Joc Oil Ltd*, a tribunal of the Foreign Trade Arbitration Commission of the USSR Chamber of Commerce and Industry held that "being an autonomous procedural contract, it requires the independent agreement of the assignee for submitting him to the jurisdiction which was chosen by the parties to the contract".[129] US courts have likewise denied the assignment of the arbitration clause.[130]

15-51 The risk of such decisions is by no means eliminated. Stemming from the fact that the assignee is not a signatory to the agreement to arbitrate, the

---

[128] *Fisser v. International Bank*, 282 F 2d 231, 241 (2d. Cir. 1960); *Certain Underwriters at Lloyd's London v. Colonial Penn Insurance Co* (SDNY, 11 June 1997); *Banque de Paris et des Pays-Bas v. Amoco Oil Co*, 573 F Supp 1464, 1469 (SDNY 1983); *Wells Fargo Bank International Corp v. London Steam-ship Owners' Mutual*, 408 F Supp 626, 629 (SDNY, 1976).

[129] *All-Union Foreign Trade Association (Sojuzneftexport) v. Joc Oil Ltd*, Foreign Trade Arbitration Commission of the USSR Chamber of Commerce and Industry, Award of 9 July 1984 in Case No. 109/1980 reprinted in XVIII YBCA 92 (1993) para 17; likewise *Re Application of IMP Group (Cyprus) Ltd for Enforcement of the Arbitral Award*, Ruling of the Judicial Collegium for Civil Cases of the Moscow District Court, 21 April 1997, reported in XXIII YBCA 745-749 (1998).

[130] See Girsberger and Hausmaninger, supra note 2, referring to e.g., *Kaufman v. William Iselin & Co, Inc* 143 NE 780, and *Lachmar v. Trunklin LNG Co* 753 F 2d 8 (CA 2d Cir, 1985) at 9-10.

reality is that an arbitration will always be vulnerable to efforts by assignees or the signatory counterparties to compel or resist arbitration, whether by invoking the applicable local laws, arbitration rules or perhaps treaties. Attempts will continue to be made to have awards set aside, recognition and enforcement refused, where parties involved have not themselves signed the agreement to arbitrate.

15-52 English law takes a robust, common-sense approach, consistent with the other jurisdictions discussed. The rationale for this sort of approach can be found in the *bona fide* principle and the fair and reasonable expectations of the parties. It takes account of the needs of modern commerce and trade which cannot be dependent upon idiosyncratic national laws. Consistent with this, Craig, Park and Paulsson observe that it is a general rule in ICC arbitration that an assignee may invoke an arbitration clause contained in an assigned contract.[131] UNIDROIT seems to have picked up on this thread and in its 2004 edition of the *Principles of International Commercial Contracts*, Article 9.1.14 of which provides that

> the assignment of a right transfers to the assignee: ... (b) all rights securing performance of the right assigned.[132]

With these developments we may be getting closer to the uniform substantive rule to regulate the issue preferred by Girsberger and Hausmaninger in their 1992 comparative study on "Assignment of Rights and Agreement to Arbitrate".[133] Should we ever get there we would enjoy the benefits of a solution which does not focus on national laws as such. However, we are not there yet, so for the time being the parties in international commercial arbitration, where applicable substantive and procedural laws vary, will remain subject to the peculiar foibles of different national legal systems.

---

[131] Craig, Park and Paulsson, supra note 19, 78-79.

[132] Notably there is no specific mention of arbitration clauses in the Principles or whether assignment transfers not only the rights, but also the obligations embodied in an arbitration clause. The "black letter" rules of the 2004 UNIDROIT Principles are available online at: www.unidroit.org/english/principles/contracts/principles2004/blackletter2004.pdf and are published in hard copy together with commentary by UNIDROIT, *UNIDROIT Principles of International Commercial Contracts* (Rome: UNIDROIT, 2004). See further, Michael Joachim Bonell, "UNIDROIT Principles 2004 – The New Edition of the Principles of International Commercial Contracts adopted by the International Institute for the Unification of Private Law", (2004) *Uniform Law Review* 5.

[133] Girsberger and Hausmaninger, supra note 2, 163; also Veeder, supra note 1, 291.

*Paul Friedland**

CHAPTER 16

THE AMICUS ROLE IN INTERNATIONAL ARBITRATION

16-1 This chapter considers
  i.   whether *amicus curiae* submissions, now on the fringe of international arbitration, are likely to enter the arbitration mainstream, and
  ii. how to manage the differential impact of *amicus* submissions on the arbitrating parties.

I. AMICUS CURIAE FRINGE OR MAINSTREAM

16-2 There are two sets of requisites for submission of amicus briefs. The first is intrinsic to the arbitral process: arbitrators must find themselves empowered to accept *amicus* submissions, and then must exercise that power to accept *amicus* submissions. The second is extrinsic to the arbitral process: there must be *amici* (consumer groups, environmental groups or others) with a vital interest in the subject matter and with the energy and financing to mobilise themselves to submit *amicus briefs*.

16-3 On the first requirement – arbitral power to accept *amicus* submissions – the decisions which have received the most attention are those by two NAFTA tribunals (*Methanex*[1] and *UPS*[2]). The issue is whether the rulings in those cases foreshadow the direction of investor/state disputes and international arbitration

---

* Partner, White & Case LLP (New York). The author thanks Stefan Ebaugh, an associate in White & Case's international arbitration group, for his contribution to this chapter.
[1] *Methanex v. United States*, Decision of the Tribunal on Petitions from Third Persons to Intervene as "Amicus Curiae," available at http://www.international-economic-law.org/Methanex/ Methanex%20-%20Amicus%20Decision.pdf (hereinafter Methanex).
[2] *United Parcel Service v. Canada*, Decision of the Tribunal on Petitions for Intervention and Participation as Amici Curiae, available at http://www.dfait-maeci.gc.ca/tna-nac/documents/IntVent_oct.pdf (hereinafter UPS).

gcncrally, or whether they are more likely to be precedents for NAFTA cases only.

1. Methanex v. United States

16-4 *Methanex* was a claim by a Canadian investor that California's ban on an environmentally unfriendly gasoline additive caused it compensable harm. The *amici* were environmental groups, who argued that the investor's claim would have a chilling effect on the willingness of state and federal governments throughout North America to implement environmental legislation. The investor opposed the proffer by the *amici*. The US, the respondent in the case, favoured the *amicus* submission. Canada also supported the *amicus* submission, notwithstanding that its national, the claimant, opposed the submission. Mexico opposed the submission.

16-5 The *Methanex* Tribunal held that it had the power to accept the *amicus* submission under Article 15(1) of the UNCITRAL Rules.[3] It found that this holding was supported by the practice of the Iran/US Claims Tribunal[4] (although

---

[3] *Methanex,* at para 47:

> The Tribunal concludes that by Article 15(1) of the UNCITRAL Arbitration Rules it has the power to accept *amicus* submissions (in writing) from each of the Petitioners…

[4] *Methanex,* at para 32. The *Methanex* Tribunal cited Note 5 of the Iran-US Claims Tribunal Notes to Article 15(1) of the UNCITRAL Rules, which provides:

> The arbitral tribunal may, having satisfied itself that the statement of one of the two Governments – or, under special circumstances, any other person – who is not an arbitrating party in a particular case is likely to assist the arbitral tribunal in carrying out its task, permit such Government or person to assist the arbitral tribunal by presenting written and [or] oral statements.

Ibid. (alteration in original) (quoting Iran-US Claims Tribunal Rules of Procedure, reprinted in Charles Brower & Jason Brueschke, *The Iran-United States Claim Tribunal* 742 (1998)). The *Methanex* Tribunal concluded that

> [f]or present purposes, the [Iran-US Claims Tribunal Note 5 to Article 15(1) of the UNCITRAL Rules] and [one of the awards of the Iran-US Claims Tribunal] demonstrate that the receipt of written submissions from a non-party third person does not necessarily offend the philosophy of international arbitration involving states and non-state parties.

Ibid. (citing *Iran v. United States*, Case A/15, Award No. 63-A/15-FT, 12 Iran-US CTR 40, 43 (20 August 1986) ("On 13 December 1983, certain interested United States banks submitted a Memorial that was accepted for filing in accordance with Article 15, Note 5, of the Tribunal Rules.").

it appears that this practice has been limited).[5] The Tribunal found that its ruling was also supported by WTO practice[6] (although, again, it appears that a WTO Appellate Body has accepted unsolicited *amicus* briefs in only two cases and in neither case was the *amicus* brief actually considered by the Appellate Body).[7] On the issue of whether to exercise this power, the *Methanex* Tribunal found that it was appropriate to do so on two bases: first, the significance of the public interest at stake, which the Tribunal found much greater than the public interest impacted by the usual commercial arbitration;[8] and second, the fact that the two

---

5 See, e.g., *Henry F. Teichmann, Inc. and Carnegie Foundry and Machine Company v. Hamadan Glass Company*, Case No. 264, Award No. 264-264-1 (12 November 1986), available at 1986 WL 424360 ("The Tribunal considers that the position enjoyed by the Government of Iran by virtue of Article 15 of the Tribunal Rules renders unnecessary its participation as a respondent in a case such as this"). Under Article 15, Note 5, the Tribunal may, "having satisfied itself that the statement of one of the two Governments - or, under special circumstances, any other person - who is not an arbitrating party in a particular case is likely to assist the tribunal in carrying out its task, permit such Government or person to assist the tribunal by presenting oral or written statements.") (quoting Iran-US Claims Tribunal Rules of Procedure, reprinted in Charles Brower & Jason Brueschke, *The Iran-United States Claim Tribunal* 742 (1998)); *Islamic Republic of Iran v. United States*, Case No. A25 (11 October 1989), 21 Iran-US CTR 283, 284 ("Phillips Petroleum Company Iran is invited, pursuant to Article 15, Note 5, of the Tribunal Rules to file, if it so wishes, on or before 20 December 1989 a Memorial....").

6 *Methanex,* at para. 33:

> For present purposes, this WTO practice demonstrates that the scope of a procedural power can extend to the receipt of written submissions from non-party third persons, even in a juridical procedure affecting the rights and obligations of state parties; and further it also demonstrates that the receipt of such submissions confers no rights, procedural or substantive, on such persons..

7 *GATT Appellate Body Report on US-Import Prohibition on Certain Shrimp and Shrimp Prods*, WT/DS58/AB/R, para 91 (12 October 1998), available at 1998 WL 720123:

> We admit, therefore, the briefs attached to the appellant's submission of the United States as part of that appellant's submission. At the same time, considering that the United States has itself accepted the briefs in a tentative and qualified manner only, we focus in the succeeding sections below on the legal arguments in the main U.S. appellant's submission.;

> GATT Appellate Body Report on US-Imposition of Countervailing Duties on Certain Hot-Rolled Lead and Bismuth Carbon Steel Prods., WT/DS138/AB/R, para 42 (10 May 2000), available at 2000 WL 569563:

> We are of the opinion that we have the legal authority under the DSU to accept and consider amicus curiae briefs in an appeal in which we find it pertinent and useful to do so. In this appeal, we have not found it necessary to take the two amicus curiae briefs filed into account in rendering our decision..

8 *Methanex* at para 49:

governments directly connected to the dispute had expressed their support for the transparency of the NAFTA process.[9]

2. UPS v. Canada

16-6 *UPS* was a claim by a US company that a Canadian state monopoly unfairly limited its ability to compete in the Canadian express courier services business. The *amici* were the Canadian Postal Workers Union and the Council of Canadians. They argued that the UPS claim would harm the employment status of Canadian postal workers and the services provided to those who depended upon Canada Post. UPS opposed the *amicus* proffer. Canada and the U.S. both again supported the proffer, but with constraints, in particular, a 20 page limit on the *amicus* submission.[10] Mexico opposed the proffer.

16-7 The *UPS* Tribunal, following *Methanex*, ruled that it had the power under the UNCITRAL Rules to accept the *amicus* submission.[11]

3. NAFTA and ICSID

16-8 In the wake of these rulings, a NAFTA Commission developed and issued guidelines for *amicus* submissions, including a 20 page limit.[12]

16-9 There is some basis in the rulings by the *Methanex* and *UPS* Tribunals for the proposition that the power to accept *amicus* submissions exists under the UNCITRAL Rules and that such power is to be exercised where the public interest is as significant as it was in *Methanex* and *UPS*.[13] Stated that way, the

---

> There is an undoubtedly public interest in this arbitration. The substantive issues extend far beyond those raised by the usual transnational arbitration between commercial parties.

[9] *Ibid.*

> There is also a broader argument, as suggested by the Respondent and Canada: the Chapter 11 arbitral process could benefit from being perceived as more open or transparent; or conversely be harmed if seen as unduly secretive.

[10] *UPS*, at para 54.
[11] *UPS*, at paras 61, 73. See also Loukas Mistelis, "Conflidentiality and Third Party Participation, 21(2) *Arb Int* 205 (2005), 213-223.
[12] NAFTA Free Trade Commission, *Statement of the Free Trade Commission on Non-Disputing Party Participation* B(3)(b) (7 October 2003), available at http://www.ustr.gov/assets/Trade Agreements/Regional/NAFTA/asset_upload file660_6893.pdf (last visited 14 March 2005).
[13] *Methanex*, at paras 47 – 49 (the Tribunal found that strong public interest in the subject matter was a "factor" in determining whether to exercise its discretion and accept the proffered *amicus* briefs); *UPS*, at para 70:

NAFTA cases can apply to many investors/state cases, and even to many international commercial disputes, because other sets of international rules give arbitrators powers similar to the broad grant of powers found in the UNCITRAL Rules, Article 15,[14] and because many international arbitrations involve public interest issues no less significant than those at stake in *Methanex* and *UPS*.

16-10   This statement of the rule established by the *Methanex* and *UPS* cases would, however, omit the heart of the matter. The two NAFTA Tribunals relied on the fact that the two governments directly connected to the cases – one as a party, the other as the country of the claimant – told the Tribunals in both cases that they supported the *amicus* submissions.   It is unsurprising that in such context the Tribunals favored the values of transparency and public access. That is a context that is unique to NAFTA (aside from the new US Model BIT, discussed below).

16-11   This view of the *sui generis* nature of NAFTA is supported by a recent ICSID case, *Aguas del Tunari v. Bolivia* (2003). According to publicly–available documents, the case involved rates charged by a foreign investor to Bolivians for water use. In response to perceived rate hikes, there were massive protests, and the government cancelled the concession. The investor claimed expropriation. The *amici* were 300 health and safety and environmental organizations from five continents. They argued that water rights belong to the Bolivian people and that an ICSID arbitration on this issue should be open to the public and permit the

---

The Tribunal returns to the emphasis which the Petitioners, with considerable cogency, have placed both on the important public character of the matters in issue in this arbitration and on their own real interest in these matters... The Petitioners have made out a case for their being permitted to make written submissions on appropriate matters as determined, on application, by the Tribunal.

[14]   See LCIA Rules, Article 14.2:

Unless otherwise agreed by the parties under Article 14.1, the Arbitral Tribunal shall have the widest discretion to discharge its duties allowed under such law(s) or rules of law as the Arbitral Tribunal may determine to be applicable.;

AAA International Rules, Article 16.1:

Subject to these rules, the tribunal may conduct the arbitration in whatever manner it considers appropriate, provided that the parties are treated with equality and that each party has the right to be heard and is given a fair opportunity to present its case.;

ICC Rules, Article 20(1):

The Arbitral Tribunal shall proceed within as short a time as possible to establish the facts of the case by all appropriate means.

But see ICSID Rule 34, infra note 19.

submission of an *amicus* brief.[15] The ICSID Tribunal ruled that party consent was required for non-party participation because ICSID arbitration belongs to the parties, and nothing in the applicable BIT said otherwise.[16] Because consent was absent (both sides opposed the submission), the Tribunal rejected the *amicus* submission.[17]

16-12 Part of the reason why the NAFTA practice was not followed in the *Aguas del Tunari* case may be that the ICSID Rules contain nothing as broad as the grant of powers given to arbitrators by UNCITRAL Rules Article 15(1).[18] But it is doubtful that this adequately explains why the *amicus* submission was not accepted in the *Aguas del Tunari* case: had the Tribunal been so minded, it might have found that the ICSID Rules (Article 34) gave it enough discretion to justify accepting the amicus submission.

16-13 It is also doubtful that the difference lies in the relative significance of the public interest at stake in the *Aguas del Tunari* case. The social issues impli-

---

[15] Petition of Amici to the Arbitral Tribunal, para 18 (29 August 2002), available at http://www.earthjustice.org /news/documents/boliviapetition.pdf (last visited 14 May 2005).

[16] Letter from David D Caron, President of the *Aguas del Tunari* Tribunal, to J Martin Wagner, Director of the International Program of Earthjustice, dated 29 January 2002, available at http://www.earthjustice.org/news/documents/2-03/ICSIDResponse.pdf (last visited 14 May 2005):

> The interplay of the two treaties involved (the Convention on the Settlement of Investment Disputes and the 1992 Bilateral Agreement on Encouragement and Reciprocal Protection of Investments between the Kingdom of the Netherlands and Bolivia) and the consensual nature of the arbitration places the control of the issues you raise with the parties, not the Tribunal.

[17] The Tribunal did not specifically rule on whether the Tribunal, on its own initiative, could accept the proffered *amicus* submission. *Ibid.*:

> [T]he Tribunal is of the view that there is not at present a need to call witnesses or seek supplementary non-party submissions at the jurisdictional phase of its work. We hold this view without in anyway prejudging the question of the extent of the Tribunal's authority to call witnesses or receive information from non-parties on its own initiative.

[18] See ICSID Rule 34, entitled "Evidence: General Principles," which empowers the Tribunal to "be the judge of the admissibility of any evidence adduced" or, in its discretion, to "visit any place connected with the dispute or conduct inquiries there." The phrase "or conduct inquiries there" may or may not be broad enough to permit the Tribunal to accept written amicus briefs. Rule 34's use of the word "adduced" may also limit the written evidence that a Tribunal may admit to evidence advanced by one of the parties. The *Aguas del Tunari* Tribunal did not rule on the scope of Rule 34. See supra note 18.

cated by the water use concession were at least as important as the ecological interests at stake in *Methanex* and the monopoly issues in *UPS*.

16-14 The distinction also surely does not lie in the relative suitability of the *amici*. The *amici* in the *Aguas del Tunari* case included major NGOs from around the world.

16-15 The likely difference, rather, is that, unlike the NAFTA situation, no ICSID member states – let alone two-thirds of them – were telling the Tribunal in the *Aguas del Tunari* case that transparency and public access were central features of the ICSID system.

16-16 If this reading of these NAFTA and ICSID rulings is correct, then NAFTA will remain a process apart from the rest of the world of international arbitration, unless or until either (i) arbitral rules are changed in order to em-power tribunals to accept *amicus* submissions, or (ii) governments express their acceptance of *amicus* submissions in other international instruments that provide for international arbitration. There is, in fact, an important recent instance of the latter: the current US model BIT, which explicitly empowers arbitral tribunals to accept *amicus* submissions and to open hearings to the public.[19] This model BIT language is now found in three current US BITs, with Chile, Singapore and Morocco.

16-17 We cannot know if other BITs will follow the US example. But even if some do, it would not inevitably follow that *amicus* submissions will become anything like a commonplace feature of the world of international arbitration. That is due to *inter alia* the second set of requisites for *amicus* submissions, namely, the need for civic activism in the form of interest groups with the financing and energy to present an *amicus* submission to an arbitral tribunal.

---

[19] US 2004 Model BIT, Art 28(3):

> The tribunal shall have the authority to accept and consider *amicus curiae* submissions from a person or entity that is not a disputing party;

ibid. at Art 29(2):

> The tribunal shall conduct hearings open to the public and shall determine, in consultation with the disputing parties, the appropriate logistical arrangements.

The US 2004 Model BIT is available at http://www.ustr.gov/assets/Trade_Sectors/Investment/ Model_BIT/asset_upload_file847_6897.pdf (last visited 14 May 2005).

16-18   North America is one of the areas where this kind of civic activism can be found. North America is home to NGOs and consumer groups whose awareness of investor/state matters is facilitated by FOIA statutes. These circumstances undeniably affect the NAFTA situation and the rulings of the NAFTA Tribunals. The world-wide ecology movement is another source of potential *amici*. That is a source of *amicus* submissions which is not limited to North America, although many environmental NGOs are headquartered in North America. Other than these settings, it is uncertain how often *amici* will present themselves.

16-19   For now, therefore, the *amicus* process is bound to remain basically a NAFTA phenomenon.

II. DIFFERENTIAL IMPACT ON THE ARBITRATING PARTIES

16-20   Although arbitration exists first and foremost for the parties, it need not be blind to the social impact of the awards which it generates. Where, however, the greater social good is sought through the mechanism of *amicus* submissions, equality of treatment of the parties will always be sacrificed to some extent.

16-21   Hardly anything is neutral in arbitration. It is almost always the case that one side opposes an *amicus* submission and the other welcomes it or feigns neutrality. The differential impact is obvious with respect to cost. The party opposing an *amicus* submission incurs greater cost in fighting to keep out the *amicus* submission, and then in responding on the substance if the submission is accepted. The cost can be lessened by limiting the issues which an *amicus* submission can address and by fixing page limits. There is no way, however, to eliminate the differential. One possible remedy is for the arbitral tribunal to require the *amicus* to pay in advance a lump sum to cover the attorneys' fees of the party opposing the submission, as a form of security for costs. The security would then be allocated at the time of the final award, and potentially returned to the *amicus*.

16-22   From a party's perspective in a NAFTA case, the *amicus* role must be a cost that is anticipated. The same is now true if one brings or defends a claim under the current generation of US BITs. Otherwise, the *amicus* process is not a cost that a party should anticipate, and this is not a short-fall of the system. When an *amicus* brief is presented and accepted, it will often serve as a weapon for one side and an expensive burden for the other.

*Norah Gallagher**

CHAPTER 17

PARALLEL PROCEEDINGS, *RES JUDICATA* AND *LIS PENDENS*: PROBLEMS AND POSSIBLE SOLUTIONS

I. INTRODUCTION

17-1 The implications of parallel proceedings in international arbitration have generated much debate recently. It has been identified as a problem because such proceedings can result in conflicting awards by different tribunals arising out of the same set of facts. This could seriously undermine the very existence of the arbitral process. Arbitration is the preferred dispute resolution option for international transactions largely due to its finality, commercial certainty and neutrality. The main cause of concern is that there seems to be something inherently unfair about a claimant being able to take more than one chance against a respondent based on the same events and essentially the same claim.

17-2 It can, and indeed has, resulted in multiple cases against a respondent state at the same time dealing with substantially the same dispute. This can lead to a number of obvious problems, not just for the parties involved. The principle of finality of awards, certainty in commercial matters and coherence in the application of international legal principles are all brought into question. The now notorious cases of *CME v. Czech Republic* and *Ronald Lauder v. Czech Republic*[1] illustrate the problem clearly. Two international arbitral tribunals rendered awards reaching different conclusions based on the same set of circumstances but initiated under different investment treaties. There are divergent views on the legitimacy of pursuing such parallel proceedings. It runs contrary to the accepted

---

* BCL, LLM, MA, Senior Fellow, School of International Arbitration, Queen Mary, University of London; Solicitor, International Arbitration Group, Herbert Smith, London.
[1] Awards available on the Czech Ministry of Finance website at www2004.mfcr.cz/index_en.php.

Loukas A. Mistelis and Julian D.M. Lew (eds), Pervasive Problems in International Arbitration, 329-356
© 2006 Kluwer Law International. Printed in the Netherlands

principle that a party should not be subjected to multiple and costly legal proceedings.

17-3 This phenomenon can be understood in the context of the rapid change in the international legal framework within which foreign direct investment is made. The main reason that this issue has arisen recently is a direct result of the dramatic proliferation of bilateral investment treaties (BITs). The large number of BITs entered into by states, over the past 15 years in particular, has given investors direct recourse against a host state for alleged breaches of international law where previously it would not have been possible. This has resulted in a marked increase in the number of international investment arbitrations both institutional[2] and *ad hoc*. In addition, an investor may now have several dispute resolution options available under the growing number of BITs.[3] This has greatly increased the potential for multiple claims arising under different BITs relating to the same circumstances. It is this possibility that has been identified as a contemporary problem for the purposes of this collection of essays.

17-3 The main focus of this chapter is to look at the problem of parallel proceedings in investor state arbitration. It will try to analyse whether the legal doctrines of *res judicata* and *lis pendens* can be applied to arbitrations under investment treaties to prevent multiple proceedings and possibly conflicting awards. Some of the recent international cases will be reviewed to see how these doctrines have been applied. Can they prevent parallel proceedings and if not, what alternative solutions should be considered? There has been much speculation on how best to redress the problem.[4] Whether parallel proceedings along the

---

[2] For example, the cases filed at ICSID went from 3 in 1995 to 31 in 2003. The majority of recent cases are based on alleged breaches of BIT obligations, details at www.worldbank.org/icsid/cases/pending.htm. For a discussion of some procedural problems arising out of this large increase in investment arbitration see David Williams, "Review and Recourse against Awards Rendered under Investment Treaties", 4(2) *J World Inv & Trade* 251 (2003).

[3] See Antonio Parra, "Provisions on the Settlement of Investment Disputes in Modern Investment Laws, Bilateral Investment Treaties and Multilateral Instruments", 12 *ICSID Rev - FILJ* 287 (1997) and Rudolf Dolzer & Margrete Stevens, *Bilateral Investment Treaties* (Kluwer Law International 1995). For texts of over 2000 BITs see the UNCTAD website collection at http://www.unctadxi.org/templates/DocSearch____779.aspx.

[4] Vaughan Lowe, "Overlapping jurisdiction in international tribunals", 20 *Australian Yb Int'l Law* 191-204(1999); Iain Scobbie, *"Res judicata*, precedent and the International Court: a preliminary sketch", 20 *Australian Yb Int'l Law* 299-317 (1999); Peter Barnett, "The Prevention of Abusive Cross-border Re-litigation", 51(4) *ICLQ* 943-957 (2002); Bernard Hanotiau, "The *res judicata* effect of arbitral awards, in ICC Bulletin, special supplement, *Complex arbitrations*, 43-51(2003); Jeremy Carver, "How to Avoid Conflicting Awards: the Lauder and CME Cases",

line of the Czech arbitrations will ultimately adversely affect the international arbitration process in the long run remains to be seen. It is hoped that parties would want to avoid the cost and inconvenience of such multiple litigation.

II. PARALLEL PROCEEDINGS

1. Introductory Remarks

17-4 There are a number of possibilities where parallel proceedings can arise in international arbitration including, for example, an international court and an international tribunal[5]; a state court and an international arbitral tribunal[6] and two international arbitral tribunals. It is this latter situation that has given rise to recent discussion and as this volume is about contemporary problems[7] this chapter will concentrate on the position where two arbitral tribunals are considering the same issue. We must start from the premise that in international arbitration each tribunal is constituted to determine the particular dispute between the parties. The tribunal in *Joy Mining v. Egypt* noted that there

> has been much argument regarding recent cases, notably *SGS v. Pakistan* and *SGS v. Philippines*. However, this Tribunal is not called upon to sit in judgment on the views of other tribunals. It is only called to decide this

---

[5] 5(1) *J World Inv & Trade* 23-29 (2004); Hans Bagner, "How to Avoid Conflicting Awards: the Lauder and CME Cases, 5(1) *J World Inv & Trade* 31-35 (2004); Wolfgang Kühn, "How to Avoid Conflicting Awards: the Lauder and CME Cases", 5(1) *J World Inv & Trade* 7-17 (2004). E.g., the orders issued by the Annex VII tribunal in *MOX Plant Case (Ireland v. England)* to suspend proceedings pending the outcome of the ECJ. The tribunal in Procedural Order 3 stated

> bearing in mind considerations of mutual respect and comity which should prevail between judicial institutions both of which may be called upon to determine rights and obligations as between two States, the Tribunal considers that it would be inappropriate for it to proceed further with hearing the Parties on the merits of the dispute...Moreover, a procedure that might result in two conflicting decisions on the same issue would not be helpful to the resolution of the dispute between the Parties.

Para 28 available at www.pca-cpa.org.

[6] See for examples and discussion on asymmetrical jurisdictional conflicts Zachary Douglas, "The Hybrid Foundations of Investment Treaty Arbitration", *74 BYbIL* 151 (2003) at 267. See also *Fomento de Construcciones y Contratas SA v. Colon Container Terminal SA,* Bundesgericht [Swiss Federal Court] (4P 37/2001) (Unreported, 14 May 2001) extracts in *ASA Bulletin* (3) 2001, 544 and Case note Laurent Levy, "Switzerland: Applying the Principle of Litispendence", 4(4) *Int ALR* N28-29 (2001).

[7] See the problems identified at the opening conference of the School of International Arbitration in Julian Lew (ed), *Contemporary Problems in International Commercial Arbitration* (Centre for Commercial Law Studies, 1986).

dispute in the light of its specific facts and the law, beginning with the jurisdictional objections.[8]

17-5 Each tribunal has jurisdiction to consider the particular dispute before it without regard to other tribunals or awards. Of course, decided awards are routinely referred to before tribunals and are cited by the parties to support or distinguish their own case.[9] For example, in the NAFTA award of *ADF Group Inc v. USA* the tribunal referred to the conclusion in *Mondev International Ltd* on the application of Article 1105 on fair and equitable treatment.[10]

17-6 The increasing number of international courts and tribunals[11] makes it more of a challenge to ensure consistent application and interpretation of international law. Although there is no coherent system or hierarchy as such, international judicial bodies traditionally have adopted a common sense approach to competing jurisdictions. Although the current ad hoc common sense approach may prove more problematic in the future. A judge sitting on the International Criminal Tribunal for the Former Yugoslavia observed that "In international law, every tribunal is a self-contained system (unless otherwise provided)."[12] This can lead to two or more related claims taking place in different international fora.

17-7 "BITs have given foreign investors the possibility of relying on dispute resolution options that best suit their needs."[13] Although this was not necessarily the intention of states at the time of entering into BITs, investors now structure their investments so as to benefit from the protections of at least one BIT. In fact,

---

[8] *Joy Mining Machinery Ltd v. Egypt,* ICSID Case no. ARB/03/11, Award on Jurisdiction, 6 August 2004, para 80. The tribunal declined jurisdiction being unpersuaded by the claimants arguments on the application of the umbrella clause in the UK/Egypt BIT to what it concluded were purely contractual claims (annulment proceedings pending) at www.worldbank.org/icsid.

[9] Raj Bhala, "The Myth about Stare Decisis and International Trade Law (Part One of a Trilogy)", *14 Am. U. Int Law Rev. 845* (1999)

[10] *ADF Group Inc v. USA,* Case No. ARB(AF)/00/1, para 184

> We understand Mondev to be saying… that any general requirement to accord "fair and equitable treatment" and "full protection and security" must be disciplined by being based upon State practice and judicial or arbitral case law or other sources of customary or general international law.

Available at www.naftaclaims.com.

[11] See work being done by the Project on International Courts and Tribunals at www.pict.org.

[12] *Prosecutor v. Tadic,* Decision on the Defence Motion for Interlocutory Appeal on Jurisdiction, Case No. IT-94-1-AR72, para 11 (2 October 1995), 35 ILM 32 (1996).

[13] Lew, Mistelis & Kröll, *Comparative International Commercial Arbitration,* para 28-25 (Kluwer Law International, 2003).

in recent arbitrations the investor has been able to avail of more favourable dispute resolution provisions in an unrelated BIT of the host state by relying on a most favoured nation clause.[14] There were suggestions for an investment arbitration appellate body to address inter alia this issue. An appellate body, however, may not necessarily put an end to parallel proceedings under BITs. The fact is that each entity instituting proceedings has a legitimate legal basis for its claim under a relevant investment treaty. It is also legitimate to try to find a relevant BIT, be it one that links the investor company with the host State or one that links individual shareholder with the host State. Tribunals and courts have not been willing to pierce the corporate veil or refuse jurisdiction to hear a minority shareholder's claim.[15]

2. The Czech Republic Arbitrations[16]

17-8 The current problem is best exemplified in the parallel arbitrations of CME and Ronald Lauder against the Czech Republic. The dispute arose out of the control of a Czech company (CNTS) that ran the first somewhat controversial independent TV station, TV Nova, in the Czech Republic. Essentially the local director (Dr Zelezny) of CME fell out with the American investor. Through the efforts of Dr Zelezny the TV licence was revoked. This greatly reduced the value of CNTS and thus the investment made by CME. Lauder in his individual

---

[14] See *Maffezini v. Spain,* ICSID Case No. ARB/97/7, where the claimant relied successfully on the most-favoured-nation clause in the Argentina-Spain BIT to avail of the dispute resolution provisions in the Chile-Spain BIT allowing for direct access to international arbitration; thereby avoiding any mandatory waiting periods or requirement to seek redress in the national courts. See also *Siemens v. Argentina,* ICSID Case No. ARB/02/8, where the award on jurisdiction went so far as to allow the investor rely on the more attractive provisions for dispute resolution in the Chile/Argentina BIT while avoiding the fork in the road provision to which a Chilean investor would have been bound. However, for a more restrictive application see *Salini v. Jordan,* ICSID Case No. ARB/02/13, where the claimant was refused in his request to apply the MFN clause in the Italy/Jordan BIT to avail of the dispute resolution provisions of the Jordan/US BIT, para 119 and more recently *Plama Consortium Limited v. Bulgaria,* ICSID Case No. ARB/03/24. All cases available on line at www.worldbank.org/icsid.

[15] *CMS Gas Transmission Company v. Argentina,* Decision on Jurisdiction, 17 July 2003, 42 ILM 788 (2003), Final award, 15 May 2005 against respondent in the amount of $133.2 million; the final award is available at http://ita.law.uvic.ca/documents/CMS_FinalAward_000.pdf.

[16] This dispute generated more proceedings than the two UNCITRAL arbitrations that will be discussed here (including court proceeding in Czech Republic taken by CNTS and CET21). See, e.g., *CME Media Enterprises BV v. Zelezny,* 10 September 2001 (SD NY (US)) on the enforcement of an ICC award rendered in Amsterdam discussed in Jason Fry, "Quasi in rem Jurisdiction and discovery in Enforcing an Arbitration Award: Understanding CME Enterprises BV v. Zelezny", 6(3) *Int ALR* 100 (2003).

capacity as a controlling – though minority (no more than 30%) – shareholder in CME commenced UNCITRAL arbitration proceedings in London under the US/Czech BIT. Six months later, CME also filed a claim against the Czech Government under the Netherlands/Czech BIT pursuant to the UNCITRAL rules.

17-9 The London tribunal dismissed all of the claims made by Mr Lauder in its final award of 3 September 2005. However, the CME tribunal sitting in Stockholm found the Czech Republic had in fact violated the BIT in its dealings with the company and awarded CME damages in the amount of $268,814,000 plus interest. Two eminent international tribunals considering the same set of facts, with related parties, under similar BITs reached different conclusions. It is this outcome that has caused such concern, not least because it "is easy to see that the CME case will not remain an isolated incident."[17] The existing legal doctrines only go some way to ensure multiple and vexatious legal proceedings are kept to a minimum.

III. THE PRINCIPLES OF *RES JUDICATA* AND *LIS PENDENS*

17-10   The applications of such principles as *res judicata* and *lis pendens* have been recognised and accepted as "general principles of international law."[18] They are principles known both to international law and domestic law.[19] They are doctrines based on public policy considerations: finality of litigation, economy of justice and fairness.[20] They aim to prevent a party having to defend itself twice for the same action, thereby reducing costs and promoting legal coherence.[21]

---

[17] August Reinisch, "The Use and Limits of *Res Judicata* and *Lis Pendens* as Procedural Tools to Avoid Conflicting Dispute Settlement Outcomes", 3 *Law & Practice of Int'l Courts & Tribunals* 37 (2004) at p 41.

[18] International Court of Justice (ICJ) Statute Article 38(1)(c). See also Bin Cheng, *General Principles of Law as Applied by International Courts and Tribunals* (Cambridge University Press, 1953) 336 and the ILA International Commercial Arbitration Committee Interim Report on *Res Judicata* and Arbitration, Berlin Conference 2004 (hereinafter "ILA Interim Report"), Section V, p 18. The Report is available at www.ila-hq.org.

[19] See Dicey & Morris *Conflicts of Laws* (Sweet & Maxwell 2000, 13th Edition, Lawrence Collins (Ed)); Cheshire & North's *Private International Law* (Butterworths 1999, 13th Edition, Peter North & James Fawcett (Eds)); Peter Barnett, *Res Judicata, Estoppel and Foreign Judgments The Preclusive Effects of Foreign Judgments in Private International Law* (OUP, 2001).

[20] See ILA Interim Report, supra note 18, Section VII where it identifies the policy considerations underpinning *res judicata* and asks "whether they are the same for international arbitration as for domestic litigation" p 25.

[21] See, for example, *Allen v. McCurry* 449 US 90, 94 (1980) where the court confirmed that the doctrine

They do go some way to preventing identical claims being pursued in different fora.

1. Res Judicata

17-11 *Res judicata* (judged or decided matter) essentially is a claim, issue, or cause of action, settled by a judgment, decree, award, or other determination that is considered final as to the rights, questions, and facts involved in the dispute. It is a legal principle or doctrine that generally bars relitigation or reconsideration of the particular matters settled. In the decision in *Waste Management, Inc v. Mexico*[22] the tribunal confirmed that there was

> no doubt that *res judicata* is a principle of international law, and even a general principle of law within the meaning of Article 38(1)(c)

of the ICJ Statute.[23]

17-12 In the *Corfu Channel* case the ICJ in its judgment on 15 December 1949 on the assessment of the amount of compensation payable, rejected Albania's submission that it had no jurisdiction to decide on quantum. It confirmed that

> in accordance with the Statute (Article 60) which, for the settlement of the present dispute, is binding upon the Albanian Government, that Judgment is final and without appeal, and that therefore the matter is *res judicata*.[24]

Certain requirement must be fulfilled before the doctrine of *res judicata* applies.[25] These include the triple identity test: identity of parties; identity of cause and

---

> relieves parties of the cost and vexation of multiple law suits, conserve[s] judicial resources....

See also *International Air Response v. US*, Court of Appeals for the Federal Circuit 01-5117, 4 September 2002 for a more recent application of the principle. Available at http://laws.lp.findlaw.com/fed/015117.htm.

[22] ICSID Case No. ARB(AF)/00/3. Mexico's Preliminary Objection concerning the Previous Proceedings is available on www.naftaclaims.com.

[23] Although it appears that the rules of *res judicata* in international criminal procedure are still developing. See Rosa Theofanis, "The doctrine of *Res Judicata* in International Criminal Law", 3(3) *Int Criminal L Rev*, 195 (2003).

[24] *The Corfu Channel Case (UK v. Albania)*, ICJ Reports 244 at p 248 (1949).

[25] See ILA Interim Report, supra note 18, which reviews the requirements of the doctrine in the common law, civil law and international law. See also Case Note on Res Judicata, 6 *ERPL* 105 (1998) for a review on how the doctrine applies in selected European countries.

identity of subject matter.[26] It is the application of this test in recent arbitrations that has led to tribunals finding that they can continue to determine the case before them without regard to any other tribunal.[27]

17-13   It seems that it "is now commonly accepted that arbitral awards have *res judicata*"[28] effect. In *the Administrative Tribunal* case the ICJ confirmed that it was a well established principle of law that

> a judgment rendered by such a judicial body is *res judicata* and has binding force between the parties to the dispute.[29]

Although its exact scope and application to international arbitration is currently under review by the International Law Association's Commercial Arbitration Committee.[30]

17-14   One of the clearest statements of the application of the principle of *res judicata* in international law was set out by the second tribunal in *Amco v. Indonesia*.[31] The second ICSID tribunal in its award on jurisdiction of 10 May 1988 considered in detail which parts, if any, of the original award remained in place between the parties after the annulment proceedings. The parties accepted that when an ICSID ad hoc committee makes a partial annulment of an award, a subsequent tribunal constituted under Article 52(6) ICSID Convention must treat the annulled sections of the award as *res judicata* and binding on the parties.[32]

---

[26]   See Vaughan Lowe, "*Res Judicata* and the rule of Law in International Arbitration", 8 *African J Int'l L* 38 (1996) at p 40, citing dissenting opinion of Judge Anzilotti in *Chorzow Factory Case,* (1927) PCIJ Ser. A No. 13, 23-27.

[27]   Bernard Hanotiau, "Complex – Multicontract-Multiparty – Arbitrations", 14 *Arb Int* 369 (1998) 393.

[28]   Bernard Hanotiau, "Problems Raised by Complex Arbitrations Involving Multiple Contracts– Parties–Issues – An Analysis", 18(3) *J Int'l Arb* 253 (2001) at 357, Part X. See also *Pious Fund Arbitration (USA v. Mexico)* (1916) Hague Court Reports (Scott) 1 at 5; *Trail Smelter Case (USA v. Canada)* 3 UNRIAA 1905 at 1950; *Amco v. Indonesia,* ICSID Case No. ARB/81/1, (Resubmission: Jurisdiction Award) 89 ILR 552.

[29]   Effect of Awards of Compensation Made by the United Nations Administrative Tribunal, Advisory Opinion 13 July 1954, *ICJ Reports* 47, 54. See also Chile/Argentina *Laguna Del Desierto* arbitration where the tribunal confirmed "the authority of res judicata as a universal and absolute principle of international law." 113 ILR 1, 43. See also *Trail Smelter Arbitration* (Canada/USA) 3 UNRIAA (1938) 1905 and *Orinoco Steamship Company* arbitration 11 UNRIAA (1910) 227.

[30]   See the ILA Interim Report, supra note 18.

[31]   The award of the first ICSID tribunal had been annulled save as to the findings on the armed taking of the hotel. *Amco Asia Corp v. Indonesia,* Decision on Annulment, 16 May 1986, 1 *ICSID Reports* 509.

[32]   In fact the tribunal identified the problem as being one of deciding

17-15 The *Amco* tribunal referred to the decision in *The Orinoco Steamship Company* case[33], which confirmed that

> [t]he general principle, announced in numerous cases is that a right, question, or fact distinctly put in issue and distinctly determined by a court of competent jurisdiction as a ground of recovery, cannot be disputed.

This essentially prescribes the triple identity test. Although the second tribunal in *Amco* still had to determine whether the reasoning of the ad hoc committee rather than the operative part of the award was also *res judicata*

> It is by no means clear that the basic trend in international law is to accept reasoning, preliminary or incidental determinations as part of what constitutes *res judicata*.[34]

The second tribunal therefore accepted that each determination (although not all of the reasoning) by the ad hoc committee were *res judicata*. Although they refused to allow Amco to raise matters decided by the first tribunal but not raised at the annulment stage. These remained binding on the parties as *res judicata* of the first award and could not be relitigated.

17-16 The scope and extent of the doctrine of *res judicata* can be problematic not just for international tribunals. The extent, for example, to which an arbitral tribunal should take into consideration an award rendered in a separate but connected arbitration was considered recently by the courts in England. The High Court had to decide whether a tribunal's findings on the application of certain provisions in a reinsurance contract were binding on a second arbitration. There was no identity of parties (only one party was involved in both arbitrations) in the case. Despite this, Toulson J noted that the House of Lords should determine the rules about the extent to which an award between A and B could be relied on by or against B in proceedings between B and C. He concluded that

---

> whether reasons of the ad hoc committee are to be treated as res judicata, even if that has the effect of rendering annulled parts of the Award as effectively closed off from redetermination.

Ibid, para 15. For the distinctions on the exact scope of the res judicata see the ILA Interim Report, supra note 18, Section C, p 16.

[33] Hague Court Reports (1916) 226.

[34] *Amco Asia Corp v. Indonesia,* Decision on Jurisdiction of May 10, 1988, 1 *ICSID Reports* 543, para 20. See also para 26

> So far as international law practice is concerned, authors have not been able to show a clear trend towards the acceptance of reasons as *res judicata*.

The modern tendency when tackling the diverse problems of serial litigation involving a common issue has been to move away from technical rules towards a broader consideration of what is fair. Thus the rules of *res judicata* and issue estoppel have been supplemented by the court's jurisdiction to strike out claims or defences where the issue has been previously determined, not necessarily between the same parties...[35]

This finding was overruled by the Court of Appeal.

2. Lis Pendens

17-17 *Lis pendens*, literally meaning "a suit pending," is a related doctrine aimed to prevent two judicial bodies dealing with the same dispute at the same time.[36] *Lis pendens* applies a stage earlier than *res judicata* where a judgment or award already exists. Similar policy consideration underlie the *lis pendens* doctrine, namely to prevent multiplicity of actions and to ensure "legal certainty."[37] *Lis pendens* therefore prevents the initiation of new proceedings on a matter if there is already an existing case pending before a court or tribunal. By refusing to hear a case it prevents the possibility of contradictory judgments. This is what the EC Regulation on Jurisdiction and the Recognition and Enforcement of Judgments in Civil and Commercial Matters seeks to prevent.

17-18 The EC Regulation provides that once a court is first seized of a dispute the other courts must stay proceedings relating to that dispute. Article 27(1) states:

Where proceedings involving the same cause of action and between the same parties are brought in the courts of different Member States, any court other than the court first seised shall of its own motion stay its proceedings until such time as the jurisdiction of the court first seised is established.[38]

---

[35] *Sun Life Assurance Company of Canada, American Phoenix Life and Reassurance Company, Phoenix Home Life Mutual Insurance Company v. The Lincoln National Life Insurance Company,* [2004] All ER (D) 429 para 92.

[36] Rolf Schütze, "*Lis Pendens* and Related Actions", 4(1) *European J of Law Reform* 57 (2002).

[37] Hans van Houtte, "Parallel Proceedings before State Courts and Arbitration Tribunals: Is there a Transnational *lis alibi pendens*-exception in Arbitration or Jurisdiction Conventions", in Pierre Karrer, Arbitral Tribunals or State Courts Who Must Defer to Whom? *ASA Special Series No.* 15 (2001) p 35.

[38] EC Council Regulation No. 44/2001 of 22 December 2000 on Jurisdiction and the Recognition and Enforcement of Judgments in Civil and Commercial Matters, OJ 2001 L 12, p 1. See for discussion Schütze, supra note 36.

Lis pendens imposes similar criteria as *res judicata* before it will apply: the same cause of action and the same parties.[39] Otherwise no stay of proceedings is required. There is no equivalent treaty at the global level providing for the 'first come first seised' rule. Of course the strict application of "*lis pendens* cannot resolve all problems."[40]

17-19 In the *Benvenuti & Bonfant* arbitration the ICSID tribunal had to consider its jurisdiction in light of the objections made by the Congolese Government based on *lis pendens*. The tribunal was not persuaded that it should relinquish the case to the Revolutionary Court of Justice as

> the pendency of a case was in order only in the event of the identity of the parties, of the subject matter, and of the cause of the suits pending before the two tribunals.[41]

In the *Fomento* case, the Swiss Supreme Court confirmed that an arbitral tribunal that had failed to stay proceedings pending the outcome of an appeal before Panamanian courts had violated Swiss public policy. The ICC tribunal should

> have complied with the principle of (international) litispendence, which also binds arbitral tribunals…[42]

17-20 The Committee on International Civil and Litigation at the ILA London Conference in 2000 noted that *lis pendens* was more a description of a problem, parallel litigation, rather than an approach towards solving it.[43]

> *Lis pendens* may be seen as part of a wider issue of related actions in international litigation…it is perhaps unfortunate that the issues raised by related actions have always been overshadowed by consideration of the

---

[39] See English High Court decision in *JP Morgan Europe Ltd v. Primacom AG* [2005] EWHC 508 where Cooke J. had to consider whether, for the purposes of Article 27 EC Regulation, the English and German proceedings involved "the same cause of action" (para 33). In concluding they were he had to order a stay of proceedings despite the existence of an exclusive jurisdiction clause in favour of the English Courts.

[40] Thalia Kruger, "The Anti-Suit Injunction in the European Judicial Space: *Turner v. Grovit*", 53(4) *ICLQ* 1030 (2004) at p 1036.

[41] *Benvenuti & Bonfant v. People's Republic of the Congo,* ICSID Case No. ARB/77/2, VIII YBCA 144 (1983).

[42] *Fomento de Construcciones y Contratas SA v. Colon Container Terminal SA,* Swiss Tribunal 14 May 2001, XXIX YBCA 809 (2004).

[43] Citing Fawcett 'General Report' in James J Fawcett (ed), Declining Jurisdiction in Private international law (Oxford 1995) 27 -43.

much stricter rules which may be necessary where the competing proceedings are on all fours with each other.[44]

The European Court of Justice has confirmed that *lis pendens* can only apply to a particular case where the parties are identical.[45]

17-21   Despite these formal requirements, tribunals do defer in certain circumstances. In the *MOX Plant* case, for example, the tribunal suspended the arbitration proceedings pending the outcome at the ECJ. The tribunal in the *Southern Bluefin Tuna* case also declined jurisdiction to consider the case brought by Australia and New Zealand against Japan. The tribunal constituted under Article 286 UNCLOS upheld the submission of Japan that the Convention on the Conservation of Southern Bluefin Tuna 1993 precluded compulsory jurisdiction for disputes arising under it and another treaty such as UNCLOS. However, the five member tribunal did confirm that a dispute could arise under more than one international treaty. The tribunal acknowledged that

> it is a commonplace of international law and State practice for more than one treaty to bear upon a particular dispute. There is no reason why a given act of a State may not violate its obligations under more than one treaty.[46]

However, in most instances it would seem that only one international body was ultimately seized of a particular dispute, until recently.

IV. APPLICATION OF DOCTRINES IN RECENT INTERNATIONAL CASES

17-22   The application of these legal principles is more problematic in international investor-state arbitration. Each tribunal is hermitically sealed deriving its jurisdiction from the relevant investment treaty. The parties may be the same, or related, but each action is based on a different treaty. In the *CME* arbitration, the Czech Government argued that the UNCITRAL tribunal sitting in Stockholm was bound by the findings of the UNCITRAL tribunal in London on liability for certain events. The London tribunal had dismissed Mr Lauder's claims in its final award of 3 September 2001. The Czech Government had submitted that the

---

[44]   ILA Report of the Sixty-Ninth Conference 25-29 July 2000 (ILA, 2000) p 143.

[45]   Case C-406/92, *Owners of the cargo lately laden on board the Tatry v. Owners of Maciej Rataj (The Tatry),* [1994] ECR I-5439.

[46]   *Southern Bluefin Tuna Case (Australia and New Zealand v. Japan)* Award on Jurisdiction and Admissibility, 4 August 2000, para 52 available at www.worldbank.org/icsid/bluefintuna/award080400.pdf.

multiplicity of proceedings amounted to an abuse of process that could result in different findings by the two treaty tribunals.

17-23 However, the London tribunal concluded that the claimant was entitled to initiate proceedings under the US/Czech Republic BIT so long as the dispute related to an investment within the meaning of that BIT. The tribunal affirmed that

> the Respondent's recourse to the principle of *lis alibi pendens* to be of no use, since all the other court and arbitration proceedings involve different parties and different causes of action.[47]

There was no abuse of process arising out of the multiple proceedings as the parties rights could only be protected under the BIT in those arbitral proceedings.[48] The CME tribunal in Stockholm similarly had the power to decide whether there had been a breach of the Dutch/Czech BIT.

17-24 The CME tribunal issued its partial award on liability on 13 September 2001, ten days after the London award. The tribunal rejected the respondent's assertions that the parallel proceedings were an abuse of process and not contemplated by the BIT. So long as there is an investment within the terms of the BIT, a claimant is free to pursue its claim. Thus,

> The argument of abusive Treaty shopping is not convincing. A party may seek its legal protection under any scheme provided by the laws of the host country. The Treaty as well as the US Treaty are part of the laws of the Czech Republic and neither of the treaties supersedes the other. Any overlapping of the results of parallel processes must be dealt with on the level of loss and quantum but not on the level of breach of treaty.[49]

17-25 The tribunal was not persuaded by the respondent's arguments that it should decline jurisdiction to hear the claims made by CME. The Czech Government had pointed out that the tribunal was:

---

[47] *Lauder v. Czech Republic* UNCITRAL Award, para 171.
[48] The London tribunal also noted that not only had Mr Lauder commenced the arbitration before the CME claims

> the Respondent itself did not agree to a de facto consolidation of the two proceedings by insisting on a different arbitral tribunal to hear CME's case.

Ibid at para 173.
[49] *CME v. Czech Republic* Partial Award, para 419.

faced with the danger of incompatible and ostensibly "final" decisions being made not only in the various Czech court proceedings but also by another tribunal set up under the US Treaty and by the ICC arbitral tribunal ruling between CME and Dr. Železný. This is precisely the prospect of disorder that the principle of lis alibi pendens is designed to avert.[50]

17-26 The tribunal confirmed its jurisdiction. The mere fact that another claim existed under a separate BIT, whether deriving from the same facts and circumstances or otherwise, did not deprive one of the claimants of jurisdiction, once jurisdiction was valid under the relevant BIT. Furthermore, the CME tribunal in its Final Award on quantum of 14 March 2003 rejected the submissions made by the Czech Republic on the *lis pendens* and *res judicata* effect of the London Award. The tribunal found that not only had they been waived but

> even disregarding the Respondent's waiver with regard to *lis pendens* and *res judicata*, the principle of *res judicata* cannot apply in relation to the London Award.[51]

It did not apply the principle of *res judicata* in this case because the requirements were not met. The parties were not identical, nor were the subject matter and cause of action the same. The two different BITs "create rights that are not in all respects exactly the same, different claims are necessarily formulated."[52]

17-27 The respondent challenged the CME partial award in Sweden and sought an adjournment of the arbitration proceedings pending the outcome in the Stockholm court.[53] The Svea Court of Appeal in its judgment on 15 May 2003 rejected the argument of the Czech Republic that notwithstanding that Mr Lauder and CME were not formally the same legal entity, they should be treated as the same party with respect to the issues of *lis pendens* and *res judicata*. Essentially, Mr Lauder and CME were just shareholders of CNTS at different levels of the chain. The Svea Court of Appeal instead found that the fact that the two cases were commenced under two different BITs "militates against these legal principles being applicable at all." Furthermore,

> With respect to piercing the corporate veil, no international cases have been presented in the case in which, in an actual situation of *lis pendens* and *res*

---

[50] *Ibid*, para 309.
[51] *CME v. Czech Republic* Final Award para 437.
[52] *Ibid*, para 433.
[53] Procedural Order regarding adjournment of arbitration pending annulment proceedings before a state court, *SchiedsVZ* 1/2004, p 56.

judicata, a controlling minority shareholder has been equated with the company.

According to Swedish law, one of the fundamental conditions for *lis pendens* and *res judicata* is that the same parties are involved in both cases. As far as is known, the same condition applies in other legal systems which recognize the principles in question. Identity between a minority share-holder, albeit a controlling one, and the actual company cannot, in the Court of Appeal's opinion, be deemed to exist in a case such the instant one [*sic*]. This assessment would apply even if one were to allow a broad determination of the concept of identity.[54]

So the respondent's submission was rejected because of a lack of identity of parties and secondly because the Czech Republic had waived its right to challenge on this ground The Svea Court of Appeal rejected the application of *lis pendens* and *res judicata* in this case because the conditions were not met.

17-28 In the more recent case of *SGS v. Pakistan*, the respondent challenged the tribunal's jurisdiction on the grounds of *lis pendens*, waiver and estoppel. Pakistan submitted that the contractual choice of forum should prevail

> where it broadly provides for mandatory arbitration of all disputes, the parties are identical, the claims for breach of the BIT include a pure claim for breach of contract, and the Claimant when it filed its ICSID request was already participating in contract arbitration proceedings with overlapping claims concerning the same facts and circumstances and seeking the same relief. As a result, the application of the *lis pendens* doctrine requires dismissal of the second proceeding.[55]

The *SGS v. Pakistan* panel noted that both tribunals in *Lauder v. Czech Republic* and *CME v. Czech Republic* case rejected the respondent's *lis pendens* submissions because they involved different parties and different causes of action (under different BITs).[56]

17-29 Pakistan also argued that as the claimant could have raised the alleged BIT breaches before the national court under the "general principles of *ne bis in*

---

[54] *Czech Republic v. CME Czech Republic BV*, Svea Court of Appeal Case no. T 8735-01, p 98, available at http://ita.law.uvic.ca/documents/CME2003-SveaCourtofAppeal_001.pdf; also at 42 ILM 919.

[55] *SGS v. Pakistan*, ICSID Case No. ARB/01/13, para 52, available at www.worldbank.org/icsid/cases/awards.htm.

[56] *Ibid* para 115 and note 134.

idem and *res judicata*, the fact that it did not do so is irrelevant."[57] The tribunal concluded that as it did not have jurisdiction over the purely contractual claims the:

> *lis pendens* doctrine has no application in this case. Pakistan asserted that the doctrine of *ne bis in idem* dictates a dismissal; however, if the claims are not *idem*, *bis* does not arise. As the causes of action are not identical, the doctrine of *lis pendens* cannot operate to preclude us from exercising jurisdiction over the BIT claims.[58]

17-30 A subsequent tribunal in the *SGS v. Philippines* case involving similar facts noted that:

> The ICSID Convention provides only that awards rendered under it are "binding on the parties" (Article 53(1)), a provision which might be regarded as directed to the *res judicata* effect of awards rather than their impact as precedents in later cases. In the tribunal's view, although different panels constituted under the ICSID system should in general seek to act consistently with each other, in the end it must be for each tribunal to exercise its competence in accordance with the applicable law, which will by definition be different for each BIT and each Respondent State.[59]

In the operative part of the SGS v. Pakistan award the tribunal withdrew its earlier order that the PSI Agreement arbitration be stayed.[60]

17-31 In the *Loewen* Decision on Respondent's Request for a Supplementary Decision the tribunal dismissed the contention that it had failed to deal with the claimant's Article 1116 claim. In its decision the tribunal affirmed that the

> dismissal was a consequence of the reasoning expressed in paras 213-216 … that reasoning was not merely "obiter dicta". It was the reasoning on

---

[57] *Ibid*, para 71.

[58] *Ibid*, para 182.

[59] *SGS v. Philippines,* http://ita.law.uvic.ca/documents/SGSvPhil-final_001.pdf, para 97. The tribunal in that case confirmed it had jurisdiction but stayed proceedings pending the determination on quantum by the local courts in accordance with the contract provisions.

[60] Supra note55, at para 190. See also the finding in *Plama Consortium Limited v. Bulgaria*, ICSID Case No. ARB/03/24 (Energy Charter Treaty). Decision on Jurisdiction, 8 February 2005. See, in particular, paras 136 and 181 on *res judicata* where "The Tribunal rejects the Respondent's application to suspend the proceedings pending the final outcome of the litigation concerning Dolsamex and Mr. O'Neill." Also para 240.

which that part of the Award was based and it is not open to the Tribunal to reconsider it.[61]

Thus the tribunal itself was prevented from reviewing the matter as it was *res judicata*. This is a clear example of the application of the strict rule of *res judicata*.

17-32 The application of the principle of *res judicata* arose in a recent award under the Energy Charter Treaty (ECT). In *Petrobart v. Kyrgyz Republic*[62] the tribunal constituted under the Stockholm Chamber of Commerce Rules rejected the arguments made by the Kyrgyz Government that the dispute was *res judicata*. There had been several previous actions arising out of a gas supply contract between Petrobart and a state owned company, KGM. First, the Kyrgyz Republic initiated domestic proceedings seeking a ruling from the Bishkek court that Petrobart had not made a foreign investment. The court by a decision of 26 December 2000 confirmed that no investment had in fact been made by Petrobart.[63] The second set or proceedings were initiated by Petrobart under the Foreign Investment Law of the Kyrgyz Republic in March 2000. However, in its award in 2003, the UNCITRAL tribunal declined jurisdiction. The tribunal concluded that Petrobart had not made an investment within the meaning of Article 1 paragraph 2 of the Foreign Investment Law.[64] Petrobart started proceedings under the ECT in September 2003.

17-33 It is not surprising in the circumstances that *res judicata* arguments were raised by the respondent state in the ECT proceedings. Why should they again defend the same case? There were already two separate decisions from a domestic court and an international tribunal that no foreign investment existed. However, in a very carefully drafted award the ECT tribunal rejected the submissions by the Kyrgyz Republic. The domestic court proceedings were dismissed by the tribunal as that process involved the interpretation and application of

---

[61] *The Loewen Group Inc and Raymond L Loewen v. USA,* ISCID Case No. ARB (AF)/98/3, paras 20-21.

[62] *Petrobart Limited v. Kyrgyz Republic*, SCC Arbitration No. 126/2003, 29 March 2005 available at http://ita.law.uvic.ca/documents/petrobart_kyrgyz.pdf.

[63] Petrobart did not participate in the proceedings before the Bishkek court as it had already commenced arbitration proceedings under the Foreign Investment Law by way of Arbitration Notice of 2 March 2000.

[64] Article 1 para 2 Foreign Investment Law provides "investments appearing as contributions of foreign investors into objects of economic activity in the territory." This was further explained in the Foreign Investment Interpretation Law promulgated on 30 May 2000.

Kyrgyz domestic law only, the ECT not being at issue in the case at all. Further, the ECT at Article 26 gives an investor but not a contracting state the right to commence proceedings. The domestic proceedings had been initiated by the State and could not thus be used to deprive an investor of his right to have his claim heard at the international level.

17-34 The UNCITRAL arbitration had been commenced by Petrobart but the ECT tribunal distinguished it as the claim was based on the Kyrgyz Foreign Investment Law and not the ECT. Thus the question of whether the respondent had violated its obligation under the ECT had not been considered before. The Kyrgyz Republic submitted that Petrobart ought to have raised the ECT claims before the UNCITRAL tribunal.[65] It argued that this could even have been done by way of concurrent proceedings

> since the claim would have been adjudicated efficiently, judicial/arbitral resources would have been preserved, and the Republic would have enjoyed finality.[66]

The ECT tribunal although holding that Petrobart could have raised its ECT claims before the UNCITRAL tribunal was not under any obligation to have done so. The ECT did not compel Petrobart

> to initiate proceedings ... at a particular time to conduct the arbitration jointly with other domestic or international proceedings...[67]

17-35 The government's submissions on collateral estoppel were also dismissed by the tribunal. As the UNCITRAL tribunal had not seised itself of the matter, the merits of the case were not *res judicata* even though the parties and the dispute were the same. Thus echoing the conclusion reached by the tribunal

---

[65] This rule is known in England as the rule in *Henderson v. Henderson* (1843) 3 Hare 100. Sir James Wigram V-C stated that

> The plea of *res judicata* applies, except in special cases, not only to points upon which the court was actually required by the parties to form an opinion and pronounce a judgment, but to every point which properly belonged to the subject of litigation, and which the parties, exercising reasonable diligence, might have brought forward at the time.

p 115. See for application of the rule *Talbot v. Berkshire County Council* [1994] QB 290.

[66] *Petrobart v. Kyrgyz Republic*, SCC Award, supra note 62, p 65.

[67] *Ibid*, p 66. The tribunal noted that the Kyrgyz Republic was not a Contracting Party listed in Annex ID which precludes parties from resubmitting the same dispute to international arbitration.

in the *Waste Management* award that a decision not dealing with the merits of a case

> even if it deals with issues of substance, does not constitute *res judicata* as to those merits.[68]

V. POSSIBLE SOLUTIONS TO THE CURRENT PROBLEM

17-36 This brief review of recent cases involving multiple proceedings reveals that *res judicata* and *lis pendens* are limited in application. Parallel proceedings (involving the same set of facts, the same or related parties, arising under different investment treaties) determined by individual tribunals fall outside the strict application of these legal doctrines. The large number of BITs in place increases the risk of duplication of proceedings in the future. Investors are now structuring their investments so as to be able to avail themselves of as many BITs as possible, for example, making an investment through a company incorporated in a state that already has a BIT with the host state. Thus ensuring it can rely on its provisions should it be necessary in the future.

17-37 Many believe that the need to identify ways to avoid such multiple proceedings "is likely to be a major challenge for investor-State arbitration in the near future."[69] Although in addressing the possibility of such multiple claims the Iran US Claims tribunal remarked

> As to the alleged risk that the Respondents could be subject to multiple liabilities, the Tribunal notes that, in any event, the principles of *res judicata* or estoppel would bar Amoco in most, if not all, legal systems, from successfully prosecuting a claim, the merits of which have been finally determined by this Tribunal.[70]

17-38 In international commercial arbitration party autonomy is paramount. Parties can include in their contracts a provision expressly dealing with joinder and consolidation of related claims. In complex multiparty arbitration, e.g., in

---

[68] *Waste Management, Inc v. United Mexican States* (Number 2), ICSID Case No. ARB(AF)/00/3 Award on Jurisdiction , June 26, 2002 para 43.

[69] Bernardo Cremades and David Cairns, "Contract and Treaty Claims and Choice of Forum in Foreign Investment Disputes", in Norbert Horn (ed), *Arbitrating Foreign Investment Disputes: Procedural and Substantive Legal Aspects* (Kluwer, 2004), 332.

[70] Iran-US Claims Tribunal, Case No. 56 (Chamber Three) Award No. 310-56-3, Partial Award, 14 July 1987, para 18.

large construction contracts where there are many different parties (contractor, sub-contractors, owners, operators,) there is often a protocol to the main agreement setting out in detail the consent of all parties to arbitrate disputes in one set of proceedings.[71] This avoids having a string of related arbitral proceedings going on at the same time under the various contracts essentially relating to the same set of facts. However, this is not the case in investor state arbitration. It is possible that there could be parallel proceedings between, e.g., the government and the main contractor, a shareholder and the government; thus increasing the risk of "incompatible determinations of fact and liability."[72]

17-39 In *CMS v. Argentina,* the tribunal confirmed jurisdiction to hear a claim brought by a minority shareholder of Transportadora de Gas del Norte (TGN) a gas transportation company. The tribunal noted that ICSID

has made every effort possible to avoid a multiplicity of tribunals and jurisdictions, but that it is not possible to foreclose rights that different investors might have under different arrangements. The Tribunal also notes that, while it might be desirable to recognize similar rights to domestic and foreign investors, this is seldom possible in the present state of international law in this field. Finally, it is not for the Tribunal to rule on the perspectives of the negotiation process or on what TGN might do in respect of its shareholders, as these are matters between Argentina and TGN or between TGN and its shareholders.[73]

Essentially the possibility of a large number of cases against the same state arising out of the same circumstances was not for that tribunal to remedy. It could only decide on the jurisdiction and merits of the claim under the terms of the relevant BIT.

17-40 It is clear therefore, that

---

[71] See Paul Friedland, *Arbitration Clauses for International Contracts* (Juris Publishing, 2000), Chapters 6-8 and Annex 27 on Multi-party Contracts.

[72] John Collier & Vaughan Lowe, *The Settlement of Disputes in International Law* (OUP, 2000) 262. See also Jean-Louis Devolvé, "Final Report on Multiparty Arbitrations of the ICC Commission on International Arbitration", 6(1) *ICC Bulletin* 24 (1995); Patrice Level, "Joinder of Proceedings, Intervention of Third Parties and Additional Claims and Counterclaims", 7(2) *ICC Bulletin* 36 (1996); and Douglas Reichert, "Problems with Parallel and Duplicate Proceedings: The Litispendence Principle and International Arbitration", 8 *Arb Int* 237 (1992).

[73] *CMS Gas Transmission Company v. Argentina,* ICSID Case No. ARB/01/8. Award on Jurisdiction, 17 July 2003, para 86, 42 ILM 788 (2003) online at www.asil.org/ilib/cms-argentina.pdf.

Investor-State arbitration differs fundamentally from traditional international commercial arbitration in that its basis lies in treaties between states (either multilateral or bilateral), rather than in private agreements.[74]

This lack of privity between the parties makes it difficult for a state to preclude or revise (to provide for consolidation) the dispute resolution options in a BIT with individual investors.[75] A number of possible solutions to this problem have been suggested including

(i)   a more robust/flexible application of the legal doctrines;
(ii) drafting new BITs to expressly exclude such eventualities;
(iii) drafting a new multilateral treaty to deal with the matter;
(iv) consolidation/joinder of related claims and
(v)   the creation of a standing appellate body for investment disputes.

17-41   (i) It has been suggested that perhaps a more flexible application of the legal principles to investor state arbitration would solve the problem. The principles of

> *res judicata* and *lis pendens* have the potential to be flexibly applied in order to serve their ultimate object and purpose to avoid multiplication of proceedings.[76]

To achieve this end the focus must be on issues and facts rather than on the parties involved. This might prevent the Czech and Petrobart multiple proceedings as the issues and facts were the same but the basis of the claims were different. Yet this surely is changing the nature of the existing legal doctrines and could lead to even greater uncertainty. The Svea Court of Appeal was not prepared to entirely disregard one of the central tenets of the *res judicata* doctrine in its decision upholding the CME partial award. It concluded that even allowing for a broad determination of the concept it would still reach the same conclusion.

17-42   In England, the more robust approach adopted by the High Court in *Sun Life v. Lincoln Insurance* was completely rejected by the Court of Appeal. The case dealt with the extent to which an award on the interpretation of a reinsurance

---

[74] Cremades and Cairns, supra note 69, at 339.
[75] See, e.g., *Azurix Corp v. Argentina,* ICSID Case No. ARB/01/12, at www.worldbank.org/icsid, where an express waiver in a concession agreement of all fora other than that agreed to in the contract was held not to preclude the claimant's treaty claim. Perhaps a more robustly drafted waiver clause would remedy this finding and provide states with a way of limiting future BIT arbitrations in concession agreements.
[76] Reinisch, supra note 17, at p 77.

contract between A and B was binding on B in a second arbitration between B and C. The High Court acknowledged that the policy issue should be determined by the House of Lords, that is, the extent of the binding nature of the first award over the second tribunal. It concluded that there had been a move away from the strict application of technical rules in multiple litigation. This pragmatic or flexible approach was entirely rejected by the Court of Appeal. Lord Justice Mance in his comments on *res judicata* started out with "some basic propositions. The principles of *res judicata* and issue estoppel apply between parties to the original proceedings or their privies."[77] There was no foundation in legal principle to extend the doctrine in this way. The Court of Appeal were unmoved by arguments based on "general justice."[78] In view of the reasoning of the tribunals in the CME and Lauder awards it is unlikely that such a flexible approach will be adopted by an international panel either.

17-43 (ii) The format of BITs could be changed to expressly preclude multiple proceedings. It was noted in the CME partial award that

> Treaty proceedings are barred by civil law proceedings only if the respective investment treaty contains such a provision. Modern bilateral investment treaties usually do not contain judicial limitations like that.[79]

States currently negotiating the terms of BITs could include provisions precluding more than one arbitration being commenced relating to the same circumstances. Essentially the commercial relations between states and private investors (individuals or corporate entities) are governed by a plethora of investment treaties. These treaties are intended to encourage foreign direct investment while allegedly protecting the interests of both the capital importing and capital exporting state. These instruments create

> an enforceable right to damages via international arbitration in the event that investors can prove breaches of a few, basic and long-established international standards for the treatment of foreign investment.[80]

---

[77] *Sun Life Assurance Company of Canada, American Phoenix Life and Reassurance Company, Phoenix Home Life Mutual Insurance Company v. The Lincoln National Life Insurance Company* [2004] All ER(D) 171 para 53.

[78] *Ibid*, para 66.

[79] *CME v. Czech Republic* Partial Award, para 409.

[80] Para 42, Affidavit of J. Crawford submitted in Support of the Respondent, 15 July 2004, in *Council of Canadians and CUPW v. Attorney General of Canada*, Ontario Superior Court of Justice, File No. 01-CV-208141, 8 July, 2005 available online at www.dfait-maeci.gc.ca/tna-nac/disp/cupw_archive-en.asp.

It remains to be seen whether states will perceive the risk of parallel proceedings like the Czech Republic cases as sufficient incentive to change the existing format of BITs.

17-44 Any new provision would require careful consideration to ensure it effectively precludes all such possibilities. Historically, the procedural issues of the dispute resolution options in a BIT were not set out in any great detail. This has changed somewhat in the more recent Model BITs, for example the USA and Canada. The ECT does have an express provision that allows contracting states to prohibit the possibility of an investor from taking multiple claims. This qualified consent is set out in Article 26 (3)(b)(i) and provides,

> The Contracting Parties listed in Annex ID do not give such unconditional consent where the Investor has previously submitted the dispute under subparagraph (2)(a) or (b).

Where (a) and (b) are national courts or tribunals and previously agreed dispute resolution options respectively. Less than half the signatory states availed of this option.[81] Clearly it would have prevented the multiple proceedings taken against the Kyrgyz Republic by Petrobart.

17-45 (iii) The creation of a new comprehensive multilateral investment treaty has been suggested as a means of dealing with the potential inconsistencies in investment arbitrations. The exact form and content of this treaty has not been set out. It is, however, rather unlikely given the failure to reach agreement on the terms of the Multilateral Agreement on Investment at the OECD for there to be any real hope of a single unifying treaty for investment arbitration. There seems to be little political appetite for a further international treaty.

17-46 (iv) The possibility of joinder or consolidation is often the first suggestion made on how to prevent multiple proceedings. Although joinder may be one way of eliminating the possibility of parallel proceedings in international arbitration, consent is an issue. Most national legal systems require the consent of both parties to order consolidation.[82] The Dutch Civil Code allows for consolidation to

---

[81] ECT and Annexes available at www.encharter.org.

[82] Netherlands is an exception: see Dutch Code of Civil Procedure, section 1046 included after much lobbying from the construction industry. It provides that if an arbitration is commenced and concerns

> a subject matter which is connected with the subject matter of arbitral proceedings commenced before another arbitral tribunal in the Netherlands, any of the parties may,

be ordered by the district court if the arbitrations have the same subject matter. There does not have to be identity of parties. Obviously, the court has the discretion on whether or not to order consolidation. However, unless parties agree to consolidate, the courts in nearly every major jurisdiction will refuse to order consolidation of arbitrations arising under separate contracts. The result is that if proceedings

> cannot be consolidated, there is a risk that several proceedings are conducted in parallel and the common elements of the dispute are decided in a conflicting manner.[83]

17-47 In *Sun Life* the Court of Appeal noted that arbitration was a consensual, private process.

> The resulting inability to enforce the solutions of joinder of parties or proceedings in arbitration, or to try connected arbitrations together other than by consent, is well-recognised ... Different arbitrations on closely inter-linked issues may as a result lead to different results, even where, as in the present case, the evidence before one tribunal is very largely the same as that before the other. The arbitrators in each arbitration are appointed to decide the disputes in that arbitration between the particular parties to that arbitration.[84]

Although in the Court's view this problem does not seem to have affected the popularity of arbitration. The same problem exists in investor-state arbitration.

17-48 At the international level some investment treaties have made provision for consolidation by the tribunal. In NAFTA, for example, where more than one investor is taking a claim against a contracting party based on the same event, a tribunal may order consolidation "in the interests of fair and efficient resolution of the claims."[85] This provision is seen as one of the more radical innovations of

---

unless the parties have agreed otherwise, request the President of the District Court in Amsterdam to order a consolidation of the proceedings.

Jan Paulsson (ed), *ICCA International Handbook on Commercial Arbitration,* Suppl 7 (April 1987) 1.

[83] Michael Schneider, "Multi-Fora Disputes", 6(2) *Arb Int* 101 (1990) at p 111.

[84] *Sun Life v. The Lincoln National Life* [2004] All ER(D) 171, para 68.

[85] Article 1126, North American Free Trade Agreement. Text available on the NAFTA Secretariat site at www.nafta-sec-alena.org. The US Model BIT has a similar provision at Article 33 allowing a tribunal to decide whether there are claims that "have a question of law or fact in common and arise out of the same events or circumstances..." See also the Group of Three (Columbia, Mexico & Venezuela) Free Trade Agreement which also provides for consolidation provided one party will not be prejudiced. Both texts available at www.sice.oas.org.

the NAFTA regime. The tribunal that decides whether the cases should be consolidated is appointed by the ICSID Secretary-General. The tribunal can if it deems consolidation necessary, assume jurisdiction over one or all of the claims.[86] Such a provision may have been helpful to Argentina in dealing with the multiple ICSID cases currently pending against it.

17-49 The majority of these cases arise out of the same set of circumstances, namely the decision of the Argentine government to address their currency imbalance by devaluation in 1999. In addition, they changed certain existing arrangements in many concession contracts where repayment was pegged to the dollar. Although, the ICSID arbitration rules have no provision for joinder of related arbitration cases, one set of proceedings involving Argentina has already been consolidated. The tribunal having sufficient discretion to do so once all parties consented. In contrast, the Czech Republic did not consent to have the cases consolidated or heard concurrently by the same tribunal, despite requests to do so.

17-50 Concurrent hearings are a less formal, though equally effective way of avoiding conflicting awards. Basically the same tribunal would hear all of the claims arising out of the same set of circumstances. There were, for example, three arbitrations filed at ICSID on 17 July 2003 relating to disputes over a concession contract for water supply and sewage services. The same tribunal members have been appointed in all cases.[87] The claims are being brought by foreign shareholders under BITS between Argentina and each of France, Spain and the UK. The same tribunal is also sitting in an ad hoc case under UNCITRAL administered by ICSID being brought by Anglian Water Group. Nominating the same tribunal eliminates the likelihood of obtaining conflicting

---

[86] See Order of the Consolidation Tribunal, 7 September 2005 where the NAFTA consolidation tribunal ordered the consolidation of the Canadian soft wood lumber companies claims (*Canfor Corporation, Tembec Investments and Terminal Forest Products Limited*) against the USA. This was the first successful application for consolidation of parallel investor – state arbitrations under NAFTA. An earlier decision by the first ever NAFTA consolidation tribunal had rejected Mexico's application to have the two arbitrations commenced by producers of sweetener used in soft drinks *(Corn Products International and ADM - Archer Daniels Midlands Company)* and *Tate & Lyle)* merged. See Order of the Consolidation Tribunal, 20 May 2005. Both texts are available online at www. naftaclaims.com

[87] *Aguas Provinciales de Santa Fe SA, Suez, Sociedad General de Aguas de Barcelona SA and Interagua Servicios Integrales de Agua, SA v. Argentina*, ICSID Case No. ARB/03/17; *Aguas Cordobesas, SA, Suez, and Sociedad General de Aguas de Barcelona, SA v. Argentina*, ICSID Case No. ARB/03/18 and *Aguas Argentinas SA, Suez, Sociedad General de Aguas de Barcelona, SA and Vivendi Universal, SA v. Argentina*, ICSID Case No. ARB/03/19.

awards. It may not always be possible for the parties to agree to such measures. Party autonomy being paramount in international arbitration the choice of arbitrator can not be imposed save in certain limited circumstances.

17-51   (v) Finally, another option to try to address parallel proceedings is the possibility of creating a single appellate body for investment treaty claims. In the Centre's Working Paper on Possible Improvements of the Framework for ICSID Arbitration[88], Section VI draws attention to the fact that states are currently entering into investment treaties that actually refer to a future appellate body.[89] The ICSID paper predicts that

> By mid-2005, as many as 20 countries may have signed treaties with provisions on an appeal mechanism for awards rendered in investor-to-State arbitrations under the treaties. Most of these countries are also Contracting States of the ICSID Convention.[90]

In the interests of consistency, coherence and economy ICSID are considering creating a single appeal mechanism to avoid a multiplicity of appellate bodies under various bilateral or multilateral treaties. However, the mere existence of such a body would not necessarily of itself do away with the possibility of an investor being able to initiate claims under different BITs. And it appears that the prediction was not proven right.

17-52   The creation of such an appellate body is still some way off. In the second Working Paper of 12 May 2005 on Suggested Changes to the ICSID Rules and Regulations there was

> general agreement that, if international appellate procedures were to be introduced for investment treaty arbitrations, then this might best be done

---

[88]   Copy available at www.worldbank.org/icsid/improve-arb.pdf.

[89]   See Article 28(10)US Model BIT of 15 September 2004 which essentially confirmed that should a multilateral treaty set up an investment appellate body the parties will try to reach agreement that this body would be able to review awards rendered under the BIT. Text available at www.state.gov/documents/organization/38710.pdf. As to whether the US would be more willing to accept decisions from such an appellate body rather that the ICJ remains to be seen. See most recently *Avena Case (Mexico v. USA)* ICJ 2004 discussed in Aceves, "Consular Notification and the Death Penalty: The ICJ's Judgment in Avena", *ASIL Insights* (April 2004) at www.asil.org.

[90]   ICSID Secretariat Discussion Paper on Possible Improvements Of The Framework For ICSID Arbitration, 22 October 2004, para 20.

through a single ICSID mechanism rather than by different mechanisms established under each treaty concerned.[91]

However the consensus seems to be that this option would be premature. A standing appellate body would essentially act in a similar way to the International Court of Justice (ICJ). Although even the ICJ Statute at Article 59 provides that:

> The decision of the Court has no binding force except between the parties and in respect of that particular case.[92]

So the judgment is *res judicata* only as been the parties to the dispute which still would not preclude the Czech type cases.

VI. CONCLUSION

17-53   It is without doubt that the "process of choosing the most advantageous forum for a particular suit is a universal one."[93] If it is opportune to choose two available fora this will also be true. In truth, commercial reality often dictates against pursuing multiple proceeding against a respondent.

17-54   The principles of *res judicata* and *lis pendens* are well recognised principles of international law. The concepts necessary to fulfilling the *res judicata* doctrine

> final judgment, identity of object, identity of parties, and identity of cause raise a host of subsidiary questions[94]

The same is also true for *lis pendens*. It appears from a review of recent cases, that they only go so far in addressing the *CME/Lauder* phenomenon. The risk of different, though possibly related, entities taking multiple claims based on similar facts under separate BIT persists. Whether the prediction that these types of cases will erode the integrity of international arbitration remains to be seen.

17-55   There are several options that might in the future successfully reduce the risk of conflicting awards in such parallel proceedings. The most likely to succeed is the adoption of a new form of BIT expressly precluding such multiple proceedings similar to the ECT. Alternatively, new treaties might provide for

---

[91]   ICSID Secretariat Working Paper on Suggested Changes to the ICSID Rules and Regulations, 12 May 2005, para 4. Available at www.worldbank.org/icsid/052405-sgmanual.pdf.

[92]   At www.icj-cij.org/icjwww/ibasicdocuments/ibasictext/ibasicstatute.htm#CHAPTER_III.

[93]   ILA Report of the Sixty-Ninth Conference 25-29 July 2000 (ILA, 2000) p 140 para 9.

[94]   Theofanis, supra note 23, at p 207.

consolidation of such multiple claims like NAFTA. In the meantime under the existing regime of investment treaties parties involved could do worse than resort to a more pragmatic triple test of common sense, courtesy and commercial reality.

*Stefan M. Kröll**

CHAPTER 18

ARBITRATION AND INSOLVENCY PROCEEDINGS – SELECTED PROBLEMS

I. INTRODUCTION

18-1 Arbitration is predicated on the principles of party autonomy and privity. It is received wisdom that "arbitration is simply a matter of contract between the parties"[1] and therefore "a party can be forced to arbitrate only those issues it specifically has agreed to submit to arbitration."[2] Consequently no third party can join or be joined to an arbitration unless the parties to the arbitration agreement have consented to the joinder.[3]

18-2 The principles of party autonomy and privity collide head on with these governing insolvency law in cases where one of the parties to the arbitration agreement files for bankruptcy. In general insolvency regimes are based on a system of ranking the claims and guaranteeing to the greatest extent possible equal treatment among members of each class of creditors. This implies that individual claims become part of a (single) collective proceeding and may no longer be brought outside the insolvency proceedings. In light of these particular features of the insolvency regimes a US Court has held that under the relevant U.S. legislation, the relation of arbitration and insolvency law

---

* Dr iur, LLM, Rechtsanwant, Cologne; German national correspondent to UNCITRAL for arbitration.
[1] US Supreme Court, *First Options Chicago Inc v. Kaplan et al*, 514 US 938, 943, 115 S Ct 1920, 1924 (1995).
[2] *Ibid.* 1925.
[3] See Julian D M Lew/Loukas Mistelis/Stefan Kröll, *Comparative International Commercial Arbitration* (Kluwer Law International, 2003), para. 16-30.

Loukas A. Mistelis and Julian D.M. Lew (eds), Pervasive Problems in International Arbitration, 357-376
© 2006 Kluwer Law International. Printed in the Netherlands

presents a conflict of near polar extremes: bankruptcy policy exerts an inexorable pull towards centralization while arbitration policy advocates a decentralized approach towards dispute resolution."[4]

18-3 Insolvency law has been very aptly described as "a crossroad where all the elements of the Legal System in question meet."[5] How the "traffic" between the various elements – in our case arbitration and insolvency law – is regulated, in particular which element must give way depends in the end on the decisions by the national legislator in each country. However, there are some common features in the various insolvency laws which allow to at least delineate the potential problems which may arise in trying to reconcile the conflicting premises of arbitration and insolvency law.

18-4 Given the breadth of the topic addressed, this contribution focuses primarily on disputes arising in connection with contracts containing arbitration agreements that were entered into prior to the insolvent party's bankruptcy filing. Such "contract disputes" include claims brought against the insolvent party which are contested either as to their existence or quantum, actions to include or exclude assets from the estate, and claims brought by the insolvent party against another party. Arbitration agreements concluded after the filing for insolvency are not addressed,[6] nor are the so-called "pure" or "stricto sensu"[7] bankruptcy disputes. Despite different terminology, the latter category of dispute consists of administrative matters pertaining to the insolvency proceedings themselves, such as the opening of the proceedings, the appointment of the trustee or the actual distribution of the assets. The purpose of such proceedings is not the settlement of disputes between the parties, but rather the collective execution or reorganization of the debtor.

---

[4] *In re United States Lines, Inc*, 197 F 3d 631, 640 (2d Cir 1999), cert. denied, 120 S Ct 1532 (2000) (citing *In re Distrigas Corp*, 80 BR 606, 610 (D Mass 1987)). For the different starting points of arbitration and insolvency see also Philippe Fouchard, "Arbitrage et faillite", *Rev Arb* 1998, 471, 473.

[5] Didier, "La Problématique du droit de la faillite internationale/The Problems Surrounding the Law of International Insolvency", 3 *RDAI/IBLJ* 201 (1989), 203.

[6] For such agreements see Vesna Lazić, *Insolvency Proceedings and Commercial Arbitration*, (Kluwer Law International, 1998), 107 et seq.; Fouchard, supra note 4, 471, 492 et seq.

[7] The terminology is not used consistently and often these disputes are also called "core" bankruptcy disputes. In particular the term "core" disputes may also covers some varieties of non-administrative contract claims, as is for example the case in the US.

II. OVERVIEW OF THE BASIC PRINCIPLES AND FEATURES OF INSOLVENCY LAW

18-5 The purpose of insolvency law is to provide a workable framework for dealing with the competing interests and claims involved where the debtor lacks sufficient means to fulfil all its obligations. The objectives pursued in the various legal systems differ and depend to a great extent also on the type of proceeding envisaged. In reorganization proceedings survival of the undertaking and maintaining employment are of primary importance. By contrast in liquidation proceedings the main focus is on securing (at least partial) satisfaction of the creditors.[8] How the often contradictory interests are balanced is a political and social choice to be made by each national legislator.[9]

18-6 Notwithstanding the many differences existing among the various national insolvency laws, however, two common features can be observed, i.e., rules are intended (a) to maximize the value of the estate and (b) to ensure an equal treatment of creditors in the same class. To attain these objectives, limits are imposed on the contractual freedom of the debtor and the creditors and certain alterations are made to the general contract law. In accordance with these shared aims, a number of substantive and procedural tools are commonly encountered in the national insolvency regulations.

18-7 First, the debtor is usually deprived of the right to manage and to dispose of the estate upon commencement of liquidation proceedings.[10] These rights are usually vested in the trustee.[11] As a consequence the debtor no longer has the right to bind the estate and loses the right to sue and be sued in legal proceedings concerning the estate.[12] Second, jurisdiction over all claims concerning the estate is vested in a single court and the right of the parties to bring claims in different

---

[8] For an overview of the various objectives pursued by the national insolvency laws see for Germany: § 1 InsO; for France, Art L 620-1; for further examples see Lazić, supra note 6, 12 et seq.

[9] Vesna Lazić, "Arbitration and Insolvency Proceedings, Claims of Ordinary Bankruptcy Creditors", 3(3) *EJCL* 2 (December 1999); Laurent Lévy, "Insolvency in Arbitration (Swiss Law)", 8 *Int ALR* 23 (2005).

[10] E.g. Germany, §§ 80 et seq. InsO; for further examples Lazić, supra note 6, 36 et seq.

[11] In defining its scope of application in Article 1(1), EC Regulation 1346/2000 on Insolvency Proceedings considers "the partial or total divestment of a debtor and the appointment of a liquidator" to be the key features of the so-called "collective insolvency proceedings".

[12] In reorganization proceedings the debtor often retains the right to manage the estate or is only limited in certain regards; see, for example, US Chapter 11, 11 USCA sections 1107-1174.

courts is limited, in order to ensure a collective procedure.[13] In this regard, existing proceedings may be stayed[14] or even transferred to the court that has general jurisdiction over the insolvency. Third, the trustee is given special powers to increase the value of the estate by challenging pre-filing transactions by the debtor. Security interest may be invalidated,[15] preferential pre-filing payments and fraudulent transfers may be avoided,[16] and the transfer of property may be challenged if it was made shortly before filing. Furthermore, the trustee has the prerogative to decide whether to take up or terminate existing contracts that are still executory, i.e. not yet fully executed.

III. POSSIBLE AREAS OF CONFLICT

18-8 The initiation or continuation of arbitration proceedings to which the insolvent debtor is a party may run afoul of a number of the above features and provisions of the applicable insolvency laws. The basic rule found in most national systems is that in cases involving a *true* conflict between the insolvency provisions and arbitration the former will prevail. The general interests protected by insolvency law are considered to override the individual interests protected by arbitration.[17]

18-9 The clearest case of a true conflict between arbitration and insolvency exist when the execution of an award is at issue. The execution of an award in favour of one creditor would satisfy the claim of that creditor while simultaneously diminishing the value of remaining estate and thereby other creditors' chances to receive payment.

18-10 However, depending on the applicable provisions and the scope of the principle of equal treatment a conflict may already arise at a much earlier stage. The existence of a title against the debtor may result in elevating a formerly unsecured creditor into a different class of creditors entitled to preferential treatment. While this would improve the chances of this creditor to see its claims satisfied, it would also reduce the amount available for distribution to the unsecured creditors. In addition, arbitration proceedings cost money. As this money

---

[13] France: Art L 621-40 Code de Commerce (ex Art 47, L 25 Jan. 1985); Fouchard, supra note 4, 471, 475 et seq.; Germany, §§ 2, 3, 87 InsO; Lazić, supra note 6, 38.

[14] Germany, § 240 ZPO (Code of Civil Procedure).

[15] E.g. 11 USCA § 544.

[16] E.g. 11 USC § 547(b) (2000), 11 USCA § 548.

[17] See Fouchard, supra note 4, 471, 474 et seq.

has to come from the estate, one could even argue that already the mere initiation of arbitration proceedings affects the principles to be protected by the insolvency law.[18]

18-11   The effects and consequences flowing from these potential conflicts differ, depending on the national insolvency law and the specific limits it imposes on party autonomy.

18-12   First, the various provisions of the applicable insolvency law may already affect the jurisdiction of the arbitral tribunal in several respects. They may either exclude the arbitrability of the dispute in question, limit the capacity of the actors involved to be a party to the arbitration agreement, or render the arbitral agreement not binding on the trustee who has not signed it.

18-13   Second, even where the general jurisdiction of the tribunal is not affected, the insolvency provisions may have a bearing on the conduct of the proceedings. New parties in form of the trustee or the other creditors may have to be included in the proceedings, procedural steps may have to repeated, new rights to challenge the tribunal may arise or the proceedings may be halted for some time to give the trustee time to familiarize with the case.

18-14   The third potential area where the insolvency provisions may affect arbitration proceedings relates to the remedies available to the tribunal. The tribunal might be limited to the rendering of declaratory awards, if payment orders or order for specific performance are excluded.

IV. THE BINDING FORCE OF INSOLVENCY PROVISIONS FOR COURTS AND TRIBUNALS

18-15   The preceding sketch of potential conflicts demonstrates that questions as to the influence of the insolvency of a party on arbitration may arise at various stages of the proceedings and in different factual settings. For example, the issue of the tribunal's jurisdiction may arise before a bankruptcy court where the trustee tries to bring a claim against one of the creditors who then invokes the existence of the arbitration agreement as a bar to the proceedings.[19] Courts may also have to deal with questions concerning the arbitral tribunal's jurisdiction

---

[18]   See for this aspect the decision of the Hong Kong Court of First Instance in *Re UDL Contracting Ltd*, [2000] 1 HKC 390.

[19]   See *Hays & Co v. Merrill Lynch, Pierce, Fenner & Smith, Inc* 885 F.2d 1149 (3rd Cir 1989).

when asked to appoint arbitrators or at the post award stage, when the lack of a valid arbitration agreement is invoked as a defence in setting aside or enforcement proceedings. In addition, the issue of the arbitral tribunal's jurisdiction may arise before a tribunal that has to decide on its own jurisdiction when it has been challenged by one of the parties – in general the trustee – in arbitral proceedings initiated by the other side.[20]

18-16 When the tribunal's jurisdiction or other questions raised by the filing for insolvency arise before a court in the country where the insolvency proceedings were initiated, the court will apply its insolvency law in so far as its provisions are mandatory and supersede the otherwise applicable provisions of the relevant arbitration law. On the other hand, when such questions arise before a court outside the country of insolvency, the application of the insolvency law depends on the relevant conflict of laws rules in that court. In general, courts will not apply the foreign insolvency law, absent an exequatur of the foreign court decision opening the insolvency proceedings.[21]

18-17 Unlike courts, the arbitral tribunal is not part of a judicial system of any given country. It owes its allegiance only – or at least primarily – to the parties. In particular, when the place of arbitration is outside the country of insolvency and a different law is applicable to the merits, the arbitral tribunal is faced with the question of whether to honour the restrictions imposed by the relevant insolvency law or not. This involves a balancing of the various interests involved and the repercussions a deviation from mandatory provisions may have on the enforceability of an award. In light of the likelihood that arbitral tribunals will not consider themselves bound by a given national insolvency law some states try to enforce their mandatory insolvency law provisions, in particular the mandatory stay of any other proceedings, by injunctions enjoining the parties or even the arbitrators from taking any further steps in the arbitration.[22]

---

[20] For the various stages where the jurisdiction of the tribunal may be challenged see Lew/Mistelis/ Kröll, supra note 3, paras 14-2 et seq.

[21] See, for example, the French view in Cour d'appel de Paris, 12 January 1993, *République de Côte-d'Ivoire et autres c Société Norbert Beyrard et autres,* Rev Arb 1994, 685, 690 et seq.; for Germany see Oberlandesgericht Düsseldorf, 18 July 1997, XXIVa *YBCA* 303 (1999).

[22] See, for example, US Court of Appeal 4th Cir. *In Re White Mountain Mining Company, LLC,* No. 04-1586, 1 April 2005.

V. Effects of the Exclusive Jurisdiction and Mandatory Stay Provisions on Arbitration

18-18   The provisions on exclusive jurisdiction of the bankruptcy court and the mandatory stay of all other proceedings generate the most obvious conflicts between arbitration and insolvency law. They are meant to ensure a collective procedure guaranteeing equal treatment of all creditors and are therefore often considered to be part of national and international public policy.[23] The relevant provisions of the national insolvency law often contain merely a general order for the stay of legal proceedings without explicitly mentioning arbitration proceedings. Nevertheless it is clear also in these legal systems that the restrictions involved in the stay of proceedings should in general also apply to arbitration.[24] Consequently the question arises whether these mandatory stay provisions do not generally exclude post-filing arbitrations with the original debtor rendering the disputes to be non-arbitrable.

18-19   The denial of arbitrability, however, is only the most dramatic possible means for a court to enforce the mandatory stay provision *vis-à-vis* arbitration and many countries have provided for different and less severe means to fulfil the purpose underlying the mandatory stay provisions.

1. The Effects on Objective Arbitrability

18-20   Whether and to what extent the public interests involved and the restrictions imposed by the national insolvency laws restrict the arbitrability of a dispute is a question to be determined by each national legislator. Neither the New York Convention nor any other international instrument contains any substantive rules on objective arbitrability. Quite to the contrary, such instruments always explicitly refer the question of arbitrability to the national legislator. Under the New York Convention, for example, the obligation in Article II to recognize and enforce arbitration agreements in writing only exists with respect to agreements concerning a "subject matter capable of settlement by arbitration". The general freedom for the national legislator to define which disputes are arbitrable becomes even more obvious if one looks at Art V(2)(a). It provides that the obligation to recognize and enforce an award does not exist if "the subject matter of the difference is not capable of settlement by arbitration under the law of that country."

---

[23]   Cour de cassation, 5 February 1991, *Société Almira Films v. Pierrel*, Rev Arb 1991, 625, 627.
[24]   See for France, Fouchard, supra note 4, 471, 476.

(a) The American View: Limitations on Objective Arbitrability

18-21   In the U.S. the question of arbitrability of a claim generally arises in the context of an application by a creditor to grant relief from the mandatory stay under section 362 US Bankruptcy Code. According to section 362(a), the filing of a petition in bankruptcy results in a broad stay of litigation and other proceedings against the debtor and the debtor's property. While arbitration is not expressly mentioned in section 362(a), it is clear from the legislative materials that the stay also extends to arbitration proceedings.[25] Consequently the question of arbitrability of a dispute generally arises within the context of an application to the bankruptcy courts to lift this mandatory stay and refer the parties to arbitration. Section 362(d)(1) of the Bankruptcy Code provides that the bankruptcy court shall grant relief from the stay "for cause", without however defining the notion of "cause". The existence of an arbitration agreement could constitute such a "cause" if the dispute is arbitrable.

18-22   The relevant test for the arbitrability of a dispute can be found in the Supreme Court's decision in *Shearson/American Express Inc v. MacMahon*.[26] To overcome the strong presumption in favour of arbitration underlying the Federal Arbitration Act, a party denying arbitrability must

> show that Congress intended to preclude a waiver of judicial remedies for the statutory rights at issue. If Congress did intend to limit or prohibit waiver of a judicial forum for a particular claim, such an intent "will be deducible from [the statute's] text or legislative history," [...] or from an inherent conflict between arbitration and the statute's underlying purposes [references omitted].[27]

18-23   Accordingly, the arbitrability of a dispute in relation to an insolvent party depends on whether the text or the legislative history of the Bankruptcy Code excludes arbitration of this dispute or that arbitrating the dispute would lead to an irreconcilable conflict with the purpose of the Bankruptcy Code.

---

[25] José Rosell / Harvey Prager, "International Arbitration and Bankruptcy, United States, France and the ICC", 18 (4) *J Int'l Arb* 417 (2001).

[26] *Shearson/American Express, Inc. et al v. Eugene McMahon et al* 482 US 220, 107 S Ct 2332 (1987).

[27] *Ibid.* p 2337.

18-24 The currently prevailing view is well expressed in the Second Circuit's decision in *Re United State Lines*.[28] That court based its finding on the third prong of the *Shearson/MacMahon* test since it found no guidance in the text or the legislative history of the Bankruptcy Code as to whether it was intended to supersede the FAA.[29] In relation to "irreconcilable conflict" test the Court distinguished between core claims and other claims. While the latter were considered to be in general arbitrable,[30] the court held in relation to core proceedings that

> ... even a determination that a proceeding is core will not automatically give the bankruptcy court discretion to stay arbitration. Certainly not all core bankruptcy proceedings are premised on provisions of the Code that inherently conflict with the Federal Arbitration Act; nor would arbitration of such proceedings necessarily jeopardize the objectives of the Bankruptcy Code. However, there are circumstances in which a bankruptcy court may stay arbitration, and in this case the bankruptcy court was correct that it had discretion to do so.
>
> In exercising its discretion over whether, in core proceedings, arbitration provisions ought to be denied effect, the bankruptcy court must still carefully determine whether any underlying purpose of the Bankruptcy Code would be adversely affected by enforcing an arbitration clause. ... The Arbitration Act as interpreted by the Supreme Court dictates that an arbitration clause should be enforced unless [doing so] would seriously jeopardize the objectives of the Code.
>
> In the instant case, the declaratory judgment proceedings are integral to the bankruptcy court's ability to preserve and equitably distribute the Trust's assets. Furthermore, as we have previously pointed out, the bankruptcy court is the preferable venue in which to handle mass tort actions involving claims against an insolvent debtor. The need for a centralized proceeding is further augmented by the complex factual scenario, involving multiple claims, policies and insurers [references omitted].[31]

---

[28] *United States Lines, Inc et al (US) v. American Steamship Owners Mutual Protection and Indemnity Association, Inc, et al (US), In re United States Lines*, XXV YBCA 1057 (2000) = 197 F 3d 631, 640 (2d Cir 1999).

[29] For a critical analysis of this finding, see Note, "Jurisdiction in Bankruptcy Proceedings: A Test Case for an Implied Repeal of the Federal Arbitration Act", 117 *Harv L Rev* 2296 (2004), 2304 et seq.

[30] The Court held that non-core proceedings "are unlikely to present a conflict sufficient to override by implication the presumption in favor of arbitration".

[31] *Ibid*, para 14-16; in an earlier decision in *National Gypsum*, the Fifth Circuit went even further and determined that the Bankruptcy Courts only retained their discretion over those core claims

18-25 As the decision shows these so-called "core proceedings" are not to be confused with so-called "pure bankruptcy" matters. What constitutes a core matter in the context of the test promulgated by the Second Circuit is defined in section 157b.[32] Basically, any substantial claim affecting the value of the estate can be considered to be a core matter. The courts have explicitly rejected the suggestion that only claims arising under the Bankruptcy Code are "core" disputes.[33]

18-26 This position has been criticised in the literature as being inconsistent with the international legal obligations of the US arising from the New York Convention.[34] At first sight this criticism seems to lack foundation. Formally the New York Convention does not contain an autonomous definition of what matters are arbitrable, but rather seems to leave this question to the unfettered discretion of the national legislature. From this perspective, the American legislator would not have been prevented from declaring core bankruptcy disputes to be non-arbitrable.

18-27 However, the problem with this approach is that no such clear decision was taken in the Bankruptcy Code. According to the prevailing view in the U.S., the arbitrability of a dispute is basically left to the discretion of the Bankruptcy Court. This comes close to allowing a court to determine at its own discretion whether or not to enforce an arbitration agreement. Furthermore the *Shearson/ MacMahon* test is based on Congressional intent. Either the Congress intended that the Bankruptcy Code would override the pro-arbitration presumption of the FAA by making the dispute non-arbitrable, or absent such intent, the dispute should be arbitrable. The test as promulgated in *Shearson/MacMahon* does not leave any room for individualized discretionary determinations on a case by case basis.[35] Notwithstanding the problems posed by the approach taken by the Second Circuit at the pre-award stage there is also case law which gives hope that American courts would not refuse the recognition of an award rendered in

---

that involve bankruptcy rights under the Bankruptcy Code, while in regard to other core questions no inherent dispute between the two statutes existed sufficient to justify overriding the pro-arbitration policy of the FAA.

[32] 28 USC § 157(b).

[33] *In re Mirant*, 311 BR 234 (Bankr. ND Texas 2004).

[34] Robert Schwartz, "The US Bankruptcy Courts' Failure to Interpret the New York Convention as a Treaty Obligation", 14 *Arb Int* 231 (1998).

[35] See also Note, supra note 29, 2304 et seq.

foreign arbitration proceedings which took place despite the a stay of proceedings according to US law.[36]

(b) Arbitrability According to the European View

18-28 In the major European arbitration venues only "pure" bankruptcy disputes, such as the opening of insolvency proceedings or appointment of the trustee, are considered to be non-arbitrable. Since these issues affect the right of all creditors and the public at large, they fall within the exclusive jurisdiction of the competent state courts.[37]

18-29 By contrast the arbitrability of contractual claims against a party in insolvency proceedings generally presents no problem in these countries. In fact the issue is often not even discussed by the courts or arbitral tribunals, as is for example the case in Germany. The published case law only addresses questions of whether the trustee is bound or whether a certain dispute is covered by the arbitration agreement.[38] These findings presuppose, however, that the dispute as such is arbitrable.

18-30 In Germany and other legal systems where the national arbitration law expressly defines arbitrability on the basis of criteria such as "economic interest"[39], the arbitrability of contract disputes with an insolvent party can be directly derived from the arbitration law. It is beyond doubt that contract claims against or by an insolvent party concern "economic interests". The arbitrability of such contract disputes is less obvious where according to the relevant definition arbitrability is dependent on what can be called a "free disposal" or "compromise" criteria. For example the French Code Civil provides in Art 2059:

> Any person may submit to arbitration the rights of which he has full disposition

---

[36] *Fotochrome, Inc v. Copal Co*, 517 F.2d 512 (2d Cir 1975); Rosell/Prager, supra note 25, 425 et seq.

[37] See the overview at Lazić, supra note 6, 154 et seq.; for the French Law: Jean-Louis Devolvé/Jean Rouche/Gerald Pointon, *French Arbitration Law and Practice,* (Kluwer Law International 2003), para 73; for Switzerland: Lévy, supra note 9, 28, according to whom, however, this conclusion is not necessarily one based on arbitrability but rather results from interpreting the arbitration agreement.

[38] See BGH, 20 November 2003, *DZWiR* 2004, 161 (with note Flöther).

[39] Section 1030(1) ZPO provides: "Any claim involving an economic interest can be the subject of an arbitration agreement"; for a comparable definition of arbitrability see also Switzerland, Art 177(1) PILA ("any dispute involving property"); see Lévy, supra note 9, 27 et seq.

18-31 The problem is that the debtor no longer has full disposition of its rights, neither has the trustee. Irrespective of this the arbitrability of disputes arising under the original contract has not been a major issue before the French Courts.[40] Where awards were set aside or not enforced the reason was not the non arbitrability of the dispute but violations of rules forming part of French international public policy. The same applies to Italy.[41]

18-32 By contrast under Dutch law only non-monetary claims against the estate are arbitrable, while claims for payment have to be settled by the special *renvoi procedure* if they are contested in bankruptcy.[42]

18-33 The underlying rationale of not excluding the arbitrability of such contract claims in most of the European legal systems is that while these claims may also affect third parties, the interest of these parties are sufficiently protected by the participation of the trustee in the arbitration proceedings.[43]

2. Other Restrictions Imposed in Connections with the "Collective Procedure Principles"

18-34 In numerous jurisdictions the provisions on the mandatory stay of all proceedings, though not excluding the general arbitrability of contract disputes, nevertheless have a bearing on arbitration proceedings.

(a) Filing Requirements and Temporary Stays

18-35 Already for practical reasons most parties will register their claims with the trustee in the insolvency proceedings. The estate is generally only distributed among the registered creditors and if the trustee accepts a claim, there is usually no further need to pursue it in arbitration. Under French law such registration is even a prerequisite for the continuation of arbitration proceedings. Articles 1465 and 369 no 3 NCPC provide for an interruption of arbitration proceedings by a

---

[40] See, for example, Cour de Cassation, 19 May 1987, *Caille et Jobart v. Société Peter Cremer France*, Rev Arb 1988, 142, 143; Devolvé/Rouche/Pointon, supra note 37, para 73; Lazić, supra note 6, 162 with further references.

[41] Tribunale Lodi, 13 February 1991, *Adda Officine Elettromeccaniche e Meccaniche et al v. Alsthom Atlantique SA et al*, XXI YBCA 580 (1996) para 6.

[42] See the Dutch Bankruptcy Act (Faillissementsrecht) Article 122; see also Lazić, supra note 6, 164 et seq; for an overview of the legal situation in Hong Kong: Soo, "Impact of Insolvency on Hong Kong Arbitration", 3 *Int ALR* 103 (2000).

[43] Lévy, supra note 9, 30; see also ICC case no 4415, *Clunet* 1984, 952, 954.

creditor against the debtor until the creditor has registered his claim in the insolvency proceedings. The French courts consider this registration obligation to form part of the French international public policy. As a consequence, this obligation even applies to arbitration in France which is not subject to French law.[44]

18-36 By contrast in German law § 240 ZPO providing for a mandatory stay of all proceedings after the initiation of insolvency proceedings, does not impose comparable restrictions. The primary purpose of this provision is to ensure that the divestment and substitution of the original debtor results in a change of parties in ongoing proceedings and that the trustee has sufficient time to evaluate and prepare its case.[45] The same probably also applies to Swiss law where Art. 207 LP does also not impose a mandatory stay of arbitration proceedings.[46] While under both laws the respective provisions are considered not to be binding on the parties, the due process requirement of the national arbitration law may require at least an extension of time limits.

(b) Limitations on the Remedies Available

18-37 In some countries the provisions to ensure a collective procedure also affect the remedies available to an arbitral tribunal. For example, under French law the tribunal only has the power to determine the existence and the amount of claims against the insolvent debtor but cannot order payment.[47] Such an order is considered to violate the principle of equal treatment. No such restrictions exist under Swiss or German law.[48]

18-38 The underlying principle of equal treatment of all creditors, however, excludes in all jurisdictions orders for set off or orders to provide security for claims in the arbitration proceedings. In both cases the chances that the party in

---

[44] See Cour de cassation, 5 February 1991, *Société Almira Films v. Pierrel*, Rev Arb 1991, 625 (applicable though decision as amiable compositeur,); see also Devolvé/Rouche/Pointon, supra note 37, para 200.

[45] See Flöther, "Schiedsverfahren und Schiedsabrede unter den Bedingungen der Insolvenz", *DZWiR* 2001, 89, 90.

[46] Lévy, supra note 9, 29.

[47] Cour d'Appel de Paris, 27 February 1992, *Me Sohm v. Société Simex*, Rev Arb 1992, 590 note Ancel; Rosell/Prager, supra note 25, 423.

[48] For Swiss law see Lévy, supra note 9, 29 Fn 33.

whose favour the orders are made will see its claims fulfilled are enhanced to the detriment of the other creditors.[49]

VI. EFFECTS OF "DIVESTMENT AND SUBSTITUTION" PROVISIONS ON ARBITRATION

18-39 The provisions on divestment of the original debtor and the transfer of power to manage the estate to the trustee raise a number of questions in relation both to the tribunal's jurisdiction as well as to the conduct of the proceedings. The most important of these are whether and to what extent the trustee or the estate as such may be bound by the arbitration agreement signed by the original debtor, and whether the participation of the trustee requires the repetition of procedural steps or any other adaptations to procedure.[50]

1. Effects on the Tribunal's Jurisdiction: The Personal Scope of the Agreement

18-40 In dealing with the effects of the arbitration agreement on the trustee a distinction has to be made between disputes arising out of the original contract (debtor derived claims) and disputes relating to the exercise of powers granted by the insolvency law to the trustee (non debtor derived claims). In both cases the question of extension of the arbitration agreement to the trustee is governed by the law applicable to the arbitration agreement.[51]

(a) Debtor Derived Claims

18-41 The prevailing view in the jurisdictions examined here is that the trustee is bound by the debtor's consent to the arbitration agreement.[52] The exact

---

[49] See ICC case no 7205, in: Arnaldez/Derains/Hascher, *Collection of ICC Arbitral Awards* 1991-1995, 1997, 622; ICC case no 6697 reported in Fernando Mantilla-Serrano, "International Arbitration and Insolvency Proceedings", 11 *Arb Int* 51 (1995) 70 et seq.

[50] Further questions relate to the capacity of the original debtor/trustee/estate to be a party to the arbitration agreement (see on this Lévy, supra note 9, 26; Mantilla-Serrano, *ibid*, 64 et seq.); and the role of the original debtor in the arbitration proceedings and its participation in the proceedings (see on this Flöther, supra note 45, 90 et seq.).

[51] Lévy, supra note 9, 26 et seq.

[52] For Germany see BGH, 28 February 1957, *BGHZ* 24, 15, 18 (Konkursverwalter (receiver) under the old Bankruptcy Law); BGH, 20 November 2003, *DZWiR* 2004, 161 (note Flöther) with further references (Insolvenzverwalter (trustee) under the new Insolvency Law); see also Stein/Jonas/Schlosser, *ZPO Kommentar*, 22. ed. (Beck 2002), § 1029 para. 35; Musielak/Voit, *ZPO Kommentar*, 4th ed. (Vahlen 2005, § 1029 paras 8 and 12; Lüke in Kübler/Prütting (ed.), *InsO-Kommentar* (Looseleaf: RWS 2005) § 85 para 33; for a different view see Ludwig Häsemeyer,

doctrinal justification depends on the concrete status accorded to the trustee under the national insolvency law. The underlying rationale for this view is, however, that in relation to debtor derived claims the trustee is considered to be the successor of the debtor. The German Supreme Court justified this view with the argument that with the beginning of insolvency proceedings the trustee takes up the legal position of the debtor as it stands.[53]

18-42 Problems in this regard may arise from the fact, that under numerous bankruptcy laws, trustees do not only represent the original debtor but also must act in the interest of the other creditors.[54]

(b) Non Debtor Derived Claims

18-43 The various insolvency laws considered here generally provide for special claims and remedies that go beyond the claims arising directly out of contracts concluded with the original debtor. They concern on the one hand rights of preferred creditors to exclude certain property from the estate and on the other hand powers of the trustee to invalidate pre-filing fraudulent transactions or leading to an unequal treatment of creditors.

(i) Rights of preferred creditors

18-44 Preferred creditors are often accorded the right to withdraw certain assets from the estate. For example, German insolvency law (§ 47 InsO) allows creditors who have a right *in rem* or a personal right to an object in the possession of the original debtor to exclude it from the estate. The German Supreme Court held that the trustee is bound by the arbitration clause in connection with these rights.[55] The underlying rationale for such a view is that the insolvency law primarily affects the timing of the exercise of a right. The creditor's claim to ask for the return of certain assets originates in the underlying contract and the insolvency law only affects the time when it can be exercised.

(ii) Right of the trustee to challenge pre-filing transactions

18-45 To ensure equal treatment of the creditors, the various national insolvency laws often empower the trustee to challenge transactions by the original debtor entered into shortly before the filing, where these transaction

---

Insolvenzrecht, 3th ed. (Carl Heymanns 2003), para 13.28; for Switzerland: Lévy, supra note 9, 27; Lazić, supra note 6, p. 183 et seq.
[53] BGH, 20 November 2003, *DZWiR* 2004, 161 (note Flöther).
[54] Note, Jurisdiction in Bankruptcy Proceedings, supra note 29, 2307.
[55] BGH, 20 November 2003, *DZWiR* 2004, 161 (note Flöther).

would favour certain creditors or diminish the estate's value.[56] Disputes as to whether pre-filing transactions can be challenged under the relevant provisions and about claims arising from the special powers of the trustee are not rare.

18-46 The prevailing view is that these disputes do not fall within the ambit of the arbitration law. The German Supreme Court based such a finding on the fact that these rights are not based on the contract concluded by the debtor but originate in the person of the trustee.[57] They are statutory causes of action arising out of the insolvency law and not out of the contract, as often required by the arbitration clause.[58]

2. Effects on the Arbitration Proceedings

18-47 The divestment of the original debtor and the transfer of the power to manage the estate to the trustee constitute a change of parties, or at least have similar effects. Where arbitration proceedings were already under way before the filing, this "change of parties" may influence their further conduct.

18-48 First, the change of parties may influence the composition of the arbitral tribunal. If, for example, the trustee unlike the original debtor has close connections with one of the arbitrators (such as being partners in the same law firm), the question arises whether this affects the independence of the arbitrator. A German court had to deal with the converse situation in which the trustee in proceedings between the insolvent company and one of its directors challenged the arbitrator appointed by the original debtor for lack of independence. The court removed the arbitrator from the panel.[59]

18-49 Second, it appears reasonable to extend time limits to give the trustee sufficient time to become familiar with the case and to evaluate whether and how to continue the proceedings. That seems to be the prevailing attitude in practice unless it is clear that the filing for insolvency was merely a tool to delay the

---

[56] See, for example, the insolvency laws of Germany: §§ 129 et seq InsO.
[57] BGH, 20 November 2003, *DZWiR* 2004, 161, 162; see also under the old law BGH, 17 October 1957, *NJW* 1956, 1920.
[58] Lévy, supra note 9, 30.
[59] KG Berlin, 11 August 2004, *SchiedsVZ* 2005, 100 with note Lachmann.

arbitration proceedings or the proceedings were already closed so that no further action was required.[60]

18-50 Another question is whether certain steps in the proceedings, such as the hearing of witnesses, should be repeated at the request of the trustee. As the trustee just steps in the shoes of the original debtor, the general rule should be that he takes the proceedings as they stand. Otherwise the original debtor might benefit from its insolvency as procedural rights already lost are available to the estate.

VII. Effects of Trustee's Statutory Powers to Avoid Executory Contracts on Arbitration

18-51 The statutory powers given to the trustee to avoid executory contracts have the potential to affect the tribunal's jurisdiction. If a generous interpretation is given to these powers they may also extend to the arbitration agreement and allow the trustee to terminate the agreement at least in cases where proceedings have not been initiated.

18-52 Such an interpretation of the relevant provisions has been supported in parts of the literature in the US.[61] While there is no direct decision by US courts on the issue with precedential value, the various decisions where bankruptcy courts have referred the parties to arbitration are based on an at least implicit rejection of this view. Otherwise the start of court proceedings by a trustee would have been interpreted as a termination of the still "executory arbitration agreement" and no referral to arbitration would have been possible

18-53 In Germany the trustee has no choice of whether or not to renounce the arbitration agreement. The Supreme Court held that while the arbitration agreement is an executory contract it is not a "gegenseitiger Vertrag" (synallagmatic contract) as required by § 103 InsO.[62] It is also unlikely that the arbitration agreement as such may be successfully challenged under the provisions for unbalanced

---

[60] See the reports on ICC cases in Mantilla-Serrano, supra note 49, 60 et seq; see also Cour de cassation, 5 February 1991, *Société Almira Films v. Pierrel*, Rev Arb 1991, 625.

[61] Note, Jurisdiction in Bankruptcy Proceedings, supra note 29, 2313; see also for the special powers existing under the McCarron-Ferguson Act dealing with insolvent insurances, Frank Koranda, "On hostile ground: Ohio's notice to insolvent insurance companies with arbitration agreements", 2004 *J Disp Resol* 493.

[62] BGH, 20 November 2003, *DZWiR* 2004, 161; see also Flöther, supra note 45, 89, 94.

pre-filing transactions. It is hard to see how the conclusion of an arbitration agreement can negatively affect the value of the estate.[63]

VIII. ARBITRATION PRACTICE

18-54 As indicated above arbitral tribunals which owe allegiance primarily to the parties may not be bound at all or at least not in the same way as courts by the provisions of the national system in which they are situated. As a result tribunals, when requested by one of the parties, have often rendered awards despite restrictions by a given insolvency law.[64] The willingness to do so may differ depending on whether the place of arbitration and the place where the insolvency proceedings were initiated are in the same country or not.

18-55 In cases where the place of arbitration was outside the country of insolvency tribunals have, upon the request of one party, often disregarded the restrictions imposed by the applicable insolvency law.[65] The underlying rationale is that though the award may not be enforceable in the country of insolvency it may be enforceable in other countries.

18-56 A different approach seems to prevail where insolvency proceedings have been initiated at the place of arbitration. In such cases, there is some tendency for tribunals to observe the limitations imposed by the national insolvency law.[66] Most of such limitations belong to the international public policy of the state. Consequently an award rendered in violation of these provisions could be set aside in that country for the underlying violation of public policy. Since only few countries enforce awards annulled in their country of origin,[67] the award

---

[63] See Flöther, *DZWiR* 2004, 163; however, under German law the impecuniosities of a party may lead to the inoperability of an arbitration agreement which might be another tool available to the trustee to avoid the arbitration agreement; see BGH, 14 September 2002, *BGHZ* 145, 116 generally on this issue see DIS (ed) *Financial Capacity of the Parties – A Condition for the Validity of Arbitration Agreements?* (2004); for the Swiss position see Lévy, supra note 9, 24 et seq.

[64] See the examples of ICC cases by Mantilla-Serrano, supra note 49, 57 et seq.

[65] See awards in ICC Cases no 1350, *Clunet* 1975, 931; no 2139, III *YBCA* 220 (1978); no 4415, *Clunet* 1984, 952; no 6057, *Clunet* 1993, 1016; for further unpublished references see Mantilla-Serrano, supra note 49, 58 et seq.

[66] In relation to the French prohibition to order payment see the awards rendered by tribunals sitting in Paris referred to in Mantilla-Serrano, supra note 49, 72 et seq.

[67] This is primarily the case in France, Cour de cassation, 23 March 1994, *Hilmarton v. Omnium de Traitement et de Valorisation (OTV)*, XX YBCA 663 (1995) and the US, *Chromalloy Aeroservices Inc (US) v. The Arab Republic of Egypt*, 939 F Supp 907, XXII YBCA 1001 (1997) (DDC 1996); US Court of Appeal 5th Cir, *Karaha Bodas Co v. Perusahaan*

might be of little value to the claimant, since in all other New York Convention states, such an annulment would constitute a reason to resist enforcement under the relevant national provisions of Art V(1)(e). However, even in the face the likely de facto non enforceability of any award in its favour a claimant may still have an interest in continuing the arbitration proceedings. For example, the award may be primarily needed for presentation to an insurer or a guarantor the like. In such cases it has been submitted that the tribunal should go ahead since there is no one who knows better what is good for a party than the party itself.[68]

18-57 At least in cases with an international element the latter approach is, with certain limitations, preferable. The obligation to enforce agreements entered into by the parties has correctly been considered to be a principle of international public policy relevant for the proper functioning of international commerce.[69] Even where it collides with other principles of public policy it should not be completely ignored but both should be modified in a way to reconcile them. Furthermore, in particular where the place of arbitration has been chosen by the tribunal or an institution it is difficult to see why nearly identical cases should be treated differently merely for the choice of a place of arbitration. To give the tribunal discretion to continue the proceedings despite restrictions in the national insolvency law may also prevent an abuse of the insolvency proceedings for completely different purposes.[70]

18-58 Irrespective of the will of the parties involved the tribunal should, however, ensure that the principles of due process and of equality of the creditors are not violated by the proceedings. Correctly understood both can be considered to be principles of what is sometimes called transnational public policy.[71] In this respect, however, one has to keep in mind that the national understanding of these two principles as enshrined in the national insolvency law may differ from what actually forms part of the transnational principle. As shown above the national understandings of the principles of equality of treatment and due process differ considerably, as is evidenced by the different restrictions imposed in the various legal systems. Consequently the arbitration tribunal should not yield to

---

Pertambangan Minyak Dan Gas Bumi Negara, 18 (6) Mealey's IAR C-1 (2003); for further examples see Lew/Mistelis/ Kröll, supra note 3, paras 26-103 et seq.

[68] Mantilla-Serrano, supra note 49, 57.

[69] Rosell/Prager, supra note 25, 425.

[70] An example is the effort by Menatep, the main shareholder in the Russian oil company Yukos to use the American Chapter 11 to prevent the public auction of Yukos' most valuable production company in Russia.

[71] On this notion see Pierre Lalive, "Transnational (or Truly International) Public Policy and International Arbitration", Sanders (ed), *ICCA Congress series no 3,* 258, 312-317.

every restriction imposed in a given national insolvency law to secure the national understanding of these two principles. This applies in particular in relation to the principle of equality of creditors. The transnational part of the equality principle pertains only to equality in the distribution of assets. Consequently, the restriction of remedies under French law, for example, should not prevent an order for payment if requested, even though the restriction serves to protect the principle of equality of creditors as it is understood in France. The mere existence of the award does not violate the equality of the party; only its execution in the estate would.[72] To ensure due process the tribunal should give sufficient additional time to the trustee to evaluate and put its case.

IX. CONCLUSION

18-59 Despite various areas where principles of insolvency law and arbitration law conflict in principle, in practice filing for insolvency in general does not frustrate the parties' agreement to arbitrate their contract claims. Arbitral tribunals in international cases rarely decline jurisdiction, even in the face of restrictions in the national insolvency laws.[73] Certain modifications to the conduct of the arbitration proceedings may be necessary. All participants involved should try to comply to the greatest extent possible with the requirements of the relevant insolvency law, not least since doing so helps to ensure the enforceability of an award.

18-60 Where that is not possible, arbitral tribunals should take a firm approach to the limitations imposed by insolvency law and only yield to those which are necessary to serve the two principles of transnational public policy, i.e., the equality of creditors and due process.

18-61 A certain caveat applies to insolvency applications in the US. Since American courts often combine the declaration of non-arbitrability with an injunction to participate in the bankruptcy proceedings, these filings for insolvency may pose a serious threat to the parties' agreement to arbitrate. In light of the strict enforcement of these injunctions against arbitrators as well as parties these injunctions often result in a stay of the arbitration proceedings, in particular, if held under the auspices of an institution which is amenable to the jurisdiction of the American courts.

---

[72] Lévy, supra note 9, 24; Rosell/Prager, supra note 25, 432.
[73] See Yves Derains, Comment on ICC case 6057, Clunet 1993, 1016; ICC case no 7205, reported in Arnaldez/Derains/Hascher, *Collection of ICC Arbitral Awards 1991-1995*, 1997, 622.

SUBJECT INDEX

1. Moshe Hirsch, *The Arbitration Mechanism of the International Center for the Settlement of Investment Disputes* (ISBN 0792319931)
2. Aida B. Avanessian, *Iran-United States Claims Tribunal in Action* (ISBN 1853339024)
3. Isaak I. Dore, *The UNCITRAL Framework for Arbitration in Contemporary Perspective* (ISBN 1853335738)
4. Christian Bühring-Uhle, *Arbitration and Mediation in International Business: Designing Procedures for Effective Conflict Management* (ISBN 9041102426)
5. Vesna Laziæ, *Insolvency Proceedings and Commercial Arbitration* (ISBN 9041111158)
6. Joachim Frick, *Arbitration in Complex International Contracts* (ISBN 9041116621)
7. Katherine Lynch, *The Forces of Economic Globalization: Challenges to the Regime of International Commercial Arbitration* (ISBN 9041119949)
8. Christoph Liebscher, *The Healthy Award: Challenge in International Commercial Arbitration* (ISBN 9041120114)
9. Hamid G. Gharavi, *The International Effectiveness of the Annulment of an Arbitral Award* (ISBN 9041117172)
10. Abdullah Sayed, *Corruption in International Trade and Commercial Arbitration* (ISBN 9041122362)
11. Gabrielle Kaufmann-Kohler and Thomas Schultz, *Online Dispute Resolution. Challenges for Contemporary Justice* (ISBN 9041123180)
12. Christopher R. Drahozal and Richard W. Naimark (eds), *Towards a Science of International Arbitration: Collected Empirical Research* (ISBN 9041123229)
13. Ali Yeşilırmak, *Provisional Measures in International Commercial Arbitration* (ISBN 9041123539)
14. Bernard Hanotiau, *Complex Arbitrations: Multiparty, Multicontract, Multi-issue and Class Actions* (ISBN 904112442X)
15. Loukas A. Mistelis and Julian D.M. Lew (eds), *Pervasive Problems in International Arbitration* (ISBN 9041124500)